Heike Paul
The Myths That Made Ai

Heike Paul teaches American Studies at the Friedrich-Alexander-Universität Erlangen-Nürnberg (Germany). Her current research interests are cultural mobility and interculturality, transnational American studies, dimensions of tacit knowledge, and contemporary North American literature.

HEIKE PAUL

The Myths That Made America

An Introduction to American Studies

[transcript]

Bibliographic information published by the Deutsche Nationalbibliothek
The Deutsche Nationalbibliothek lists this publication in the Deutsche Nationalbibliografie; detailed bibliographic data are available in the Internet at http://dnb.d-nb.de

Cover concept: Kordula Röckenhaus, Bielefeld
Cover illustration: MisterQM / photocase.com
Text editor: Sebastian Schneider
Typesetting: Stephen Koetzing
Further assistance: Klaus Lösch

Print-ISBN 978-3-8376-1485-5
PDF-ISBN 978-3-8394-1485-9

It has always seemed to me a rare privilege, this, of being an American, a real American, one whose tradition it has taken scarcely sixty years to create. We need only to realise our parents, remember our grandparents and know ourselves and our history is complete.

The old people in a new world, the new people made out of the old, that is the story I mean to tell, for that is what really is and what I really know.

GERTRUDE STEIN, THE MAKING OF AMERICANS (1926)

Perchance, when, in the course of ages, American liberty has become a fiction of the past, – as it is to some extent a fiction of the present, – the poets of the world will be inspired by American mythology.

HENRY DAVID THOREAU, "WALKING" (1862)

If you don't like it, go to Russia, retorted the others.

STUDS TERKEL, AMERICAN DREAMS: LOST AND FOUND (1980)

Contents

Acknowledgments

What began as a project for my sabbatical in the winter term of 2009/10 turned into a five-year (ad)venture. Through all delays and extended deadlines, Karin Werner, Johanna Tönsing, and Jennifer Niediek at transcript have remained patient and encouraging.

Over the years, I have had much help in matters of research, and I owe very special thanks to Tanja Aho, Jasmin Dragaschnig, Judith Lakamper, Christine Oswald, and Katrin Schmidt for their assistance. For individual chapters (at times in the shape of talks and workshops), I received much appreciated critical feedback as well as positive reinforcement from Elisabeth Bronfen, Cedric Essi, Herbert Sirois, Werner Sollors, Florian Tatschner, Harald Zapf, and Meike Zwingenberger. Alexandra Ganser and Katharina Gerund have read and commented upon larger parts of the manuscript, and they eventually were the first to 'try it out' in the Erlangen American studies-classroom. Their test-runs have helped to eliminate confusing passages as well as study questions seminar participants were reluctant to answer. After all, this is a book for students of American studies. Many thanks also go to the participants of my teacher training seminars on American mythology in Munich and Nuremberg.

Sebastian Schneider has been an admirably thorough reader and a superb text editor, who has made this project his first priority when other things were pressing. His keen eye for dispensable words (or even half-sentences), for bibliographical inconsistencies, and for stylistic improvements have made this a much better book. Stephen Koetzing has been of invaluable help in matters of research and has handled difficult inquiries of all kinds; above all, he has produced the final manuscript with painstaking diligence – as always, I should add. I am much indebted to both of you. Finally, Klaus Lösch has carried the burden of constant interpellation as local expert and has come to wonder whether he has ever known me 'without the book;' he has persistently questioned the politics of each chapter while helping me shape the argument. The final result owes much to his critical comments and helpful suggestions, not the least its title.

All efforts have been made to contact copyright holders of illustrations. Should any have unintentionally been overlooked, the necessary arrangements will be made at the first opportunity.

Erlangen, May 2014   Heike Paul

Introduction

1. INTRODUCTION

This book offers an introduction to American studies by examining 'the myths that made America,' i.e., popular and powerful narratives of US-American national beginnings which have turned out to be anchors and key references in discourses of 'Americanness,' past and present. Even if America obviously is "a continent, not a country" (Gómez-Peña, "New World Border" 750), in this study I will follow the convention of using the signifier 'America/n' to refer to the United States, and treat US-American myths only. The following chapters analyze the core foundational myths upon which constructions of the American nation have been based and which still determine contemporary discussions of US-American identities. These myths include the myth of Columbus and the 'discovery' of America, the Pocahontas myth, the myth of the Promised Land, the myth of the Founding Fathers, the myth of the melting pot, the myth of the American West, and the myth of the self-made man. Each of these foundational myths allows us to access American culture(s) from a specific angle; each of them provides and contains a particular narrative of meaningful and foundational 'new world' beginnings and developments in the history of the United States of America as well as iconic visual images and ritualistic cultural practices that accompany and enhance their impact and effect. Yet, these myths are not fixtures in the American national cultural imaginary: The explanation for their longevity and endurance lies in their adaptability, flexibility, and considerable narrative variation over time and across a broad social and cultural spectrum.

My discussion of these myths will trace their complex histories and multi-voiced appropriations as well as various semiotic/semantic changes and discursive shifts that are part of these histories. The material of each chapter consists of the manifold representations and usages of the myths in different functional areas of American society over time. In the first part of each chapter, I will outline the relevance of the particular myth, reconstruct its formation in its specific

historical moment and context, and show how its 'making' is intricately connected to the project of US-American nation-building and to the (discursive)
production and affirmation of a coherent and unified US-American *national*
identity: The United States as an "imagined community" (cf. Anderson) is constructed and affirmed by way of this repertoire of a foundational mythology that
entails the creation of a "usable past" (cf. Commager, *Search*; Brooks, "On
Creating") and the "invention" of a "tradition" (cf. Hobsbawm and Ranger) for
the new American nation complete with a national genealogy of past and present
heroes. This "imagined communal mythology" (Campbell and Kean, *American
Cultural Studies* 22) provides national narratives of individual and collective
heroism and excellence (when referring to historical individuals and groups,
such as Columbus, Pocahontas, the Pilgrims and Puritans, and the Founding Fathers) as well as narratives of collective belonging and progress (when referring
to abstract concepts such as the melting pot, the West, and the self-made man).
Taken together, they make up a powerful set of self-representations that an
American collectivity has claimed and at times appropriated from an early, pre-
national utopian imaginary of the Americas and that it has converted into powerful ways of talking about itself as a "consciously constructed new world utopia"
(Ostendorf, "Why Is" 340). Rather than as the product of a series of more or less
contingent historical events and developments, the USA appears in these myths
as a predestined entity and (still) unfinished utopian project, i.e., it is endowed
with a specific teleology. At the same time, these myths do not simply 'add up'
to a coherent and consistent national mythology free of contradictions neither in
a diachronic nor in a synchronic perspective, since the foundational national
discourse has always been marked by struggles for hegemony (e.g. between the
North and the South or the West and the East), as established regimes of representation are always being contested.

    In the second part of each chapter, I will work through the many recon-
figurations and reinterpretations that the respective myths have undergone from
subnational perspectives. Often, various immigrant and/or minority groups as
well as individual writers and artists have contested the authority of (pre)domi-
nant versions and interpretations of these myths to prescribe a "unified national
monoculture" (Pease, "Exceptionalism" 111), and thereby questioned the seeming homogeneity and coherence of US national identity. Subnational perspectives on these myths have challenged and intervened in the national regime of
representation by pointing to the voices that have been silenced, rejected, and
excluded from the American foundational mythology through acts of epistemic
violence. Yet, subnational revisionists' call for more inclusive and democratic
articulations of these myths has often left their iconic status intact; in this sense,

marginalized groups (Native Americans, women, African Americans, immigrant groups, and the working class, to name only a few) have pursued a strategy of appropriation and empowerment rather than of radical dismissal in order to articulate their experiences and claim their Americanness.

In the third and final part of each chapter, I will point to more recent (often contemporary) critiques of and commentaries on the myths under scrutiny, which at times are more radically revisionist and debunk a myth entirely. In many instances, the earlier national and subnational versions of a myth assume a *transnational* or *postnational* dimension in light of new postcolonial inter-pretations and critiques of empire that transcend the US national context and US exceptionalism as interpretive frameworks. Yet, a myth does not necessarily be-come obsolete by becoming more controversial and contested, as popular beliefs and forms of commemoration that privilege the national perspective on the one hand, and an academic, perhaps somewhat elitist revisionism articulated from subnational and transnational perspectives on the other often coexist side by side (cf. Schuman, Schwartz, and D'Arcy, "Elite Revisionists"). The resulting ten-sion, which can be described as a kind of cognitive dissonance, produces an "internally divided cultural symbology" (Rowe, *At Emerson's Tomb* 41) or a "Balkanization of the symbolic field" (Veyne, *Did the Greeks* 56) that allows for balancing different and at times overtly contradictory ways of world-making within the same discourse.

When assessing the role and relevance of the foundational US-American myths in the age of globalization, we can also discern new forms of mass-commodification and large-scale cultural export of American mythic narratives across the globe; whether this will lead to a reinvigoration of the mythic material and its often utopian appeal or to an emptying out of cultural specificity in the process of circulation, translation, and indigenization (or to both) remains to be seen, but the processing of the 'myths that made America' in any case is ongoing and unfinished.

Although I am pursuing a rough, somewhat schematic chronology in each of the chapters, a purely linear narrative often falls short of the complex adaptations and interpretations of each myth, as different versions and narratives compete with each other for dominance and hegemony. In order to reveal the biases of the myths' dominant versions and the political and economic interests of those who promote them, the discussion of the *national, subnational,* and *transnational* dimension of each myth is informed by a framework of ideology critique, within which opposition to the American consensus appears as challenging the validity of the US foundational ideology. The dominant ideological paradigm that is es-tablished, critiqued, reaffirmed or debunked is that of *American exceptionalism*:

All of the myths appear under the arc of this single most dominant paradigm in the history and practice of American studies, because the discipline has for a long time been organized around it either by way of affirmation or critique.

2. AMERICAN EXCEPTIONALISM – SOME DEFINITIONS

When the French aristocrat Alexis de Tocqueville remarked in his seminal work *Democracy in America* (1835/1840), a piece of American studies scholarship *avant la lettre* which records his 1831/32 journey through the United States, that "the position of Americans was quite *exceptional*" (*Democracy* Vol. 2, 36; my emphasis), he did not imply that Americans were exceptional or special as a people or culture, but referred to the uniqueness of the American political system. American democracy for him contrasted sharply with the situation in his native France, which for the past decades had been characterized by violent revolutions and counter-revolutions and the restoration of monarchical rule. Tocqueville saw the democratic system that he studied in the United States as God-willed and thought that it was only a matter of time before it would spread to other countries; he felt that in the US this system had taken root in 'exceptional' ways only in so far as that it had been able to do so in the absence of feudal structures and aristocratic opposition.

The passage quoted above is often taken as a foundational scholarly reference to American exceptionalism, yet, American exceptionality was soon decontextualized from this particular instance and used to describe the genesis of the American nation in much more comprehensive and sweeping terms; political scientist Byron E. Shafer for example flatly states that "American exceptionalism [...] is the notion that the United States was created differently, developed differently, and thus has to be *understood* differently – essentially on its own terms and within its own context" (Preface v). Differently from what, we may ask, and in what ways in particular? And what does this difference imply? Often, the phrase 'exceptionalism' has been used in very unspecific ways to claim American superiority vis-à-vis non-Americans and to legitimate American hegemony outside of the US; it also conveys notions of uniqueness and predestination.

American exceptionalism is an ideology that we find throughout US-American history in various forms and discourses of self-representation. It gains renewed relevance and even normativity with the formation of American studies as a discipline in the first half of the 20th century, and becomes the blueprint and guiding principle for many scholarly publications on the United States. While

American studies scholarship analyzes American exceptionalism, it may at the same time also produce new exceptionalist narratives. Even though the ideology of American exceptionalism is a fuzzy conglomerate of very different ingredients, three types can be identified that recur time and again in political, artistic, and popular discourses, past and present: a *religious* exceptionalism, a *political* exceptionalism, and an *economic* exceptionalism.

Regarding the religious dimension of American exceptionalism, Deborah Madsen reminds us that the concept of American exceptionalism "is used frequently to describe the development of American cultural identity from Puritan origins to the present" (*American Exceptionalism* 2). The Puritan rhetoric of the Promised Land can be considered to be the origin of American exceptionalism. According to Madsen, "the mythology of the redeemer nation" can be "explained with reference to seventeenth-century Puritan sermons, poetry and prose" (ibid. 16). It is in John Winthrop's image of the City upon a Hill, in William Bradford's history of Plymouth Colony as well as in Puritan journals that we find the belief of the first generation of New England settlers in their special destiny as 'God's chosen people' expressed (cf. chapter 3). This belief has been surprisingly persistent in the course of US-American history and has been modified into secular and semi-secular variations.

The political dimension of American exceptionalism comes closer to what Tocqueville may have had in mind when he used the adjective 'exceptional' in reference to the founding and development of the US-American nation. The writings of, for example, Benjamin Franklin, Thomas Jefferson, and Thomas Paine reflect the exceptionalist discourse surrounding the political founding of the American republic. When Paine declares that "[w]e have it in our power to begin the world over again" (*Common Sense* 45), he is establishing a creation mythology of the American nation that has been reaffirmed by numerous authors, for example by Seymour Martin Lipset, who calls the US "the first new nation" (cf. his book of the same title). References to founding documents and founding figures (to be addressed in chapter 4 of this study) affirm the shared sense of a secularized doctrine of US-American predestination. The particular (and to cultural outsiders often quite overbearing) type of American patriotism already considered to be somewhat annoying by Alexis de Tocqueville needs to be placed in the context of a self-image that is built on the notion of the exceptionality of American democratic republicanism.

The economic dimension of American exceptionalism is often connected to notions of a new kind of individualism that corresponds to but at the same time also exceeds the realm of the political, and valorizes self-interest as legitimate and necessary for the well-being of the body politic. American individualism is often seen as a precondition for individual success, which is mostly understood in economic terms. The notion of social mobility epitomized in the cultural figure of the self-made man – from rags to riches, "from a servant to the rank of a master" (Crèvecoeur, *Letters* 60) – prototypically illustrates the promise of economic success in America as a direct consequence of the conditions of freedom and equality, which in this context is understood as equality of opportunity. The myth of the self-made man and the idea of expressive individualism (to be addressed in more detail in chapter 7 of this book) are part of a utopian narrative that promises a better life to all those who come to the US, and thus also is very much an immigrant myth. Within the typology of the present study, this myth is identified as the secularized version of the religiously and politically informed mythic narratives of American exceptionalism. In a broader sense, it (along with the other myths) is part of the civil religious vision of the American dream, which figures as a kind of 'umbrella myth' that encompasses all others (cf. Fluck, "Kultur").

Clustered around these three strands of the ideology of American exceptionalism that champion religiosity, patriotism, and individualism, we find mythic narratives of historical figures (Columbus and Pocahontas) and models (the melting pot, the West) with which they are interrelated. Yet, one could even more broadly claim that exceptionalism is "a form of interpretation with its own language and logic" (Madsen, *American Exceptionalism* 2). American exceptionalism thus is not only about *what* is represented (historical figures, incidents, interactions, and achievements) but also about *how* American matters are depicted and emplotted – i.e., about the semiotics and politics of representation. The "language and logic" of American exceptionalism are modes of narrative framing, iconic visualization, and ritualistic enactment. Often, these modes have been identified as articulating American civil religion; the concept of civil religion (which was first used by the French philosopher Jean-Jacques Rousseau, cf. *Social Contract* 249-50) suggests not merely a utilitarian relation to religion, but one that borrows selectively from religious traditions of various denominations in order to create "powerful symbols of national solidarity" (Bellah, "Civil Religion" 239). American civil religion presents an institutionalized collection of sacred or quasi-sacred beliefs about the American nation that is distinct from denominational religions, yet shares with them a belief in the existence of a transcendent being (God); it centers on the idea that the American nation is subject to God's laws and that the United States will be guided and protected by God. Symbolically, this civil religion is expressed in America's founding documents and made concrete in phrases such as 'In God We Trust' (ibid. 228). The American exceptionalist logic conceptualized as American civil religion by

Robert Bellah and others had earlier also been called the American Creed: "America is the only nation in the world that is founded on a creed. That creed is set forth with dogmatic and even theological lucidity in the Declaration of Independence" (Chesterton, *What I Saw* 7). Gunnar Myrdal refers to the "American Creed" as "a social *ethos*" and as a "political creed" which functions as "the cement" in the structure of the nation and is identified with "America's peculiar brand of nationalism" (*American Dilemma* 1, 5). Both Gilbert K. Chesterton and Gunnar Myrdal, cultural outsiders (from England and Sweden, respectively) for who the US was an object of scholarly interest, developed influential interpretations of American patriotism's ideals as well as its deficits.

Whereas we can clearly see the symbolic languages of politics and religion coming together in the notion of a civil religion and an American creed, the economic aspect also plays an important role as the genuine "promise of American life" (cf. Croly's study of the same title), which entails the promise of economic self-improvement and gain, just as, in turn, the proverbial "gospel of wealth" (cf. Carnegie, "Wealth") connects economic success to communal obligation in the framework of national solidarity and belonging. In its dominant and recurring themes as well as in its overall rhetorical structure, American exceptionalism informs and structures American *self-representations*. It has been important in fashioning internal coherence and has also often been used as an ideological tool to project American hegemony outside the US. American myths thus play a crucial role in the symbolization and affirmation of the US nation; it is their cultural work, so to speak, to make discursive constructions of the nation plausible and self-evident, to create internal solidarity and commitment to the nation state and its policies, and to represent the US to outsiders. Myth in general, as it operates on the level of (often tacit) belief rather than rationality, can be seen as the prime discursive form of ideology; the myths discussed in this book can then be assumed more specifically to reinforce the basic tenets of American exceptionalism also and maybe even mainly below the level of awareness whenever they are evoked.

American studies and American exceptionalism have been connected in precarious ways from the beginning. During the emergence and consolidation of American studies as a discipline around the beginning of the 'Cold War' era, American exceptionalism was a powerful hegemonic construct that proliferated in the form of "an academic discourse, a political doctrine, and a regulatory ideal assigned responsibility for defining, supporting, and developing the U.S. national identity" (Pease, "Exceptionalism" 109). For the practitioners of American studies, this meant that

[h]istorians and political theorists [as well as scholars from other disciplines, HP] approached the past in search of historical confirmations of the nation's unique mission and destiny. Examining the past became for scholars who were steeped in exceptionalist convictions a personal quest whereby they would understand the meaning of their "American" identity by uncovering the special significance of the nation's institutions. (ibid. 110)

Historically, American studies in part have thus been complicit in establishing and maintaining discourses which sought to justify US imperial policies in the 'Cold War' – and beyond.

3. AMERICAN STUDIES SCHOLARSHIP – AN OVERVIEW

American exceptionalism and American myths can be examined more specifically in regard to their national, subnational, and transnational contexts and frames of reference, which correspond with the three major phases in the history of the discipline of American studies and the concomitant transformations of its research practices and modes of thought.

Whereas various early individual works from Alexis de Tocqueville's aforementioned *Democracy in America* to Vernon Parrington's three-volume *Main Currents in American Thought* (1927-30) have been discussed as the first pieces of American studies scholarship, the discipline really only took institutional shape and developed in more formalized ways from the late 1930s onwards. During its inception period from the late 1930s to the 1950s, scholars of the so-called Myth and Symbol School looked for and identified myths and symbols that allegedly attested to the specificity or even uniqueness of the US, and thus sought to affirm American exceptionality. The name of this loosely connected school of thought derives from the subtitle of Henry Nash Smith's seminal study *Virgin Land: The American West as Symbol and Myth* (1950); Smith, the first scholar to receive his PhD in the field of American studies (in 1940 from Harvard University), defined his approach in the following way:

I use the words ['myth' and 'symbol'] to designate larger or smaller units of the same kind of thing, namely an intellectual construction that fuses concept and emotion into an image. The myths and symbols with which I deal have the further characteristic of being collective representations rather than the work of a single mind. I do not mean to raise the question whether such products of the imagination accurately reflect empirical fact. They exist on a different plane. But as I have tried to show, they sometimes exert a decided influence on practical affairs. (*Virgin Land* vii)

Smith sees the 'Virgin Land' as one prominent symbol that is embedded in resonant mythic narratives about European encounters with North America, such as
the frontier myth and the agrarian myth, readily conceding that myths (and the
corresponding symbols) may be seen as fiction and thus may contain some
degree of wishful thinking or even falseness. Alongside Smith, other influential
Myth and Symbol scholars like R.W.B. Lewis and Perry Miller similarly investigated the nature of the American experience and its historical protagonists.
Lewis suggests the image of the 'American Adam' in order to characterize the
prototypical 'new world' settler as a figure of origin and an emblem of 'new
world' beginnings:

[T]he American myth saw life and history as just beginning. [...] The new habits to be
engendered on the new American scene were suggested by the image of a radically new
personality, the hero of a new adventure: an individual emancipated from history, happily
bereft of ancestry, untouched and undefiled by the usual inheritances of family and race;
an individual standing alone, self-reliant and self-propelling [...]. It was not surprising, in
a Bible-reading generation, that the new hero [...] was most easily identified with Adam
before the Fall. (*American Adam* 4)

Perry Miller's American genealogical narrative is similarly steeped in religious
discourse; he puts the Puritans' "errand into the wilderness" (cf. his book of the
same title), a God-willed quest for a utopian community, at the center of the
early American experience and therefore also at the center of American studies.
17th-century Puritan theology is thus seen as having had a lasting impact on the
cultural imaginary of the nation. Miller shares with Sacvan Bercovitch, another
prominent scholar of Puritanism, the sense that "the Puritan origins of the American self" (cf. Bercovitch's book of the same title) have guided the formation of
the US nation-state through the "capacity for self-creation that Puritan theology
attributes to believers" (Madsen, *American Exceptionalism* 13).

Overall, an evocative American primal scene is constructed by the first group
of American studies scholars as they imagine the 'American Adam' in the 'Virgin Land' on an 'Errand into the Wilderness' (cf. Pease, "New Americanists").
The early phase of this new field of study is often referred to as "the American
Studies movement" (cf. Marx, "Thoughts"), indicating a critical stance toward
traditional disciplinary configurations that had been dominant in the English de-
partments of many American universities, which seemed to imply some sort of
political agenda. As the US felt increasingly pressured to explain (and advertise)
itself to the world beyond its borders, the scholars of the Myth and Symbol
School both identified and created powerful images for a national imaginary. It

is no coincidence that American studies programs and projects received major funding after the end of World War II and throughout the 1950s, and became quite a corporate enterprise (cf. Wise, "'Paradigm Dramas'" 181). In the wake of the 'Cold War,' 'America' was imagined in American studies in somewhat essentialist terms as a largely unified and homogenous entity. All of the Myth and Symbol scholars would probably have agreed that there is something like the "American mind" that can be studied in the intellectual history of the United States (ibid. 179). Furthermore, the exceptionality claimed for the object of study, i.e. the USA, was also claimed for the new discipline of American studies that sought to investigate the US "as a whole" rather than in distinct disciplinary pockets. When Henry Nash Smith asked, "can American studies develop a method?" (cf. his essay of the same title), he answered his question to the effect that he saw the "scholarship" of "American culture, past and present" (ibid. 207) carried out not so much within the framework of a particular methodology or theoretical approach but in the form of an interdisciplinary venture centering on a common subject, i.e. America. From the beginning, many scholars envisioned American studies as "an arena for disciplinary encounter and staging ground for fresh topical pursuits" (Bailis, "Social Sciences" 203). Myth and Symbol scholarship invoked American studies as the new ideal of scholarly and disciplinary coherence, yet by emphasizing the unity and uniqueness of American society, it often lacked a sufficient analytical distance from the object under investigation and scrutiny (cf. Claviez, *Grenzfälle* 209). Since the Myth and Symbol scholars did not thoroughly reflect their own positionality, their ideological presuppositions to a certain degree predetermined their findings, and their scholarly endeavors mainly produced an affirmation (rather than any precise definition or critique) of those American myths, symbols, and images on which the field imaginary of American studies relied so strongly.

In the mid-1960s, the Myth and Symbol scholarship of the first American studies cohort was challenged by many critics who began to question the unequivocal nature and the political implications of the American myths allegedly uncovered and categorized by the preceding generation of scholars. In the wake of the social protest movements of the 1960s and 1970s, among them the civil rights movement, the women's movement, and the anti-war movement, many critics proposed alternative genealogies of America and American identity formation that cast American history in a more critical light and contested the 'innocence' of the American Adam cultivating his 'garden' in the 'wilderness.' The dominant version of American beginnings, which had been privileging certain groups while marginalizing or entirely leaving out others, was no longer accepted as representative of *the* American experience. What about the American 'Eve'? Or, more broadly, what about the experiences of women and non-white people in the United States, past and present? What about Native American removal from the 'wilderness' and slavery's role in cultivating the 'garden'? The representatives of the so-called Critical Myth and Symbol School, the second important group in the history of American studies, examined aspects such as violence, racism, sexism, and genocide as foundational for American culture. Whereas the symbols and myths carved out in the first phase of American studies were often not entirely debunked, they were now interpreted differently and seen in a much more critical light. This reorientation produced less flattering accounts of the making of America than the narratives produced by the Myth and Symbol School, which now appeared as idealized and romanticized accounts of the evolution of a white patriarchal America. Take, for instance, Henry Nash Smith's prominent symbol of the Virgin Land: Annette Kolodny in *The Lay of the Land* reinterprets this image's gendered symbolism as a metaphor of rape and patriarchal exploitation, and Richard Slotkin, another leading protagonist of the Critical Myth and Symbol School, more generally explicates violence (rather than innocence) as the foundational American experience (cf. chapter 6).

While the Critical Myth and Symbol School was also concerned with grasping the specificity and particularity of the United States, it was not concerned with affirming the superiority of American culture and society but with critiquing the ideology of American exceptionalism; its critical reevaluation of US founding texts and myths led to a transformation of American studies research and practice as it addressed the national project from subnational perspectives and thus brought to light that the notion of a homogeneous nation and a single 'American' history was the product of a hegemonic master narrative that excluded the perspectives and histories of internal others. This revisionism coincided with the articulation of a 'negative' US exceptionalism and the development of new fields within and alongside American studies such as black studies, women's studies, popular culture studies, Native American studies, ethnic studies, and labor studies, to name only a few. These new fields addressed and tackled cultural and social hierarchies (i.e., asymmetrical power relations between men and women, whites and non-whites, as well as economically privileged and economically disadvantaged Americans) that were deeply inscribed in Myth and Symbol scholarship. This counter-hegemonic scholarship valorized the particular over the universalized American experience by addressing issues of identity below the level of the nation. In the process of deconstructing hierarchies, distinctions between high culture and low (or popular) culture have also been called into question, and the study of popular culture has become a centerpiece of American studies scholarship (cf. Cawelti, *Adventure*; Tompkins, *Sensational Designs*).

By emphasizing the heterogeneity of American society and by focusing on power asymmetries in the field of representation, the Critical Myth and Symbol School aimed at a more inclusive narration and representation of America and at a recognition of its multicultural legacy, privileging the heterogeneity of American society over any one-dimensional view of America 'as a whole' as the object of study; the American studies scholarship of this second phase thus was pluralistic rather than holistic in perspective and shattered conventional notions of 'Americanness' in the course of several decades. As this new cohort of American studies scholars (among them Leslie Fiedler, Alan Trachtenberg as well as the aforementioned Annette Kolodny and Richard Slotkin) became more prominent, scholars such as Henry Nash Smith felt obliged to revise their Myth and Symbol narratives:

I proposed to use the terms "myth" and "symbol" to designate "larger or smaller units of the same kind of thing [...]." I might have avoided some misunderstandings of what I was about if I had introduced the term "ideology" at this point by adding that the intellectual constructions under consideration could not be sharply categorized but should be thought of as occupying positions along a spectrum extending from myth at one end, characterized by the dominance of image and emotion, to ideology at the other end, characterized by emphasis on concepts, on abstract ideas. ("Symbol" 22)

An institutionalization of these new perspectives occurred in the reformulation of university degree programs and with the so-called canon debates of the 1980s. These often fierce debates (also referred to as 'culture wars') saw an at times dramatic confrontation between those who fought to preserve a supposedly universal "Western Canon" (cf. Bloom's book of the same title) and those who aimed at diversifying the narratives of America by substituting the universalist US master narrative (*grand récit*) with a plurality of 'small' narratives (*petites histoires*) and proposed to canonize texts (especially by women and minorities) that so far had not been canonical. Works such as Paul Lauter's *Reconstructing American Literature* (1983), Jane Tompkins's *Sensational Designs* (1986), Henry Louis Gates's *Loose Canons* (1992), and A. LaVonne Brown Ruoff and Jerry W. Ward's *Redefining American Literary History* (1990) are exemplary publications on the 'new' canon which include formerly excluded or marginalized voices that express a particular, subnational (or subaltern) view instead of claiming to be representative of the nation as a whole. While 'weak' versions of multiculturalism merely advocate adding 'new' texts to school curricula and college reading lists, 'strong' versions advocate more pivotal revisions concerning cultural legacies and the canon:

"Multicultural" is not a category of American writing – it is a *definition* of all American writing. [...] The concept of "mainstream" culture and "minority" cultures is the narrow view. Redefining the mainstream is the theme, the message, and the mission of [our project]." (Strads, Trueblood, and Wong, "Introduction" xi-xii)

As the national consensus around the idea of 'America' was either reformulated in more inclusive terms or questioned as a coercive concept in and of itself, subnational and multicultural approaches from the 1960s through the 1980s were strengthened; however, new constraints and limitations of the field of American studies became apparent in the process. While the Critical Myth and Symbol School successfully created sensibilities for inner-American differences and power dynamics and directed scholarly attention to the multicultural dimension of American national genesis and cultural production, it did not thoroughly question the framework of the nation as the basic conceptual category of scholarship and thus remained bound to the logic of national exceptionalism (cf. Tally, "Post-American Literature").

It is only in the third phase of American studies scholarship from the 1990s to the present after a paradigm shift or 'turn' carried by the representatives of the so-called New Americanists that the field began to pursue a transnational perspective in much of its work. Amy Kaplan and Donald Pease's seminal *Cultures of United States Imperialism* (1993) clearly marked the transition from a subnational to a transnational perspective, as the essays in this volume place the USA in a wider context of postcolonial theory and postcolonial studies. The US as empire has become the object of many scholarly endeavors that no longer regard the US as a "self-contained nation" (Bender, *Nation* 3) and see continental expansion as the result of imperial rather than domestic politics. Thus, the New Americanists of the 1980s and 1990s (Amy Kaplan, Donald Pease, John Carlos Rowe, and Robyn Wiegman, among others) have fundamentally scrutinized and questioned the paradigm of American exceptionalism and its foundational role for the discipline of American studies by drawing on the work of "scholars whose concept of the nation and of citizenship has questioned dominant American myths rather than canonized them" (Rowe et al., "Introduction" 3). The New Americanists' agenda for American studies aims "to transform the traditionally nationalist concerns of the field to address the several ways in which 'America' signifies in the new global [...] circumstances" (ibid. 3). Viewing the US as "a multicultural nation in a globalized world" (Bender, *Nation* 6) also necessitates "globalizing American studies," as Brian T. Edwards and Dilip Parameshwar Gaonkar suggest in their essay collection of the same title; nationalism here is cast as parochialism, and exceptionalism as an outdated field imaginary, provoking the questions whether "American Studies [can] exist after American exceptionalism" at all (Pease, "American Studies" 47), and whether "all American studies scholarship [is] [...] propaganda" (Castronovo and Gillman, "Introduction" 1). According to Pease, the field of American studies needs to be "grounded in a comparativist model of imperial state exceptionalisms" ("American Studies" 80) and, as Srinivas Aravamudan states, has to continue its close examination of the "relationship between the state and the discipline" ("Rogue States" 17). The turn to a relational framework of analysis along the lines of Jane Desmond and Virginia Domínguez's "cosmopolitanism" and "critical internationalism" that operates with "a non-US-centric comparativism" ("Resituating" 286) seems as important as the "engagement with Postcolonial studies" (Rowe et al., "Introduction" 7) and the use of a New Historicist methodology that has also contributed to the field's reconfiguration (cf. Michaels and Pease, *American Renaissance*). The interdisciplinarity of the field of American studies (or 'critical US studies') thus is being reinforced in the work of the New Americanists on a new theoretical basis.

In a similar vein, Shelley Fisher-Fishkin's address to the American Studies Association held on November 12, 2004 (cf. "Crossroads") focuses on an impressive range of transnationally oriented scholarly activities by herself and others, including transatlantic, transpacific, and hemispheric American studies scholarship, as well as border studies. Characteristic of this new transnational critical focus are publications such as Radway et al.'s 2009 reader *American Studies: An Anthology*, which includes in its first section entries on "nation" as well as "empire" and "diaspora." There is also a new turn to non-English languages and multilingualism (cf. Sollors, *Multilingual America*; Shell and Sollors, *Multilingual Anthology*), as transnational American studies cannot be conducted and practiced with English-only sources.

The transnational American studies approach is diachronic, going back as far as the 15th century, as well as synchronic; through the lens of a transnational perspective, American beginnings (just like any other national beginnings) appear as more accidental and contingent, more chaotic and "messy" (cf. Schueller and Watts) than is suggested by historical and mythic narratives which assert their purposefulness, coherence, and telos. The transnationality of well-known cultural, political, social, and literary phenomena has in the past often been relegated to the margins; transnational American studies moves it to the center by analyzing the US from a comparative angle as "a nation among nations" (cf. Bender's book of the same title).

To summarize: each of the following chapters addresses the three phases of American studies scholarship in terms of the national, subnational, and transnational approaches and perspectives they have generated; in the first phase, the so-called Myth and Symbol School focused on national themes and symbols; in the second phase, the so-called Critical Myth and Symbol School focused on subnational perspectives and groups that had been ignored in the first phase; and in the third phase, the so-called New Americanists questioned the nation as framework on the basis of a postnational or transnational and possibly post-exceptionalist agenda, and articulated a critique of the American empire.

However, I am not suggesting that every single piece of American studies scholarship and criticism can be subsumed under these three perspectives and in this exact chronological order. There is certainly a considerable amount of overlap, just as there are other frameworks that can be used to describe and to chronologize American studies scholarship. It also needs to be acknowledged that there is a strong connection between subnational and transnational approaches. Lisa Lowe's scholarship on Asian American history refers to "the international within the national" (cf. her article of the same title) and is emblematic of attempts to study the subnational and transnational in conjunction, as they are but two sides of the same coin: while the subnational approach frames ethnic immigrant groups within the national discursive field, the transnational does so with reference to the global; similarly, diasporic cultures can be examined as part of both subnational and transnational spheres. Yet, a national mythology is still affirmed in many current visions of the US in the face of a perceived fragmentation of traditional collectivities, and some versions of the transnational endeavor still lapse into constructing a US-centered universe.

4. AMERICAN STUDIES:
MYTH CRITICISM – IDEOLOGY CRITIQUE – CULTURAL STUDIES

There are a number of descriptions of American studies that serve to define the field. Interdisciplinarity is usually a common denominator: American studies

is a joint, interdisciplinary academic endeavor to gain systematic knowledge about American society and culture in order to understand the historical and present-day meaning and significance of the United States. (Fluck and Claviez, "Introduction" ix)

While various academic disciplines such as literary criticism, sociology, political science, history, economics, art history, geography, media studies, etc. engage in American studies, it is the discipline of cultural studies that allows us to *connect* e.g. political science to literature, art history to sociology, or history to economics and geography, and to integrate these various disciplinary perspectives into an American studies framework. Cultural studies has always operated as a discipline that in the field of American studies brings different approaches into dialog and that bridges disciplinary gaps. In what follows, all of those (sub)disciplines of American studies will be relevant for my account of core myths of the US, as myths are not specific to one particular sector of American society but are part of the larger "biography" of a nation (Anderson, *Imagined Communities* 204), answer to "the need for a narrative of 'identity'" (ibid. 205), and constitute the "National Symbolic" that is carried by "traditional icons, its metaphors, its heroes, its rituals, and its narratives" in order to "provide an alphabet for a collective consciousness or national subjectivity" (Berlant, *Anatomy* 20). Myth criticism therefore is relevant for analyzing political culture, sociological descriptions, historiographic accounts, literary texts, cartographical practices of mapping and naming, as well as national visual and commemorative culture, and may be concerned both with the semiotic as well as with the discursive dimensions of myths, i.e. with forms of (re)presentation as well as with their ideological function (cf. Hall, *Representation*). Myth criticism as practiced by literary and cultural critics, historians, sociologists, anthropologists, political scientists, etc. has allotted quite different roles, meanings, and functions to myths; I will therefore briefly sketch some of these contributions to myth theory to arrive at a working definition of myth for the present volume.

One prominent branch of myth criticism has established a critical perspective on myths by contrasting them with "truth" ("logos") or "scientific thought;" myth here is considered as false, fictional, anachronistic, "primitive," or "pathological" (Claviez, *Grenzfälle* 14). Historically, myths have often been considered to be pre-modern constructions and interpretations of the world whose powers have been waning since the onset of the Age of Enlightenment. From this perspective, myth in modernity figures negatively as a tool of propaganda, political demagogy, and manipulation (as analyzed by Horkheimer and Adorno, cf. *Dialektik* 44). In the everyday use of the word 'myth,' which equates myth with falsehood, wishful thinking, or fiction, this meaning is still present.

The denigration of the nature and cultural work of myths as outlined above contrasts with myth theories by critics such as Ernst Cassirer and Hans Blumenberg, who have instead pointed to the function of myth as a way of making sense of the world. Cassirer does not consider myths normatively as anti- or irrational but instead holds that myth provides "its own kind of reality" and rationality (*Philosophy* 4). Whereas myth seems "to build up an entirely fantastic world on the one hand" (Cassirer, *Language* 45), it is a "symbolic expression" and a "work" of "artful expression" on the other (ibid. 46, 48). Myths are "objectivations" (ibid. 47) of social experiences and contribute in meaningful ways to an intersubjective understanding of a culture or society. Cassirer's description of myth addresses its internal logic, its formal structures, and its sociocultural function, not its subject matter. Philosopher Hans Blumenberg in *Work on Myth* further elaborated on the function of myth as a fundamental human activity to "overcome the archaic alterity of the world" (Wallace, Translator's Introduction x) and to protect individuals from "the absolutism of reality" (Blumenberg, *Work* 3) by creating collective identities and solidarity. For Blumenberg, our need for myths does not dissolve with enlightenment thinking or positivistic rationality but rather figures as a timeless constant in the way we relate to the world at large (cf. ibid. 113).

Whereas it is debatable whether modern myths such as the ones discussed in this book can in fact be considered as a primary way of world-making, they are clearly part of a discursive formation and constitute a semiotic system that includes an intersubjective dimension. This intersubjective dimension, in my argument, works to establish the nation as an imagined community and extends to all those interpellated as members. The social function of myth as a popular belief system is to respond to an affective desire for ontological (re)assurance and operates in civil religious forms that create within a group (i.e., the 'nation') a semi-conscious yet deeply affective bond (cf. Bellah, "Civil Religion") which can be experienced and articulated as a kind of "public feeling" (Stewart, *Ordinary Affects* 2). The "structures of feeling" (cf. Williams's essay of the same title) that underlie these "public feelings" and "ordinary affects" sit at the intersection of individual experience and collectively intelligible explication.

Roland Barthes's *Mythologies* more critically turns to the role of myth in everyday life. Barthes conceptualizes myth as "a system of communication" (*Mythologies* 109) and as a "metalanguage" (ibid. 115) which functions on the basis of, and like a language. For Barthes, myth criticism is equivalent to ideology critique, whose task it is to continually de-naturalize and deconstruct what seems self-evident, natural, and objective: "[M]yth is constituted by the loss of the historical quality of things; in it, things lose the memory that they once were made" (ibid. 142). In this sense, myth may be instrumentalized to various ends: "*Myth hides nothing*: its function is to distort, not to make disappear" (ibid. 121). The definition of myth as a means of providing coherence is echoed by the definition of ideology as a system of cultural assumptions, or the discursive concatenation, the connectedness, of beliefs or values which uphold or oppose the social order, or which otherwise provide a coherent structure of thought that hides or silences the contradictory elements in social or economic formations. (Wolfreys, *Keywords* 101)

Sacvan Bercovitch has pointed out that scholars have often constructed a false opposition between "myth criticism and ideological analysis" which claims that myth criticism's task is "to 'appreciate' it [myth, HP] from within, to explicate it 'intrinsically,' in its own 'organic' terms" (*Rites* 358), whereas by contrast, ideology "is [an] inherently suspect" "vehicle of culturally prescribed directives for thought and behaviour" whose analysis "uncover[s], rationally, the sinister effects of its fictions:" "[t]o criticize a piece of ideology is to see through it, to expose its historical functions, necessarily from an extrinsic, and usually from a hostile perspective" (ibid.). This "double standard" (ibid.) obscures the ideological dimension/appropriation of myth and mythic texts; it is exactly this dual quality of myth – as meaningful self-representation and as ideological investment – that I will engage with in this study.

In the field of political science, Christopher Flood and Herfried Münkler have also argued against an earlier normative approach that eyed myths suspiciously and unilaterally as tools of political indoctrination without denying that political myths serve an ideological function. Flood examines mythmaking in political discourses in modern societies in the 19th and 20th centuries at the intersection of politics, (sacral) mythology, and ideology (cf. *Political Myth*). Herfried Münkler has redeemed the study of political myths as an integral part of discursively constructed modern national identities that should not be dismissed offhandedly as irrelevant or anachronistic. Pulling together much of earlier myth criticism (cf. Burkert, *Structure*; Barthes, *Mythologies*; Cassirer, *Language*; cf. also Berlant, *Anatomy*), Münkler identifies three aspects of myths: 1) (repetitive) ritual as the oldest manifestation of mythical thinking, 2) the narrative form of myth as a kind of storytelling, and 3) the visual and iconic dimension of the representation of a myth (cf. *Die Deutschen*). Again, it is the civil religious, not the purely religious aspect that is foregrounded and explored with regard to a national and cultural imaginary. All of these dimensions – the ritualistic iteration of myths in cultural practices, their various narrative patterns, and their visual quality and iconicity – will be addressed in each chapter of the present study.

Yet, the different ways in which we encounter myths in politics, art, literature, memorial culture, etc. do not exhaust the power and complexity of myth and do not even wholly explicate its meaning. We only know myth through our work on the workings of it, Blumenberg suggests, and we can never grasp myth fully through rational or other forms of explication, as it exceeds complete semiotic access. In fact, "its function may be the 'only knowable aspect' that it possesses for us" (Wallace, Translator's Introduction xviii), whereas for the community of its believers, for whom its ontological status is evident, it presents the "holy truth" (Flood, *Political Myth* 32). Ideology critique is limited by the dynamic and at the same time self-effacing character of myth and by the fact that its ideological core settles into collectively shared tacit knowledge, or what could also be called the "political unconscious" (cf. Jameson's book of the same title) or a "state fantasy" (cf. Pease, *New American Exceptionalism* 1-39). Similar to Sigmund Freud, who finds mythical patterns in the unconscious (cf. *Die Traumdeutung*), Slavoj Žižek identifies the "unknown known" (cf. "What Rumsfeld") as part of our internalized ideological repertoire, which works effectively precisely because it is that "which cannot be named" (Pease, *New American Exceptionalism* 17). It is this implicit quality of myth that immunizes it against criticism time and again and accounts for its longevity and its capacity for make-believe in spite of obvious contradictions.

The historical 'making' of American national myths defies the assumption that myths lose their power and interpretive authority and become obsolete with the development of modern democratic societies; quite to the contrary: it is with the formation of the USA as a nation and republic in the late 18th century in the context of enlightenment thinking and a natural rights philosophy that a set of modern national myths emerge or 'are made' in the name of an exceptionalist American nationalism:

Nothing in the history of American nationalism is more impressive than the speed and the lavishness with which Americans provided themselves with a usable past: history, legends, symbols, paintings, sculpture, monuments, shrines, holy days, ballads, patriotic songs, heroes, and – with some difficulty – villains. (Commager, *Search* 13)

It seems as if the anthropological and psychosocial dimensions of myths are of central importance to a national discourse that appropriates universality as an "American universality" (Claviez, *Grenzfälle* 16). The evolution of this "American universality" has been reconstructed by Richard Slotkin, who applied Jungian archetypes to a national context in order to critically identify specifically American archetypal patterns and the way in which they have been encoded in American myths. For Slotkin, "[a] myth is a narrative which concentrates in a single dramatised experience the whole history of a people in their land" by "reducing centuries of experience into a constellation of compelling metaphors"

(*Regeneration* 269; 8). In the context of memory studies, Jan Assmann has described myth, somewhat similar to Roland Barthes, as "'hot' memory" whose foundational function it is to affirm the present as predestined and self-evident (*Das kulturelle Gedächtnis* 78); I use 'foundational' in much the same way. Some of the myths that I address commemorate a glorious past (Columbus, Pocahontas, the Pilgrims and Puritans, the Founding Fathers) and connect myth to cultural memory and its various archives, while others (the melting pot, the West, and the self-made man) are myths of (geographic, cultural, and social) mobility that commemorate events and developments in the past but also envision the future of America. Yet, in Assmann's model, a myth is not necessarily always foundational but may also have a second function, namely to draw attention to a *deficit* between the commemorated mythic past and the lived-in present – this 'counter-presentist' effect may trigger social and political change, and instigate revolutionary acts.

In the context of American culture, Sacvan Bercovitch has identified the American jeremiad, a motivational sermon in the Puritan tradition, as a pervasive rhetorical structure that continually acknowledges such a deficit and postpones the closing of the gap between the 'foundational' and the 'presentist' dimension of myth without reneging on the promise of America and its utopian qualities. Even as the American jeremiad asserts that people have fallen from their (original) biblical, spiritual, or moral standard, it offers and embraces a second chance to return to or to fully realize the ideal public life with all its benefits for the individual and the community (cf. Bercovitch, *American Jeremiad*). The American jeremiad can be considered a make-believe rhetoric that time and again affirms the ideological content of American mythology by smoothing over social and political discontent and by camouflaging social and political deficiencies. Such deficiencies are addressed more specifically by Donald Pease in his account of the US after the end of the 'Cold War' and 9/11, where he identifies precisely this kind of 'gap' between the national belief system and presentist experiences. According to Pease, it is the "state fantasy work" – the state fantasy being "the dominant structure of desire out of which US citizens imagined their national identity" (*New American Exceptionalism* 1) – that closes the gap between (the old) myth (of the 'Cold War' era) and (the new post-9/11) reality as the new situation exceeds the old myth's interpretive powers:

Myths normally do the work of incorporating events into recognizable national narratives. But traumatic events precipitate states of emergency that become the inaugural moments in a different symbolic order and take place on a scale that exceeds the grasp of the available representations from the national mythology. Before a national myth can narrate

events of this magnitude, the state fantasy that supplies the horizon of expectations orient-
ing their significance must have already become symbolically effective. (ibid. 5)

The "state fantasy" in times of crisis then facilitates an adaptation of old myths
to a new situation in a way that does not shake the social and political order "by
inducing citizens to want the national order they already have" (ibid. 4). In this
logic, American exceptionalism is reiterated and reinvigorated as a state fantasy
(or a state of fantasy; cf. ibid. 20); when examining what Pease calls "the new
American exceptionalism," he in fact diagnoses the rerouting and ultimate "return of the national mythology" after 9/11, in which the "virgin land" becomes
"ground zero" (ibid. 153). A study of American myths in historical perspective,
then, is in no way obsolete, nor is it stating the obvious; even as we have come a
long way since the beginnings of the Myth and Symbol School, the entangle-
ments between historical myth and contemporary ideology are as complex as
they have ever been.

To sum up the most salient aspects of this introduction's discussion of myth:
First, a discursive rather than normative definition of myth is informing contemporary myth criticism as well as the analyses in the following chapters. Second,
myth criticism needs to take into account the relationship between myth and
ideology. Third, the power of myths derives from a seemingly paradoxical
structure that involves longevity and continuity as well as variety and flexibility.
Fourth, myth becomes manifest in narratives, icons, and rituals. Fifth, the tacit
dimension of myth is part of its power to perform and to regulate the "political
unconscious." The following chapters will discuss US foundational mythology
within this framework.

5. STUDY QUESTIONS

1. What are the different aspects of American exceptionalism outlined in the text and with which myths do they correlate most clearly?
2. Give a definition of American civil religion and name a few examples of civil religion as manifestations of exceptionalism.
3. What is the respective outlook and agenda of the different generations/cohorts of American studies scholars?
4. Discuss definitions of American studies in terms of their focus on interdisciplinarity.
5. Summarize in your own words the various dimensions of myth criticism.
6. What is the relationship of the different American myths to each other?
7. Discuss the relationship between myth and ideology as outlined in the text.
8. Research the context of this often quoted dictum: "[I]n the beginning all the world was America" (John Locke, *Second Treatise of Government* 29).
9. Research the context of then-Secretary of State Madeleine Albright's statement that "[w]e are the indispensable nation" (*The Today Show*, 19 February 1998). Discuss its claims and implications in view of the ideology of exceptionalism.
10. In a comparative framework, can you think of the myths of other modern nations and relate, compare, and/or contrast them to those of the US?

6. BIBLIOGRAPHY

Works Cited

Anderson, Benedict. *Imagined Communities: Reflections on the Origin and Spread of Nationalism.* London: Verso, 2006.

Aravamudan, Srinivas. "Rogue States and Emergent Disciplines." Castronovo and Gillman, *States* 17-35.

Assmann, Jan. *Das kulturelle Gedächtnis: Schrift, Erinnerung und politische Identität in frühen Hochkulturen.* 2nd ed. München: Beck, 1997.

Bailis, Stanley. "The Social Sciences in American Studies: An Integrative Conception." *American Quarterly* 26.3 (1974): 202-24.

Barthes, Roland. *Mythologies.* Trans. Annette Lavers. New York: Hill, 1998.

Bellah, Robert N. "Civil Religion in America." *The Robert Bellah Reader.* Ed. Robert N. Bellah and Stephen M. Tipton. Durham: Duke UP, 2005. 225-45.

Bender, Thomas. *A Nation among Nations: America's Place in World History.* New York: Hill, 2006.

Bercovitch, Sacvan. *The American Jeremiad.* Madison: U of Wisconsin P, 1978.

–. *The Puritan Origins of the American Self.* New Haven: Yale UP, 1975.

–. *The Rites of Assent: Transformations in the Symbolic Construction of America.* New York: Routledge, 1993.

Berlant, Lauren. *The Anatomy of National Fantasy: Hawthorne, Utopia, and Everyday Life.* Chicago: U of Chicago P, 1994.

Bloom, Harold. *The Western Canon: The Books and School of the Ages.* New York: Harcourt Brace, 1994.

Blumenberg, Hans. *Work on Myth.* Trans. Robert M. Wallace. Cambridge: MIT P, 1985.

Brooks, Van Wyck. "On Creating a Usable Past." *Dial* 64.7 (1918): 337-41.

Burkert, Walter. *Structure and History in Greek Mythology and Ritual.* Berkeley: U of California P, 1979.

Campbell, Neil, and Alasdair Kean. *American Cultural Studies: An Introduction to American Culture.* New York: Routledge, 1997.

Carnegie, Andrew. "Wealth." *North American Review* 391 (1889): 653-65.

Cassirer, Ernst. *Language and Myth.* New York: Dover, 1946.

–. *Philosophy of Symbolic Forms.* New Haven: Yale UP, 1955.

Castronovo, Russ, and Susan Gillman. "Introduction: The Study of the American Problems." Castronovo and Gillman, *States* 1-16.

–, eds. *States of Emergency: The Object of American Studies.* Chapel Hill: U of Carolina P, 2009.

Cawelti, John G. *Adventure, Mystery, and Romance: Formula Stories as Art and Popular Culture*. Chicago: U of Chicago P, 1976.

Chesterton, Gilbert K. *What I Saw in America*. London: Hodder and Stoughton, 1922.

Claviez, Thomas. *Grenzfälle: Mythos – Ideologie – American Studies*. Trier: Wissenschaftlicher Verlag Trier, 1998.

Commager, Henry Steele. *The Search for a Usable Past, and Other Essays in Historiography*. New York: Knopf, 1967.

Crèvecoeur, J. Hector St. John de. *Letters from an American Farmer*. London: J. M. Dent and Sons, 1912.

Croly, Herbert. *The Promise of American Life*. New York: Macmillan, 1909.

Desmond, Jane C., and Virginia R. Domínguez. "Resituating American Studies in a Critical Internationalism." *American Quarterly* 48 (1996): 483-97.

Edwards, Brian T., and Dilip Parameshwar Gaonkar, eds. *Globalizing American Studies*. Chicago: U of Chicago P, 2010.

Fisher-Fishkin, Shelley. "Crossroads of Cultures: The Transnational Turn in American Studies: Presidential Address to the American Studies Association, November 12, 2004." *American Quarterly* 57.1 (2005): 17-57.

Flood, Christopher. *Political Myth: A Theoretical Introduction*. New York: Garland, 1996.

Fluck, Winfried. "Kultur." *Länderbericht USA*. Ed. Peter Lösche. Bonn: Bundeszentrale für politische Bildung, 1998. 712-812.

Fluck, Winfried, and Thomas Claviez. "Introduction." *Theories of American Culture – Theories of American Studies*. Ed. Winfried Fluck and Thomas Claviez. Tübingen: Narr, 2003. ix-xii. Yearbook of Research in English and American Literature (REAL) 19.

Freud, Sigmund. *Die Traumdeutung*. Frankfurt/Main: Fischer, 1961.

Gates, Henry Louis. *Loose Canons: Notes on the Culture Wars*. New York: Oxford UP, 1992.

Gómez-Peña, Guillermo. "The New World Border." *The Mexico Reader: History, Culture, Politics*. Ed. Gilbert M. Joseph and Timothy J. Henderson. Durham: Duke UP, 2003. 750-55.

Hall, Stuart. *Representation: Cultural Representations and Signifying Practices*. London: Sage, 1997.

Hobsbawm, Eric, and Terence Ranger, eds. *The Invention of Tradition*. New York: Cambridge UP, 2009.

Horkheimer, Max, and Theodor W. Adorno. *Dialektik der Aufklärung*. Frankfurt/Main: Fischer, 1969.

Jameson, Fredric. *The Political Unconscious: Narrative as a Socially Symbolic Act.* Ithaca: Cornell UP, 1981.

Kaplan, Amy, and Donald E. Pease, eds. *Cultures of United States Imperialism.* Durham: Duke UP, 1993.

Kolodny, Annette. *The Lay of the Land: Metaphor as Experience and History in American Life and Letters.* Chapel Hill: U of North Carolina P, 1975.

Lauter, Paul, ed. *Reconstructing American Literature.* Old Westbury: Feminist, 1983.

Lewis, R.W.B. *The American Adam: Innocence, Tragedy, and Tradition in the Nineteenth Century.* Chicago: U of Chicago P, 1955.

Lipset, Seymour Martin. *The First New Nation: The United States in Historical and Comparative Perspective.* New York: Basic, 1963.

Locke, John. *Second Treatise of Government.* Ed. Thomas P. Peardon. New York: Liberal Arts, 1952.

Lowe, Lisa. "The International within the National: American Studies and Asian American Critique." *Cultural Critique* 40 (1998): 29-47.

Madsen, Deborah L. *American Exceptionalism.* Jackson: UP of Mississippi, 1998.

Marx, Leo. "Thoughts on the Origin and Character of the American Studies Movement." *American Quarterly* 31.3 (1979): 398-401.

Michaels, Walter Benn, and Donald E. Pease, eds. *The American Renaissance Reconsidered.* Baltimore: Johns Hopkins UP, 1989.

Miller, Perry. *Errand into the Wilderness.* Cambridge: Belknap, 1956.

Münkler, Herfried. *Die Deutschen und ihre Mythen.* Berlin: Rowohlt, 2009.

Myrdal, Gunnar. *An American Dilemma: The Negro Problem and Modern Democracy.* New York: Harper, 1944.

Ostendorf, Berndt. "Why Is American Popular Culture So Popular? A View from Europe." *Amerikastudien* 46.3 (2001): 339-66.

Paine, Thomas. "Common Sense." *The Complete Writings of Thomas Paine.* Vol. 1. Ed. Philip S. Foner. New York: Citadel, 1945. 3-50.

Parrington, Vernon Louis. *Main Currents in American Thought.* 3 vols. New York: Harcourt, 1927.

Pease, Donald E. "American Studies After American Exceptionalism? Toward a Comparative Analysis of Imperial State Exceptionalisms." Edwards and Gaonkar, *Globalizing* 47-83.

–. "Exceptionalism." *Keywords for American Cultural Studies.* Ed. Bruce Burgett and Glenn Hendler. New York: New York UP, 2007. 108-12.

–. *The New American Exceptionalism.* Minneapolis: U of Minnesota P, 2009.

–. "New Americanists: Revisionist Interventions into the Canon." *boundary 2* 17.1 (1990): 1-37.

Radway, Janice A., et al., eds. *American Studies: An Anthology*. Chichester: Wiley, 2009.

Rousseau, Jean-Jacques. *The Social Contract* and *The First and Second Discourses*. Ed. and introd. Susan Dunn. New Haven: Yale UP, 2002.

Rowe, John Carlos. *At Emerson's Tomb: The Politics of Classic American Literature*. New York: Columbia UP, 1997.

Rowe, John Carlos, et al. "Introduction." *Post-Nationalist American Studies*. Ed. John Carlos Rowe. Berkeley: U of California P, 2000. 1-21.

Ruoff, A. LaVonne Brown, and Jerry W. Ward, Jr., eds. *Redefining American Literary History*. New York: Modern Language Association of America, 1990.

Schueller, Malini Johar, and Edward Watts, eds. *Messy Beginnings: Postcoloniality and Early American Studies*. New Brunswick: Rutgers UP, 2003.

Schuman, Howard, Barry Schwartz, and Hannah D'Arcy. "Elite Revisionists and Popular Beliefs: Christopher Columbus, Hero or Villain?" *Public Opinion Quarterly* 69.1 (2005): 2-29.

Shafer, Byron E. Preface. *Is America Different? A New Look at American Exceptionalism*. Ed. Byron E. Shafer. Oxford: Clarendon, 1991. v-xi.

Shell, Marc, and Werner Sollors, eds. *The Multilingual Anthology of American Literature: A Reader of Original Texts with English Translations*. New York: New York UP, 2000.

Slotkin, Richard. *Regeneration through Violence: The Mythology of the American Frontier, 1600-1860*. Middletown: Wesleyan UP, 1973.

Smith, Henry Nash. "Can American Studies Develop a Method?" *American Quarterly* 9.2 (1957): 197-208.

–. "Symbol and Idea in *Virgin Land*." *Ideology and Classic American Literature*. Ed. Sacvan Bercovitch and Myra Jehlen. Cambridge: Cambridge UP, 1986. 21-35.

–. *Virgin Land: The American West as Symbol and Myth*. Cambridge: Harvard UP, 1950.

Sollors, Werner. *Multilingual America: Transnationalism, Ethnicity, and the Languages of America*. New York: New York UP, 1998.

Stewart, Kathleen. *Ordinary Affects*. Durham: Duke UP, 2007.

Strads, Gunnar, Kathryn Trueblood, and Shawn Wong. "Introduction: Redefining the Mainstream." *The Before Columbus Foundation Fiction Anthology: Selections from the American Book Awards, 1980-1990*. Ed. Ishmael Reed, Kathryn Trueblood, and Shawn Wong. New York: Norton, 1992. xi-xx.

Tally, Robert. "Post-American Literature." *49th Parallel* 25.1 (2011): 1-20.

Tocqueville, Alexis de. *Democracy in America.* 2 vols. Ed. Daniel Boorstein. New York: Vintage, 1990.

Tompkins, Jane. *Sensational Designs: The Cultural Work of American Fiction, 1790-1860.* New York: Oxford UP, 1986.

Veyne, Paul. *Did the Greeks Believe in Their Myths? An Essay on the Constitutive Imagination.* Trans. Paula Wissing. Chicago: U of Chicago P, 1988.

Wallace, Robert M. Translator's Introduction. *Work on Myth.* By Hans Blumenberg. Cambridge: MIT P, 1985. vii-xxxvii.

Williams, Raymond. "Structures of Feeling." *Marxism and Literature.* Oxford: Oxford UP, 1977. 128-35.

Wise, Gene. "'Paradigm Dramas' in American Studies: A Cultural and Institutional History of the Movement." 1979. *Locating American Studies: The Evolution of a Discipline.* Ed. Lucy Maddox. Baltimore: Johns Hopkins UP, 1999. 166-210.

Wolfreys, Julian. *Critical Keywords in Literary and Cultural Theory.* Basingstoke: Palgrave Macmillan, 2004.

Žižek, Slavoj. "What Rumsfeld Doesn't Know That He Knows About Abu Graib." *In These Times* 24 May 2004. 15 July 2013.

Further Reading

Adams, David K., and Cornelis A. van Minnen, eds. *Reflections on American Exceptionalism.* Staffordshire: Ryburn, 1994.

Adams, Rachel. *Continental Divides: Remapping the Cultures of North America.* Chicago: U of Chicago P, 2009.

Anderson, Wanni Wibulswasdi, and Robert G. Lee, eds. *Displacements and Diasporas: Asians in the Americas.* New Brunswick: Rutgers UP, 2005.

Anzaldúa, Gloria. *Borderlands/La Frontera: The New Mestiza.* San Francisco: Aunt Lute, 1999.

Assmann, Aleida, and Jan Assmann. "Mythos." *Handbuch religionswissenschaftlicher Grundbegriffe.* Ed. Hubert Cancik, Burkhard Gladigow, and Matthias Samuel Laubscher. Vol. 4. Stuttgart: W. Kohlhammer, 1998. 179-200.

Attebery, Brian. "American Studies: A Not So Unscientific Method." *American Quarterly* 48.2 (1996): 316-43.

Bercovitch, Sacvan, ed. *Reconstructing American Literary History.* Cambridge: Harvard UP, 1986.

Bercovitch, Sacvan, and Myra Jehlen, eds. *Ideology and Classic American Literature.* Cambridge: Cambridge UP, 1986.

Bogues, Anthony. *Empire of Liberty: Power, Desire, and Freedom.* Hanover: Dartmouth College P, 2010.

Bridgman, Richard. "The American Studies of Henry Nash Smith." *American Scholar* 56.2 (1987): 259-68.

Briggs, Laura, Gladys McCormick, and J.T. Way. "Transnationalism: A Category of Analysis." *American Quarterly* 60.3 (2008): 625-48.

Burgett, Bruce, and Glenn Hendler, eds. *Keywords for American Cultural Studies.* New York: New York UP, 2007.

Canclini, Néstor García. *Hybrid Cultures: Strategies for Entering and Leaving Modernity.* Trans. Christopher L. Chiappari and Silvia L. López. Minneapolis: U of Minnesota P, 1996.

Carter, Dale, ed. *Marks of Distinction: American Exceptionalism Revisited.* Aarhus: Aarhus UP, 2001.

Cassirer, Ernst. *The Myth of the State.* New Haven: Yale UP, 1961.

–. *Symbol, Myth, and Culture: Essays and Lectures of Ernst Cassirer, 1935-1945.* New Haven: Yale UP, 1979.

Cawelti, John G. *Apostles of the Self-Made Man.* Chicago: U of Chicago P, 1965.

Chen, Xiangming. *As Borders Bend: Transnational Spaces on the Pacific Rim.* Lanham: Rowman and Littlefield, 2005.

Clifford, James. *Routes: Travel and Translation in the Late Twentieth Century.* Cambridge: Harvard UP, 1997.

Dirlik, Arif, ed. *What Is in a Rim? Critical Perspectives on the Pacific Region Idea.* Boston: Rowman and Littlefield, 1998.

Duncan, Russell, and Clara Juncker, eds. *Transnational America: Contours of Modern US Culture.* Copenhagen: Museum Tusculanum, 2004.

Elliott, Emory. "Diversity in the United States and Abroad: What Does It Mean When American Studies Is Transnational?" *American Quarterly* 59.1 (2007): 1-22.

Engler, Bernd, and Kurt Müller, eds. *Metzler Lexikon amerikanischer Autoren.* Stuttgart: Metzler, 2000.

Fiedler, Leslie. *Love and Death in the American Novel.* Rev. ed. New York: Stein and Day, 1966.

–. *The Return of the Vanishing American.* New York: Stein and Day, 1968.

Fluck, Winfried, ed. *Transnational American Studies.* Tübingen: Narr, 2007.

Fluck, Winfried, Donald E. Pease, and John Carlos Rowe, eds. *Re-Framing the Transnational Turn in American Studies.* Hanover: Dartmouth College P, 2011.

Fousek, John. *To Lead the Free World: American Nationalism and the Cultural Roots of the Cold War.* Chapel Hill: U of North Carolina P, 2000.

Franklin, Cynthia G., Ruth Hsu, and Suzanne Kosanke, eds. *Navigating Islands and Continents: Conversations and Contestations in and Around the Pacific.* Honolulu: U of Hawai'i P, 2000.

Freese, Peter. "Westward the Course of Empire Takes Its Way: The *Translatio*-Concept in Popular American Writing and Painting." *Amerikastudien* 41.2 (1996): 265-95.

Fussel, Edwin S. *Frontier: American Literature and the American West.* Princeton: Princeton UP, 1965.

Giles, Paul. "Transnationalism and Classic American Literature." *PMLA* 11.1 (2003): 62-77.

–. *Virtual Americas: Transnational Fictions and the Transatlantic Imaginary.* Durham: Duke UP, 2002.

Gillies, Mary Ann. *Pacific Rim Modernisms.* Toronto: U of Toronto P, 2009.

Glaser, Elisabeth, and Hermann Wellenreuther, eds. *Bridging the Atlantic: The Question of American Exceptionalism in Perspective.* Cambridge: Cambridge UP, 2002.

Goh, Robbie B.H., and Shawn Wong, eds. *Asian Diasporas: Cultures, Identities, Representations.* Hong Kong: Hong Kong UP, 2004.

Gray, Richard. *A History of American Literature.* Chichester: Wiley, 2012.

Grewal, Inderpal. *Transnational America: Feminisms, Diasporas, Neoliberalisms.* Durham: Duke UP, 2005.

Grice, Helena. *Asian American Fiction, History, and Life Writing: International Encounters.* New York: Routledge, 2009.

Hannerz, Ulf. *Transnational Connections: Culture, People, Places.* London: Routledge, 2009.

Harth, Dietrich, and Jan Assmann, eds. *Revolution und Mythos.* Frankfurt/Main: Fischer, 1992.

Hebel, Udo J. *Einführung in die Amerikanistik/American Studies.* Stuttgart: Metzler, 2008.

–, ed. *Transnational American Memories: Media and Cultural Memory.* Berlin: de Gruyter, 2009.

Hietala, Thomas R. *Manifest Design: American Exceptionalism and Empire.* Ithaca: Cornell UP, 2003.

Hodgson, Godfrey. *The Myth of American Exceptionalism.* New Haven: Yale UP, 2008.

Hollinger, David A., and Charles Capper, eds. *The American Intellectual Tradition: A Sourcebook.* 2 vols. New York: Oxford UP, 1989.

Horwitz, Richard P., ed. *The American Studies Anthology*. Lanham: SR, 2004.

Huhndorf, Shari M. *Mapping the Americas: The Transnational Politics of Contemporary Native Culture*. Ithaca: Cornell UP, 2009.

Johannessen, Lene M. *Horizons of Enchantment: Essays in the American Imaginary*. Hanover: Dartmouth College P, 2011.

Kamboureli, Smaro, and Roy Miki, eds. *Trans.Can.Lit: Resituating the Study of Canadian Literature*. Waterloo: Wilfrid Laurier UP, 2007.

Kammen, Michael. "The Problem of American Exceptionalism: A Reconsideration." *American Quarterly* 45.1 (1993): 1-43.

Kaplan, Amy. "The Tenacious Grasp of American Exceptionalism." *Comparative American Studies: An International Journal* 2.2 (2004): 153-59.

Kerber, Linda. "Diversity and the Transformation of American Studies." *American Quarterly* 41.3 (1989): 415-31.

Kolodny, Annette. *The Land Before Her: Fantasy and Experience of the American Frontiers, 1630-1860*. Chapel Hill: U of North Carolina P, 1984.

Koshiro, Yukiko. *Trans-Pacific Racisms and the US Occupation of Japan*. New York: Columbia UP, 1999.

Kuklick, Bruce. "Myth and Symbol in American Studies." *American Quarterly* 24.4 (1989): 435-50.

Lenz, Guenter H. "American Studies – Beyond the Crisis? Recent Redefinitions and the Meaning of Theory, History, and Practical Criticism." *Prospects* 7 (1982): 53-113.

Levander, Caroline S., and Robert S. Levine, eds. *Hemispheric American Studies*. New Brunswick: Rutgers UP, 2008.

Lévi-Strauss, Claude. "The Structural Study of Myth." *Structural Anthropology*. Trans. Claire Jacobson and Brooke Grundfest Schoepf. New York: Basic, 1963. 206-31.

Lipset, Seymour Martin. *American Exceptionalism: A Double Edged Sword*. New York: Norton, 1996.

Lockhart, Charles. *The Roots of American Exceptionalism: History, Institutions, and Culture*. New York: Palgrave Macmillan, 2003.

Lowe, Lisa. *Immigrant Acts: On Asian American Cultural Politics*. Durham: Duke UP, 1996.

Luce, Henry. *The American Century*. New York: Farrar, 1941.

Maddox, Lucy, ed. *Locating American Studies: The Evolution of a Discipline*. Baltimore: Johns Hopkins, 1999.

Marcus, Greil, and Werner Sollors, eds. *A New Literary History of America*. Cambridge: Belknap, 2009.

Marks, Barry. "The Concept of Myth in *Virgin Land.*" *American Quarterly* 5.1 (1953): 71-76.

Marx, Leo. "American Studies – A Defense of an Unscientific Method." *New Literary History* 1.1 (1969): 75-90.

–. *The Machine in the Garden: Technology and the Pastoral Ideal in America.* New York: Oxford UP, 1964.

Merk, Frederick. *Manifest Destiny and Mission in American History: A Reinterpretation.* New York: Knopf, 1963.

Miller, Perry. *The New England Mind: The Seventeenth Century.* New York: Macmillan, 1939.

–. *Orthodoxy in Massachusetts, 1630-1650: A Genetic Study.* Cambridge: Harvard UP, 1933.

Mitchell, Katharyne. *Crossing the Neoliberal Line: Pacific Rim Migration and the Metropolis.* Philadelphia: Temple UP, 2004.

Muthyala, John. *Dwelling in American: Dissent, Empire, and Globalization.* Hanover: Dartmouth College P, 2012.

Ortiz, Fernando. *Cuban Counterpoint: Tobacco and Sugar.* Trans. Harriet de Onís. New York: Knopf, 1947.

Ostendorf, Berndt, ed. *Transnational America: The Fading of Borders in the Western Hemisphere.* Heidelberg: Winter, 2002.

Pease, Donald E. "American Exceptionalism(s) in an Extended Field: The Inauguration of International American Studies." *Conformism, Non-Conformism and Anti-Conformism in the Culture of the United States.* Ed. Antonis Balasopoulos, Gesa Mackenthun, and Theodora Tsimpouki. Heidelberg: Winter, 2008. 9-43.

Pease, Donald E., and Robyn Wiegman, eds. *The Futures of American Studies.* Durham: Duke UP, 2002.

Potter, David M. *People of Plenty: Economic Abundance and the American Character.* Chicago: U of Chicago P, 1958.

Pratt, Mary Louise. *Imperial Eyes: Travel Writing and Transculturation.* London: Routledge, 2000.

Rodgers, Daniel. "American Exceptionalism Revisited." *Raritan* 24.2 (2004): 21-47.

Romero, Fernando. *Hyperborder: The Contemporary U.S.-Mexico Border and Its Future.* New York: Princeton Architectural, 2008.

Rosaldo, Renato. *Culture and Truth: The Remaking of Social Analysis.* London: Routledge, 1993.

Rowe, John Carlos. *Afterlives of Modernism: Liberalism, Transnationalism, and Political Critique.* Hanover: Dartmouth College P, 2011.

–. *The New American Studies*. Minneapolis: U of Minnesota P, 2002.

Saldívar, José David. *Border Matters: Remapping American Studies*. Berkeley: U of California P, 1997.

Schiller, Nina Glick, Linda Basch, and Cristina Blanc-Szanton, eds. *Towards a Transnational Perspective on Migration: Race, Class, Ethnicity, and Nationalism Reconsidered*. New York: New York Academy of Sciences, 1992.

Siemerling, Winfried. *The New North American Studies: Culture, Writing, and the Politics of Re/Cognition*. New York: Routledge, 2005.

Siemerling, Winfried, and Sarah Phillips Casteel, eds. *Canada and Its Americas*. Montreal: McGill-Queens UP, 2010.

Slotkin, Richard. *The Fatal Environment: The Myth of the Frontier in the Age of Industrialization, 1800-1890*. New York: Atheneum, 1985.

–. *Gunfighter Nation: The Myth of the Frontier in Twentieth-Century America*. New York: Harper, 1993.

Smith, Anthony D. *Myths and Memories of the Nation*. Oxford: Oxford UP, 1999.

Spanos, William V. *American Exceptionalism in the Age of Globalization: The Specter of Vietnam*. Albany: State U of New York P, 2008.

Stephanson, Anders. *Manifest Destiny: American Expansion and the Empire of Right*. New York: Hill, 1995.

Trachtenberg, Alan. "Myth and Symbol." *The Massachusetts Review* 25.4 (1984): 667-73.

–. "Myth, History, and Literature in *Virgin Land*." *Prospects* 3 (1977): 127-29.

Traister, Bryce. "The Object of Study; or, Are We Being Transnational Yet?" *Journal of Transnational American Studies* 2.1 (2010): 1-23.

Tyrrell, Ian. "American Exceptionalism in an Age of International History." *American Historical Review* 96.4 (1991): 1031-55.

Umberger, Daryl. "Myth and Symbol." *Encyclopedia of American Studies*. Ed. George T. Kurian. Vol. 3. New York: Grolier, 2001. 180-84.

Weinberg, Albert K. *Manifest Destiny: A Study of Nationalist Expansionism in American History*. Baltimore: Johns Hopkins, 1935.

Wersich, Rüdiger B., ed. *USA-Lexikon: Schlüsselbegriffe zu Politik, Wirtschaft, Gesellschaft, Kultur, Geschichte und zu den deutsch-amerikanischen Beziehungen*. Berlin: Schmidt, 1996.

Wilson, Rob, and Wimal Dissanayake, eds. *Global/Local: Cultural Production and the Transnational Imaginary*. Durham: Duke UP, 1996.

Chapter I

Christopher Columbus and the Myth of 'Discovery'

---

1. WHY COLUMBUS?

> Let us begin at the most famous of beginnings.
> STEPHEN GREENBLATT, *MARVELOUS POSSESSIONS*

> Imagine the scene: it is an autumn day in the late fifteenth century. On a beach with rose-colored sand, somewhere in the Caribbean, two groups of people, the hosts and their visitors, are about to meet for the first time. The world will never again be the same.
> MICHAEL DORRIS, "MISTAKEN IDENTITIES"

The mythology of the 'new world' begins with the discourse of discovery and with powerful European projections that envision a new kind of paradise, a utopia somewhere across the Atlantic that alleviates the grievances of the 'old world' and that promises boundless earthly riches. In its traditional European version, this discourse is not so much about the 'hosts' whom the part Native American novelist and poet Michael Dorris envisions as sharing in the primal scene of encounter as it is about their 'visitors,' i.e. those Europeans who arrive and 'discover.' Although this primal scene precedes the formation of the USA as a nation-state by several hundred years, it has developed into one of its core foundational myths, and, for all its historical remoteness, has profoundly shaped the national imaginary. The story of Christopher Columbus (1451-1506) and his arrival in the Americas holds a pivotal place in an American foundational mythology that stages the 'discovery' and the subsequent settlement and colonization of the 'new world' in prophetic ways as an inevitable step forward in the course of human progress that eventually would lead to the founding of the USA and to US-American westward expansion, its 'manifest destiny.' One may wonder why, when, and "how an Italian explorer became an American hero" (cf. Bushman, *America*), or, to tease out the paradox further: why Columbus, who never set foot on the land that would later become the United States and who never knew in his lifetime that in 1492 he had not landed in Asia has been considered one of the founding figures of the US-American nation. In fact, he may be the single most important and best-known figure in the context of the 'discovery' of the 'new world' even though his place in history has for a long time been contested. I will show how the myth of 'discovery' is firmly tied to the figure of Columbus and how ideological investments determine the uses that this historical figure has been put to: Columbus "is nothing but a collection of multiple disguises assembled around a set of historical facts" (Stavans, *Imagining* xvii) with an image oscillating between "the arch-villain of the modern era for bringing genocide and pollution to an unsullied earthly paradise" and "someone worthy of sainthood" (Shreve, "Christopher Columbus" 703).

This chapter will sketch four phases in the making and unmaking of the American myth of 'discovery' and of Christopher Columbus; it will historicize the myth and its modifications and point to its various functions. My genealogy starts with the historical moment of Columbus's original 'fame' in the late 15th century and its reverberations in the context of Spanish colonialism; second, I will turn to the inauguration and consolidation of the Columbus myth in North America during the revolutionary period in the second half of the 18th century and look at the processes of translation (also in the sense of *translatio imperii*) involved; third, I will trace the myth through the late 19th and early 20th centuries to point to its enlistment in immigrant discourses that made Columbus into an ethnic hero following the Irish, Jewish, and Italian 'waves' of immigration to the United States; fourth, I will summarily discuss the recent revisionism in Native American scholarship in the context of the watershed year of 1992 (which marked the quincentennial of 'discovery') as indicative of a new take on Columbus (the man as well as the myth).

Of course, these four phases cannot be said to start or end in one year or another; instead they indicate tendencies, trends, and shifting perspectives. Throughout US-American history and for hundreds of years Columbus has served as a national icon – Columbus Day today is still a national holiday despite persistent objections to his idealization and glorification. His profile, however, disappeared from the five-dollar bill in 1923 (the last US-American bill on which he was depicted); and whereas US-American elementary school students still learn of Columbus's heroism in unequivocal terms, the city of Berkeley since 1992 has been celebrating Indigenous People's Day instead of celebrating Columbus (cf. Martin, "Literature" 16): the meaning of Columbus and the legacy

of his 'discovery' thus have been and still are contested and continually negotiated anew.

2. THE FIRST LETTER FROM THE 'NEW WORLD'

> Let us not make the mistake, now that we are about to accompany Columbus
> on his great adventure, of assuming, as is commonly done, that although he
> was not aware of it, he "really" crossed the Atlantic in quest of America and
> that the shores at which he arrived were "really" those of the American conti-
> nent.
> EDMUNDO O'GORMAN, *THE INVENTION OF AMERICA*

When reviewing the historical evidence about Columbus's journeys and about
his landing in the Americas on October 12, 1492, in a first step it is to Columbus's own writings that we turn, as he is commonly referred to as "the first
European to write the new world" (Loewenberg, *American History* 31). The
original manuscript of Columbus's log has been lost, so scholars rely on the
summary of his *Diario* composed by Bartolomé de las Casas (which is excerpted
in the *Heath Anthology of American Literature*; cf. Lauter et al.). Yet, Columbus's so-called first letter is generally considered to be the more authentic
document; he supposedly wrote the first version under the impression of an
impending shipwreck on his return from his first voyage (three more were to
follow) in order to leave a record for posterity of what he had seen and found,
waxed and sealed it, and tossed it into the sea. He made a second version of it to
be deposited on board of his ship, the *Niña*; both of these letters also were lost.
However, the almost-shipwreck seems to have made Columbus aware of the importance of leaving a record of his explorations to document the 'new world' as
well as his role in 'discovering' and claiming it. Thus, he wrote his letter for a
third time – this time in a more sober mood and in a more calculated style, we
may assume – addressing it to Luis de Santángel, treasurer of the Spanish
Crown, and, by implication, to the Spanish monarchs themselves, who sponsored
his enterprise and whom he obviously wanted to impress with what he found in
order to legitimize and extend his venture (cf. Wallisch, *Kolumbus* 6). We should
therefore not make the mistake of naively looking at this letter as simply a
faithful rendering of Columbus's travels and encounters; this would mean under-
estimating his rhetorical skill in crafting a scene that is fully intended to convey
the importance and foreboding of the historical moment, i.e. to describe it as and
thus make it a historical moment, even though he actually was rather clueless

about where he was and what he was about to initiate. Above all, Columbus's letter relies on conscious self-fashioning in its careful construction of his role as explorer and conqueror of new worlds.

Illustration 1: Columbus Takes Possession

Theodor de Bry, *Discovery of America, 12ᵗʰ of May, 1492* (1590).

To begin with, in his letter Columbus describes the Americas in *a language of wonder and awe*, conjuring up biblical images of the Garden of Eden. "Hispaniola is a marvel," he writes, "[i]t has […] fine, large flowing rivers," "mountains and peaks […] most beautiful," "trees of endless varieties, so high that they seem to touch the sky […] covered with blossoms, some with fruits," "honey, many kinds of birds, and a great variety of fruits;" the earth is "rich and fertile" ("Letter"). Columbus has found, his letter seems to suggest, an earthly paradise, a place of beauty and abundance that he describes in superlative after superlative. His expressions of amazement are not entirely genuine and sincere but are framed, in a second step, by *a language of profit and gain*. The abundance of the 'new world' promises economic profit for the Spanish Crown: not only will the Spanish be able to settle in this paradise by "planting" and "pasturage" and by "building towns and villages" but also to gain a fortune by extracting from it the resources that it holds: the Spanish monarchs will find "as much gold as they desire" as well as "spices, cotton, as much as their Highnesses may command to be shipped" (ibid.). Columbus is trying to impress the Spanish Crown in order to fulfill his original promise of return on capital at least in words and to secure further financial support for his next expeditions across the Atlantic, an investment for the monarchs, he seems to suggest, with manifold and exorbitant returns. Thus, Columbus advertises his 'discovery' as a success by all standards.

Yet, this paradise that Columbus describes is not 'empty:' it is inhabited by an indigenous population that somehow seems to stand between him and the riches he covets. The Natives figure as *inhabitants* of the islands he takes to be located east of India. These 'Indians,' however, are not portrayed as *owners* of the place they inhabit. In the very beginning of his letter Columbus describes how he *takes possession* of the 'new world' by bringing the Native population under Spanish colonial rule: "I discovered a great many islands, inhabited by numberless people; and of all I have taken possession for their Highnesses by proclamation and display of the Royal Standard without opposition" (ibid.). Stephen Greenblatt has drawn our attention to the theatricality of the event described in Columbus's letter, which is a staging that may seem strangely inappropriate, almost absurd, and quite literally somewhat 'out of place' when we keep in mind that the circumstances of the encounter between the Natives and Columbus were "drastically different" from anything that went before (*Marvelous Possessions* 55). Who among the addressees of Columbus's speech act present at the scene could have understood what was going on, let alone voiced opposition to Columbus's proclamation? How could the Native population have opposed his claim when for them it was not clear what his pompous gesturing implied or what his ritualized language meant? Columbus ostensibly plays a trick on them – with a simple formality he claims the land, and their reserve is read as forever forfeiting the right to the territory (cf. ibid. 60). Columbus constructs his subject position as an extension and an expression of the Spanish royal authority that he simply assumes in a series of speech acts: "For Columbus taking possession is principally the performance of a set of linguistic acts: declaring, witnessing, recording" (ibid. 56-57). He is obsessed with naming. Prior to any closer descriptions of the islands, Columbus details the new names he has given to them not because they were nameless – he even registers their 'Indian' names at times – but because he disregards and discards their previous names in favor of new, Spanish ones and makes their renaming part of the process of his 'discovery' and conquest (cf. Sale, *Conquest of Paradise*; Todorov, *Conquest of America* 38). In addition, his choice of names is intended to flatter the monarchs in Spain: Isabella, Fernandina, Santa María de Concepción, Juana. Translating, naming, and classifying are operations that are part of the process of colonization (cf. Hartog, *Mirror*) and intricate parts of the process of 'othering,' i.e. of turning the Native population into 'the other' and the object of European rule. In Columbus's description of the 'new world' inhabitants, there is a clear dichotomy of us (the Europeans) vs. them (the Native population) at work – both groups are portrayed as fundamentally and irreconcilably different from each other. This extreme polarization – what Hartog describes as the "excluded middle" (ibid. 258) – is another ingredient in the rhetoric of otherness that produces unbridgeable difference, introduces a steep hierarchy between 'us' and 'them,' and thus legitimizes asymmetrical power relations. Thus, the Natives are described as 'children of nature' by Columbus, as "extraordinarily timid" (in fact, they are "the most timid people in the world"), naked, instinctive, trusting, generous, gullible, and ignorant; and they have no weapons apart from "sticks of cane" ("Letter"). By inference, Columbus and his men are superior in every way. They represent culture (not nature) – and thus refinement and progress against the backdrop of the Natives' 'natural state' – in terms of their clothes, their religion (Christianity), and their technology; and they violently demonstrate their assumed superiority: Columbus takes possession of the islands and of the Natives, implying that he is authorized to do so at his will. He fleshes out the culture-nature divide between Europeans and the indigenous population, who by definition are closely related to the soil of their 'native' land. In the entire letter, there is no sense of the kind of encounter conjured up by Michael Dorris in the epigraph to this chapter, no meeting at eye level between the inhabitants of the Americas and their European visitors: the Europeans are landing and invading; the Natives are fleeing and have to be taken "by force." Overall, the latter are not portrayed as individuals but as a generalized group of "Indians" ("numberless people"). In his assessment of Columbus's hermeneutical skills, Tzvetan Todorov even contends that Columbus "was more perspicacious when he was observing nature than when he was trying to understand the Natives. His hermeneutic behaviour is not precisely the same in the one case as in the other" (*Conquest of America* 17), thereby ranking, according to Todorov, the Natives, human beings inhabiting the 'new world,' below the level of the inanimate world of nature and landscape. The cherished assumption of his own superiority registers at every level of Columbus's letter and is part of his "finalist" view – "the latter [view] no longer consists in seeking the truth but in finding confirmations of a truth known in advance (or, as we say, in wishful thinking)" (ibid. 19). All this is to the effect that Columbus offers us a narrative of first contact in which he tries to convince us of his rightful conquest of the Americas. This strategy locates the Native population clearly on the side of nature, lumped together with the wildlife and the vegetation – "Columbus speaks about the men he sees only because they too, after all, constitute a part of the landscape" (ibid. 34). We know that Columbus took several Natives from the Americas back to Spain with him – just like he took along plants, animals, and gold – and paraded them at court in front of the Spanish king and queen like animals.

Another defining aspect of Columbus's colonial hermeneutics and his 'rhetoric of otherness' is his religiosity. The letter opens and closes with references to God, and the 'discovery' is celebrated as a God-willed "glorious event, at which all Christendom should rejoice" ("Letter"). The Natives, of course, are not Christians, and in Columbus's view this is another manifestation of their primordial state of nature and their inferiority. That they supposedly take the Europeans for gods from heaven only adds to the argument that they lack a proper understanding of Christian religiosity and a comparable concept of God. Columbus's skills at reading and translating the gestures and exclamations of the Natives are certainly poor and symptomatic of his wishful thinking, yet his judgments are brought forward with utter self-confidence and with no attempt at self-reflection. Frauke Gewecke ponders the question whether he could have possibly freed himself more rigorously from his Eurocentric categories and norms in order to perceive and describe what he actually *saw* (cf. *Wie die neue Welt* 12). Clearly, in his letter it is by claiming the right to represent, define, categorize, and rule that Columbus grounds his authority over the Americas. From the perspective of postcolonial criticism, we find that Columbus's representational strategy in his letter renders the Natives mute and turns them into objects of hegemonic discourse; they have no voice in his text, and as they do not speak Spanish, they cannot participate in his discourse. Regarding Gayatri Spivak's famous question, "can the subaltern speak?" (cf. her article of the same title), in the case of the Native encounter with Columbus we would have to answer in the negative: no, they cannot.

Beyond the reception and circulation of this first letter – which laid the basis for Columbus's reputation and has been the object of much interpretation – Columbus's standing in the late 15th and early 16th centuries did not go unchallenged. In fact, power struggles between various interest groups in the newly conquered territories began the minute Columbus set foot on the Americas, proliferated after he had left to return to Spain, and continued to characterize the fate of the Spanish 'new world' colonies. His subsequent journeys to the Americas (1493-1496; 1498-1500; 1502-1504) did not consolidate his status as the 'discoverer' of new worlds. Even though Columbus quickly rose to fame in his time and day (and has remained the object of public adoration and commemoration), he fell out of grace with the monarchs toward the end of his life and was even shortly imprisoned on charges of mismanaging the colony. As Kirkpatrick Sale and others remind us, "the Admiral" died in relative obscurity; Sale describes him as somewhat disoriented and alienated, and he certainly had not yet gained the mythic status he attained later on (cf. *Conquest of Paradise*). His role as explorer and his legacy of 'discovery' seem to have been contested already during his lifetime, and have remained so after his death.

Illustration 2: Map of Columbus's Voyages

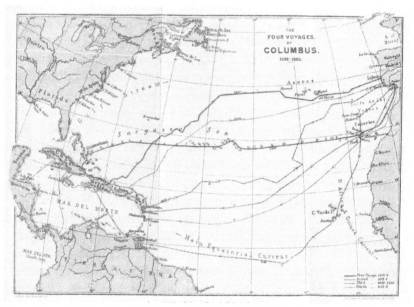

Filson Young, *Christopher Columbus and the New World of His Discoveries* (1906).

Next to Columbus's letter and Bartolomé de las Casas's summary of Columbus's logbook, it was the first biography of Columbus (written by his son, Ferdinand) that reached a wider circulation and promoted the image of Columbus as hero and 'discoverer' internationally. The narrative, titled *The Life of the Admiral Christopher Columbus by His Son Ferdinand*, was published posthumously in 1571 in Spanish, Italian, English, and Latin, and underwent many editions in the following decades and centuries (cf. Colón, *Life*). Ferdinand had his own agenda in promoting the unequivocal exoneration of his father's achievement. The bookish Ferdinand, as a member of the "Columbus Dynasty in the Caribbean" (cf. Troy Floyd's book of the same title), lived comfortably off his father's 'new world' discovery as a landowner as well as an (entirely unscrupulous) slaveholder, and thus had a strong interest in securing his inheritance and the legal titles granted to his father, which in the meantime had been revoked by the Spanish Crown. It appears that many passages in the book had originally been written for a litigation procedure against the Spanish courts. Ferdinand claims that Columbus and nobody else before and after him had discovered the Americas and that he deserved unqualified praise for that; like many others, Ferdinand never questioned this 'discovery' by taking into account the fact that his father never knew or fully realized where he had been. Texts like Ferdinand's continued to shape the image of Columbus as the agent of 'discovery,' and furthered the perpetuation of the idea of a 'discovery' of the Americas in general.

Even as the horrors of Spanish colonialism in the Americas – such as the brutal mistreatment of the indigenous population – became known in Spain and Europe at large, the reputation of Christopher Columbus as 'discoverer' did not diminish, and seems to have been largely immune to revision in the long run. In his famous *History of the Indies*, the foremost critic of Spanish colonialism, Bartolomé de las Casas, judges Columbus mildly; first of all he sees Columbus, whom he accompanies on his second journey, as chosen by God for "the fulfillment of a divine plan" (O'Gorman, *Invention* 19), and his 'discovery' as providence (cf. Roa-de-la-Carrera, *Histories* 138); and even as he indicts the horribly cruel treatment of the population by the Spanish and acknowledges Columbus's role in the establishment of the *encomienda* system of slave labor, he largely exempts Columbus from criticism and does not blame him directly for the enslavement and torture of the indigenous population in the Americas. According to de las Casas, Columbus's good intentions turned into an evil practice in the hands of the greedy and ruthless Spanish colonizers: "Columbus discovered America; others explored and colonized it" (Loewenberg, *American History* 44). De las Casas is not alone in separating Columbus's 'discovery' and his journeys from what followed in the course of the Spanish colonization of the Americas, thus setting him apart from other figures of colonization such as the notorious Hernán Cortés or the even more infamous Francisco Pizarro. This strategy has clearly helped to preserve and to affirm time and again an image of Columbus as a figure of light and salvation (representing the possibility to convert the 'new world' natives) rather than as a figure of doom and destruction (representing genocide and slavery). Whereas Columbus symbolizes new possibilities, a new world, a new time, and the re-discovery of paradise, it is the successive Spanish colonists who supposedly destroyed this paradise and perverted Columbus's vision. His journey to the 'new world' thus encapsulated "a brief moment of wonder followed by a long series of disasters and disenchantments" (Baym et al., "Christopher Columbus" 25).

Whether for reasons of personal gain (as in Ferdinand's case) or to critique Spanish colonialism (as in de las Casas's case), many writers have been preserving Columbus as a heroic figure, and a steady trickle of publications through the centuries ensured Columbus's continued prominence and popularity; the myth of Christopher Columbus and his 'discovery' of the 'new world' was, and is, firmly in place.

3. COLUMBUS AS AN AMERICAN HERO

> But if an historical past and an historical memory are indeed essential ingredients for a viable nationalism, what was the new United States to do in 1776, or in 1789, or for that matter at almost any time before the Civil War? How does a country without a past of her own acquire one, or how does she provide a substitute for it? Where could such a nation find the stuff for patriotism, for sentiment, for pride, for memory, for collective character?
> HENRY STEELE COMMAGER, "THE SEARCH FOR A USABLE PAST"

Christopher Columbus, it seems, was the historical figure most useful in the "search for a usable past" (cf. Commager) which had 18th-century Americans – colonial subjects of the British Crown seeking independence – look for meaningful beginnings. It is in the last decades of the 18th century that the specifically North American myth of Columbus comes into existence and in a very brief time span is firmly consolidated and embroidered. In the process of transmission from Spanish-language to English-language sources, William Robertson's 1778 *History of America* is highly influential – this book "was available to more American colonists than was any earlier source" (Bushman, *America* 40) and devoted hundreds of pages to Columbus, who, according to Robertson, in his endeavors combined "the superiority of genius" with "ardent enthusiasm" (*History* Vol. II 104). Robertson follows de las Casas in elevating Columbus and in crediting him with the 'discovery' of a new world. Overall, the author blames the Spanish colonizers (aside from Columbus) for their violent excesses in Latin America, but unsurprisingly exempts the British colonial power exercising control in North America from any criticism.

In the context of the American anti-colonial movement directed against the British Crown shortly before, during, and particularly after the American Revolutionary War (1775-1783), the cultural work of American public intellectuals,

writers and poets was to colonize the past in order to invent a meaningful beginning, and they did so by making the figure of Columbus part of their own
colonial and postcolonial legacy. Many public figures and writers gathered
around Columbus as a historical persona to affirm North American independence, and they represented him as a figure of national consensus exemplifying
American national virtues and an American national character *avant la lettre* (cf.
Herget, "Whitewashing" 3). In political culture, in public discussions of memorial practices and naming, in poetry, non-fiction, and the visual arts, Columbus
figures as a patron and ancestor of those Americans who were demanding their
independence from England and who later became citizens of the new republic.

On October 12, 1792, Jeremy Belknap (1744-1798), founder of the recently
established Massachusetts Historical Society, delivered the Columbus Day address to a rapt audience in Boston. He lauds the "Admiral's bold powers of
mind" (Martin, "Literature" 21), suggesting that Columbus 'knew' about land
masses to the West – "from the necessity of a counterpoise in the west, for the
immense quantity of land which was known to be in the east" (Belknap, *American Biography* 19). According to this somewhat curious reasoning, Belknap
holds that Columbus was fully aware of his 'discovery' and credits him with
intelligence, skill, and vision, for which Americans owed him thanks and admiration. Therefore, Belknap suggests, America should have rightfully been named
"Columbia." He was not alone with this view. Many of his contemporaries
lamented the 'misnaming' – of the hemisphere as well as the nation – as they
considered Amerigo Vespucci's role minor in comparison to Columbus's
achievements. The geographer and mathematician Martin Waldseemüller had
introduced the name "America" for the new continent he mapped in his "Cosmo-
graphiae Introductio" in 1507 after the wide circulation of Amerigo Vespucci's
mundus novus letter about his third journey to South America in 1501 and 1502,
which had been published immediately in various languages. And the name
stuck. In the late 18th century, most accepted this 'misnaming' as a *fait accompli*
(cf. Martin, "Literature" 23). Yet, the historian Samuel Whelpley was among
those who took a somewhat extreme position when he complained that naming
the continent and the nation 'America' rather than 'Columbia' was "the greatest
act of folly, caprice, cruelty, and injustice [...] that ever mankind were guilty of"
(qtd. in ibid.). According to him, the new nation also should be strictly distinguished in name from the continent, and thus he concludes: "There are serious
and urgent reasons why the United States should have a name [of its own]"
(ibid.).

Amidst these discussions of naming the new nation, "Columbia" had been informally "adopted as an alternative to America on the eve of the American Revolution" (Bushman, *America* 41). It became a lyrical term for America envisioned as a female allegorical figure in revolutionary poetry. The African American poet Phillis Wheatley is supposedly the first to use it in her poem "To His Excellency General Washington" (1776):

Celestial Choir! enthron'd in realms of light,
Columbia's scenes of glorious toils I write.
While freedom's cause her anxious breast alarms,
She flashes dreadful in refulgent arms.
See mother earth her offspring's fate bemoan,
And nations gaze at scenes before unknown! (577; my emphasis)

Wheatley follows her male contemporaries in pairing Columbus and George Washington – commander-in-chief of the revolutionary troops and first President of the United States (and another emergent national hero for more obvious reasons) – for patriotic purposes (cf. Bushman, *America* 54; Groseclose, "American Genesis" 14). This tandem of two foundational figures is forcefully evident in highly symbolic practices of naming in the early republic: the US capital is named "Washington," whereas the government district, ceded by Virginia and Maryland in 1791, is named "District of Columbia." George Washington's farewell address is published in 1796 as *Columbia's Legacy* (cf. Bushman, *America* 55). Many place names (cities, towns, and streets) as well as a rich memorial culture remind us of the heroism credited to Columbus (and Washington, of course) in the foundational phase of the USA.

Wheatley's lyrical reference is far from singular. Philip Freneau (1752-1832), who bore the title of the "poet of the American revolution" and who is perhaps the most remarkable 18th-century American writer, refers to Columbus in many of his patriotic verses, e.g. in "Discovery," "The Rising Glory of America" (with Henry Brackenridge), and "The Pictures of Columbus." Freneau, who belongs to the new American elite, champions Columbus as an unrecognized genius, as a brilliant navigator ahead of his time, as an individualist and an idealist, and as a figure of dissent who found "new worlds for thankless kings" (Freneau, "Pictures" 122). But Freneau also addresses the dark side of Spanish conquest. In his early poem "Discovery," which he wrote in 1772, he criticizes the brutality of Spanish colonialism, which under the cloak of missionary work usurped the continent by using physical and epistemic violence:

How few have sailed on virtue's nobler plan,
How few with motives worthy of a man! –
While through the deep-sea waves we saw them go
Where'er they found a man they made a foe [...]. (86)

Whereas Freneau singles out Pizarro as the villain of Spanish colonialism (cf. ibid.), Columbus is not explicitly mentioned in his critique of the Spanish empire. Like many others, the poet disconnects Columbus's 'discovery' from Cortés's and Pizarro's conquests (cf. Bushman, *America* 48) and thinks Columbus is deserving mostly of praise, as his famous poem "The Rising Glory of America" evidences:

The Period famed when first Columbus touched
These shores so long unknown – through various toils,
Famine, and death, the hero forced his way,
Through oceans pregnant with perpetual storms,
And climates hostile to adventurous man. (49)

In "The Pictures of Columbus," Freneau finds Columbus imprisoned on false charges and disowned from his rightful claims. Freneau anticipates a compensation for this lack of recognition in the distant future:

My toils rewarded, and my woes repaid;
When empires rise where lonely forests grew,
Where Freedom shall her generous plans pursue. (122)

The newly formed US republic – we can infer – is a late recompense for Columbus's suffering as a tragic hero in his own time.

Next to the poems of Freneau, Joel Barlow's *The Columbiad* (1807), which is an expanded version of his *The Vision of Columbus* (1787), is another key text for tracing how Columbus and the narrative of 'discovery' were represented in North American poetry of the 18th and early 19th centuries. Its author was a statesman, political writer, and poet whose epic introduces a new word to the English language: Columbiad – echoing the *Iliad*, which recounts the fall of Troy. Barlow calls his work a "patriotic poem" (*Columbiad* 375); it celebrates Columbus as "one of the wisest and best among the benefactors of mankind," whereas it condemns Cortés as "the perfidious butcher of its [America's] ancient race" (ibid.). Its preface as well as its first lines echo the Greek source text:

I sing the Mariner who first unfurl'd
An eastern banner o'er the western world
And taught mankind where future empires lay
In these fair confines of descending day
Who swa'd a moment, with vicarious power
Iberia's sceptre on the new found shore
Then saw the paths his virtuous steps had trod
Pursued by avarice and defiled with blood
The tribes he foster'd with paternal toil
Snatcht from his hand, and slaughter'd for their spoil
Slaves, kings, adventurers, envious of his name
Enjoy'd his labors and purloin'd his fame
And gave the Viceroy, from his high seat hurl'd
Chains for a crown, a prison for a world. (413-14)

Barlow acknowledges, as does Freneau, that things have gone awry after the 'discovery' because of the greed of the Spanish colonizers. Yet, with the republican future secured by US-American independence, Columbus's legacy will be honored and cherished, Barlow writes. This perspective is offered to Columbus as a consolation (*consolatio*); in Barlow's epic, as in Freneau's "Pictures," Columbus is imprisoned and awaiting his death when Hesper, the angel of the West, shows him in a dream the subsequent history of the Americas. Columbus is desperate when he sees the destruction of Mexico by Cortés, curses his 'discovery,' and begs God for forgiveness. Only at the end of his dream does the angel make him see North America, a hopeful vision, to brighten his mood:

A happier hemisphere invites thy view [...]
there Europe's better sons their seats shall trace
and change of government improve the race. (427)

Columbus then looks with paternal contentment on his North American descendants. He can now rest assured that in spite of the years of agony and suffering (both of the peoples of the Americas and his own), his 'discovery' has been meaningful and a blessing for humanity. The United States of America are to prove this and are an embodiment of Barlow's "idea of progress" (Pearce, *Continuity* 65). Barlow turns to classical antiquity in order to integrate Columbus and the history of the USA into the master narrative of Western civilization; Barlow's *translatio imperii* anticipates the greatness of the new US nation with its republican ideals. He, like Freneau, writes in the neoclassical mode of his literary period, often "forc[ing] his new world into archaic literary dress" (Elliott, *Revolutionary Writers* 124), yet his coinage of terms such as 'Columbiad' shows how he wrestles with the limitations of conventional language to adequately describe the history of America: we note "the strange and awkward neologisms by which the language of the poem is disfigured," writes scholar Samuel Kettell in 1829 ("Joel Barlow" 11). As Helmbrecht Breinig and Susanne Opfermann suggest, the neologisms in Barlow's work indicate how early American literature is creating an artistic language for a new political entity and national culture (cf. "Die Literatur" 43; cf. also Pearce, *Continuity* 67).

The historians Belknap and Whelpley and the poets Freneau, Barlow, and Wheatley are only a few examples of the larger phenomenon of Columbus worship. Why him? And what are the reasons and rhetorical strategies used to appropriate Columbus as an American hero?

First of all, Columbus was a convenient historical figure for the simple reason that he was *not British* and thus not implicated in British colonialism; the notion of Columbus as a Founding Father establishes a non-English patrimony for the United States (cf. Groseclose, "American Genesis" 12) at the height of the conflict between the colonial power and its colonies. Second, the writers of the American revolutionary era sympathized with Columbus's dependency on monarchical good will and clearly cast him as an anti-monarchical, almost revolutionary figure; they established a somewhat skewed analogy between Columbus's suffering under the yoke of greedy monarchs who did not appreciate his genius and the fate of North American colonists under the rule of George III. The events of the age of 'discovery' are cast in a typological manner and become symbolic of the revolutionary period (cf. Herget, "Whitewashing" 3-5). Third, Columbus's quest for a "passage to India" (Smith, *Virgin Land* 20) can be seen as prefiguring American westward expansion – with the aim to found "a mighty nation reaching from coast to coast" (Bushman, *America* 49). Columbus is a "symbol of ongoing expansion" and "of expansive destiny" (Martin, "Literature" 20). From the turn of the century onward, Columbus's "daring, perseverance, and intrepidity were championed as necessary ingredients to the transcontinental endeavour" and he "became the very embodiment of an American pathfinder" (Groseclose, "American Genesis" 14). Fourth, it is argued that Columbus's willpower and stamina in the face of sheer insurmountable obstacles embodied the highest degree of individualism – a core American virtue in early discourses of the republic – which "makes Columbus an American by temperament" (Martin, "Literature" 22). Fifth, the sense of providence that surrounds Columbus in historical sources can be attributed to both religious as well as secular designs. In the North American invention of tradition, he becomes part of "the negotiation of an uncharted intellectual and artistic path from a dominant religious vision of America to a new nationalist ideology" (Elliott, *Revolutionary Writers* 17) in the age of enlightenment, in which American writers could envision Columbus "[w]ith all the moral fervor of eighteenth-century American Calvinism behind them and the expanse of an open cultural horizon before them" (ibid. 11). Thus, the glorification of Columbus concurs with the first phase of the formation of an American civil religion.

The 'Americanization' of Columbus in the revolutionary period continued into the 19th century. Washington Irving's comprehensive biography of Columbus as well as George Bancroft's *History of the United States* are two of the most prominent examples signifying this trend. Washington Irving, one of America's first writers of short stories and its first canonized as well as internationally popular writer, is considered by Shreve still to be "one of the first true Columbus scholars" ("Christopher Columbus" 704). His voluminous *Life and Voyages of Christopher Columbus*, written in the Alhambra in Granada, Spain on the basis of archival manuscripts, embraces the historical figure as a bridge-builder between the 'old' and the 'new' world:

It is the object of the following work, to relate the deeds and fortunes of the mariner who first had the judgment to divine, and the intrepidity to brave the mysteries of this perilous deep; and who, by his hardy genius, his inflexible constancy, and his heroic courage, brought the ends of the earth into communication with each other. The narrative of his troubled life is the link which connects the history of the old world with that of the new. (Irving, *Life* 10)

The historian George Bancroft indicates with his choice of title – *History of the United States of America, from the Discovery of the American Continent* – that he includes the narrative of Columbus's 'discovery' in US-American national history and, beyond that, dwells on this first period because "it contains the germ of our institutions" (6):

Imagination had conceived the idea, that vast inhabited regions lay unexplored in the west; and poets had declared, that empires beyond the ocean would one day be revealed to the daring navigator. But Columbus deserves the undivided glory of having realized that belief. During his lifetime he met with no adequate recompense. The self-love of the Spanish monarch was offended at receiving from a foreigner in his employ benefits too vast for requital; and the contemporaries of the great navigator persecuted that merit which they could not adequately reward. Nor had posterity been mindful to gather into a finished picture the memorials of his career, till the genius of Irving, with candor, liberality, and original research, made a record of his eventful life, and in mild but enduring colors sketched his sombre inflexibility of purpose, his deep religious enthusiasm, and the disinterested magnanimity of his character. (6-7)

A portrayal could hardly be more laudatory, and Irving and Bancroft are only two among many praising voices. As Matthew Dennis points out in his overview, "[w]ithin fifty years of the American Revolution, versions of Columbus's name graced the titles of some sixteen periodicals, eighteen books, and a half dozen scholarly societies" ("Reinventing" 128).

Illustration 3: Neo-Classicist Depiction of Columbus's Landing

John Vanderlyn, *Landing of Columbus at the Island of Guanahaní, West Indies* (1846).

Columbus also quickly advanced to become an American icon in visual culture, and his landing in the Americas became a powerful "image of American genesis" (cf. Groseclose). The two most representative examples of early American paintings that depict Columbus's arrival in the Americas are David Edwin's depiction of Columbus in *The Landing of Christopher Columbus* (1800), which is uncannily similar to Charles Willson Peale's 1779 portrayal of George Washington in his *George Washington at Princeton* (cf. ibid. 14), and John Vanderlyn's painting *The Landing of Columbus at the Island of Guanahaní, West Indies*

(1846), displayed in the rotunda of the United States Capitol in Washington D.C.; Vanderlyn hierarchizes the 'discoverer' and his objects of 'discovery' (dressed versus naked, proud and upright versus timid and huddled, Christians versus non-Christians) and culturally translates the Caribbean setting into a more unspecified, possibly North American one in a transposition that we are already familiar with: the lone tree in the painting "is not a palm but instead looks very much like a specimen that might grow in a temperate climate such as one finds in the United States" (ibid. 16).

In sum, the public discourse commemorating Columbus's 'discovery' – the poetry by Philip Freneau and Joel Barlow, Washington Irving's biography, early historiography, as well as early American visual culture representing the landing of Columbus – evidences the elevation of Christopher Columbus and his 'discovery' to a national myth. The 1792 celebrations of the 'discovery's' Tercentennial constituted a first climax in the glorification of this figure, after 1592 and 1692 had come and gone without much notice in either the 'old' or the 'new' world. Disregarding historical evidence, Christopher Columbus was elevated to a *homo americanus*; he was depicted as a good colonist (if a colonist at all), a scientist, scholar, and humanist, as a profoundly religious man, as an Enlightenment figure ahead of Enlightenment, and thus as a tragic figure. It may not always be easy or even feasible to distinguish the 'historical Columbus' from the 'heroic Columbus,' as Sale suggests we must (cf. *Conquest of Paradise*), yet in the case of US-American mythmaking in the late 18th century, the extreme divergence between historical evidence and narrative embellishment is quite apparent in the way that Columbus serves as a figure of empowerment regardless of the specificity of his historical, cultural, and religious context. The far-reaching consequences of this foundational narrative for all of the Americas and its treatment in historiography have been pointed out by historian James Loewen: "Columbus was so pivotal that, like Jesus, historians use him to divide history: the Americas before 1492 are called 'pre-Columbian'" (Loewen, *Lies* 1).

4. WHOSE COLUMBUS? THE MAKING OF AN ETHNIC HERO

> [T]he age created him and the age left him. There is no more conspicuous example in history of a man showing the path and losing it.
> JUSTIN WINSOR, *CHRISTOPHER COLUMBUS*

In the second half of the 19th century we witness the first phase of revisionism regarding the mythical status of Christopher Columbus in the United States. For one thing, other more genuinely 'American' foundational narratives had by then developed, and were continuing to take shape (for example the myth of the Founding Fathers, the myth of the West, and the myth of the self-made man), which made Columbus's 'discovery' as a story of American beginnings less singular and less important. At the same time, the Columbus myth as such was more closely scrutinized in light of ongoing discussions about changes and developments in American society and its demographic composition. The adoption of Columbus as a foundational figure in American national discourses of the late 18th and early 19th centuries had reflected little on a number of aspects that now surfaced: that he was an Italian sailing for the Spanish Crown, that he did not actually land in North America but in the Caribbean, and that he was Catholic. Why did Americans become aware of these facts regarding Columbus's 'discovery' now, one hundred years after they had made him their national hero?

In the 19th century, the USA was receiving millions of immigrants from Europe – the so-called first wave of immigrants from Northern and Western Europe in the 1840s and 1850s, and the so-called second wave of immigrants mainly from Southern and Eastern Europe in the 1870s and the following decades: "From 1880 to 1924, some four million immigrants from southern Italy came to America, joining an earlier group of Italian immigrants, mainly from the northern peninsula" (Dennis, "Reinventing" 140). In response to the large numbers of newly arriving immigrants, the American-born population often reacted with anxiety and hostility. The last decades of the 19th century have often been characterized as a period of extreme xenophobia, racism, and nativism, a specifically American term to describe the phenomenon of "intense opposition to an internal minority on the grounds of its foreign (i.e. 'un-American') connections" (Higham, *Strangers* 4). Many social and political groups formed to protect what they considered to be a distinctively American way of life. John Higham discerned three major themes in American nativism: anti-Catholicism, anti-radicalism, and racial nativism based on an Anglo-Saxon tradition and the assumption of Anglo-Saxon superiority in the United States (ibid. 5-11). Historian Matthew Jacobson has traced the heated debates around the racial composition of the USA in the 19th century, when 'race' was not merely used to distinguish 'blacks' from 'whites' but 'Anglo-Saxons' from 'Celtic,' 'Slavic,' 'Teutonic,' 'Nordic,' 'Iberic,' 'Latin,' and other supposedly 'foreign' elements and lineages (cf. *Whiteness* 7). In this logic, immigrants from different parts of Europe – particularly those from Catholic countries – were viewed with distrust and skepticism, a reaction that often caused massive discrimination and sometimes even physical violence. The heated debate around the dangers of 'foreign infiltration' culminated in the Immigration Act of 1924, which put a stop to mass immigration to the United States.

This nativist intellectual climate affected the attitude toward Christopher Columbus as a national hero. Lawyer and diplomat Aaron Goodrich, author of *A History of the Character and Achievements of the So-Called Christopher Columbus* (1874), and historian Justin Winsor, founding member of the American Historical Association and author of *Christopher Columbus and How He Received and Imparted the Spirit of Discovery* (1890), were among those who contested the 'truthfulness' and merit of the narrative of 'discovery,' which, they argued, derived mostly from Columbus's own writings. According to Goodrich, Columbus in fact was "his own historian and eulogist" (*History* 128) and thus left out a great many aspects that would cast him in a less positive light. Goodrich radically revised the Columbus myth and pointed to previously neglected sources and archival records; one has to add that since American independence, many new sources had become available for the study of early transatlantic mobility and were then used by scholars to different ends (cf. Henige, *In Search*). Based on his research, Goodrich portrays Columbus as a "pirate" and a "slave trader" who already had "a history of piracy and crime" before entering Spain for dubious reasons in 1485, and journeyed out of the basest motives, intending merely to raid any place he might find (*History* 129); Columbus did neither deserve commemoration as an individual nor did he deserve credit for any kind of 'discovery.' Goodrich claims that the arrival of Leif Erikson in North America was the actual moment of 'discovery' of the Americas 600 years prior to Columbus's arrival, and that it was the "heroic character of the Northmen" – rather than the "shabby grandeur" of a slave trader from Southern Europe (ibid. 336) – that lastingly shaped the American character. In that, Goodrich concludes, "the American might well feel relief and pride" (ibid. 87). Justin Winsor, the leading historian of his day, similarly denounces the Italians, who may produce capable individuals such as Christopher Columbus or Amerigo Vespucci every once in a while, but as a nation are incapable of holding their own:

You and I have not followed the maritime peoples of western Europe in planting and defending their flags on the American shores without observing the strange fortunes of the Italians, in that they have provided pioneers for those Atlantic nations without having once secured in the New World a foothold for themselves. (*Christopher Columbus*)

Although Columbus may have been a somewhat exceptional figure, his enterprise lacked sustainability, and his 'discovery' was a "blunder" (ibid. 512) – shortcomings that are also attributed to the 'nature' of Italians. 19th-century

American stereotypes concerning Italian immigrants cast them as innately criminal, lazy, unfit for democracy, and, as one Secret Service report has it, "a menace to the country" (Jacobson, *Whiteness* 61). Although Winsor's text is less explicit than Goodrich's, it still breathes the common racist sentiments of the time; both Goodrich and Winsor use stereotypes in profiling Columbus individually and Italians as a 'race' collectively. From a New Historicist perspective, we see the 19th-century discourses on 'race' and Anglo-Saxon superiority reflected in the historiography and mythmaking of American 'origins.' What had made Christopher Columbus attractive in the founding phase of the US – that he was not British – now made him suspect.

Of course, these new voices in American historical scholarship did not completely debunk the Columbus myth – far from it; it continues to have a firm place in popular discourses of commemoration and other forms of public and popular culture. The World's Columbian Exposition of 1893 (originally scheduled for 1892) in Chicago was a grandiose event, described as "a spectacle of surpassing significance" (Sale, *Conquest of Paradise* 350) that celebrated the historical figure in more abstract terms: the long water pool – the centerpiece of the "White City" exhibition grounds – symbolized the long voyage Columbus took to the 'new world;' the statue placed next to it, however, was not one of Columbus but of the republic. Rather than merely as a patriotic figure, Columbus is cast here as a symbol of progress and civilization par excellence. As such, it seems that his journey only makes sense in the context of the newly emergent US empire and its self-proclaimed exceptionalism. Yet, we can also observe that the meaning of Columbus as a foundational figure and national icon is becoming contested, even controversial. Dennis refers to the 1892 celebrations as a "confused Columbian discourse" ("Reinventing" 145). The celebration of Columbus as hero and of America as Columbia (cf. John Gast's 1872 painting *American Progress*) was accompanied by some white American intellectuals' disenchantment with Columbus on the one hand, and identification with Columbus on the part of newly arrived immigrants (particularly those who were stigmatized as foreigners in the United States) on the other. Since the late 19th century, the myth of Columbus and the 'discovery' of America thus no longer functions as an unequivocal universal national myth but is enlisted in new minority discourses by Jewish, Italian, and Irish immigrants to America who claim him as their foundational figure. He thus remains a figure of dissent, of heroism and of, at times, unrecognized achievement, albeit in a modified ideological configuration – he becomes an ethnic hero. This new turn in the troping of Columbus as hero is manifested in the cultural and memorial practices of the immigrants, in their poetry and literature, as well as their politics.

Illustration 4: Columbia Moves West

John Gast, *American Progress* (1872).

It comes as no surprise in this context that the 1892 commemoration of Columbus's 'discovery' is clearly accentuated by Italian Americans, who celebrate Christopher Columbus as their ancestral figure. After all, he was a native of Genoa and sailed for the Genoese fleet before he went to Portugal, and later to Spain. On the occasion, the Italian Americans of New York City erected a 75-feet high marble statue by Gaetano Russo with an inscription that is supposed to remind all Americans of Columbus's achievements:

TO

CHRISTOPHER COLUMBUS
THE ITALIANS RESIDENT IN AMERICA,
SCOFFED AT BEFORE,
DURING THE VOYAGE, MENACED,
AFTER IT, CHAINED,
AS GENEROUS AS OPPRESSED,

TO THE WORLD, HE GAVE A WORLD.
JOY AND GLORY
NEVER UTTERED A MORE THRILLING CALL
THAN THAT WHICH RESOUNDED
FROM THE CONQUERED OCEAN
IN SIGHT OF THE FIRST AMERICAN ISLAND
LAND! LAND!

Illustration 5: Columbus Monument in New York (Historical Postcard)

Brooklyn Postcard Co. Inc., *Columbus and Maine Monuments* (1914).

This memorial is an indication of the trend to transform Cristóbal Colón into Cristoforo Colombo, a specifically Italian hero embraced both by native Italians hungry for progenitors of their new nation (united in 1861) and by the growing numbers of Italian immigrants in the United States eager to claim an authentic "American" figure as their own. (Sale, *Conquest of Paradise* 351)

Today, in New York City alone there are eleven memorials to Christopher Columbus, ranging from the marble statue in Central Park to less extravagant pieces in Brooklyn and the Bronx, many of which are part of Italian American institutions and/or were commissioned by Italian American organizations. The enlistment of Columbus in Italian American cultural practices continues into the present: Columbus Day parades in major American cities are organized by Italian American communities; Italian American author Mario Puzo (of *The Godfather* fame) wrote a screenplay for *Christopher Columbus – The Discovery* (1992); and the HBO television drama series *The Sopranos* dedicated an episode titled "Christopher" to a controversial celebration of Columbus Day in New York (cf. Bondanella, *Hollywood Italians* 303-4).

Yet, at the end of the 19th century not only Italian Americans took recourse to Columbus in their search for a 'usable past.' Emma Lazarus, the Jewish American poet famous for her sonnet "The New Colossus" (which is inscribed on the pedestal of the Statue of Liberty), titles one of her poems "1492," which is here quoted in full:

> Thou two-faced year, Mother of Change and Fate,
> Didst weep when Spain cast forth with flaming sword,
> The children of the prophets of the Lord,
> Prince, priest, and people, spurred by zealot hate.
> Hounded from sea to sea, from state to state,
> The West refused them, and the East abhorred.
> No anchorage the known world could afford
> Close-locked was every port, barred every gate.
> Then smiling, thou unveil'dst, O two-faced year,
> A virgin world where doors of sunset part,
> Saying, "Ho, all who weary, enter here!
> There falls each ancient barrier that the art
> Of race or creed or rank devised, to rear
> Grim bulwarked hatred between heart and heart!"

Lazarus's poem acknowledges two momentous historical events that occurred in 1492: the Jewish expulsion from Spain under King Ferdinand and Queen

Isabella, and their support for Columbus's journey across the Atlantic. In 1888, Lazarus's poem depicts the USA as a haven for refugees who are in need of a new home. The poet may have been aware of the rumors indicating that Columbus himself was partly Jewish. Although there is still little evidence to corroborate this long-standing speculation, we may yet reflect on the 'timing' of the expulsion of the Jews from Spain and his journey, and agree with Morison and Vignaud that even if Columbus himself was not Jewish it is likely that Jews who hoped to find a new home somewhere in the West were among his crewmembers (cf. Morison, *Admiral*; Vignaud, *Letter* and "Christopher Columbus"). More recently, Steve Berry's *The Columbus Affair* (2012) picks up on this possibility and makes it the center of a contemporary conspiracy-thriller plot.

Apart from Lazarus's patriotic Columbus poem, Jewish American literature and popular culture – from Mary Antin's autobiography *The Promised Land* (1912) to the Marx Brothers' comedies – often took issue with the glorification of Columbus. "A curse on Columbus!" became a frequent pun "in ironic response to the nation's official narrative" (Weber, "Accents" 136; cf. Sollors, *Beyond Ethnicity* 33; Goldsmith, "Curse"). In the novel *Jews without Money* (1930) by the socialist Jewish American writer, journalist, and activist Michael Gold one character exclaims in a somewhat typical fashion: "'It is all useless. A curse on Columbus! A curse on America, the thief! It is a land where the lice make fortunes, and the good men starve!'" (79). Jewish American author Philip Roth declares "Goodbye Columbus" in his 1959 novella of the same title in commenting on the story of initiation of a young Jewish American man into the complex system of Jewish American class distinctions and on the subsequent failure of a love relationship.

Columbus became not only an ancestral figure for different ethnic groups but was also considered a patron by Catholics in Protestant America. Catholic (mostly Irish and Italian) immigrants to America strongly felt the anti-Catholic and anti-papal sentiments in American nativist attitudes, and reacted by forming their own institutions. In 1882, the Knights of Columbus are founded by an Irish American Catholic priest in New Haven, Connecticut; this organization was intended as a "fortress" against discrimination, dedicated itself to "Columbianism," and tried to "demonstrate the compatibility of Roman catholicism and American democracy" (Kauffman, *Faith* 276). According to historian Christopher Kauffman, who was commissioned by the order to write numerous histories and documentations, the organization's ideology is shaped by "a blend of popular fraternalism, American Catholic patriotism and traditional Catholicism" (*Columbianism* 29).

[The Knights of Columbus] viewed the discovery of America as a Catholic event, just as Anglo-Saxon Protestants viewed the landing at Plymouth Rock as a Puritan event. The Knights of Columbus were implicitly celebrating the landing of the *Santa Maria*, the Catholic counterpart to the Protestants' *Mayflower* and a ship which had arrived 128 years earlier. (Kauffman, *Faith* 276)

The Catholic order quickly expands across the country: 6.000 knights participate in the 1892 Columbus parade (cf. Kauffman, *Faith* 91); by 1893, the order has 550.000 members in the Boston area and by 1905, it has spread to all American states as well as to Mexico and Canada. Kauffman's *Faith and Fraternalism* is published on the occasion of the 100th anniversary of the Knights in 1982, and reprinted for the Quincentenary of Columbus's arrival in the Americas in 1992. The order today prides itself on more than 125 years of history, during which it has also seen internal debates, phases of historical revisionism, discussions of racism and gender discrimination, as well as criticism from the Catholic Church because of its name – amidst revisionists, suggestions have been made to rename the order the "Knights of Christ," or any other less controversial, i.e. political name (cf. Dennis, "Reinventing" 157).

Overall, Columbus ceased to be a symbol of national unity and cohesion by the end of the 19th century as different groups staked their claim to 'America' by placing themselves in the tradition of Columbus and his 'discovery,' and this trend continued throughout the 20th century. Yet, around 1992, the second and most forceful phase of revisionism set in. As the 500th anniversary of the 'discovery' of the Americas approached, the question of what and who was to be celebrated seemed ever more pressing.

5. 1992 AND THE COLUMBUS CONTROVERSY

For many Native Americans, to be asked to celebrate Columbus is the equivalent of asking Jews to celebrate Hitler.
ELLA SHOHAT AND ROBERT STAM, *UNTHINKING EUROCENTRISM*

Der Amerikaner, der den Kolumbus zuerst entdeckte, machte eine böse Entdeckung.
GEORG CHRISTOPH LICHTENBERG

Lichtenberg's aphorism points to the fact that until the period of the American Revolutionary War, the term 'American' referred to the native inhabitants of the

American continent, not to the English settlers. Lichtenberg's unusual perspective on who was being discovered in the Americas (Columbus, not the Natives) is used in many discussions and new publications of the early 1990s to reconfigure the Eurocentric view on the 'new world.' The quincentennial of 'discovery' in 1992 has been a watershed for questioning the status of Columbus as hero, adventurer, opportunist, slave trader, and slaveholder in revisionisms that come in many different shapes and manifestations.

Literature and film are two prime media in which the claim to·Columbus's legacy has not only been contested but in which the very idea of 'discovery' has also been outright refuted. For many Native Americans, Columbus's arrival in the Americas marks the beginning of colonialism, genocide, rape, slavery, expropriation and displacement, as well as cultural death. Columbus stands at the beginning of a new and for many inhabitants of the Americas deadly era.

Authors of multicultural American literature and Native American writers in particular have published essays, novels, poetry, and histories on these issues. In 1992, the Before Columbus Foundation, established in 1976 by the writers Ishmael Reed, Victor Hernández Cruz, Shawn Wong, and Rudolfo Anaya, put out *The Before Columbus Foundation Fiction Anthology* with the agenda of going before and "beyond" Columbus (Strads et al., "Introduction" xi). Going 'beyond' Columbus and his 'discovery' is also at the core of Native American rewritings of 'discovery.' Many of these texts are exploring the dark areas of history, often with a postmodern fantastic twist (cf. McHale, *Postmodernist Fiction*), as do Louise Erdrich and Michael Dorris in *The Crown of Columbus* (1991) or, even more radically, Gerald Vizenor in *The Heirs of Columbus* (1991). The first use a present-day campus romance to revisit the historical evidence and site of 'discovery,' the latter invents a trickster figure who revises the historical legacy by rendering Columbus a part-Native "crossblood."

Humor and re-invention are also part of several other re-envisionings: Osage writer and poet Carter Revard presents a parodic reversal of the discovery scene, this time set in Europe:

It may be impossible to civilize the Europeans. When I claimed England for the Osage Nation, last month, some of the English chiefs objected. [...] So I said the hell with England for this trip and went to France and rented a little Renault in Paris and drove past the chateaux to Biarritz, stopping only to proclaim that everything the Loire and Seine flowed past was ours. [...] The people there talk differently from those in London, but their signs are much the same – they use a lingua franca so to speak – so they recognized my visa card and gave the Renault gasoline much like that in Oklahoma, globalized enough so they are not completely benighted. Whether they understood that France now belongs to us was not clear, but they were friendly and they fed me well, accepting in return some pieces of beautifully painted paper and metal discs with allegorical figures on them, with which they seemed almost childishly pleased [...]. ("Report" 333-34)

Revard's travel account about a journey to Europe intertextually engages with Columbus's first letter from the 'new world' and inverts the European perspective of 'discovering' and 'civilizing' the Americas. Columbus's proclamation about taking possession of the Americas on behalf of the Spanish Crown is reconfigured in the voice of the Native discoverer signifying on the ignorance and 'childishness' of the Europeans, i.e. the French, in an anachronistic postmodern fashion that allows the Native American protagonist who is 'colonizing' Europe – and who in the European imagination has of course been linked predominantly to a state of nature – to drive around by car and to use money and credit cards. The comparison "much like that in Oklahoma" echoes the comparison in Columbus's writing between the 'new world' nature and climate to that of particular Spanish regions: Columbus's Andalusia is Revard's Oklahoma. Revard's irony is matched in the self-reflexive reimagining of first contact by African American comedian Flip Wilson. When his Columbus, conversing with Queen Isabella in African American Vernacular English, sets out for America in order to discover Ray Charles, he meets Natives celebrating among themselves:

It's a big holiday in America that day, a big holiday called "Not-Having-Been Discovered-Yet-Day." All the Indians on the beach, they are celebrating. They got sandwiches, six-packs, three or four bags of whatever it is they putting in the pipe. Chris leans over the rail of the ship, he says, "Hey y'all. Y'all. Where is this? [...] My name is Christopher Columbus. I'm a discoverer. I'm gonna discover America. I'm going to discover y'all." ("Christopher Columbus")

It is only when "the Indians are throwing rocks, spears, flaming arrows, tree trunks [...] yelling out a bunch of profanities about Chris's mother and everything" (ibid.) that Wilson's Columbus, unsuccessful at colonization, decides to turn the boat around and to leave any further 'discoveries' in the 'new world' to the Puritans. Wilson's Columbus provides us with a metafictional commentary on the narrative of discovery and the precarious claims to truth it has held, and counters long-cherished notions of European superiority as well as indigenous naiveté.

In Native American poetry, Jimmie Durham in his poem "Columbus Day" (1983) addresses the Native American experience in the American school system almost ten years prior to the culmination of the Columbus controversy:

> In school I was taught the names
> Columbus, Cortez, and Pizarro and
> A dozen filthy murderers.
> A bloodline all the way to General Miles,
> Daniel Boone and General Eisenhower. (10)

Durham's speaker makes no distinction between Columbus on the one hand and Cortés and Pizarro on the other, as did the poets of the American Revolution: here, all of them are part of the same criminal history of exploitation. And this history is extended to US-American historical figures who are placed in a continuum with the Spanish conquerors and who figure as agents of westward expansion, Manifest Destiny, and war.

Further critical, historiographical, fictional, and lyrical perspectives are collected in numerous anthologies. To name only two: *America in 1492* is an alternative history in which Alvin Josephy has gathered together renowned writers and scholars, among them N. Scott Momaday and Francis Jennings, in order to describe and promote an understanding of "America and its traditions on the eve of the Columbus voyages. Its point of reference is America, not Europe" (Josephy, "Introduction" 7); editor Joseph Bruchac's *Returning the Gift: Poetry and Prose from the First North American Native Writers' Festival* is the result of a gathering of more than 300 Native writers held in Norman, Oklahoma, in 1992. Festival historian Geary Hobson calls it a "showcase of Native American literature" ("On a Festival" xxvii). In addition, Coco Fusco and Guillermo Gómez-Peña have produced "Radio Pirata: Colón Go Home!," which aired on National Public Radio and was printed in Fusco's *English Is Broken Here* (179-95).

The most prestigious Hollywood project in the context of the quincentennial is Ridley Scott's *1492: Conquest of Paradise* (1992), which is "erratically revisionist but fundamentally protective of Columbus's good name. Here the scintillating beauty of the cinematography enfolds the violence of conquest into the ideology of the aesthetic" (Shohat and Stam, *Unthinking* 64). Whereas we may be hesitant to identify an "ideology of the aesthetic," the film in no uncertain terms takes over the perspective of the 'discoverers' and thus coheres with an overall pattern: "Most discovery narratives place the reader on a European ship, the land is sighted (usually through an anachronistic telescope), and the 'Indians' are glimpsed on the beach or behind the trees" (ibid. 71).

　　More clearly revisionist films produced around the 1992 debates range from *Surviving Columbus* (1992) and *Columbus on Trial* (1992) to Robbie Leppzer's

Columbus Didn't Discover Us (1992). These films privilege the perspective of the indigenous inhabitants over that of the European invaders; they reconstruct tribal traditions, the history of Native tribes in various North American regions, and the suffering of Native Americans due to white aggression, missionary politics, and cultural and physical displacement.

In addition to revisionist literature and film, we find another kind of historical 'rescue' attempt, namely an archaeological project that seeks to go 'before' Columbus rather than 'beyond.' Charles C. Mann has investigated the pre-contact Americas in *1491: New Revelations of the Americas Before Columbus* and, most recently, in *Before Columbus: The Americas of 1491*. Drawing on findings by anthropologists, archaeologists, and paleolinguists, Mann refutes many stereotypes about pre-contact Native life. For one thing, the Americas, he suggests,

were a far more urban, more populated, and more technologically advanced region than generally assumed; and the Indians, rather than living in static harmony with nature, radically engineered the landscape across the continents, to the point that even "timeless" natural features like the Amazon rainforest can be seen as products of human intervention. (*1491*, book cover)

This perspective refuses to subscribe to the view that the history of the Americas only begins with European knowledge of the continent and thus constitutes another critique of Eurocentric historiography and the doctrine of discovery. With all these revisionist publications drawing attention to the fact that Columbus was complicit in introducing a discourse of violent ethnocentricity to the Americas, it comes as no surprise that the public festivities to commemorate the Quincentenary were controversial, to say the least. *Sinking Columbus* (2000) documents how the original plan of the organizing commission appointed by the US government to 'celebrate the discovery of America' in 1992 failed. However, the authors, Stephen Summerhill and John Alexander Williams, who were both involved in these preparations, paradoxically see this failure as a success: as the official Quincentenary "struggled unsuccessfully to escape being an anachronism" (*Sinking* 181), it was superseded by "an unofficial, *other* Quincentenary that gave voice to the subaltern" (ibid. 126). Rather than affirming the Columbian legacy of the United States in a patriotic spirit, as had been done in both the 1792 and 1892 celebrations, the 1992 commemorations clearly also belonged to those who were victimized by this legacy; thus, the event introduced a new kind of national memorial culture and a new kind of critical patriotism.

Illustration 6: Columbus: Savage

Poster created for AIM Denver, Colorado by Walt Pourier,
Oglala Lakota (Creative Director, Nakota Designs).

On the occasion of the Columbus Day festivities, October 12, 1992, poster art, cartoons, buttons, and pamphlets reinforced the Native American perspective and protest with epigrams such as "Discover Columbus's Legacy: 500 Years of Racism, Oppression & Stolen Land," "Wanted for Genocide: Christopher Columbus," and "Columbus: Savage." A more recent, post 9/11 image indicates that fighting terrorism – more or less successfully – has been a Native American activity since the arrival of Columbus and thus provocatively parallels the destruction of Native American culture with the 2001 destruction of the World Trade Center in New York City.

In 1992, Native American organizations also were joined by other oppositional voices. Dennis speaks of an "anti-Columbus coalition – American Indians, some religious groups, environmentalists, peace activists, political protesters, and others" ("Reinventing" 156). Yet the main Columbus Day parade in 1992 engaged in by Italian Americans in New York City (many others had been cancelled) to the great relief of the authorities went smoothly: Columbus may have been contested but he still was a figure of consensus for many Americans – and as good as any other reason to have a day off from work, or school.

Illustration 7: Fighting Terrorism Since 1492

"Homeland Security (Geronimo's Band)," *Azusa Publishing* (Web, 5 March 2014).

Apropos school: despite recent shifts in perspective, in American elementary schools the teaching of Columbus's heroism is a mandatory part of the curriculum – a situation that will not change any time soon. And thus, Shohat and Stam remind us of the larger ramifications of the Columbus myth:

[T]he Columbus story is crucial to Eurocentrism, not only because Columbus was a seminal figure within the history of colonialism, but also because idealized versions of this story have served to initiate generation after generation into the colonial paradigm. For many children in North America and elsewhere, the tale of Columbus is totemic; it introduces them not only to the concepts of "discovery" and the "New World," but also to the idea of history itself. (*Unthinking* 62)

James W. Loewen has devoted an entire booklet to how the myth of Columbus's 'discovery' is taught in American schools. His revisionist publication is titled provocatively *Lies My Teacher Told Me About Christopher Columbus* (1992) and surveys, among other things, fifteen widely used high school and middle school textbooks of American history to see what they have to say about Christopher Columbus. His findings show that "almost everything [written about Columbus] is either wrong or unknowable. The textbooks have taken us on a trip of their own, away from the facts of history, into the realm of myth" (*Lies* 1).

Still, since 1992 "a distinct American Indian version of the holiday" (Kubal, *Cultural Movements* 75) has been established in various states and locales (mostly college campuses): an "American Indian memory of national origins" (ibid.) is no longer completely ignored by official discourses on 1492. Timothy Kubal has recently used political process theory in order to show how ethnic and political minorities have used the occasion of Columbus Day over time in order to empower themselves and their political visions and to mobilize through social movements and activism connected to the festivities of one particular holiday. The counter-festivities of groups such as AIM (American Indian Movement) or the Indians of All Tribes have effectively changed the meaning and perception of Columbus Day within the national imaginary, a change that is also beginning to trickle down through the different levels of educational institutions.

6. CONCLUSION

> One day in 1474, when Amerigo Vespucci was only ten, his mother woke
> him up and said to him: "Amerigo, I had a beautiful dream last night. I dreamt
> that you will become a great explorer and that one day a whole new continent
> will be named after you. It will be called North Vespuccia."
> ITALIAN JOKE

> It saddens Norwegians that America still honors this Italian, who arrived late
> in the New World and by accident, who wasn't even interested in New
> Worlds but only in spices. Out on a spin in search of curry powder and hot
> peppers – a man on a voyage to the grocery – he stumbled onto the land of
> heroic Vikings and proceeded to get the credit for it. And then to name it
> *America* after Amerigo Vespucci, an Italian who never saw the New World
> but only sat in Italy and drew incredibly inaccurate maps of it. *By rights, it
> should be called Erica, after Eric the Red, who did the work five hundred
> years earlier. The United States of Erica. Erica the Beautiful. The Erican
> League."*
> GARRISON KEILLOR, *LAKE WOEBEGONE DAYS*

> It was wonderful to find America, but it would have been more wonderful to
> miss it.
> MARK TWAIN

To reconstruct the genesis – the making and unmaking – of the Columbus myth
is also to acknowledge that, after all, the narrative of past events can only be told
in many different versions. There is a sense of inscrutability and a certain
amount of contingency to processes of cultural mobility like those that fashioned
Columbus – him, and not others – first into an American icon, and then re-
fashioned him into a villain.

Today, we are left with a somewhat uneasy coexistence of multiple 'Colum-
buses' both heroic and shameful and alternatively American, Spanish, Jewish,
Italian American, part-Native, Catholic, etc. The myth of Columbus and the
controversy surrounding it reveal ideological conflicts at the heart of American
scholarly and popular historiography. Whether this shows that the project
'America' is still evolving and unfinished (cf. Campbell and Kean, *American
Cultural Studies* 20) or whether it indicates that it has been thwarted from the
beginning is a question still widely debated. In any case, we have to pay
attention to the "emplotment" (cf. White, *Metahistory*) of history to find out just

how narrative, causality, and a 'good' story are constructed and produced: a story that can appeal to and sway many people over a long stretch of time, a story both of 'newness' and of 'discovery.'

I would like to end this chapter with a transnational perspective. Columbus is not only a foundational myth of the US – of course, he is at the center of much 'old world' mythmaking about the 'new' – but also a European myth, perhaps even a global one; and in the age of globalization he may take on new symbolic meanings. In the Spanish film *También la lluvia* (*Even the Rain*, 2010) by Iciár Bollaín, a Mexican film team travels to Bolivia in order to shoot a film about Christopher Columbus and his 'discovery' at seemingly authentic (and yet cheap) sites, even as the film early on acknowledges the problematic conflation of the natives of Bolivia with the natives of the Caribbean, a conflation which the producer justifies by commenting on the ostensible 'sameness' of all indigenous peoples. In the process of shooting the film, the film team is caught up in the 2000 Cochabamba protests directed against the privatization of the city's water supply company. The main Native actor in the film project is also crucially involved in the water war. The film indicates the various levels of historical-colonial and present-day neo-colonial exploitation by cutting back and forth between film scenes and protests, and the various levels of narration often become entangled in powerful visual images that disorient us in time. The shooting of the film, it is suggested, exploits the historical conquest as the (only) cultural capital of the indigenous population of the Americas while it uses them as cheap extras. We recognize in the brutal police force that uses dogs to go after the water activists in the city the Spanish colonizers and their bloodhounds who hunted fugitive Natives in order to re-enslave or kill them. Both the present-day protestors and the captives of colonialism are bound and beaten when caught. In a remarkable scene in the film, the film director asks a group of indigenous women with babies to pretend to drown their children as an act of anti-colonial resistance: the translator tells them that they are to walk into the water, quickly exchange the babies for dolls, and then hold those dolls underwater for filmic effect. Whereas the director tries to insist on this scene as part of his artistic vision and the camera tantalizingly cuts back and forth between him and the faces of the (crying) babies, the women simply refuse to comply. The translator explains to the exasperated director that they could not even imagine what it is that he is asking of them. As they resist the director's instruction, the women refuse to enact his version of their historical suffering. *Even the Rain* conjures up the myth of 'discovery' in the context of a continuous and/or renewed and global exploitation of the Americas. By simultaneously returning us to the primal scene of encounter in a make-believe filmic scenario and addressing present-day economic asymmetries, the film can be read as a powerful critique of a globalization that follows a neoliberal logic. Such representations point to a hemispheric, even global perspective on the Columbus myth, and continue the cultural work surrounding one of America's key foundational narratives.

7. STUDY QUESTIONS

1. Discuss the semantic implications of 'discovery,' 'exploration,' and 'landing.' Which other terms might be used to describe Columbus's geographic mobility?

2. What are the rhetorical strategies Bartolomé de las Casas, Ferdinand Columbus, and others employ to depict Columbus in a positive light?

3. Give the various aspects that made Columbus seem an appropriate and usable national hero around the time of the founding of the US.

4. Describe the process by which Columbus became appropriated as an Italian American ancestor figure.

5. Discuss Walt Whitman's poems "A Prayer of Columbus" and "A Thought of Columbus," and explicate their representational strategies.

6. Discuss the implications of Native American revisionist critiques of the Columbus myth as both subnational and transnational interventions. What does, in this context, the neologism 'Columbusing' refer to?

7. Compare the representation of Columbus in different history and/or school books. How do they reflect on various versions of the myth?

8. Check out Tatzu Nishi's 2012 installation "Discovering Columbus" at Columbus Circle, New York City (www.publicartfund.org/view/exhibitions/5495_discovering_columbus). How does this art project reflect on the mythic quality of the historical figure?

9. Can you think of other (American) stories of 'discovery' and/or 'landing' that perpetuate, reproduce, or converge with that of Columbus?

10. In a comparative hemispheric framework, you can study the ways in which Columbus is represented in Latin American literature, e.g. in Rubén Darío's poem "A Colón" (1892), in Alejo Carpentiers *El arpa y la sombra* (1979), and/or in Augusto Roa Bastos's *Vigilia del almirante* (1992). What are differences and similarities to the US-American Columbus discourse?

8. BIBLIOGRAPHY

Works Cited

Antin, Mary. *The Promised Land.* 1912. New York: Penguin, 1997.

Bancroft, George. *A History of the United States from the Discovery of America to the Present Time.* Vol. 1. Boston: Bowen, 1834.

Barlow, Joel. *The Columbiad.* Washington City: Milligan, 1825.

Bastos, Augusto Roa. *Vigilia del almirante.* Buenos Aires: Editorial Sudamericana, 1992.

Baym, Nina, et al. "Christopher Columbus (1451-1506)." *The Norton Anthology of American Literature.* Shorter 6th ed. Ed. Nina Baym, et al. New York: Norton, 2003. 25.

Belknap, Jeremy. *American Biography, or, An Historical Account of Those Persons Who Have Been Distinguished in America as Adventurers, Statesmen, Philosophers, Divines, Warriors, Authors: Comprehending a Recital of the Events Connected with Their Lives and Actions, Vol. II.* Boston: Thomas, 1798.

Berry, Steve. *The Columbus Affair.* New York: Ballantine, 2012.

Bondanella, Peter. *Hollywood Italians: Dagos, Palookas, Romeos, Wise Guys, and Sopranos.* New York: Continuum, 2004.

Breinig, Helmbrecht, and Susanne Opfermann. "Die Literatur der frühen Republik." *Amerikanische Literaturgeschichte.* 2nd ed. Ed. Hubert Zapf. Stuttgart: Metzler, 2004. 35-84.

Bruchac, Joseph, ed. *Returning the Gift: Poetry and Prose from the First North American Native Writers' Festival.* Tucson: U of Arizona P, 1994.

Bushman, Claudia L. *America Discovers Columbus: How an Italian Explorer Became an American Hero.* Hanover: UP of New England, 1992.

Campbell, Neil, and Alasdair Kean. *American Cultural Studies: An Introduction to American Culture.* London: Routledge, 1997.

Carpentier, Alejo. *El arpa y la sombra.* 1979. *Narrativa Completa.* Vol. 7. Madrid: Ediciones Acal, 2008.

Colón, Fernando. *The Life of the Admiral Christopher Columbus by His Son, Ferdinand.* [*Historie des S. D. Fernando Colombo.* 1571.] Trans. Benjamin Keen. 1958. New Brunswick: Rutgers UP, 1992.

Columbus, Christopher. "The Letter of Columbus to Luis De Sant Angel Announcing His Discovery (1493)." *US History.* http://www.ushistory.org/documents/columbus.htm. 30 Sept. 2013.

Columbus Didn't Discover Us. Dir. Robbie Leppzer. Turning Tide Productions, 1992.

Columbus on Trial. Dir. Lourdes Portillo. Xochitl Productions, 1992.

Commager, Henry Steele. "The Search for a Usable Past." *The Search for a Usable Past and Other Essays in Historiography.* New York: Knopf, 1967. 3-27.

Darío, Rubén. "A Colon." 1892. *Nicaragua: Erasmo Gutierrez's Home Page.* http://www.oocities.org/erasgu2/colon.html. 30 Sept. 2013.

Dennis, Matthew. "Reinventing America: Columbus Day and Centenary Celebrations of His Voyage of 'Discovery,' 1792-1992." *Red, White, and Blue Letter Days: An American Calendar.* Ithaca: Cornell UP, 2002. 119-61.

Dorris, Michael. "Mistaken Identities: False Perceptions and Self-Fulfilling Prophesies." *The American Columbiad: 'Discovering' America, Inventing the United States.* Ed. Mario Materassi and Maria Irene Ramalhode Sousa Santos. Amsterdam: VU UP, 1996. 312.

Durham, Jimmie. "Columbus Day." *Columbus Day.* Albuquerque: West End, 1983. 10-12.

Elliott, Emory. *Revolutionary Writers: Literature and Authority in the New Republic, 1725-1810.* New York: Oxford UP, 1986.

Erdrich, Louise, and Michael Dorris. *The Crown of Columbus.* New York: Harper, 1991.

Floyd, Troy S. *The Columbus Dynasty in the Caribbean, 1492-1526.* Albuquerque: U of New Mexico P, 1973.

1492: Conquest of Paradise. Dir. Ridley Scott. Paramount, 1992.

Freneau, Philip. "Discovery." Freneau, *Poems* 85-88.

–. "The Pictures of Columbus. " Freneau, *Poems* 89-122.

–. *The Poems of Philip Freneau.* Vol. 1. Ed. Fred Lewis Pattee. New York: Russell and Russell, 1963.

–. "The Rising Glory of America." Freneau, *Poems* 49-83.

Fusco, Coco, and Guillermo Gómez-Peña. "Radio Pirata: Colón Go Home!" *English Is Broken Here: Notes on Cultural Fusion in the Americas.* Ed. Coco Fusco. New York: New, 1995. 179-95.

Gewecke, Frauke. *Wie die neue Welt in die alte kam.* Stuttgart: Klett-Cotta, 1986.

Gold, Michael. *Jews without Money.* 1930. New York: Avon, 1972.

Goldsmith, Arnold J. "A Curse on Columbus: Twentieth-Century Jewish-American Fiction and the Theme of Disillusionment." *Studies in American Jewish Literature* 5 (1979): 47-55.

Goodrich, Aaron. *A History of the Character and Achievements of the So-Called Christopher Columbus.* New York: D. Appleton, 1874.

Greenblatt, Stephen. *Marvelous Possessions: The Wonder of the New World.* Chicago: U of Chicago P, 1991.

Groseclose, Barbara. "American Genesis: The Landing of Christopher Columbus." *American Icons: Transatlantic Perspectives on Eighteenth- and Nineteenth-Century American Art.* Ed. Thomas W. Gaehtgens and Heinz Ickstadt. Santa Monica: Getty Center for the History of Art and the Humanities, 1992. 11-32.

Hartog, François. *The Mirror of Herodotus: The Representation of the Other in the Writing of History.* Trans. Janet Lloyd. Berkeley: U of California P, 1988.

Henige, David. *In Search of Columbus: The Sources for the First Voyage.* Tucson: U of Arizona P, 1991.

Herget, Winfried. "'Whitewashing the Tragedy of Discovery:' Die Rehabilitation des Kolumbus im amerikanischen Traum." *Amerika: Entdeckung, Eroberung, Erfindung.* Ed. Winfried Herget. Trier: Wissenschaftlicher Verlag Trier, 1995. 1-10.

Higham, John. *Strangers in the Land: Patterns of American Nativism, 1860-1925.* 1955. New Brunswick: Rutgers UP, 1988.

Hobson, Geary. "On a Festival Called Returning the Gift." Bruchac, *Returning* xxiii-xxix.

Irving, Washington. *The Life and Voyages of Christopher Columbus.* 1828. *The Complete Works of Washington Irving.* Ed. Richard Dilworth Rust, et al. Vol. 11. Ed. John Harmon McElroy. Boston: Twayne, 1981.

Jacobson, Matthew Frye. *Whiteness of a Different Color: European Immigrants and the Alchemy of Race.* Cambridge: Harvard UP, 1997.

Josephy, Alvin M. "Introduction: The Center of the Universe." *America in 1492: The World of the Indian Peoples Before the Arrival of Columbus.* Ed. Alvin M. Josephy. New York: Knopf, 1992.

Kauffman, Christopher J. *Columbianism and the Knights of Columbus: A Quincentenary History.* New York: Simon, 1992.

–. *Faith and Fraternalism: The History of the Knights of Columbus.* 1982. Rev. ed. New York: Simon, 1992.

Keillor, Garrison. *Lake Woebegone Days.* New York: Penguin, 1985.

Kettell, Samuel. "Joel Barlow." *Specimens of American Poetry with Critical and Biographical Notices.* Vol. 3. Boston: Goodrich, 1829. 1-27.

Kubal, Timothy. *Cultural Movements and Collective Memory: Christopher Columbus and the Rewriting of the National Origin Myth.* New York: Palgrave Macmillan, 2008.

Lauter, Paul, et al., eds. *The Heath Anthology of American Literature.* Boston: Houghton, 2004.

Lazarus, Emma. "1492." 1888. *The Norton Anthology of American Literature.* Shorter 6th ed. Ed. Nina Baym, et al. New York: Norton, 2003. 1220-21.

–. "The New Colossus." 1883. *The Norton Anthology of Poetry.* 4th edition. Ed. Margaret Ferguson, Mary Jo Salter, and Jon Stallworthy. New York: Norton, 1996. 1172.

Loewen, James. *Lies My Teacher Told Me About Christopher Columbus: What Your History Books Got Wrong.* New York: New, 1992.

Loewenberg, Bert James. *American History in American Thought: Christopher Columbus to Henry James.* New York: Simon, 1972.

Mann, Charles C. *1491: New Revelations of the Americas Before Columbus.* New York: Vintage, 2006.

–. *Before Columbus: The Americas of 1491.* New York: Atheneum, 2009.

Martin, Terence. "Literature: Columbus in American Literature." *The Christopher Columbus Encyclopedia.* Vol. 2. Ed. Silvio A. Bedini. Basingstoke: Macmillan, 1992. 433-35.

McHale, Brian. *Postmodernist Fiction.* New York: Methuen, 1987.

Morison, Samuel Eliot. *Admiral of the Ocean Sea: A Life of Christopher Columbus.* 1942. Boston: Northeastern UP, 1983.

O'Gorman, Edmundo. *The Invention of America: An Inquiry into the Historical Nature of the New World and the Meaning of Its History.* Bloomington: Indiana UP, 1961.

Pearce, Roy Harvey. *The Continuity of American Poetry.* Princeton: Princeton UP, 1961.

Revard, Carter. "Report to the Nation: Repossessing Europe." *Nothing But the Truth: An Anthology of Native American Literature.* Ed. John Purdy and James Ruppert. Upper Saddle River: Prentice Hall, 2001. 333-44.

Roa-de-la-Carrera, Cristián A. *Histories of Infamy: Francisco López de Gómara and the Ethics of Spanish Imperialism.* Trans. Scott Sessions. Boulder: U of Colorado P, 2005.

Robertson, William. *The History of America.* Vol. 2. London: Strahan, 1778.

Roth, Philip. *Goodbye, Columbus and Five Short Stories.* Boston: Houghton, 1959.

Sale, Kirkpatrick. *The Conquest of Paradise: Christopher Columbus and the Columbian Legacy.* New York: Knopf, 1990.

Shohat, Ella, and Robert Stam. *Unthinking Eurocentrism: Multiculturalism and the Media.* London: Routledge, 2001.

Shreve, Jack. "Christopher Columbus: A Bibliographic Voyage." *Choice* 29 (1991): 703-11.

Smith, Henry Nash. *Virgin Land: The American West as Symbol and Myth.* Cambridge: Harvard UP, 1950.

Sollors, Werner. *Beyond Ethnicity: Consent and Descent in American Culture.* New York: Oxford UP, 1986.

Spivak, Gayatri Chakravorty. "Can the Subaltern Speak?" *Marxism and the Interpretation of Culture.* Ed. Cary Nelson and Lawrence Grossberg. London: Macmillan, 1984. 24-28.

Stavans, Ilan. *Imagining Columbus: The Literary Voyage.* New York: Palgrave, 2001.

Strads, Gundars, et al. "Introduction: Redefining the Mainstream." *The Before Columbus Foundation Anthology: Selections from the American Book Awards, 1980-1990.* Ed. Ishmael Reed, et al. New York: Norton, 1992.

Summerhill, Stephen J., and John Alexander Williams. *Sinking Columbus: Contested History, Cultural Politics, and Mythmaking during the Quincentenary.* Gainesville: UP of Florida, 2000.

Surviving Columbus: The Story of the Pueblo People. Dir. Diane Reyna. KNME-TV, et al., 1992.

También la lluvia [Even the Rain]. Dir. Iciár Bollaín. Vitagraph Films, 2010.

Todorov, Tzvetan. *The Conquest of America: The Question of the Other.* New York: Harper, 1984.

Vignaud, Henry. "Christopher Columbus a Spaniard and a Jew?" *The American Historical Review* 18.3 (1913): 505-12.

–. *The Letter and Chart of Toscanelli on the Route to the Indies by Way of the West, Sent in 1474 to the Portuguese Fernam Martins, and Later on to Christopher Columbus: A Critical Study of the Authenticity and the Value of These Documents and the Sources of the Cosmographical Ideas of Columbus, Followed by the Various Texts of the Letter, Several Facsimiles and Also a Map.* 1902. Freeport: Books for Libraries, 1971.

Vizenor, Gerald. *The Heirs of Columbus.* Hanover: Wesleyan UP, 1991.

Wallisch, Robert. *Kolumbus: Der erste Brief aus der neuen Welt.* Stuttgart: Reclam, 2000.

Weber, Donald. "Accents of the Future: Jewish American Popular Culture." *The Cambridge Companion to Jewish American Literature.* Ed. Hana Wirth-Nesher. Cambridge: Cambridge UP, 2003. 129-48.

Wheatley, Phillis. "To His Excellency General Washington." 1776. *The Heath Anthology of American Literature*. Ed. Paul Lauter. Boston: Houghton, 2004. 577.

White, Hayden. *Metahistory: The Historical Imagination in Nineteenth-Century Europe*. Baltimore: Johns Hopkins UP, 1973.

Whitman, Walt. *Leaves of Grass and Other Writings*. Ed. Michael Moon. New York: Norton, 2002.

–. "A Prayer of Columbus." Whitman, *Leaves* 354-56.

–. "A Thought of Columbus." Whitman, *Leaves* 491.

Wilson, Flip. "Christopher Columbus." *The Black Columbiad: Defining Moments in African American Literature and Culture*. Ed. Werner Sollors and Maria Diedrich. Cambridge: Harvard UP, 1994.

Winsor, Justin. *Christopher Columbus and How He Received and Imparted the Spirit of Discovery*. London: Low, 1890.

Further Reading

Adams, Charles Francis. "Columbus and the Spanish Discovery of America." *Proceedings of the Massachusetts Historical Society* 8 (1982-1984): 24-44.

Badger, R. Reid. *The Great American Fair: The World's Columbian Exposition and American Culture*. Chicago: Nelson Hall, 1979.

Bedini, Silvio A., ed. *The Christopher Columbus Encyclopedia*. 2 vols. Basingstoke: Macmillan, 1992.

Bitterli, Urs. *Alte Welt – Neue Welt: Formen des europäisch-überseeischen Kulturkontakts vom 15. bis zum 18. Jahrhundert*. München: Beck, 1986.

Bodnar, John. *Remaking America: Public Memory, Commemoration, and Patriotism in the Twentieth Century*. Princeton: Princeton UP, 1992.

Bump, Charles Weathers. "Public Memorials of Columbus." *Columbus and His Discovery of America*. Ed. Herbert B. Adams and Henry Wood. Baltimore: Johns Hopkins P, 1892. Johns Hopkins U Studies in Historical and Political Science Series 10 No. 11. Appendix II. 69-88.

Crosby, Alfred W. *The Columbian Exchange: Biological and Cultural Consequences of 1492*. Westport: Greenwood, 1972.

–. *The Columbian Voyage, the Columbian Exchange, and Their Historians*. Washington: American Historical Association, 1987.

Curtis, William Eleroy. "Columbus Monuments." *The Chautauquan: A Monthly Magazine* 16 (1892-93): 138-46.

Deschamps, Bénédicte. "Italian-Americans and Columbus Day: A Quest for Consensus between National and Group Identities, 1840-1910." *Celebrating*

Ethnicity and Nation: American Festive Culture from the Revolution to the Early Twentieth Century. Ed. Geneviève Fabre, Jürgen Heideking, and Kai Dreisbach. New York: Berghahn, 2001. 124-39.

Dunbar, Paul. "Columbian Ode." *The Complete Poems of Paul Laurence Dunbar*. 1913. New York: Dodd/Mead, 1946.

Fernández de Oviedo, Gonzalo. *De la natural historia de las Indias*. Toledo: Petras, 1526.

–. *La historia general de las Indias*. Sevilla: Cromberger, 1535.

Fryd, Vivien Green. *Art and Empire: The Politics of Ethnicity in the United States Capitol, 1825-1860*. New Haven: Yale UP, 1992.

Gerbi, Antonelli. *The Dispute of the New World: The History of a Polemic, 1750-1900*. Pittsburgh: U of Pittsburgh P, 1973.

Handlin, Lilian. "Discovering Columbus." *American Scholar* 62.1 (1993): 81-95.

Heydenreich, Titus, ed. *Columbus zwischen zwei Welten: Historische und literarische Wertungen aus fünf Jahrhunderten*. 2 vols. Frankfurt: Vervuert, 1992.

Kadir, Djelal. *Columbus and the Ends of the Earth: Europe's Prophetic Rhetoric as Conquering Ideology*. Berkeley: U of California P, 1992.

Kammen, Michael. *Mystic Chords of Memory: The Transformation of Tradition in American Culture*. New York: Knopf, 1991.

Lehmann, Hartmut. "Columbus als amerikanischer Nationalheld im 19. und 20. Jahrhundert." *Geschichte in Wissenschaft und Unterricht* 45 (1994): 240-49.

Loock, Kathleen. "Goodbye Columbus, Hello Abe! Changing Imagery on U.S. Paper Money and the Negotiation of American National Identity." *Almighty Dollar*. Ed. Heinz Tschachler, Simone Puff, and Eugen Banauch. Wien: LIT, 2010. 81-101.

MacNamara, Brooks. *Day of Jubilee: The Great Age of Public Celebrations in New York, 1788-1909*. New Brunswick: Rutgers UP, 1997.

Prescott, William Hickling. *History of the Reign of Ferdinand and Isabella, the Catholic*. 1837. Ed. C. Harvey Gardiner. London: Allen and Unwin, 1962.

Schlereth, Thomas J. "Columbia, Columbus, and Columbianism." *Journal of American History* 79.3 (1992): 937-68.

Wawor, Gerhard. "Columbus: Der Augenblick der Landung in Wort und Bild." *Kritische Berichte* (1992): 82-92.

Wawor, Gerhard, and Titus Heydenreich. *Columbus 1892/1992: Heldenverehrung und Heldendemontage*. Frankfurt: Vervuert, 1995.

Wenger, Beth S. "Rites of Citizenship: Jewish Celebrations of the Nation." *The Columbia History of Jews and Judaism in America*. Ed. Marc Lee Raphael. New York: Columbia UP, 2008. 366-84.

Wolanin, Barbara A. "The Artist of the Capitol." *The United States Capitol: Designing and Decorating a National Icon.* Ed. Donald R. Kennon. Athens: Ohio UP, 2000. 171-95.

Chapter II

Pocahontas and the Myth of Transatlantic Love

---

1. WHY POCAHONTAS?

> When the first permanent English settlers arrived in America in 1607, their
> sponsors had not given up hope of an integrated biracial community.
> EDMUND S. MORGAN, *AMERICAN SLAVERY, AMERICAN FREEDOM*

> A shipload of single men founded Jamestown, and yet Virginia's origin myth
> revolves around a female.
> ANN UHRY ABRAMS, *THE PILGRIMS AND POCAHONTAS*

The figure of Pocahontas is at the core of an American foundational myth that
for a long time has been considered the first love story of the 'new world' and
thus paradigmatic for casting intercultural relations in the early colonial history
of the Americas as harmonious and peaceful. As a Native American female
foundational figure, Pocahontas may seem less prominent than the male European Christopher Columbus and his myth of discovery (due to her gender and
ethnicity), yet her story has had an enormous circulation. The romanticization of
Pocahontas and her encounter with the English settlers has become one of the
most enduring narratives of American culture: this story was "recast and retold
more often than any other American historical incident during the colonial and
antebellum periods" (Tilton, *Pocahontas* 1), pointing to the "evolution of an
American narrative" (cf. ibid.) over the course of two centuries and to the debate
and refashioning of this narrative in the centuries to follow.

Unlike Columbus, Pocahontas did not leave letters or diaries, and many
scholars have dwelled upon the voicelessness of this American heroine, who was
appropriated by contemporaries – John Smith is the only writer to actually refer
to words she ostensibly addressed to him verbatim – as well as by historians,
writers, and critics from the 17th to the 21st centuries. Although less historically

remote than Columbus's 'discovery,' the historical sources of the myth of Pocahontas and of her apparent romantic interest in various Englishmen thus have to
be viewed with skepticism and caution. My reconstruction of the narratives
about her shows how she became the centerpiece of a foundational myth that
often is presented "in the guise of history" (Jenkins, "Princess" 8) and that is
heavily invested in ideologies of US-American nation-building and identity
politics. As much as she has been used as a trope in colonial tales of assimilation, she has also variably been cast as a foundational figure in a non-Eurocentric
narrative of American beginnings.

With Sharon Larkins and Peter Hulme, the following 'facts' of Pocahontas's
life can be considered as corroborated by historical evidence: that she was born
around 1595; that she encountered Captain John Smith immediately after the
arrival of the first English settlers at what was to become Jamestown (named
after King James I of England) in 1607 (in the most prominent version of the
story of this encounter she rescued Smith from death at the hands of her father,
Powhatan, chief of a powerful Native confederacy); that she helped the people of
Jamestown and continued to have a relationship with Smith; that Smith was
injured in an accident and returned to England in 1609, Pocahontas believing
him to have died; that she was abducted by Captain Argall in 1612 and held captive in Jamestown by the English; that she was converted to the Christian faith in
1613 while living in Jamestown; that she married John Rolfe in 1614 and that
she gave birth to her son Thomas in 1615; that she traveled to England in 1616
and was a great success as the 'Indian princess' now called 'Lady Rebecca' at
the English court; that in January 1617 she attended the famous *Twelfth Night*
masque; that she was visited by John Smith during her stay and that they had one
last conversation; that she died and was buried at Gravesend in 1617 on her way
back to America (cf. Larkins, "Using;" Hulme, *Colonial Encounters* 140-41).

In the various retellings of her life, Pocahontas's narrative often falls into
two parts: her friendship with John Smith, the 'rescue' incident, and Smith's
return to England constitute the first part; the second part includes her captivity
among the English, her conversion, her marriage to John Rolfe, the birth of her
son, and her visit to England. In all these variations on the level of discourse, the
underlying story of first contact takes on mythic significance as an allegorical
narrative of the birth of a new (American) society. It is also the first American
love story between the colonizer and the colonized which has us believe (at least
in its conventional version) that Pocahontas was "sacrificing her life to rescue
her (White) love object from her barbarian tribe, a reading which excludes the
narrative of rape, cultural destruction and genocide" (Shohat and Stam, *Unthinking* 44).

The historical figure of Pocahontas, alias Matoaka, alias Lady Rebecca Rolfe has been represented as Indian 'girl,' 'princess,' female 'noble savage,' mediator, and indigenous femme fatal, depending on the respective ideological investment, ranging from national, regional, feminist, and ethnic agendas, to name only a few. This chapter tracks the myth of the 'Indian princess' and her transatlantic love story through four phases. First, it will historicize the myth in early modern discourses of expansion and in the context of early American colonial culture and history since 1607, the year in which Jamestown, the first permanent English settlement was founded and in which Pocahontas first met the English arrivals. Before 1607 we already find conventional gendered allegories of the 'new world' as a woman, a fact with which I will deal briefly in the next section. After a reconstruction of the early Jamestown years and the Pocahontas narrative in the 17th century, second, I will turn to the uses made of the Pocahontas tale in the period of the early republic and revisit the fabrication of the romantic love story between Pocahontas and John Smith in the first decades of the 19th century. Third, I will discuss the ways in which Pocahontas was made into an American 'founding mother' by various groups throughout the 19th, 20th, and 21st centuries. And fourth, I will look at the most recent versions of this myth in American popular culture and literature, in which the revisionism of the second half of the 20th century has led to new accentuations; rather than privileging the so-called rescue scene and the friendship between Pocahontas and John Smith, recent scholarship and rewritings often focus on her marriage to John Rolfe instead. Again, these phases and trends do not start and end in one particular year or decade; rather, they reveal discursive formations and shifts over a period of more than four hundred years.

2. AMERICA IS A WOMAN: A PREFACE

> The novelty of America was always perceived in overtly sexual terms.
> PETER HULME, *COLONIAL ENCOUNTERS*

To understand the troping of Pocahontas as a paradigmatic 'new world' woman and a female 'noble savage' we need to first contextualize her in a discourse that at the time of the first English settlements depicted the Americas as an allegorically feminized space. These representations were part of "a full allegorical tradition in which continents – Europe, Asia, Africa and now America – were portrayed as women surrounded by the representative attributes of their respective parts of the world" (Hulme, "Polytropic Man" 17). Hugh Honour has examined this tradition with regard to the Americas, showing how North America as the "land of allegory" is visually embodied as woman in ambiguous illustrations by European artists such as Philip Galle, Jan Sadeler, Simon van de Passe, Theodor Galle and Jan van der Straat (cf. Honour, *New Golden Land*). In North America, the practice of imagining the continent or its regions as female is also evident in Walter Raleigh's naming of 'Virginia' at the end of the 16th century; Raleigh had been exploring the American coast in an unsuccessful attempt to establish a permanent settlement and colony at Roanoke, the coastal region of what today is North Carolina, between 1584 and 1590 – an attempt that obviously did not engender a foundational myth of American origins and that has been commonly referred to as the "lost" or the "abandoned colony" of Roanoke (cf. Kupperman, *Roanoke*). Raleigh had named the entire territory Virginia, in honor of Queen Elizabeth (1533-1603), the 'virgin queen,' who, for a time, supported his venture. This territory, Raleigh's choice of name insinuates, was waiting in supposedly feminine passivity for the European traveler to arrive and colonize it. The gender-specific attribution of America as 'Virginia' presupposes a male traveler who encounters the (virginal, i.e. empty) feminized space and takes possession of it; it is thus highly suggestive of a sexualized relationship between both, which is constructed as a libidinal bond between traveler and territory (cf. Schülting, *Wilde Frauen* 49). Therefore, in 1607 Virginia already figured as a mysterious feminine/feminized space to be penetrated, conquered, and domesticated by the English settlers.

The ambivalence that such gendered representations may entail is paradigmatically encoded already in a late 15th-century engraving of "America" by the Dutch artist Jan van der Straat on a 1619-copperplate by Theodor Galle. It depicts Amerigo Vespucci's encounter with an allegorical female figure that represents the continent named after him. Vespucci is equipped with all the insignia of a European explorer (flag, cross, and astrolabe), while a voluptuous America lies naked on a hammock, stretching out her hand and beckoning the visitor to come closer. She is part of a pastoral scene, tempting, seductive, and enticing. A closer look, however, reveals disturbing details: in the background of the picture, Natives are roasting something over a fireplace that looks suspiciously like a human leg, and another leg can be seen next to the fireplace. Eroticism and cannibalism here appear side by side, and the dangers of intercultural contact are envisioned; for all the claimed superiority of the European traveler in terms of religion and technology, the alterity of the Native is perceived as tempting and threatening at the same time and thus seems to be beyond the Europeans' control. Could this 'new world' beauty's invitation to the traveler have a hidden agenda? At the same time, this scene of seduction conceals European colonial aggression toward the indigenous 'new world' population behind a myth of erotic encounter, perhaps even love, correlating the relationship between Europeans and Natives with the allegedly 'natural' order of the sexes: the distinguished European male is to the 'new world' native as man is to woman: i.e., superior (cf. Schülting, *Wilde Frauen* 14).

Illustration 1: Amerigo Vespucci 'Discovers' America

Theodor Galle, *America* (1619).

Not only has the 'new world' often been allegorically depicted as a woman, but more specifically, "[i]n English prints and engravings, [it] was often shown as an unclothed Indian princess" (Bushman, *America* 50). E. McClung Fleming has detailed the historical phases in which America appeared first as "Indian Queen," then as an "Indian Princess presented as the daughter of Britannia," and finally by representations of "an Indian Princess whose attributes were the symbols of United States sovereignty" ("American Image" 65). In fact, the Indian princess was the "oldest and most durable representation of the United States" before representations increasingly turned to classicism in the 19th century (Fleming, "From Indian" 39). The allegory of America as the 'Indian princess' thus paves the way for the troping of Pocahontas in first-contact scenarios against a backdrop of the foundational mythology of the 'new world.'

In an already symbolically feminized space, she appears as the first flesh-and-blood Native female we encounter in European narratives of North America. In fact, as Werner Sollors points out, "[a]llegories of America as an Indian princess have often been combined with Captain John Smith's Pocahontas story" (*Beyond Ethnicity* 79). The label "Indian princess" refers to her status as the daughter of chief Powhatan and describes Native tribal relations using the European classificatory system of aristocratic distinction which obviously is itself an act of symbolic domination. Therefore, the first English narrative about the first permanent English settlement in the 'new world' centers on the story of a woman native to the American continent who is discursively appropriated and put to use in various guises for the purpose of legitimizing European conquest: as an allegorical representative of the 'new world' in accordance with the connotations of exotic femininity, as a cultural mediator and supporter of European colonialism, and as a model for assimilation and conversion.

3. THE FIRST LOVE STORY FROM THE 'NEW WORLD'?

> [T]he story of Pocahontas and John Smith tells of an "original" encounter of which no even passably "immediate" account exists, a blank space which has not been allowed to remain empty. [...] The founding but most problematic moment of that story is the "rescue."
> PETER HULME, *COLONIAL ENCOUNTERS*

> From the *Aeneid* of Virgil onward, intercultural romance was a preferred beginning of colonial narratives.
> GESA MACKENTHUN, *METAPHORS OF DISPOSSESSION*

> Pocahontas was a child at the time of her interactions with Smith.
> LEIGH H. EDWARDS, "THE UNITED COLORS OF POCAHONTAS"

The status of the focal point of the Pocahontas myth – the 'rescue' scene in which she supposedly intervenes on behalf of John Smith and stops his execution – has been the subject of discussion and scrutiny by generations of scholars wavering between enthusiastic affirmation of its truthfulness and utter skepticism. Catchy titles such as *Did Pocahontas Save Captain John Smith?* by J.A. Leo Lemay reveal the almost obsessive dedication to this question, and thus the contested origins of American mythmaking. What is at stake in Lemay's question is the Native woman's desire to save the white man and to show him that he is not considered an intruder and colonizer in North America; in this sense, Pocahontas's "famous supposed rescue of Captain John Smith has become a rescue of America" (Edwards, "United Colors" 147) and thus a legitimization of the colonial endeavor.

For various reasons, the authenticity of the famous rescue scene has come to be doubted in contemporary scholarship. In order to fully comprehend this skepticism, we have to turn to the historical sources of the story. The textual evidence of the historical encounter in North America between the first English settlers and the indigenous inhabitants is scarce and one-sided. As to the encounter between John Smith and Pocahontas, it is Smith's own writing in his *A True Relation of Such Occurrences and Accidents of Note as Happened in Virginia* (published in 1608 and then worked into subsequent editions and versions) that we need to turn to first. Pocahontas herself did not leave any textual records, only traces in the texts of others which enlist her story in the authors' own ideological maneuvers.

In his first account of the cultural encounter with the North American natives, John Smith narrates his captivity among the Algonquians as well as the early skirmishes between English settlers and Natives, and although he mentions Pocahontas in this early document as a messenger between Powhatan and the settlers, he does not credit her with having saved his life (neither is this mentioned in his *Proceedings* of 1612). Other early 17th-century sources, such as the texts by Samuel Purchas, Ralph Hamor and William Strachey, are equally silent on the matter of any such rescue.

William Strachey, Secretary of the Resident Council in Virginia and author of *The Historie of Travaile into Virginia Britannia* (1612), an important textual record of the colony's early history, refers to Powhatan's many wives and children, among them "younge Pocahunta, a daughter of his, using sometime to our fort in tymes past" (54). Later he recounts how

the before remembered Pochahontas, a well featured, but wanton yong girle, Powhatan's daughter, sometimes resorting to our fort, of the age then of eleven or twelve yeares, get the boys forth with her into the market place, and make them wheele, falling on their hands, turning up their heeles upwards, whome she would followe and wheele so her self, naked as she was, all the fort over. (65)

Whereas Strachey renders Pocahontas as a kind of elfish girl (later texts would refer to her as the "forest princess"), Ralph Hamor records the details of her captivity, conversion, and marriage in his *True Discourse of the Present Estate of Virginia* (1615), and Samuel Purchas in *Hakluytus Posthumus Or Purchas His*

Pilgrimes (1625) decribes Pocahontas's fabulous reception in London, where "she carried her selfe as the Daughter of a King, and was accordingly respected" (Vol. 19 118). These are the main historical sources. Even if these texts were written by contemporaries of Pocahontas, this does not mean that they are per se more authentic or reliable than the romantic biographies of the 19th century, as the English authors had their own agenda in describing the North American natives. And still, the absence of the rescue scene, which is central to American mythology, in all of the early textual records is puzzling.

It is in 1624, 17 years after the publication of his first text on the early years of the Virginia Colony, that John Smith for the first time describes the rescue scene in his *The Generall Historie of Virginia, New-England, and the Summer Isles* in the following words, referring to himself in the third person:

> At his [John Smith's] entrance before the King [Powhatan], all the people gaue a great shout. The Queene of Appamatuck was appointed to bring him water to wash his hands, and another brought him a bunch of feathers, instead of a Towell to dry them: having feasted him after the best barbarous manner they could, a long consultation was held, but the conclusion was, two great stones were brought before *Powhatan*: then as many as could layd hands on him, dragged him to them, and thereon laid his head, and being ready with their clubs to beate out his brains, Pocahontas the Kings dearest daughter, when no entreaty could prevaile, got his head in her arms, and laid her owne upon his to saue him from death. (49)

Smith thus adds this rescue scene to his account of the initial intercultural contact in North America almost two decades after the incident had supposedly occurred and only after Powhatan as well as Pocahontas had died. Apart from this addition the account is quite similar to the 1608 version, and "no totally convincing explanation has ever been offered for the rescue's absence from the 1608 account" (Hulme, *Colonial Encounters* 140). Scholars have speculated – based on the premise that the scene actually took place – that Smith was at first embarrassed to include his rescue by a young girl for fear of undermining his image as a heroic soldier able to look out for himself (cf. Mackenthun, *Metaphors* 210); after all, his coat of arms was *Vincere est Vivere* – to conquer is to live. Others concluded that Smith embroidered his original version for political purposes and a more dramatic self-fashioning, and that his 1624 publication is by no means accidental in view of the occurrences in the colony.

Combining colonial discourse analysis with a New Historicist sensibility, historian Peter Hulme links the appearance of the rescue scene in Smith's 1624 account to the so-called Indian massacre of 1622 in the Jamestown area which lastingly reconfigured English-Native relations as inimical and aggressive (cf. Mackenthun's discussion of Hulme in *Metaphors* 211). Hulme suggests that Smith could then, many years after Pocahontas's death, glance back at the primal scene of intercultural encounter nostalgically and present her as a model:

[T]he rescue can be articulated into a narrative in which Pocahontas has an increasingly central role to play as evidence that Algonquian recognition of the values of European culture could have provided the basis for a harmonious relationship, had not the inherent viciousness of [other natives] destroyed all hope of peaceful co-operation. (*Colonial Encounters* 172)

This 'viciousness' became evident, according to the English chroniclers, in the massacre of 1622 and led to a change of English policy against the Natives. Opechancanough, an uncle of Pocahontas and Powhatan's half-brother, understood that the English settlers had come to stay and led the Algonquian resistance against the continuing incursions of the English settlers into Native land. Unsurprisingly, he is cast by the English as the prototypical 'evil savage' who shows resistance to rather than compliance with English colonialism. The attacks in 1622 killed a third of the colony's population, i.e. "more than three hundred colonists," and could have wiped out the entire colony if not for the hit-and-run tactics employed by the English, which ultimately allowed for a counteroffensive (Kelly and Clark Smith, *Jamestown* 69). John Rolfe, then already a widower who had in his last years in the colony introduced and revolutionized the planting and processing of tobacco, also died in that conflict (cf. Woodward, *Pocahontas* 190), a fact that connects the story of Pocahontas and the massacre on yet another level: whereas Pocahontas, the 'good Indian,' had loved and married John Rolfe, her uncle's 'evil scheming' later caused his violent death.

After the relations between the English and the Natives had irrevocably turned from bad to worse, Smith emphasizes the historical moment where a different course of events had still been fathomable if Natives had only followed the path Pocahontas had chosen: conversion and intermarriage. Yet, they did not. In fact, throughout the 18th century historical accounts blame Native American resistance to intermarriage and reluctance to mingle more intimately and on a broader scale with the English for the continuously deteriorating English-Native relations. It has been argued somewhat speculatively that in terms of phenotype, outward appearance and cultural habits, Native Americans were mostly repulsed by the English settlers due to their masses of facial and bodily hair and their odorous perspiration.

Another problem facing the colony in its early years was the high number of settlers who left the English settlement in order to live with the Natives and who were "rapidly and unproblematically assimilated" (Hulme, *Colonial Encounters* 143; cf. Crèvecoeur, *More Letters* 137), thus undermining any ideological construction of English superiority. Indigenization of the English, i.e. 'going native' was a common phenomenon and posed a threat to the very existence of the colony not least by harming promotional efforts in England geared toward attracting more people to settle in Virginia: what kind of colony had its residents run off into the 'wilderness' of an unknown continent to live with 'uncivilized' people they did not even know? Therefore, the story of Pocahontas came in handy for those advocating colonization and was widely used in the promotional literature encouraging further immigration from England. While the trend of 'going native' among the English settlers was hushed up, the Pocahontas tale at the same time was ideologically exploited as it advertised Native American acceptance of the superiority of the English culture. Pocahontas sided with the invaders, and became as the anglicized heroine of the American colonial romance – "the non-pareil," as Smith calls her and as she is frequently referred to in early American scholarship (cf. Garnett, *Pocahontas*) – a model for all to emulate. "Pocahontas's crossing of the cultural rift – however that crossing is interpreted – [...] was quite exceptional" (ibid. 142) simply because she was the only one who did cross it. The Pocahontas narrative "has come to validate in the national psyche the presence by a mythical indigenous consent of Europeans in America" by playing off Pocahontas as the "exotic peacekeeper" against the rest of the Natives as "bloodthirsty savages" (Baringer, "Captive Woman" 2).

Coming back to Smith's text, we can register at least two further interpretive complications. First of all, Smith's text resembles other classical narratives which he obviously took as a model; Peter Hulme points to similarities between Odysseus's encounter with Polyphemus and the Cyclops in Homer and Ovid and Smith's own rendering of his interaction with Powhatan and the Algonquians (cf. *Colonial Encounters* 153f.). Even the rescue scene has features of classical storytelling drawing on an intercultural love story to dramatize cultural conflict. Smith's rescue scene furthermore resembles other parts of his own text quite conspicuously; he "claims to have been aided by beautiful ladies at least twice during his earlier adventurous career in Turkey and Tartaria [...] and includes 'that blessed Pocahontas' in his list of those women who 'oft saved my life'" (Mackenthun, *Metaphors* 217; cf. Smith, *Generall Historie* 41-42). In fact, Smith is not the only one to tell such stories: we find parallels in rescue stories of other travelers of that time, as the "'enamoured princess' was a literary topos, or trope rather, derived from Orientalist discourse" and was chosen by Smith as the "organizing discourse" of his 1624 narrative (Mackenthun, *Metaphors* 217).

After those qualifications, we should, however, take one last look at the rescue scene that Smith describes, if only to complicate matters even further. When taking the story itself at face value we may come to yet another conclusion: That Smith's experience was not a rescue in the strict sense but a kind of adoption ritual of the Algonquians. Philip Barbour first suggested this reading in his 1969 study *Pocahontas and Her World*: "The ceremony of which Smith had been the object was almost certainly a combination of mock execution and salvation, in token of adoption into Powhatan's tribe" (24). Most scholars have come to agree with Barbour that Smith did not lie about what happened and that his memory did not fail him either but that he misread the Native rituals and practices which were unintelligible to him. The thesis of the cultural misreading of an adoption ritual is based on "our conjectures on well-attested Indian practices" (ibid. 23) and has been corroborated by many scholars over the past decades. Barbour even argues that Smith had included the scene in the earlier versions of his texts but that his London editor deleted it (cf. ibid. 24).

Reading the rescue scene as a ritual of adoption also seems plausible in light of the last encounter between Pocahontas and Smith in England. Peter Hulme unravels the dialogue between Smith and Pocahontas in England briefly before her death, upon whose truthfulness we should take a chance, he suggests, because what Pocahontas tells Smith is obviously incomprehensible to him yet quoted by him at some length; these are perhaps the only 'original' words of her that we have (cf. Hulme, *Colonial Encounters* 151-52). When meeting at Brentford, after years of separation and silence, Smith finds Pocahontas distant. The words she directs to him are recorded by Smith as follows:

You did promise Powhatan what was yours should bee his, and he the like to you; you called him father being in his land a stranger, and by the same reason so I must doe you: which though I would haue excused, I durst not allow of that title, because she was a Kings daughter; with a well set countenance she said, Were you not afraid to come into my father Countrie, and caused feare in him and all his people (but mee) and feare you here I should call you father; I tell you then I will, and you shall call mee childe, and so I will bee fore euer and euer your Countrieman. They did tell vs you were dead, and I knew no other til I cam to Plimoth; yet Powhatan did command Vttamatomakkin to seeke yu, and know the truth, because your Countriemen will lie much. (*Generall Historie* 122-3)

Pocahontas reminds Smith of his duties and obligations to her and to her people. She demands reciprocity and commitment due to the ritual of adoption enacted in 1607, which made them kin. Smith, not familiar with the Algonquian communal culture of reciprocity, seems unable, or at least reluctant, to comment on her words although he quotes them at length.

Smith's text of 1624, the *Generall Historie*, "differs from earlier texts in that it is the first English text that attempts to write a historical narrative of British America – and such a national narrative [...] can only develop when it is based on a coherent and meaningful beginning" (Mackenthun, *Metaphors* 210). In 1624, the first phase of colonization – the masking and downplaying of the colonial project in the encounter with the Natives – was over: the English no longer pretended to have come to North America only temporarily (as Smith had told Powhatan during one of their first meetings), and the Natives no longer pretended that they did not mind the white presence. The English conquest of North America had begun. Smith's integration and prioritization of the rescue scene in his narrative has been tremendously effective for colonial politics, as it successfully marginalized other elements of the Pocahontas story that may have been less suitable for the making of a colonial, i.e. national myth. First, the construction of an intercultural love story effaces the story of Pocahontas's captivity among the English to such a degree that we rarely think about her as a captive at all. The genre of the early American captivity narrative on the other hand dramatizes – by inversion – the captivity of white settlers among the Natives. Rebecca Faery shows how the famous captivity narrative of Mary Rowlandson about her experiences during King Philip's War (1675/76) overwrites the story and experience of Pocahontas and thus codes captivity lastingly as the captivity of whites among 'evil savages' as a legitimizing strategy of colonial expansion (cf. *Cartographies*; cf. also Robertson, "First Captive"). Second, the construction of a romantic interest between Pocahontas and John Smith and later between Pocahontas and John Rolfe also obscures the fact that in the interim years between her encounter with John Smith and before her capture, Pocahontas supposedly had been married to Kocoum, a member of her tribe about whom we know very little. This is mentioned by William Strachey (cf. *Historie* 54). Thus, when Captain Argall kidnapped her in order to put pressure on her father Powhatan, she may have already been married. "If William Strachey's report that Pocahontas had been married in 1610 to 'a private captain,' Kocoum, were true, [...] then the English had kidnapped a married woman and thus condoned bigamy" (Robertson, "First Captive" 97; cf. Barbour, *Pocahontas* 98-99). However, this earlier "shadowy marriage" (Barbour, *Pocahontas* 99) seemingly was an impediment neither to her conversion nor to her marriage to Rolfe. Pocahontas's first marriage is omitted in most of the romanticized narratives about her, since it was considered to be a 'heathen' ritual without any meaning before God or the Law.

During his stay with his wife and son in England, John Rolfe writes his own pro-motional tract, *A True Relation of the State of Virginia* (cf. the transcription on the *Encyclopedia Virginia* webpage), to satisfy sponsors of the colony. While his marriage "symbolized an uneasy truce" (Hulme, "Polytropic Man" 168) in English-Native relations, after his return to Virginia as a widower, he was about to witness an eruption of violence that was to change English-Native relations in North America forever.

Throughout the second half of the 17th century and the 18th century Poca-hontas and John Rolfe figured as "the great archetype of Indian-white conjugal union" (Sheehan, *Seeds* 175). At the same time, however, Virginia was the first colony to introduce anti-miscegenation laws: in 1662, the legislature passed the Racial Integrity Act to prohibit the intermarriage of whites and blacks as well as whites and Natives. And still, Pocahontas and John Rolfe continued to be seen as foundational figures and as a blueprint for an alternative version of what American race relations *could* have been. This crucially entailed the insight that it all had – and irreversibly so – developed differently. The solution of racial conflict and territorial disputes via intermarriage and miscegenation seemed less and less feasible. Thomas Jefferson was perhaps one of the last Americans to publicly give voice to this vision and to encourage "an amalgamation of the races as a real possibility" (Tilton, *Pocahontas* 24; also cf. chapter 5), if only to assuage Americans' guilt-ridden conscience in the face of Native displacement and death. Over all, miscegenation became an increasingly taboo subject to dwell on. Pocahontas and John Rolfe certainly were "the first, and perhaps the only, Anglo-Indian marriage in Virginia's early history" (Nash, "Image" 215). Following American independence, Pocahontas attained her iconic mythical status in American culture and literature. The utopia of interracial love that was symbolized by the Pocahontas figure develops into a myth of the past while at the same time the policy of 'Indian removal' is implemented and carried out.

4. POCAHONTAS AND THE ROMANTIC TRADITION

> In the woods of Powhattan,
> Still 'tis told by Indian fires,
> How a daughter of their sires,
> Saved the captive Englishman.
> WILLIAM MAKEPEACE THACKERAY, "POCAHONTAS"

> When I think of Pocahontas, I am ready to love Indians.
> HERMAN MELVILLE, *THE CONFIDENCE-MAN*

Scholars agree that it is after the American Revolutionary War and, more prominently, at the beginning of the 19th century that the mythical dimension of the Pocahontas narrative evolved most powerfully (cf. Young, "Mother" 395; also cf. Tilton, *Pocahontas*). Thus, it is in the age of Indian removal – an official policy of deportation resulting in the death of thousands of Native Americans on the Trail of Tears – that Pocahontas becomes a full-fledged American icon and myth.

In order to mythologize Pocahontas in the context of profound anti-Native sentiments, a number of discursive strategies had to be employed: first of all, most texts and visual representations cast Pocahontas as the savior of John Smith rather than as the wife of John Rolfe; the second part of the narrative becomes lastingly marginalized in order to avoid the issue of miscegenation – by then an even stronger cultural taboo than in the 17th century. Second, Pocahontas figures somewhat nostalgically as a heroine of the past and of an innocent American beginning. The split between "the peace-loving and Christian Pocahontas" (Uhry Abrams, *Pilgrims* 127) on the one hand and her allegedly treacherous, violent and uncompromising indigenous male counterparts on the other is continued and deepened. This profound feminization of the narrative avoided the contradictions between racial discourse and foundational mythmaking. Third, the Pocahontas narrative underwent a turn to sentimentalism that further diverts attention from the brutality of colonial politics and that champions her as a romantic symbol of voluntary cultural contact and self-chosen assimilation to the white culture.

It is in 19th-century plays, literature, poetry as well as visual culture that we find manifestations of the gendering of the Pocahontas myth that still echo in contemporary cultural productions. Pocahontas made her first American schoolbook appearance in the 1797 edition of Noah Webster's *An American Selection of Lessons in Reading and Speaking*, yet the first author whose claim to fame the Pocahontas story would become was John Davis, an Englishman who had come to the United States as a visitor at the beginning of the 19th century. Davis quickly realized the potential of this early American legend and first worked it anecdotally and in a somewhat garbled fashion into his *Farmer of New Jersey* (1800), where he made John Smith an 'Indian trader' and Pocahontas a 'squaw' who saves him. Three years later, in *Travels of Four Years and a Half in the United States of America During 1798, 1799, 1800, 1801, and 1802* (1803) he expands the anecdote by drawing on Smith's texts, local lore, and his own imagination to recount the Pocahontas story in a "thirty-seven page segment" (Jenkins, "Princess" 14). Although his book is, strictly speaking, a travel report, Davis presents us here with the first fictionalized treatment of the topic; akin to a short story, the narrative displays markers of fictionality rather than an investment in historicism (cf. ibid.). Davis expands on the Pocahontas story and is credited by many scholars with the fabrication of the love story between Pocahontas and John Smith, a young girl and an older man by 17th-century standards. The manner in which he processed the story can be sensed from the following excerpt, a scene that follows upon Pocahontas bringing food to Smith and the Jamestown settlers:

The acclamations of the crowd affected to tears the sensibility of Pocahontas; but her native modesty was abashed; and it was with delight that she obeyed the invitation of Captain Smith to wander with him, remote from vulgar curiosity, along the banks of the river. It was then she gave loose to all the tumultuous ectasy of love; hanging on his arm and weeping with an eloquence more powerful than words. (*Travels* 278)

While we may glimpse from this paragraph why Davis's sentimentalist narrative never became canonical, we cannot overestimate the cultural work his texts performed in the context of an American foundational ideology: he "unearthed" the story of Pocahontas; he "popularized and perpetuated it; but most of all, he romanticized it and made historical fiction of it" (Jenkins, "Princess" 19). Davis further expanded the historical material by adding *Captain Smith and Princess Pocahontas* and *The First Settlers of Virginia, a Historical Novel* (both 1805) to his oeuvre, paving the way for numerous "romantic reconstructions of the narrative in the nineteenth century" at a time "when Americans had begun to scan the colonial past in search of figures like Pocahontas and Smith who could be rewarded retroactively for their proto-nationalist sentiments" (Tilton, *Pocahontas* 33). Again, Commager's phrase of the "search for a usable past" comes to mind. With his timely but now mostly forgotten writings Davis, who is generally considered "a prolific but minor English novelist-poet" (Jenkins, "Princess" 8), secured the enduring popularity of the Pocahontas story *as a romance* in the post-revolutionary period in the United States. However, Davis also contributed to a major shift in the reception of the story. Davis as well as the writers and poets who followed him focused mostly on the rescue scene, at times all but ignoring the story of her marriage and the fact that she had a mixed-race child with an English husband. As Jenkins puts it somewhat flippantly,

if Smith [...] made Pocahontas a sixteenth-century "cover girl for his come-hither pamphlets," then Rolfe, perhaps, made her the first of those who might be labelled "American Mother of the Year," and Davis, by his imaginative treatment of the love interests of the Indian princess, may have qualified her as the first American girl who was worthy of the title of "Miss America." (ibid. 19)

Following Davis, other American authors would take up the figure of the Native American woman and use recognizable elements of the Pocahontas story in plots of cultural contact, captivity, and love, e.g. Catharine Maria Sedgwick, who in her novel *Hope Leslie* (1827) uses the character of the Native American woman Magawisca to demythologize the Pocahontas narrative, and James Fenimore Cooper, who in his lesser-known novel *The Wept of Wish-Ton-Wish* (1829) inverts the Pocahontas story by addressing the indigenization of a white captive raised by a Native tribe (cf. Opfermann, "Lydia Maria Child," and Haselstein, *Die Gabe*).

Pocahontas is mentioned by American historians from William Stith (cf. *History of the First Discovery*) and Jeremy Belknap (cf. *American Biography*) to George Bancroft (cf. *History of the Colonization*); however, unlike Columbus, she did not have a biographer like Washington Irving to sing her praises. Instead, it is in the dramatic tradition – aside from Davis's prose – that she is most profoundly commemorated. The so-called Indian plays of the 19th century popularized stories about Pocahontas and similar, fictive figures in a mode of retrospective nostalgia. The Indian hero or heroine is cast as a melancholic figure, doomed to disappear with the advance of 'civilization;' Pocahontas's assimilation into white culture and the trope of the vanishing Indian thus were two dominant modes of representing this disappearance.

In 1808, one year after the bicentennial of the founding of Jamestown, the first play in English about Pocahontas was published: James Nelson Barker's *The Indian Princess, or, La Belle Sauvage*. Barker presents the same version as Davis's texts: one individual act of heroism – Pocahontas's rescue of John Smith – is dramatized as the key moment of American national prehistory (cf. Tilton, *Pocahontas* 48). The play mentions John Rolfe, yet leaves the marriage unconsummated, a standard feature of most of the 19th-century versions, which did not give a lot of attention to the fact that John Smith was not the only Englishman in Pocahontas's life.

Throughout the 19th century, Pocahontas plays abounded: "Pocahontas plays, as well as Indian plays in general, became a fixture on the American stage during the first half of the nineteenth century" (Jaroff, "Opposing Forces" 485). Approximately forty plays were performed between 1825 and 1869 (cf. ibid.; Quinn, *Exciting Adventures* 275). Aside from Barker's play, antebellum dramatist George Washington Custis's *Pocahontas, or the Settlers of Virginia* (1830) is among the most important ones. Custis was a descendant of George Washington; his play fit well into the nationalistic and patriotic spirit of the time and presented one exceptionally popular "Indian drama" (Tilton, *Pocahontas* 72). And yet, the publication of the play in 1830 also coincided with the Indian Removal Act, which the US Congress passed in the same year. Overall, the seeming paradox between the policy of Indian removal and the popularity of the Indian plays is compelling. As the quotation from Herman Melville's novel in the epigraph to this chapter illustrates, the idealization of Pocahontas as a foundational figure was in complete opposition to the demonization of Native Americans in 19th-century public discourse. We have already noted how 'good,' i.e. acceptable, and 'bad,' i.e. unacceptable attributes of the 'other' are distributed into complementary stereotypes, such as the 'noble savage' and the 'ignoble savage' (or 'evil heathen'): on the one hand, the championing of Native Americans as a marker of difference had a central function in revolutionary discourses that tried to dissociate the US from England: "the figure of the Indian became a convenient base upon which to build a uniquely American character" (Jaroff, "Opposing Forces" 485). Thus, Pocahontas figures in a history and tradition in which white Americans used Native Americans as figures of empowerment: "Pocahontas's consent gives the chosen people of white Americans a new fictional line of noble Indian ancestry" (Sollors, *Beyond Ethnicity* 79). Eventually, those white Americans would even dress up as 'Indians' in order to protest colonial rule (the transcultural phenomenon of 'playing Indian' has been extensively addressed by Philip Deloria; cf. his book of the same title). Yet, on the other hand, in internal negotiations of difference, the indigenous population is anything but representative of America. Carolyn Karcher comments on this paradox: "white Americans win their political freedom at the expense of the Indians they exterminate and [...] they achieve their cultural independence by expropriating the cultures of the peoples they have systematically debased, devalorized, and deprived of an independent identity" (Introduction xxxiii). In this discourse, Pocahontas appears prominently as "the selfless Indian princess" (Jaroff, "Opposing Forces" 486). Custis's play and the Indian Removal Act thus present two different but related strategies of the same colonial and racist discourse of white hegemony – and "[t]he rarer actual American Indians became in the United States, [...] the more accessible their history became to appropriation by a national culture in search of legitimating traditions of identity" (Loeffelholz, "Miranda" 59).

In contrast to the conventional romanticization of Pocahontas in the popular Indian plays, some dramas avoided the by then predictable racial and gender stereotypes, of which I will briefly mention two. Charlotte Barnes's *The Forest Princess* (1844) does not employ the standard repertoire of the Pocahontas narrative, nor does the author center her play on the rescue scene or on any romantic investments; rather, it "subverts popular Indian plays of the day supplying Pocahontas with a voice, granting her political status, and allowing her to reject colonial domination" (Jaroff, "Opposing Forces" 483). Its representational strategies contrast with Custis's patriotic championing of the national agenda of Indian removal.

John Brougham's 1855 parody *Po-ca-hontas, or the Gentle Savage* turns on the dramatic tradition of the Pocahontas play in order to make fun of it. His heroine is referred to as "Pokey," and Brougham's play closes with the marriage of Pocahontas and John Smith, leaving Rolfe to complain on the sidelines. Brougham – nicknamed "American Aristophanes" by his contemporaries (Hutton qtd. in Moody, Introduction 402) – ridicules the fashionable mythologizing of Pocahontas, and his play is "a wonderful parody of the archetypal Indian heroines of drama and romance, all of whom were ultimately based primarily on John Smith's representations of the original Powhatan princess" (Tilton, *Pocahontas* 75). For decades, Brougham's play was

the standard burlesque afterpiece in New York and in theatres across the country. It was also popular as a soldier show in Civil War army camps. In the almost thirty years of its stage life no theatrical season in any American city was complete without a few performances of "Pokey." (Moody, Introduction 401; also cf. Sollors, *Beyond Ethnicity*)

Both Brougham and Barnes present exceptions to the rule: most of the 19th-century renderings of the Pocahontas narrative focused on its first part because it seemed less problematic and offensive and could be staged as an intercultural encounter based on notions of romantic love (cf. Tilton, *Pocahontas*). The rescue scene also made a much better "colonial beginning," in the words of Peter Hulme (*Colonial Encounters* 141); obviously, the marriage to John Rolfe could not be cast as the happy ending to her aborted relationship with John Smith, if the latter was to be seen as '*the* romance of the republic:' a fateful, larger-than-life intercultural infatuation.

Illustration 2: Portrait of Pocahontas

Simon van de Passe, Engraving (1616).

In visual culture the rescue scene also figures prominently: "Smith's rescue by a scantily clad Pocahontas became a favourite topic for a number of popular prints that flooded the market from the 1830s well into the 1870s" (Uhry Abrams qtd. in Tilton, *Pocahontas* 94). It is the most canonical element of the Pocahontas story throughout the 19th century and beyond, and is to this day used in American schoolbooks to teach an ideologically fraught, orthodox version of American beginnings. In the 19th century many painters tried to visualize this crucial moment in early American history – a moment without which, it was assumed, there would not have been any *American* history to begin with. These visual representations of Pocahontas range from exoticist/primitivist to classicist, either depicting her as a nude female Native or as a (to all appearances) white young woman. Let me briefly discuss the most prominent examples in American art, portraiture, and painting. The most famous portrait of Pocahontas is probably the 1616 "Matoaka, alias Rebecca" copperplate by Simon van de Passe, which depicts her as an English lady – 'Lady Rebecca' is the name given to her by the English in reference to the biblical Rebecca, whom Abraham arranged to be brought to Canaan from his birthplace as a wife for his son Isaac. This portrait is heavily stylized – there is no trace of the Native woman, not even in her features – and follows contemporary conventions of court portraiture in order to affirm the new Christian identity of Powhatan's daughter as well as her noble background.

In the United States, the memorial culture centering on Pocahontas in the 19th century produced several works of art that particularly in terms of their location are highly important. One of them would be the 1825 relief by Antonio Capellano which is located over the west door of the rotunda of the Capitol in Washington, D.C.: "Its inclusion in the Capitol at this early date makes clear that the rescue of Smith by Pocahontas had long been perceived as a crucial generative moment in the history of the United States" (Tilton, *Pocahontas* 95). In 1825, Americans had already adopted Pocahontas as a figure of national consensus.

Illustration 3: Pocahontas Becomes a Christian

John Gadsby Chapman, *The Baptism of Pocahontas* (1839).

One of the most famous images produced in the 19th century, however, one which also inscribes Pocahontas into American cultural memory and whose importance cannot be stressed enough, is the painting of Pocahontas's baptism by John G. Chapman (1839), which is exhibited in the rotunda of the US Capitol, at the 'heart of the nation.' This painting is remarkable in many ways. First of all, for its topic: it is not the famous rescue scene with John Smith, nor her marriage to John Rolfe, nor Pocahontas and her son, the offspring of this remarkable intercultural union, that we find depicted here; rather the painting shows Pocahontas's baptism, "shrewdly choosing the moment when European ritual symbolized her rejection of her own culture and her incorporation into the ranks of the saved" (Hulme, *Colonial Encounters* 170).

As part of a "Jamestown series" (Uhry Abrams, *Pilgrims* 121), Chapman had commemorated earlier scenes such as *The First Ship, The Landing at James-town, The Crowning of Powhatan, The Warning of Pocahontas* and, of course, also an image of the rescue scene, titled *Pocahontas Saving the Life of Captain John Smith*. For his work commissioned by the United States Congress, how-ever, he depicts a different scene: the baptism of Pocahontas. Historicist in the classical sense, Chapman avoids showing Pocahontas's entire face; rather we see her profile. Tilton suggests that Chapman subordinates Pocahontas to the event that is portrayed, the baptism, and that this kind of depiction later became con-ventional also for representations of the rescue scene which no longer featured her as the prime actor (cf. *Pocahontas* 112). From what we do see of her, we can ascertain that "Pocahontas is lighter in skin tone than the other Indians in the painting. [...] This conventional depiction allows Chapman to suggest that a blanching of any distinctively Indian racial features has occurred through this Christianization process" (ibid. 113). Her pose is reminiscent of the kneeling Virgin Mary found in nativity scenes (cf. ibid. 114). Also, she has her back turned to the other Natives, who are traditionally clad; her white gown, by con-trast, symbolizes virginity, innocence, and rebirth. The English officials, Thomas Dale and John Rolfe, frame Pocahontas and Reverend Alexander Whitaker. The lighting guides our gaze to the central hierarchy between the kneeling Pocahon-tas and the upright representative of the English clergy. The scene, faithful to historical fact, does not include John Smith; it does include, however, various other historical figures of the colony's early history. Pocahontas to this day is the only female foundational figure or 'founding mother,' as she is sometimes re-ferred to, enshrined in the rotunda of the US Capitol among an otherwise all-male series of prominent figures.

The choice of Pocahontas's baptism was not unequivocally accepted by all of Chapman's contemporaries. Critics such as William Gilmore Simms saw the baptism not as a "foundational scene" related to the founding of the United States (cf. "Pocahontas"). Simms, among others, chided Chapman for *not* rep-resenting the rescue scene. "By placing Pocahontas in the role of the recipient, Chapman reminds his audience that she was, ironically, a heathen at the moment of her most Christian act (the rescue) and puts forward the idea that her baptism can be seen as a type of reward for, or a tangible acknowledgment of, her well-known heroism" (Tilton, *Pocahontas* 126). The baptism also puts her in a passive role, while she is seen as active in the rescue scene.

John Rolfe had stressed in a letter to Thomas Dale that he wanted to convert and marry Pocahontas not "with the unbridled desire of carnall affection but for the good of this plantation, for the honour of our countrie, for the glory of God" (Letter 240). The baptism scene most crucially displays the ideological twist and the central paradox in the making of the Pocahontas myth. Whereas she is seen as the Native 'other,' her baptism constitutes – in the way Chapman portrays it, at any rate – a forceful ritual of *de-indigenization*. The narrative of her baptism, i.e. the narrative of her conversion, creates a new perspective on her experience of captivity as a kind of liberation/emancipation and return:

Pocahontas was removed, literally and spiritually, from her birth parents and was "returned" to her true father, Christ. [...] Pocahontas's removal from her blood family which began with her capture by Captain Argall was maintained voluntarily because she had been educated by her God-parents to make the correct choice. (Fudge, "Pocahontas's Baptism" 24)

This was the reasoning of John Smith and others. The version of "conversion as return" appeared to be in accordance with the logic of the Reformed faith adhered to, among others, by Alexander Whitaker himself. With this rendering of events, Chapman and others have lastingly eclipsed Pocahontas's narrative of captivity in favor of one of conversion.

The painting is a milestone in the making of the Pocahontas myth, but it also points to some ambiguities in the making of the myth in the first half of the 19th century. Uhry Abrams, for instance, suggests that Chapman "seems to have been affected by the Trail of Tears, which had occurred two years before he installed his mural in the Capitol. The reality of that tragic march may explain why he featured the Indians more prominently in the final version of the painting than in the preliminary sketch" (*Pilgrims* 124), which gave them only a marginal presence. Overall, Chapman's painting relied on or took up tendencies of commemorating Pocahontas in the realm of narrative fiction, drama, and poetry. Following Chapman's painting of 1840, William McCarthy's 1842 edition of patriotic American songs includes three songs on Pocahontas (282-3, 287-8, 370-1), thus affirming her presence in yet another popular American medium.

5. WHOSE POCAHONTAS?

> [A]n estimated two million [...] people [...] to this day trace their ancestry
> back to the Indian girl.
> PHILIP YOUNG, "THE MOTHER OF US ALL."

While we can reconstruct the process in which Pocahontas became the protagonist in a national foundational myth with universal appeal, we can also complicate these findings by tracing the myth through the ages with more attention to
detail and differences. The making of this myth may have been propelled by
national ideology, yet it was also influenced by other, widely differing political
discourses: while Pocahontas was claimed in the 19th century as the "first mythic
Indian" (Fiedler, *Return* 64) and enthroned as a national heroic figure, she was
also claimed in the name of many other agendas.

First of all, many writers and critics have drawn upon Pocahontas as the central figure of a specifically *southern* myth of origin – as the "guardian angel" of
the oldest American colony, Virginia (Young, "Mother" 396), and many patriotic publications have come out of this. Much scholarship by southern critics from
David Garnet to Leo Lemay has time and again stressed the importance of
Pocahontas in a regionalist context of southern traditions. These publications
about the South and its cultural and literary traditions also deal with Pocahontas
as a central figure in southern historiographic and literary texts (cf. Kindermann,
Geschichte). Most comprehensively and convincingly, Ann Uhry Abrams has
argued for Pocahontas as an "origin myth of Virginia" (cf. *Pilgrims*), which she
juxtaposes with that of Massachusetts (the Puritans and the Pilgrims, to be dealt
with in the next chapter). This juxtaposition – "the Pilgrims and Pocahontas" –
historically unfolds as a kind of rivalry, at times even as a battle for national
dominance in which the southern heritage and legacy is frequently pitted against
that of New England. Uhry Abrams places the Pocahontas story as the foundational female savior tale of Virginia in contrast to the origin myths of Massachusetts' patriarchal colony (ibid. 149). Pocahontas as a Virginian founding
mother becomes particularly important in the context of the American Civil War
(1861-65). In the war between North and South, Pocahontas was frequently
invoked by both sides: the North tried to discredit the narrative of John Smith in
order to debunk the credibility of the first white 'Southerner.' After 1860,
authors from the North, among them Charles Deane and Henry Adams, fervently
"challenge[d] the veracity of the rescue story" with a polemical "anti-Smith
thrust" (Tilton, *Pocahontas* 172). By contrast, the South countered these attacks
and affirmed the truth of Smith's narrative, in particular the rescue scene. Over

all, "Pocahontas and her narrative were crucial to the South's growing sense of otherness" (ibid.). Constructing Pocahontas as a southern ancestress and, more literally, as a progenitrix of many members of the Virginia elite, many writers and scholars, such as James Kirke Paulding, place her among the "tutelary deities" of Virginia (*Letters* Vol. 1 25). As Anne Norton writes in *Alternative Americas*:

In the South the Pocahontas myth became increasingly expressive of a peculiar sectional culture. The chivalrous conduct in the myth recalled the Cavalier, the rank and marriage of Pocahontas assured the legitimacy of the present residents. As an Indian princess, Pocahontas united a natural, Indian, character of noble savagery and natural virtue with a conventional pre-eminence, reconciling the conflicting demands of Jefferson and an ideology derived from the Enlightenment, with the Cavalier model. As Southern sentiment for rebellion [...] increased, Pocahontas was evoked with increasing frequency. These evocations associated Pocahontas as a sectional symbol with the violent independence considered characteristic of Indians in general. (183)

Thus, the story of Pocahontas became the bone of contention in a heated controversy, and it is not without irony in this context that the United States Navy, which routinely named its battleships after Native tribes and individuals, would send its battleships *Powhatan* and *Pocahontas* (the only American warship named after a woman at this point) to serve in the war *against* the southern secessionists who claimed her as their ancestor (cf. Tilton, *Pocahontas* 146). Summarily, we have to acknowledge that the attempts at discrediting the Pocahontas narrative on the part of many Northerners during the years of national crisis failed, as by that time "the name and the accomplishments of the Indian princess Pocahontas were deeply ingrained in the collective American consciousness. By the second half of the nineteenth-century, her heroic identity was far beyond the scope of any such attempts at demythologization" (ibid. 175).

Second, in a quite different vein, Pocahontas has been cast as an early American *feminist*. Mary Hays's 1803 *Female Biography* depicted Pocahontas as a model woman, as a "princess politician" and as a manifestation of "nineteenth-century resolute womanhood" (Dyer, "Transatlantic Pocahontas" 302). In varying versions, her story has been offered as a narrative of empowerment for women, investing her with a specifically female agency in a patriarchal context of male saber-rattling. In Charlotte Barnes's play, *The Forest Princess*, we have seen traces of this feminist agenda, which often also sidesteps the hyperbolic romantic fashioning of the story in favor of presenting Pocahontas as a self-confident, single-minded Native woman. The gender-specific implications and the feminist potential of the Pocahontas myth have been addressed by various authors at different times. Particularly in the context of first-wave feminism in the United States, Pocahontas was discovered as an ancestor figure. The dissemination of the idea and trope of the 'new woman' coincided with the search for a usable feminist past. While women were campaigning for their right to vote in the US (granted in 1920 by the 19th Amendment to the United States Constitution), Pocahontas was featured in a number of plays and poems that used her as a model feminist: Margaret Ullmann's play *Pocahontas* (1912) has the heroine self-confidently refuse John Smith's attempt to seduce her when they meet for the last time. Nathalia Crane's *Pocahontas* (1930) envisions in heroic couplets a worldwide communist conspiracy threatening the nation, a future which only the last descendant of the 'Indian' princess Pocahontas can avert, who in Crane's poem is enlisted to protect and to save the American nation.

Mary Dearborn examines the uses that were made in ethnic women's writing of the story of Pocahontas as "the single most important received metaphor of female ethnic identity" (*Pocahontas's Daughters* 97) in American intellectual and literary history, and identifies Pocahontas as a signifier of American femininity as well as ethnicity and as a paradigmatic model for negotiating the intricacies of a position between two and more cultures. By examining how "gender and ethnicity function in American culture" (ibid. 189), Dearborn points to "ancestry" and "community" as crucial categories in American ethnic women's writing that also give shape to the Pocahontas narrative; the poles of kinship/descent on the one hand and of love, marriage and consent on the other hand are the crucial aspects of her tale whose tension with each other American indigenous and immigrant ethnic women writers from Mourning Dove to Gertrude Stein, from Nella Larsen to Maxine Hong Kingston have time and again tried to articulate (ibid. 192). According to Dearborn, ethnic women writers are "Pocahontas's daughters" in the sense that they give voice to what Pocahontas could have said in order to "fill her silence with words" (ibid. 193) in yet another appropriation of the historical figure in the context of feminist identity politics.

Illustration 4: Pocahontas Stamp

US Postal Service, *Pocahontas 5¢* (1907).

Whether prototypically feminine or feminist, Pocahontas is not only claimed as a founding mother by female ethnic writers but throughout also remains a national symbol, as evidenced by the 5-cent stamp that comes out in 1907 to commemorate the 300th anniversary of the founding of Jamestown, Virginia. There is, thirdly, a full-fledged Pocahontas cult after World War I among a group of American modernist writers, who also discover her as an American 'founding mother' and as a central emblem of American indigenous traditions to be contrasted with European traditions. Vachel Lindsay's poem "Our Mother Pocahontas" is an early manifestation of this notion. Although this poem may not be written in a specifically modernist style, it captures the mood of this modernist sentiment very well, as this excerpt shows:

> Because we are her fields of corn;
> Because our fires are all reborn
> From her bosom's deathless embers,
> Flaming
> As she remembers
> The springtime
> And Virginia,
> Our Mother, Pocahontas.
> John Rolfe is not our ancestor.
> We rise from out the soul of her
> Held in native wonderland,
> While the sun's rays kissed her hand,
> In the springtime,

In Virginia,
Our mother, Pocahontas. (116-117)

The Pocahontas figure is to be found in the works of many modernists. In one of his short stories, Ernest Hemingway wonders "[w]ere there two sides to Pocahontas? Did she have a fourth dimension" ("Banal Story" 334), and she appears, most prominently, in Hart Crane's long poem *The Bridge* (in the part titled "Powhatan's Daughter"), which is described by Leslie Fiedler as a "handbook of American mythology" (*Return* 119). The references to Pocahontas in modernist literature reverberate with the general fascination with the 'primitive' and the exotic in literature and art typical of that period; in its specifically American variant, this fascination pursues the symbolic appropriation of Native Americans as embodiments of a primordial, authentic way of life and thus as objects of nostalgic longing (cf. Vizenor, *Fugitive Poses*; Hutchinson, *Indian Craze*).

But whether as a Southerner or as a feminist or as modernist muse, none of these framings do affect Pocahontas's status as a *national* icon; instead they seem to further magnify it. They also signal, however, the way in which the historical figure and her encounter with the English have been taken as a "blank space" (Hulme, *Colonial Encounters* 138) and have been used for different ideological inscriptions in different phases of American history.

6. POCAHONTAS, THE SURVIVOR – NATIVE AMERICAN AND POSTCOLONIAL PERSPECTIVES

> Pocahontas's child is crucial to the story's meaning.
> ELLA SHOHAT AND ROBERT STAM, *UNTHINKING EUROCENTRISM*

> Survivance.
> GERALD VIZENOR

Certainly the most important revisionist perspective on "America's Ur-miscegenation story" (Edwards, "United Colors" 147) is that of Native Americans, which has been articulated quite forcefully since the 1960s. Native American revisionism of the myth of Pocahontas challenges, as in the case of Columbus, the very notion of an American beginning on the terms that have been described so far. Of course, there is not *one* single homogenous Native American response to the multi-layered 'white' mythologization of Pocahontas; we can, in a brief overview, identify several tendencies which range from the deconstruction of popular stereotypes of Native Americans in general and of Pocahontas in particular to various new interpretations of the historical moment of cultural contact between Pocahontas and the English settlers/invaders and its consequences.

Many contemporary Native American writers have tried to imagine what Pocahontas could or might have thought or said as we simply do not have any records. The Native American poet Paula Gunn Allen has given a voice to Pocahontas in one of her poems titled "Pocahontas to Her English Husband, John Rolfe," in which the speaker reminisces:

Had I not cradled you in my arms
Oh beloved perfidious one,
You would have died.
And how many times did I pluck you
From certain death in the wilderness –
My world through which you stumbled
as though blind?
[…]
Still you survived, oh my fair husband,
And brought them gold
Wrung from a harvest I taught you
To plant. Tobacco.
[…]
I'm sure
You wondered at my silence, saying I was
A simple wanton, a savage maid,
Dusky daughter of heathen sires
Who cartwheeled naked through the muddy towns
Who would learn the ways of grace only
By your firm guidance, through
Your husbandly rule:
No doubt, no doubt.
I spoke little, you said.
And you listened less
[…]
I saw you well
I understood your ploys and still
Protected you, going so far as to die
In your keeping – a wasting,
Putrefying Christian death – and you,

Deceiver, whiteman, father of my son,
Survived, reaping wealth greater
Than you had ever dreamed
From what I taught you and from the wasting of my bones. (8f.)

The poem outwardly simulates the poetic mode of Puritan poetry by women (such as Anne Bradstreet's well-known 1678 poem "To My Dear and Loving Husband") in addressing the beloved partner; yet it does not recreate the conventional topoi of modesty and submission, nor does it, as does Bradstreet's text, describe a harmonious and passionate union – rather it constructs a stance of superiority on the part of Pocahontas vis-à-vis her husband John Rolfe. Referring to the strategies of colonial othering, the speaker reverses well-known stereotypes: it is he who is 'the other' – ignorant, childlike, helpless, and dependent; it is she who rescues him not once, but many times; and yet, in his world/discourse she does not have a voice. Ultimately, she holds him responsible for her death, which is intricately connected to his acquisition of fame and fortune.

Pocahontas's "bones" mentioned in the last line of the poem are also at the center of Gerald Vizenor's postmodern rendering of the Pocahontas story in *The Heirs of Columbus*. Picking up the debates on repatriation triggered by the Native American Graves Protection and Repatriation Act (NAGPRA) of 1990, the novel has a protagonist who seeks to retrieve and rebury the remains of Pocahontas, yet is murdered by an alliance of the Brotherhood of American Explorers and intelligence agents referred to as "the savages of intelligence." In this novel, which tries to deconstruct the master narrative of colonial expansion in myriad ways, much is at stake in the retrieval of these bones – which miraculously vanish in a shamanistic ritual from the rooms of an anthropological museum and thus from the archive of Native American dispossession.

From a Native American perspective, the story of Pocahontas is not a story of conversion, assimilation, and sacrifice, but a story of Native survival. This, of course, fits into a general postcolonial framework, as Shohat and Stam have pointed out (cf. *Unthinking*). Pocahontas not only survived the first contact but delivered a child that may be seen as the beginning of an alternative "cross-blood" American genealogy (cf. Vizenor, *Landfill Meditation*). Such a counter-hegemonic construction of 'national' beginnings stands in stark contrast to the strange cultural practice of whites claiming a remote – not to say metaphorical – Native American ancestry (one, however, that is contained in their 'whiteness'), such as those two million Americans who claim to be Pocahontas's kin. Apart from genealogically documented lineages there seems to be a longing for

Pocahontas as an 'honorary white' founding mother (stripped of her indigenous otherness) that registers in the ambiguous cultural trope of the "Indian grandmother," which has been described by Vine Deloria as the Indian grandmother complex:

Whites claiming Indian blood generally tend to reinforce mythical beliefs about Indians. All but one person I met who claimed Indian blood claimed it on their grandmother's side. I once did a projection backward and discovered that evidently most tribes were entirely female for the first three hundred years of white occupation. (*Custer* 3)

The trope of the 'Indian princess' as an ancestor figure extrapolates from Pocahontas to become "everyone's Indian grandmother." Native American (Shoshone/Chippewa) poet nila northSun puns on the same trope that is no longer restricted to the Pocahontas figure – in fact, the Cherokee used to be the most 'fashionable' tribe to be descended from for a long time. In her poem "stupid questions" the speaker quips:

you know, my great-grandmother was a Cherokee princess
(you know, she must have been one helluva whore cause everybody has the same great-grandmother) (217)

Responding both to white colonial mythmaking and to the marginalization of women within Native American studies, Paula Gunn Allen suggests "putting women [like Pocahontas] at the center of the tribal universe" in order to "recover[] the feminine in American Indian Traditions" (*Sacred Hoop* 264). For Allen – who takes the rescue scene seriously – the fact that Pocahontas could successfully intervene on behalf of John Smith and against her father shows the absence of European patriarchal structures and the power women had in gynocratic tribal societies such as those of the Algonquians (cf. *Pocahontas* 6, 172-3). Pocahontas is imagined as part of a female continuum in the context of Allen's specific brand of Native American feminism.

Native American revisionism of the Pocahontas myth takes place in all kinds of media and art forms including poetry, fiction, nonfiction, and musical and visual culture; examples would be Native American composer George Quincy's mini-opera *Pocahontas at the Court of James I and Choctaw Diaries* (2008) or R.L. Morgan Monceaux' visual image titled "Matowaka" (1992).

Illustration 5: Pocahontas in Contemporary Art

R.L. Morgan Monceaux, *Matowaka* (1992).

A postcolonial perspective on the Pocahontas narrative is provided by the Caribbean-American author Michelle Cliff in her novel *No Telephone to Heaven* (1987). Her displaced mixed-race female protagonist with the telling name Clare Savage is Caribbean-born and lives in the United States as well as in Britain. At the British seaside she encounters Pocahontas:

She stood and walked toward it [the monument, HP] – from a distance her training sus-
pected allegory. Bronze. Female. Single figure. Single feather rising from the braids.
Moccasined feet stepping forward, as if to walk off the pedestal on which she was kept. A
personification of the New World, dedicated to some poor soul who perished in pursuit of
it. Clare came closer. It was not that at all. No; this was intended to signify one individual
and mark her resting place. The letters at the base of the statue told her this ... Pocahontas.
(136)

Cliff's narrator tries to de-allegorize and demythologize the figure of Pocahontas, to come to her 'face to face' and to see her as another human being. Down-
sizing the myth in favor of the individual is a strategy that many contemporary
authors have employed.

In addition, Native American representational critique in different shapes and
media is flanked by white-authored critiques of the romantic myth. Early on,
Leslie Fiedler has examined the troping of an "anti-Pocahontas" (*Return* 81) in
American culture. The American writer John Barth, for instance, substitutes this
negative image for the idealized version of Pocahontas in his postmodern novel
The Sot-Weed Factor (1960); in Barth's revision of the Pocahontas myth, Smith
has to rape Pocahontas at her father's request in order to save his life and that of
his men. Barth's highly ironic text points to the misogynist and racist streak in
American culture and literature that performs a degradation of Pocahontas into
"anti-Pocahontas," from redeeming Princess into prostitute, "a whore begging to
be screwed" (Fiedler, *Return* 153). From a postcolonial perspective, this hyperbolic representation of the first contact may be read as an indictment of the
predominantly violent nature of European-Native interactions. Against this background, mythologizing one Native American woman as an "Indian princess" is
but a form of displacing white guilt and has never prevented the denigration and
negative stereotyping of Native American women in general, thus re-affirming
the virgin/whore dichotomy firmly established in Western patriarchal culture. As
Leslie Fiedler points out, "princess" in colloquial diction for a long time was the
derogatory expression for a Native American prostitute (ibid. 81). Similarly,
expressions such as "squaw" and even "Pocahontas" have frequently been used
as slurs, as the Native American actress Irene Bedard, who lends her voice to
Disney's Pocahontas, remembers well (cf. Edgerton and Jackson, "Redesigning"
95).

7. CONTEMPORARY COMMODIFICATIONS OF THE LOVE STORY

> Captain Smith and Pocahontas
> Had a very mad affair,
> When her Daddy tried to kill him, she said,
> "Daddy-o don't you dare"
> He gives me fever, with his kisses,
> FEVER when he holds me tight.
> FEVER – I'm his Missus,
> Oh Daddy won't you treat him right.
> PEGGY LEE, "FEVER"

> She wanted to devour him with love. Her body acted as if it was no longer a part of the woman she knew. [...] She felt as if she were part of the man whose body gave her such joy, as if his skin were hers, as if their hearts were one. At other times she felt she would swoon with the deliciousness of her captivity.
> SUSAN DONNELL, *POCAHONTAS*

> I wish I was a trapper
> I would give a thousand pelts
> To sleep with Pocahontas
> And find out how she felt.
> NEIL YOUNG, "POCAHONTAS"

In spite of Native American criticism and controversies about her status as a foundational American heroine, the figure of Pocahontas is very much alive in American popular and mass culture, and romance continues to be the central paradigm of her narrativization. In his classic study of formula fiction, John Cawelti has identified the romance formula as one prominent archetype of formulaic writing:

The crucial defining characteristic of romance is not that it stars a female but that its organizing action is the development of a love relationship, usually between a man and a woman [...]. The moral fantasy of the romance is that of love triumphant and permanent, overcoming all obstacles and difficulties. Though the usual outcome is a permanently happy marriage, more sophisticated types of love story sometimes end in the death of one or both of the lovers, but always in such a way as to suggest that the love relation has been of lasting and permanent impact. (*Adventure* 41-42)

Illustration 6: Pocahontas in Popular Fiction

Cover of *Pocahontas* by S. Donnell (Berkley Books, 1991).

Popular Pocahontas narratives operate with the romance formula when representing Pocahontas as saving John Smith out of love. The rescue scene dramatizes the conventional 'love is stronger than death' topos as well as the notion of
sacrificial love, i.e. love as selfless altruism that makes one willing to give one's
life so that the other's may be spared. In the Pocahontas narrative, this "fantasy
of the all-sufficiency of love" (ibid. 42) overcomes linguistic barriers as well as
cultural difference – and, needless to say, does away with all questions of colonial power relations.

In the course of the 20th century, these love plots have become more daring
and more explicit in their handling of English-Native sexuality and sexual re-

lations while at the same time being hopelessly anachronistic. Susan Donnell's historical romance *Pocahontas* (1991) is one among a plethora of such retellings of the Pocahontas story as a popular love story. The author, a self-proclaimed "direct fourteenth-generation descendant" of Pocahontas, declares that she writes "from heart and history" (Author's Note viii); her novel's suggestive cover reads: "She was a princess, a lady and a legend, her story is the story of America." Again, the story of Pocahontas appears as a foundational narrative of the nation. As the second epigraph to this section shows, Pocahontas's 'captivity' is metaphorically cast as one of desire and captivation, not one of forceful abduction and political struggle. Pocahontas is completely de-indigenized on the cover of Donnell's book, apart from her dress and three feathers in her black hair, which are stereotypical attributes in Western depictions of indigenous attire. This strategy of de-indigenizing Pocahontas – which we have already found at work in many 19th-century representations – was continued most prominently in our era of late capitalism by a cultural production that brought new and unprecedented fame to the old legend: Walt Disney's *Pocahontas* (1995). This animated motion picture started a veritable Pocahontas craze fuelled by "a $125 million marketing blitz" (Edwards, "United Colors" 162) that "crested in the summer of 1995 in a wave of Pocahontas backpacks, balloons, napkins, pillows, nightgowns, cupcake tins and plastic figurines tied in to the Disney animated feature" (Robertson, "First Captive" 73). Pocahontas merchandize also included a tanned and black-haired Pocahontas Barbie doll accompanied by her animal friends, the Native 'warrior' Kocoum, and John Smith.

The Disney film has been viewed positively as a balanced, politically correct representation of first contact in North America, even as "the single finest work ever done on American Indians by Hollywood" (qtd. in Edgerton and Jackson, "Redesigning" 34), but it has also been criticized as another romantic fantasy about 'Indians' glossing over a history of genocide and dispossession (cf. ibid.), and thus, as romanticizing colonialism (cf. Turner, "Playing"). Leigh Edwards's superb analysis of Disney's *Pocahontas* takes issue with "the film's attempt to fashion Jamestown into the birthplace of multiculturalism" ("United Colors" 149). The makers of the Disney film, as Edwards points out, "change[] her [Pocahontas's, HP] age so that a romance between them [Pocahontas and John Smith, HP] becomes more feasible" (ibid. 151). After a friendship has formed and Pocahontas has rescued Smith from execution, the film includes a second rescue scene in which Smith takes a bullet for Powhatan; seriously injured, Smith has to return to England to recover, thereby providing the plot with a rationale to separate him from his beloved Pocahontas. This narrative maneuver "displaces actual miscegenation from the narrative frame" (ibid.), which the film also does by omitting Pocahontas's relationship with John Rolfe. Visually, the film depicts Pocahontas as "an historically-impossible multiethnic body," a body that was manufactured by Disney animator Glen Keane as "an ethnic blend whose convexly curved face is African, whose dark, slanted eyes are Asian and whose body proportions are Caucasian" (Keane qtd. in Tillotson, "Cartoons" C8). Pocahontas thus incorporates multiculturalism as an "undifferentiated visual compilation of non-white ethnicities" (Edwards, "United Colors" 152) and as an "icon of Western standards of exoticized female beauty" (ibid. 154). We may consider Walt Disney's Pocahontas as a postfeminist emblem who at the same time becomes "Disney's multicultural educator" (ibid. 155); in the spirit of political correctness, even the 'new world' crop, tobacco, is exchanged for corn. Overall, the story is awkwardly sanitized: there is no mention of Pocahontas's captivity or the eruption of violence in white-Native relations. The film uncritically imagines and celebrates what Leslie Fiedler has called the US-American "myth of love in the woods" (*Return* 50). Of course, the popularity of this version of the Pocahontas narrative speaks to archetypal patterns of the human imagination. We like to think about cultural contact not in terms of violence but in terms of love and affection. The possibility of Europe and America coming together in a peaceful encounter leading to friendship and love rather than to war and genocide is a fantasy people still like to entertain.

Terrence Malick's film *The New World* (2005) offers a highly aestheticized though at the same time less anodyne version of the historical narrative that casts Pocahontas as "the perfect tribal Eve" (Weatherston, "When Sleeping" 11) for the English "Adam" in the 'new world' and that tries to do justice to the ambiguities of the narrative by telling it to its (not so happy) ending instead of leaving off after Smith's rescue and departure. For Malick, Pocahontas clearly is the first American.

Most recently, the longevity of the Pocahontas narrative in US-American culture has been evidenced by the (unadjusted for inflation) currently highest-grossing film of all times, James Cameron's *Avatar* (2009), a science-fiction version of the Pocahontas story with an anti-colonialist agenda. The film's white hero is rescued twice by the Native Pocahontas character: the first time she helps him to survive in the 'wilderness' of the fictive moon of Pandora, the second time she rescues him from his fellow colonizers. In the end, it is he who becomes completely and irrevocably indigenized, rather than her being de-indigenized. The military-industrial, (neo-)colonial enterprise from earth is successfully thwarted on Pandora – to stay with the analogy: the Jamestown on Pandora is wiped out. Cameron's blockbuster may at first glance be conventional in its enactment of intercultural romance and admittedly celebrates indigenous traditions that are accessible only through the most advanced technology (cf. Theweleit, "Menschliche Drohnen"), yet its insistence on the indigenization of the hero from earth into Pandora's Na'vi culture constitutes a powerful critique of US-American neoimperialism. In a timely fashion, Cameron's film combines a re-fashioning of the Pocahontas story with a critique of US-American military interventionism as part of an interracial love story between a man from earth and a Pandoran woman. With the Pocahontas myth in mind, we can read *Avatar* as a comment on and as an update of a core foundational American myth in the age of globalization. In Cameron's retelling for 21st-century American and global audiences we can glimpse the subversive, anti-foundational potential and critical impetus of the revised Pocahontas myth.

8. CONCLUSION

> Shopworn by sentimentality, Pocahontas endures and stands with the most appealing of our saints. She has passed subtly into our folklore, where she lives as a popular fable.
>
> PHILIP YOUNG, "THE MOTHER OF US ALL"

Having traced the Pocahontas myth through several centuries of US-American history and culture, we find the strategy of de-indigenization intricately inter-twined with that of de-politicization. In a project of encyclopedic scope, Klaus Theweleit has examined the reverberations of the Pocahontas narrative as a prime example for the sexualization of violence in the context of colonization (cf. *"You Give Me Fever"*). Beyond all seemingly innocent configurations of romantic love and intercultural altruism, Theweleit argues (in an at times im-pressionistic and associative style) that it is the relationship between indigenous sexuality and the violence of the colonizer that is at the center of the Pocahontas narrative – a relationship that may be specifically US-American in some ways and in some aspects, yet also fits one of the most archetypal tropes in Western cultural history from antiquity to the present. From a transnational, hemispheric perspective, we can discuss Pocahontas alongside a figure such as Malinche, translator for Hernán Cortés during his conquest of Mexico, or in the context of similar colonial romantic plots that organize libidinal intercultural energies and validate patriarchal notions of white superiority in contexts of violent coloniza-tion.

Even though Pocahontas may appear as only "half-raced" in versions of the myth that de-indigenize her, assimilate her, and claim her as a convert to Christianity and Western ways, as a figure in colonial and colonizing plots she is nonetheless "fully sexed" (cf. "Pocahontas" at the U of Virginia webpage), i.e. sexualized and eroticized according to Western standards of 'exotic beauty.' On the other hand, as Indian princess and female noble savage, Pocahontas is one of the most prominent and most ubiquitous female figures in American children's books (cf. Young, "Mother") and to this day is one of the most popular Halloween costumes for girls; thus, for better or worse, she remains every schoolgirl's (and schoolboy's) dream.

9. STUDY QUESTIONS

1. Which elements of the Pocahontas narrative make it so useful in the context of constructing a meaningful beginning/a foundational myth?
2. What relevance does the category of gender carry in the early colonial encounters and how does Pocahontas figure in these relations?
3. What can we say about the selection processes that had the 'rescue scene,' Pocahontas's conversion, and/or her marriage to John Rolfe appear at various instances of historical commemoration? What would you consider the most important image of Pocahontas, i.e. the most important part of the Pocahontas narrative for the construction of a national beginning?
4. Recapitulate the different ideological investments and strategies with which the Pocahontas narrative has been appropriated throughout the centuries by Southerners, feminists, etc. How do these appropriations reflect on images of American identity?
5. Analyze the lyrics in the songs by Neil Young ("Pocahontas") and Peggy Lee ("Fever").
6. Analyze the visual representation of the myth in Walt Disney's *Pocahontas* and Terence Malick's *The New World*. Which similarities and differences do you detect?
7. Consider and discuss the narrative and visual aspects of Pocahontas as the heroine of children's books, for instance by Ingri and Edgar Parin D'Aulaire (*Pocahontas*, 1946); Clyde Robert Bulla and Peter Burchard (*Pocahontas and the Strangers*, 1971), and Joseph Bruchac (*Pocahontas*, 2003).
8. The trope of the "Indian princess" is most prominently connected to Pocahontas, yet, there are also other indigenous female figures who have played similar roles. Investigate the figure of Sacagawea in US cultural history, memorial culture, and filmic representations (e.g. in *The Far Horizons*, 1955).
9. Compare representations of Pocahontas and Malinche in terms of their symbolic 'careers.' Which differences and similarities can you find?
10. How does Arno Schmidt's 1953 novel *Seelandschaft mit Pocahontas* relate to the American myth?

10. BIBLIOGRAPHY

Works Cited

Allen, Paula Gunn. *Pocahontas: Medicine Woman, Spy, Entrepreneur, Diplomat*. New York: Harper, 2003.

–. "Pocahontas to Her English Husband, John Rolfe." *Life Is a Fatal Disease: Collected Poems 1962-1995*. Alberquerque: West End, 1997. 6-7.

–. *The Sacred Hoop: Recovering the Feminine in American Indian Traditions*. Boston: Beacon, 1986.

Avatar. Dir. James Cameron. 20th Century Fox, 2009.

Bancroft, George. *History of the Colonization of the United States*. Vol. 1. Boston: Little and Brown, 1841.

Barbour, Philip. *Pocahontas and Her World*. Boston: Houghton, 1969.

Baringer, Sandra. "'Captive Woman?' The Rewriting of Pocahontas in Three Contemporary Native American Novels." *Studies in American Indian Literatures: The Journal of the Association for the Study of American Indian Literatures* 11.3 (1999): 42-63.

Barker, James Nelson. *The Indian Princess, or, La Belle Sauvage*. Philadelphia: T. and G. Palmer, 1808.

Barnes, Charlotte. *The Forest Princess Or, Two Centuries Ago*: *Plays, Prose, and Poetry*. Philadelphia: Butler, 1848.

Barth, John. *The Sot-Weed Factor*. Garden City: Doubleday, 1960.

Belknap, Jeremy. *American Biography: Or, An Historical Account of Those Persons Who Have Been Distinguished in America, as Adventurers, Statesmen, Philosophers, Divines, Warriors, Authors, and Other Remarkable Characters. Comprehending a Recital of the Events Connected with Their Lives and Actions*. Vol. 1. Boston: Thomas, 1794.

Bradstreet, Anne. "To My Dear and Loving Husband." *The Works of Anne Bradstreet*. Ed. Jeannine Hensley. Foreword by Adrienne Rich. Cambridge: Harvard UP, 1967. 225.

Brougham, John. *Po-ca-hontas, or the Gentle Savage*. 1855. *Dramas from the American Theatre, 1762-1909*. Ed. Richard Moody. Cleveland: World, 1966. 397-421.

Bruchac, Joseph. *Pocahontas*. Boston: Houghton, 2003.

Bulla, Clyde Robert, and Peter Burchard. *Pocahontas and the Strangers*. New York: T.Y. Crowell, 1971.

Bushman, Claudia L. *America Discovers Columbus: How an Italian Explorer Became an American Hero*. Hanover: UP of New England, 1992.

Cawelti, John C. *Adventure, Mystery, and Romance: Formula Stories as Art and Popular Culture*. Chicago: U of Chicago P, 1976.

Cliff, Michelle. *No Telephone to Heaven*. New York: Plume, 1996.

Cooper, James Fenimore. *The Wept of Wish-Ton-Wish: A Tale*. New York: Hurd and Houghton, 1868.

Crane, Hart. *The Bridge*. New York: Liveright, 1933.

Crane, Nathalia. *Pocahontas*. New York: E.P. Dutton, 1930.

Crèvecoeur, J. Hector St. John de. *More Letters from the American Farmer*. Ed. Dennis D. Moore. Athens: U of Georgia P, 1995.

Custis, George Washington Parke. *Pocahontas, or the Settlers of Virginia: A National Drama, in Three Acts*. Philadelphia: Alexander, 1830.

D'Aulaire, Ingri, and Edgar Parin D'Aulaire. *Pocahontas*. Garden City: Doubleday, 1946.

Davis, John. *Captain Smith and Princess Pocahontas: An Indian Tale*. Philadelphia: Plowman, 1805.

–. *The Farmer of New Jersey, or, a Picture of Domestic Life: A Tale*. New York: Furman and Loudon, 1800.

–. *The First Settlers of Virginia, a Historical Novel*. New York: Riley, 1805.

–. *Travels of Four Years and a Half in the United States of America During 1798, 1799, 1800, 1801, and 1802*. Bristol: Edwards, 1803. *Google Books*. 8 March 2010.

Dearborn, Mary V. *Pocahontas's Daughters: Gender and Ethnicity in American Culture*. New York: Oxford UP, 1986.

Deloria, Philip Joseph. *Playing Indian*. New Haven: Yale UP, 1998.

Deloria, Vine. *Custer Died for Your Sins: An Indian Manifesto*. New York: Houghton, 1969.

Donnell, Susan. Author's Note. Donnell, *Pocahontas* xii-xiii.

–. *Pocahontas*. New York: Berkley, 1991.

Dyer, Gary. "The Transatlantic Pocahontas." *Nineteenth-Century Contexts* 30.4 (2008): 301-22.

Edgerton, Gary, and Kathy Merlock Jackson. "Redesigning Pocahontas: Disney, the 'White Man's Indian,' and the Marketing of Dreams." *The Journal of Popular Film and Television* 24.2 (1996): 90-98.

Edwards, Leigh H. "The United Colors of Pocahontas: Synthetic Miscegenation and Disney's Multiculturalism." *Narrative* 7.2 (1999): 147-67.

Faery, Rebecca Blevins. *Cartographies of Desire: Captivity, Race, and Sex in the Shaping of an American Nation*. Norman: U of Oklahoma P, 1999.

Fiedler, Leslie. *The Return of the Vanishing Indian*. New York: Stein and Day, 1968.

Fleming, E. McClung. "The American Image as Indian Princess: 1765-1783." *Winterthur Portfolio* 2 (1965): 65-81.

–. "From Indian Princess to Greek Goddess: The American Image, 1783-1815." *Winterthur Portfolio* 3 (1967): 37-66.

Fudge, Erica. "Pocahontas's Baptism: Reformed Theology and the Paradox of Desire." *Critical Survey* 11.1 (1999): 15-30.

Garnett, David. *Pocahontas, Or the Nonpareil of Virginia*. London: Chatto and Windus, 1933.

Hamor, Ralph. *True Discourse of the Present Estate of Virginia*. London: n. p., 1615.

Haselstein, Ulla. *Die Gabe der Zivilisation: Kultureller Austausch und literarische Textpraxis in Amerika, 1682-1861*. München: Fink, 2000.

Hays, Mary. *Female Autobiography*. London: Richard Phillips, 1803.

Hemingway, Ernest. "Banal Story." *The First Forty-Nine Stories*. Oxford: Alden, 1944. 333-34.

Honour, Hugh. *The New Golden Land: European Images of America from the Discoveries to the Present Time*. London: Allen Lane, 1976.

Hulme, Peter. *Colonial Encounters: Europe and the Native Caribbean, 1492-1797*. London: Methuen, 1986.

–. "Polytropic Man: Tropes of Sexuality and Mobility in Early Colonial Discourse." *Europe and Its Others: Proceedings of the Essex Conference on the Sociology of Literature, July 1984*. Ed. Francis Barker. Colchester: U of Essex P, 1985. 17-32.

Hutchinson, Elizabeth. *The Indian Craze: Primitivism, Modernisn, and Transculturation in American Art, 1890-1915*. Durham: Duke UP, 2009.

Jaroff, Rebecca. "Opposing Forces: (Re)playing Pocahontas and the Politics of Indian Removal on the Antebellum Stage." *Comparative Drama* 40 (2006): 483-504.

Jenkins, William Warren. "The Princess Pocahontas and Three Englishmen Named John." *No Fairer Land: Studies in Southern Literature Before 1900*. Ed. J. Lasley Dameron and James W. Mathews. Troy: Whitston, 1986. 8-20.

Karcher, Carolyn. Introduction. *Homobok and Other Writings on Indians*. By Lydia Maria Child. Ed. Carolyn Karcher. New Brunswick: Rutgers UP, 1986. i-xliv.

Kelly, James, and Barbara Clark Smith. *Jamestown, Quebec, Santa Fe: Three North American Beginnings*. Washington: Smithsonian, 2007.

Kindermann, Wolf. *Geschichte und historische Reflexion in der Literatur der amerikanischen Südstaaten*. Berlin: Verlag für Wissenschaft und Bildung, 1992.

Kupperman, Karen Ordahl. *Roanoke: The Abandoned Colony*. Lanham: Rowman and Littlefield, 1984.

Larkins, Sharon. "Using Trade Books to Teach About Pocahontas." *Georgia Social Sciences Journal* 19.1 (1988): 21-25.

Lemay, J.A. Leo. *Did Pocahontas Save John Smith?* Athens: U of Georgia P, 1992.

Lindsay, Vachel. "Our Mother Pocahontas." *The Chinese Nightingale and Other Poems*. New York: MacMillan, 1917. 39-42.

Loeffelholz, Mary. "Miranda in the New World: *The Tempest* and Charlotte Barnes's *The Forest Princess*." *Women's Re-Visions of Shakespeare: On the Responses of Dickinson, Woolf, Rich, H.D., George Eliot, and Others*. Ed. Marianne Novy. Urbana: U of Illinois P, 1990. 58-75.

Mackenthun, Gesa. *Metaphors of Dispossession: American Beginnings and the Translation of Empire, 1492-1637*. Norman: U of Oklahoma P, 1997.

McCarthy, William. *Songs, Odes, and Other Poems on National Subjects*. Philadelphia: William McCarthy, 1854.

Melville, Herman. *The Confidence-Man: His Masquerade*. 1857. New York: Norton, 1971.

Moody, Richard. Introduction to *Po-ca-hontas. Dramas from the American Theatre, 1762-1909*. Ed. Richard Moody. Cleveland: World, 1966. 397-402.

Morgan, Edmund S. *American Slavery, American Freedom*. New York: Norton, 1975.

Nash, Gary. "The Image of the Indian in the Southern Colonial Mind." *William and Mary Quarterly* 29 (1972): 197-230.

Norton, Anne. *Alternative Americas: A Reading of Antebellum Political Culture*. Chicago: U of Chicago P, 1986.

northSun, nila. "stupid questions." *Returning the Gift: Poetry and Prose from the First North American Native Writers Festival*. Ed. Joseph Bruchac. Tucson: U of Arizona P, 1994. 217-18.

Opfermann, Susanne. "Lydia Maria Child, James Fenimore Cooper, and Catharine Maria Sedgwick: A Dialogue on Race, Culture, and Gender." *Soft Canons: American Women Writers and Masculine Tradition*. Ed. Karen L. Kilcup. Iowa City: U of Iowa P, 1999. 27-47.

Paulding, James Kirke. *Letters from the South: By a Northern Man*. Vol. 1. New York: Harper, 1835.

"Pocahontas, Half-Raced and Fully Sexed: The Almost Empty Signifier and American Iconography." *American Studies at the University of Virginia*. http://xroads.virginia.edu/~cap/poca/POC_race.html. 19 Aug. 2013.

Pocahontas. Dir. Mike Gabriel and Eric Goldberg. Buena Vista, 1995.

Purchas, Samuel. *Hakluytus Posthumus Or Purchas His Pilgrimes: Contayning a History of the World in Sea Voyages and Lande Travells by Englishmen.* 1625. Vol. 19. Glasgow: MacLehose, 1905.

Quincy, George. *Pocahontas at the Court of James I and Choctaw Diaries.* Lyrichord, 2008.

Quinn, Vernon. *The Exciting Adventures of Captain John Smith.* New York: Frederick A. Stokes, 1928.

Robertson, Karen. "The First Captive: The Kidnapping of Pocahontas." *Women, Violence, and English Renaissance Literature: Essays Honoring Paul Jorgensen.* Ed. Linda Woodbridge and Sharon Beehler. Tempe: Arizona Center for Medieval and Renaissance Studies, 2003. 73-100.

Rolfe, John. Letter from John Rolfe. *Narratives from Early Virginia, 1606-1625.* Ed. Lyon Gardiner Tyler. New York: Scribner's, 1907. 240-44.

–. *A True Relation of the State of Virginia Lefte by Sir Thomas Dale Knight in May Last 1616.* 1617. *Encyclopedia Virginia.* http://encyclopediavirginia.org/A_True_Relation_of_the_state_of_Virginia_Lefte_by_Sir_Thomas_Dale_Knight_in_May_Last_1616_1617. 8 May 2014.

Schmidt, Arno. *Seelandschaft mit Pocahontas.* 1959. Stuttgart: Klett-Cotta, 1988.

Schülting, Sabine. *Wilde Frauen, fremde Welten: Kolonisierungsgeschichten aus Amerika.* Reinbek: Rowohlt, 1997.

Sedgwick, Catharine Maria. *Hope Leslie or Early Times in Massachusetts.* London: Miller, 1827.

Sheehan, Bernhard W. *Seeds of Extinction: Jeffersonian Philanthropy and the American Indian.* New York: Norton, 1973.

Shohat, Ella, and Robert Stam. *Unthinking Eurocentrism: Multiculturalism and the Media.* London: Routledge, 2001.

Simms, William Gilmore. "Pocahontas: A Subject for the Historical Painter." *Views and Reviews in American Literature, History, and Fiction.* New York: Wiley, 1845. 88-101.

Smith, John. *The Complete Works of Captain John Smith (1580-1631) in Three Volumes.* Ed. Philip L. Barbour. Chapel Hill: U of North Carolina P, 1986.

–. *The Generall Historie of Virginia, New-England, and the Summer Isles.* 1624. Smith, *Complete Works* Vol. 2.

–. *Proceedings of the English Colony in Virginia.* 1612. Smith, *Complete Works* Vol. 1. 193-292.

–. *A True Relation of Such Occurrences and Accidents of Note as Happened in Virginia.* 1608. Smith, *Complete Works* Vol. 1. 293-372.

Sollors, Werner. *Beyond Ethnicity: Consent and Descent in American Culture.* New York: Oxford UP, 1986.

Stith, William. *The History of the First Discovery and Settlement of Virginia: Being an Essay Towards a General History of This Colony.* Williamsburg: William Parks, 1747.

Strachey, William. *The Historie of Travaile into Virginia Britannia: Expressing the Cosmographie and Comodities of the Country, Togither with the Manners and Customes of the People.* 1612. London: Hakluyt Society, 1849.

Thackeray, William Makepeace. "Pocahontas." *Complete Works.* Vol. 2. Boston: Estes and Lauriat, 1881. 274.

The New World. Dir. Terrence Malick. New Line Cinema, 2005.

Theweleit, Klaus. "Menschliche Drohnen: 'Avatar,' nominiert für neun Oscars, ist ein perverser Film." *Spiegel* 9 (2010): 132-33.

–. *"You give me fever:" Arno Schmidt,* Seelandschaft mit Pocahontas: *Die Sexualität schreiben nach WW II.* Frankfurt/Main: Stroemfeld/Roter Stern, 1999.

Tillotson, Kristin. "Cartoons and Indians: Disney Fudges Facts to Turn Indian Heroine into Everbabe." *Minneapolis Star and Tribune* 13 (1995): C8.

Tilton, Robert S. *Pocahontas: The Evolution of an American Narrative.* Cambridge: Cambridge UP, 1994.

Turner Strong, Pauline. "Playing Indian in the 1990's: *Pocahontas* and *The Indian in the Cupboard." Hollywood's Indians: The Portrayal of the Native American in Film: Expanded Edition.* 2nd ed. Ed. Peter C. Rollins and John E. Connor. Lexington: U of Kentucky P, 2003. 187-205.

Uhry Abrams, Ann. *The Pilgrims and Pocahontas: Rival Myths of American Origin.* Boulder: Westview, 1999.

Ullmann, Margaret. *Pocahontas: A Pageant.* Boston: Poet Lore, 1912.

Vizenor, Gerald. *Fugitive Poses: Native American Scenes of Absence and Presence.* Lincoln: U of Nebraska P, 1998.

–. *The Heirs of Columbus.* Hanover: Wesleyan UP, 1991.

–. *Landfill Meditation: Crossblood Stories.* Hanover: Wesleyan UP, 1991.

Weatherston, Rosemary. "When Sleeping Dictionaries Awaken: The Re/turn of the Native Woman Informant." *Post Identity* 1.1 (1997): 113-44.

Webster, Noah. *An American Selection of Lessons in Reading and Speaking: Calculated to Improve the Minds and Refine the Taste of Youth: To Which Are Prefixed Rules in Elocution, and Directions for Expressing the Principal Passions of the Mind: Being the Third Part of a Grammatical Institute of the English Language.* Hartford: Hudson and Goodwin, 1797.

Woodward, Grace Steele. *Pocahontas.* Norman: U of Oklahoma P, 1976.

Young, Philip. "The Mother of Us All: Pocahontas Reconsidered." *The Kenyon Review* 24 (1962): 391-415.

Further Reading

Allen, Paula Gunn. *Grandmothers of the Light: A Medicine Woman's Sourcebook*. Boston: Beacon, 1991.

Barker, Francis, ed. *Europe and Its Others: Proceedings of the Essex Conference on the Sociology of Literature, July 1984*. Colchester: U of Essex P, 1985.

Birkle, Carmen. "Intercultural Interfaces in Visual Representations of Pocahontas." *Intercultural America*. Ed. Alfred Hornung. Heidelberg: Winter, 2007. 239-56.

Cory, Mark E. "Romancing America: Reflections of Pocahontas in Contemporary German Fiction." *German Quarterly* 62.3 (1989): 320-28.

Döring, Tobias. "Pocahontas/Rebecca." *Figuren der/des Dritten: Erkundungen kultureller Zwischenräume*. Ed. Claudia Breger and Tobias Döring. Amsterdam: Rodopi, 1998. 179-209.

Fletcher, John Gould. *John Smith, Also Pocahontas*. New York: Brentano's, 1928.

Herzogenrath, Bernd, ed. *From Virgin Land to Disney World: Nature and Its Discontents in the USA of Yesterday and Today*. Amsterdam: Rodopi, 2001.

Jalowitz, Alan J. "The Daughters of Penelope: Tradition and Innovation in American Epics by Women." *Approaches to the Anglo and American Female Epic, 1621-1982*. Ed. Bernard Schweizer. Burlington: Ashgate, 2006. 141-58.

Joseph, Betty. "Re(playing) Crusoe/Pocahontas: Circum-Atlantic Stagings in *The Female American*." *Criticism* 42.3 (2000): 317-35.

Kirwan, James. "The Postmodernist's Journey into Nature: From Philo of Alexandria to Pocahontas and Back Again, By Way of Jean-François Lyotard." Herzogenrath, *From Virgin Land* 33-52.

Kupperman, Karen Ordahl. *The Jamestown Project*. Cambridge: Harvard UP, 2007.

Kyora, Sabine, and Uwe Schwagmeier, eds. *Pocahontas Revisited: Kulturwissenschaftliche Ansichten eines Motivkomplexes*. Bielefeld: Aisthesis, 2005.

Moran, Rachel F. *Interracial Intimacy: The Regulation of Race and Romance*. Chicago: Chicago UP, 2001.

Mossiker, Frances. *Pocahontas: The Life and the Legend*. London: Gollancz, 1976.

Neill, Edward D. *Pocahontas and Her Companions: A Chapter from the History of the Virginia Company of London.* Albany: Joel Munsell, 1869. *The Darlington Digital Library.* http://digital.library.pitt.edu/d/darlington/books.html. 8 March 2010.

Preda, Roxana. "'The Angel in the Ecosystem' Revisited: Disney's *Pocahontas* and Postmodern Ethics." Herzogenrath, *From Virgin Land* 317-40.

Scheckel, Susan. "Domesticating the Drama of Conquest: Barker's *Pocahontas* on the Popular Stage." *American Transcendental Quarterly* 10.3 (1996): 219-30.

Sundquist, Åsebrit. *Pocahontas & Co: The Fictional American Indian Woman in Nineteenth Century Literature: A Study of Method.* Atlantic Highlands: Humanities Pr. Internat., 1987.

Zuckerman, Michael. "The Fabrication of Identity in Early America." *William and Mary Quarterly* 34.2 (1977): 183-214.

Chapter III

Pilgrims and Puritans and the Myth of the Promised Land

1. WHY THE PILGRIMS AND THE PURITANS?

> [The Puritans] conceived of the American paradise as the fulfilment of
> scripture prophecy.
> SACVAN BERCOVITCH, *THE PURITAN ORIGINS OF THE AMERICAN SELF*

> It is hardly an exaggeration to say that the exodus is one of America's central
> themes.
> WERNER SOLLORS, *BEYOND ETHNICITY*

> We got one last chance to make it real
> To trade in these wings on some wheels
> Climb in back, heaven's waiting down on the tracks
> Oh come take my hand
> We're riding out tonight to case the Promised Land.
> BRUCE SPRINGSTEEN, "THUNDER ROAD"

The Pilgrims and Puritans who settled in New England in the first half of the 17th
century, arriving only a little later in America than the settlers of Jamestown,
Virginia, are the protagonists of a foundational myth which has survived across
the centuries as a story of American beginnings characterized by religiosity,
idealism, sacrifice, and a utopian vision based on theology. Many scholars have
considered the New England Pilgrims and Puritans as the 'first Americans' in
the spirit of what would later develop into the full-fledged notion of American
exceptionalism. Often, they have been contrasted favorably to the settlers in
Virginia, who were seen as "adventurers" supposedly interested in material gain
only (cf. Breen, *Puritans*), whereas the Pilgrims and Puritans, it was claimed,
came for spiritual reasons and considered themselves religious refugees (cf.

ibid.; Tocqueville, *Democracy* Vol. 1 31-32). These religious dissenters from England thus were often cast as morally superior to the men of the Virginia Company in early Americanist scholarship, and the 'cradle of American civilization' has often been located in their early New England settlements. The moral righteousness of the Pilgrims and Puritans, however, is a matter of contention. Often, they have been unfavorably and stereotypically represented as overtly pious, stoic, narrow-minded, intolerant, and even fanatic. While they claimed for themselves the right to dissent from the orthodoxies of the Church of England, they in turn, it is argued, denied those who did not conform to their own doctrines the same right of religious freedom. And while the narrative of origins told about Virginia cast Pocahontas, a Native woman, in the title role, "the Massachusetts myth centered on a patriarchal hierarchy, even though women composed a relatively large percentage of the Plymouth population" (Uhry Abrams, *Pilgrims* xv).

Who were the Pilgrims of Plymouth and the Puritans of the Massachusetts Bay Colony? They were two groups of English religious dissenters, influenced by the Reformation, in particular Calvinism, who turned away not only from the Catholic but also from the Anglican Church and sought to establish a new 'Holy Commonwealth' in North America. They considered America their Promised Land, thus taking biblical scripture as prophecy and anticipating its fulfillment in their own lived reality in North America. In history and scholarship, the terms 'Pilgrims' and 'Puritans' are sometimes used synonymously, and this conflation indicates that the two groups had many things in common. For reasons of historical accuracy, however, we should be precise about the terminology: The Pilgrims were religious separatists who reached America in 1620 on board of the *Mayflower* with William Bradford (1590-1657); when sailing for the 'new world,' they had been granted land and support by the Virginia Company, yet, landing further north on the coastline, they 'missed' Virginia – perhaps purposefully so – and founded Plymouth, as legend has it, at the site of a rock. Within a few years, the colony had 2.500 inhabitants and maintained quite a rigorous community life. The Puritans – originally having been a derogatory term, they did not refer to themselves as such – arrived in 1630 on board of the *Arbella* and several other ships under the guidance of John Winthrop (1588-1649) after they had been granted the right to settle a new colony by Charles I, and founded the city of Boston, which for a long time remained the center of the Massachusetts Bay Colony. The Pilgrims and the Puritans thus originally formed distinct communities, but interacted with each other (as well as with the Native population). The so-called Great Migration (1630-40) brought many newcomers from

England to the Massachusetts Bay Colony, which soon outnumbered Bradford's Plymouth Colony by far. By 1640, there were about 10.000 settlers. Three generations later, in 1691, English colonial politics eventually merged the two colonies into the so-called Province of Massachusetts Bay. Up until then, the inhabitants of both colonies had made formative experiences which have left, as many scholars argue, "a permanent mark upon American history" (Hall, "Introduction" 1); these marks are most evident in the national mythological repertoire of the US.

Illustration 1: The Landing of the Mayflower (Historical Postcard)

Smith's Inc., *The Mayflower, 1620, Plymouth, Mass.* (1929).

In what follows, I will reconstruct the genesis of a myth of American origins in which the Pilgrims and Puritans and the notion of America as a biblical Promised Land have been closely connected. The scriptural story of the Hebrews' escape from slavery in Egypt and their journey to a new land promised to them by God is one of the most powerful narratives of the Judeo-Christian tradition. This religious narrative was turned into a cultural myth by reconfiguring the ingredients of the biblical story – human suffering under slavery, God's sympathy for the oppressed, divine providence, a sacred journey to a Promised Land, and claims of God-given entitlement – into a potent narrative of American beginnings (cf. Mazur and McCarthy, *God* 25-6), which constitutes a core foundational myth of the United States. In order to establish a chronology of this process, I will first turn to the early history of the Plymouth and Massachusetts

Bay Colonies and to the narratives of beginnings shaped by the 17th-century post-Reformation discourse of Puritanism. To understand this discourse and its development in the years from 1620 (the landing of the *Mayflower*) and 1630 (the landing of the *Arbella*) to 1691 (the end of much of the colonies' autonomy from the British Crown), we need to take into account that America had been imagined in Europe as a utopia since the Renaissance and thus seemed an obvious place to envision and found a utopian new society at the beginning of the 17th century. Second, I will turn to the foundational period of the United States and inquire about the role of the utopian legacy of the Puritans and the Pilgrims in this context. Third, I will trace how after American independence the history of the Pilgrims and the Puritans became a foundational story that was transformed from a regional narrative of New England into a national myth, and a crucial one at that. Fourth, I will trace the myth through the 19th and 20th centuries and look at revisionist as well as affirmative references and representations. While the myth was championed against alternatives from the South, the West, and from across the Atlantic and, in the context of the American Civil War, was quite successful in overcoming other competing narratives of national genesis, the topos of the Promised Land at the same time was used as a form of cultural critique with the aim of empowering groups who had found hell rather than their Promised Land in the United States. First and foremost among those groups were African American slaves, in whose religious culture it loomed large because of its emancipatory thrust. And whereas the modernists in the early decades of the 20th century were largely critical of the Puritan legacy, the myth of the Promised Land was concurrently claimed by immigrant and ethnic writers in a religious or semi-religious fashion.

In the field of American studies, the myth was established by scholars in the formative phase of the discipline in the 1930s as the dominant genealogical narrative and can be described as the 'myth that made American studies' but has been challenged thoroughly (and lastingly) in the writings of the New Americanists since the 1980s. The latter were influenced by the social protest movements of the 1960s and 1970s, which contested the white male bias and exceptionalist teleological impetus of this foundational narrative. Tracing the American myth of the Promised Land through the centuries, we can easily see that it has been one of the most prevalent of America's national mythical narratives. Whether its claim that the settlements of the Pilgrims and Puritans contained the seeds of American democracy is tenable still is a matter of debate. Yet, articulations of this myth have not only contributed to idealized accounts of American history, but have also, as we will see, employed the trope of the Promised Land as a vehicle for radical cultural dissent.

2. AMERICA AS UTOPIA: A PREFACE

> Remarkably soon after its discovery, in fact, America became the locus for a
> variety of imaginary [...] utopian constructions.
>
> JACK P. GREENE, *THE INTELLECTUAL CONSTRUCTION OF AMERICA*

> Amerika, Du hast es besser
> als unser Kontinent, der alte.
>
> JOHANN WOLFGANG V. GOETHE, *XENIEN*

In the so-called age of discovery and exploration, Europeans often imagined the Americas as a site of utopian communities by coupling the "emerging expectations about America" with "the subsequent development of the utopian tradition;" this is paradigmatically done in Thomas More's *Utopia* (1516), in which the author "located Utopia in the Atlantic and used the experienced traveler just returned from a voyage with Vespucci from the 'unkown peoples and lands' of the New World" as his central literary device (Greene, *Intellectual Construction* 26). In the early 16th century, a number of other writers also located their visions of utopian societies in America or its vicinity: Tommaso Campanella in *City of the Sun* (1602), Johann Valentin Andreae in *Christianopolis* (1619), and Francis Bacon in *New Atlantis* (1624). Most of them have a strong religious dimension: Campanella envisions, for instance, a theocracy, Andreae a Protestant (Lutheran) utopia; Bacon's is the only one among the canonical utopian texts of that time which gives priority to science over religion.

Those geographies of the imagination however were not empirically corroborated; European explorers and travelers did not come across any marvelous utopias in the Americas. The indigenous communities they actually encountered in their eyes did not constitute extraordinary alternative ways of life worthy of emulation; constructed by their Eurocentric gaze as radical alterity rather than viable alternatives, the indigenous cultures of North America seemed worthless and inferior in comparison to those of Europe. Native Americans were considered to be barely human – as 'heathens' not readily open to Christianization, they could be forcefully removed in order to make room for the newcomers. Europeans thus increasingly replaced their hopes of discovering a utopia in the Americas with reflections on how to build one there themselves: Even before the Pilgrims and Puritans settled in the 'new world,' prospective English settlers no longer "thought in terms of *finding* an existing utopia but of *founding* one in the relatively 'empty' and inviting spaces of North America" (Greene, *Intellectual Construction* 51).

Throughout the 17th and 18th centuries many religious separatist groups existed in England and in Europe as a whole, many of which migrated to the Americas. As Mark Holloway points out, "[s]eventeenth-century Europe was full of […] sects. Persecution, however severe, did nothing to diminish their fervor. And when America had been colonised, vast numbers of them emigrated in search of religious liberty" (*Heavens* 18). The Pilgrims and the Puritans thus were the earliest and certainly the most prominent of these groups yet by no means the only ones. Other religious groups which aspired to create their own "heavens on earth" (cf. ibid.) in North America were e.g. William Penn (1644-1718) and the Quakers, Johannes Kelpius' (1673-1708) Society of Woman in the Wilderness, and Johann Conrad Beissel's (1691-1768) "Dunkers," who all settled in Pennsylvania; Mother Ann Lee (1736-1784) and the Shakers, who settled in upstate New York; and the Moravians, who came to North America in 1735 as pietistic and reformist missionaries and founded Winston-Salem in North Carolina. None of these groups – many of which still are part of the rich array of denominations in the United States today – ever came close to being as symbolically powerful as the Pilgrims and the Puritans, who are the only religious groups to form the cornerstone of a foundational narrative of the 'new world.' None of the great many utopian communities, whose number reached its historical climax in the 1840s and '50s and dwindled toward the end of the 19th century, ever elicited the same fascination as did the early settlers of New England. Throughout the 19th and 20th centuries, the notion of America as utopia has remained highly attractive for a variety of groups and newcomers, and has been modified and appropriated according to their respective agendas; these more recent visions of America as the Promised Land are still shaped and propelled by the religious rhetoric of the Pilgrims and the Puritans.

3. THE PILGRIMS IN AMERICA:
WILLIAM BRADFORD'S *OF PLYMOUTH PLANTATION*

> [N]ot having received the promises, but having seen them afar off, and were
> persuaded of them, and embraced them, and confessed that they were
> strangers and pilgrims on the earth.
> PAUL THE APOSTLE, "EPISTLE TO THE HEBREWS"

> Ideal communities have always been formed by minority movements.
> MARK HOLLOWAY, *HEAVENS ON EARTH*

Jay Parini selected William Bradford's chronicle *Of Plymouth Plantation* as one
of the "thirteen books that changed America" (cf. his book of the same [sub-]
title). Bradford in his book indeed did a lot to 'create' America as the Promised
Land of the Pilgrims and by doing so dramatically changed the America he had
found. *Of Plymouth Plantation* is a key text of 'new world' beginnings, a self-
representation of the Pilgrim experience, a crucial historical source, and a
prominent foundational text of the United States. Its author was the single most
important individual in the Pilgrim settlement of Plymouth: Bradford was the
governor of the Plymouth Colony from 1620 almost continuously until his death
in 1657 and wrote the history of the colony, seeking "through his history, to
preserve both the record and the fact of Plymouth's separate identity" (Delbanco
and Heimert, "William Bradford" 51). *Of Plymouth Plantation* covers the period
from 1606 to 1646 and encompasses two volumes: Book One describes the
history of the Pilgrims until their landing in the 'new world' (1606-1620), Book
Two recounts the early years of the Pilgrims at Plymouth (1620-1646). Bradford's work has survived as a major document about 17th-century North America. Of course, we do not know and are not able to reconstruct to what extent
Bradford's account is trustworthy; still, for our purposes it is crucial to examine
how he described and framed the Pilgrim enterprise as an Exodus from England
to the Promised Land, and thereby established a powerful foil for the interpretation of early European settlement in North America.

Yet, whereas John Smith's self-confident narrative about his experiences and
observations in Virginia and his narrative of the founding of Jamestown were
immediately available to his contemporaries in print, William Bradford's historiography, written between 1620 and 1647, was printed only in 1856. It was an
immediate literary sensation – not least because of Bradford's appended pas-
senger list, which finally enabled Americans to trace their ancestry literally back
to the *Mayflower*, an endeavor which previously had been based mostly on

speculation. Prior to the publication of Bradford's text, only a few clergymen and scholars had access to the manuscript – not least because it went missing in the Revolutionary War and only resurfaced in a London library in the 1850s – and yet it "was from these deliberately selective and didactic interpretations that the Pilgrim myth evolved" (Uhry Abrams, *Pilgrims* 23). Overall, the early clerical historians viewed the Pilgrims' voyage from Europe to America as a "religious hegira" (ibid. 24), and "for two centuries, this reading of colonial history predominated and contributed greatly to the myth that the first settlers of Massachusetts were pious Puritans who immigrated to obtain religious freedom," even though this "is not exactly the way Bradford wrote it" (ibid.). In fact, when we examine Bradford's text, we will frequently find ambiguity, doubt, skepticism, and disappointment concerning the progress of the Pilgrims in realizing their Promised Land in North America. Yet, throughout his memoirs, the key text for a study of Pilgrim mythmaking, Bradford keeps referring to the biblical tale of the Promised Land, thereby consistently contrasting present oppression and misgivings with the promise of future freedom and salvation.

In the first part, Bradford's narrative recounts the trials of the Pilgrims moving first from England to the Netherlands to escape persecution, and then back to England to prepare for their journey across the Atlantic. The narrative thus begins with the suffering of the Pilgrims in an environment hostile to their religious beliefs. According to Bradford, it is with God's help that the group then manages to escape its plight and to preserve its faith and community. During their journey to North America, God's special providence is revealed to the Pilgrims in many ways, e.g. by being delivered from the danger and terror of a heavy storm. They are also shown the consequences of blasphemy and ungodly behavior, e.g. in the somewhat drastic and highly illustrative episode about a young sailor onboard the ship who frequently mocked the Pilgrims during their journey:

There was an insolent and very profane young man, – one of the sailors, which made him the more overbearing, – who was always harassing the poor people in their sicknes, and cursing them daily with grievous execrations, and did not hesitate to tell them that he hoped to help throw half of them overboard before they came to their journey's end. If he were gently reproved by anyone, he would curse and swear most bitterly. But it pleased God, before they came half seas over, to smite the young man with a grievous disease, of which he died in a desperate manner, and so was himself the first to be thrown overboard. Thus his curses fell upon his own head, which astonished all his mates for they saw it was the just hand of God upon him. (Bradford, *Of Plymouth* 41)

Bradford uses this episode to (somewhat smugly) illustrate God's providence in guiding the Pilgrims on their sacred journey to the Promised Land and letting those perish who want to harm their progress. The spirit of companionship in God culminates in the so-called Mayflower Compact that was drawn up and signed by 41 men on board the *Mayflower*, who in so doing wrote into being a new "civil body politic:"

In the name of God, Amen. We whose names are underwritten, the loyal subjects of our dread sovereign lord, King James, by the grace of God, of Great Britaine, Franc, and Ireland, King, Defender of the Faith, etc., having undertaken for the glory of God, and advancement of the Christian faith, and honour of our king and country, a voyage to plant the first colony in the northern parts of Virginia, do by these presents solemnly and mutually in the presence of God, and one of another, covenant and combine ourselves into a civil body politic, for our better ordering and preservation, and the furtherance of the ends aforesaid and by virtue hereof to enact, constitute, and frame, such just and equal laws, ordinances, acts, constitutions, and offices, from time to time, as shall be thought most meet and convenient for the general use of the Colony, unto which we promise all due submission and obedience. (Bradford, *Of Plymouth* 49)

The Mayflower Compact is a collective speech act of a white, male elite and a pragmatic attempt to define those Pilgrims who are striving for their Promised Land in North America as a social entity unto themselves. Many accounts have idealized and mythologized this contract as the beginning of American democracy, or even as the first American constitution (among them George Bancroft's 19th-century *History of the United States*); yet, in fact, it intended to achieve the exact opposite: namely to keep power and authority in the hands of the elite, to exclude other settlers and the Natives from it, and to exert control over how the ideal society was to look like. It was both a self-empowering declaration of loyalty as well as of autonomy by the separatists.

In *Of Plymouth Plantation*, William Bradford describes the arrival in the Promised Land upon which, he writes, they fell upon their knees and blessed the God of Heaven who had brought them over the vast and furious ocean, and delivered them from all the perils and miseries of it, again to set their feet upon the firm and stable earth, their proper element (cf. 42-3). The settlement site is named Plymouth, after their place of departure in England. Yet, this site at first does not look like a Promised Land at all. Bradford, in fact, compares himself standing on the dunes of Cape Cod to Moses standing on Mount Pisgah, yet under different and more difficult circumstances, as the Pilgrims could not go up to the top of Pisgah, to view from this wilderness a more goodly country to feed their hopes; for which way soever they turned their eyes (save upward to the Heavens!) they could gain little solace from any outward objects. Summer being done, all things turned upon them a weather-beaten face; and the whole country, full of woods and thickets, presented a wild and savage view. (ibid. 43)

Thus, it is still a big leap from the "savage wilderness" to God's "heavenly king-dom" (ibid.), and it is this ambiguity – the radical discrepancy between dogma and experience, between ideological construction and empirical reality – that continues to preoccupy Bradford even as the vision of America as the Promised Land for the Pilgrims propels his narrative. This kind of interpretation of God's will and intentionality is characteristic of both Pilgrim and Puritan diction; the world and every detail in it become intelligible only as signs of God's divine plan. Bradford in this way also justifies the Pilgrims' sense of entitlement toward the 'new world,' which is "fruitful and fit for habitation, though devoid of all civilized inhabitants and given over to savages, who range up and down, differing little from the wild beasts themselves" (ibid. 13). Whereas Bradford recognizes the Natives at least nominally and acknowledges their presence even when denigrating their way of life as "brutish," another text from the first half of the 17th century claims more drastically that the extinction of the indigenous population was God's work, who by "sweeping away great multitudes of the natives by the smallpox a little before we went thither [...] [made] room for us there;" to the anonymous author, this revealed how "the good hand of God favoured our beginnings" (*New England's First Fruits* 65). It becomes apparent in these sources that the Pilgrims' notions of the Promised Land and of God's divine scheme served to justify and legitimate the displacement and destruction of other peoples.

Yet, apart from his condescending attitude toward the indigenous population and despite descriptions of early English-Native conflicts and skirmishes, Bradford overall portrays the interaction with the Natives as relatively peaceful, which is mainly due to two Native figures: Squanto and Massasoit. Squanto is introduced as a Native American who upon their arrival "came boldly among them, and spoke to them in broken English, which they could well understand, but were astonished at it" (Bradford, *Of Plymouth* 51). Squanto, the only survivor of the Patuxet tribe, spoke English because of his previous captivity on board an English ship and a seafaring life that had brought him several times across the Atlantic, to the Mediterranean Sea, all the way up to Newfoundland, and even-tually back to New England – just in time to greet the Pilgrims. His (mostly involuntary) geographic movements were quite exceptional at that time, and the Pilgrims therefore marveled at an English-speaking Native. Squanto appears as an "eccentric native," as a "disconcertingly hybrid 'native' met at the ends of the earth – strangely familiar, and different precisely in that unprocessed familiarity" (Clifford, "Travelling" 19). He carved out a space for himself as the mediator between the culture of the newcomers and that of the Natives and was extremely helpful to the Pilgrims in showing them many things they did not know, because despite their claim to be culturally, religiously, and morally superior to the indigenous population, they were in fact utterly helpless and disoriented. From Squanto they learned how to survive that first long winter – after all, they had arrived at Cape Cod in November. Not surprisingly perhaps, the Pilgrims took Squanto's presence not as an effect of the globalizing force and violence of colonialism of which they themselves were a part, but primarily as another token of God's providence, which never ceased to amaze them:

[…] Squanto stayed with them, and was their interpreter, and became a special instrument sent of God for their good, beyond their expectation. He showed them how to plant their corn, where to take fish and other commodities, and guided them to unknown places, and never left them till he died. (Bradford, *Of Plymouth* 52)

Whereas Squanto was a native informant, Massasoit was the chief of the Wampanoags, who lived in the area where the Pilgrims settled. Massasoit from the beginning met regularly with the Pilgrims and initiated and negotiated a peace treaty in 1621, the first of its kind. Little did he know that those newcomers felt they were entitled to his people's land on the basis of their interpretation of a story in a text collection compiled thousands of years before their arrival in America. Yet, the pilgrims managed to live peacefully with the Wampanoags for the first 50 years, while the nearby Puritans and the Virginians to the south were already fighting the local indigenous peoples over land and resources. The peace agreement between the Wampanoags and the Pilgrims lasted until 1675, when an armed conflict often referred to as King Philip's War broke out. But, to return to Bradford's account of English-Native relations: as already mentioned he describes them mostly positively, yet at the same time he and his fellow Pilgrims are extremely condescending toward the Natives. For all the good intentions to give a balanced, even sympathetic portrayal of the indigenous population, Bradford repeatedly echoes Columbus's representation of the American natives in his first letter from the 'new world;' a milder and more strongly religiously invested but not altogether different colonial hermeneutics emanates from Bradford's text. The religious discourse of the Pilgrims is permeated by cultural assumptions of their own (i.e., white) superiority; as we can see here, religion does not transcend (English) culture – rather, it is part of it. This is also evident in the writings of other Pilgrims; Edward Winslow for instance writes in a letter on December 11, 1621:

We have found the Indians very faithful in their covenant of peace with us, very loving and ready to pleasure us. We often go to them, and they come to us. [...] Yea, it hath pleased God so to possess the Indians with a fear of us, and love unto us, that not only the greatest king amongst them, called Massasoit, but also all the princes and peoples round about us, have either made suit unto us or been glad of any occasion to make peace with us [...]. We entertain them familiarly in our houses, and they as friendly bestowing their venison on us. They are people without any religion or knowledge of any God, yet very trusty, quick of apprehension, ripe-witted, just. The men and women go naked, only a skin about their middles. (qtd. in Young, *Chronicles* 51)

Due to the lore that has developed around the experience of the Pilgrims' first winter in North America as well as due to the absence of major hostilities in the early decades of the Plymouth Colony, the Pilgrims' settlement is often connected to notions of Native hospitality and peaceful intercultural relations – notions which inspired then-President of the United States Abraham Lincoln to make Thanksgiving a national holiday in 1863 in order to commemorate that very first 'Thanksgiving' which took place in Plymouth in 1621. However, Bradford himself does not dwell on this event in his text, which has only been fleshed out and embellished by subsequent writers. Lincoln in his efforts to promote an ideology of peace and domestic harmony at a time when the 'United' States were at war with each other (cf. Seelye, *Memory's Nation* 17) chose Thanksgiving as a day of commemoration, yet the ambiguity of Thanksgiving in the ideology of the Pilgrims is apparent: they gave thanks to God for their survival but hardly to their Native fellow men and women, who, they believed, acted not of their own accord but merely as instruments of God's will. In Bradford's text, the world is interpreted according to typological doctrine and biblical literalism in an often futile attempt to brush aside or smooth over ambiguity and uncertainty.

The second volume of Bradford's *Of Plymouth Plantation*, which accounts for the settlement's development in the early decades of its existence, is imbued with a rhetoric of damnation as well as reward; it is permeated by a sense of sinfulness and reveals that the colony was embroiled in tremendous generational conflict. It is here that Bradford's writings show a deep ambivalence about the analogy of the Promised Land. He increasingly realizes a "failure of Plymouth to fulfill its original purpose as a selfless community," and also makes note of "the concurrent completion of the Reformation through Cromwell's victories in Old England" (Delbanco and Heimert, "William Bradford" 51). Bradford implies a causal connection – that "Plymouth's congregational polity informed Massachusetts Bay and that the example of the larger colony in turn inspired the ecclesiastical revolution in England" (ibid.) – yet he also thinks that the colony is in decline because of its consolidation with the Puritan community, and nostalgically reminisces about the early 'golden days' of Plymouth, and even about the Dutch exile in Leyden. In revisiting the early days of the colony, Bradford not only chronicles history but also reminds his brethren of their vision and the strength of their faith, which he seeks to re-invigorate by calling to mind the divine signs which assured the Pilgrims of God's providence. Bradford "seems intent on showing what might have been if a deeper devotion of all to all had prevailed," and he is anxious that a great "change" will come over the colony, which he finds now devoid of "its former glory" (Rosenmeier, "With My" 100). Late in his life, William Bradford taught himself Hebrew to be able to read "that most ancient language and holy tongue, in which the Law and Oracles of God were writ" (qtd. in ibid.). About his Hebrew studies, he writes that "I am refreshed to have seen some glimpse hereof; (as Moyses saw the land of Canan a farr off)" (qtd. in ibid.). The Promised Land of William Bradford in the 1650s is no longer America but the Hebrew Scriptures, one might conclude. (Re)turning to the holy text more than thirty years after his arrival in North America, Bradford prepares for his own "resurrect[ion] to new and literal life" (ibid. 106) in a Promised Land not of this world: he dies in 1657. His history of the Pilgrims today appears to be much more complicated and ambivalent than has often been acknowledged, and moreover has in fact been straightened out and idealized by generations of religious scholars and historians, and by Americans who have celebrated Plymouth Rock – the site where the Pilgrims supposedly first set foot on American soil – as a symbol of 'new world' beginnings. Bradford sailed to the 'new world' in order to find/found a Promised Land, yet the high expectations in this self-proclaimed 'exceptional' community remained unfulfilled. As much as Bradford insisted that God had "preserved their spirits" through "crosses, troubles, fears, wants, and sorrowes" in the establishment of the colony (*Of Plymouth* 381), the whole enterprise ultimately seemed somehow incomplete, and dubious in its consequences for all parties involved – it was as if the Pilgrims had never really left the biblical wilderness and were perpetually stuck in a painful moment of delay in which the Promised Land was beckoning in the distance but could still somehow never be reached.

4. THE PURITANS AND THEIR PROMISED LAND

> We shall be as a city upon a hill.
> JOHN WINTHROP

> Hayle holy-land wherin our holy lord
> Hath planted his most true and holy word
> Hayle happye people who have dispossest
> ourselves of friend, an meanes, to find some rest
> For your poore wearied soules, opprest of late
> For Jesus-sake, with Envye, spight, and hate
> To yow that blessed promise truly's given
> Of sure reward, which you'l receve in heaven.
> THOMAS TILLAM, "UPON THE FIRST SIGHT"

> What went you out to the wilderness to find?
> SAMUEL DANFORTH, "A BRIEF RECOGNITION"

Whereas the history of the Pilgrims was primarily represented by William Bradford, there were many chroniclers, orators, and commentators among the Puritans. In fact, the New England Puritans "were highly self-conscious about their achievements and began interpreting themselves for posterity as soon as they arrived in the New World" (Morgan, *Founding* 3). In promotional tracts, sermons, histories, and autobiographical conversion narratives, the Puritans fashioned themselves as the founders of a model colony that realized God's will. Whereas the Pilgrims had arrived in North America ten years earlier than the Puritans, "with the formation of the Massachusetts Bay Company and with the arrival on the scene of Governor John Winthrop in 1630, Massachusetts became the spearhead of Puritan emigration to the New World" (ibid. vii) – although not all of the Massachusetts settlers were Puritans in the strict sense of the term, and by far not all of them were members of the rather exclusive Puritan congregation. Aside from the aforementioned John Winthrop, John Cotton, Thomas Shepard, Thomas Hooker, Samuel Danforth, Increase Mather, and Cotton Mather would also become influential Puritan theologians. New England Puritanism was not homogeneous though and cannot be interpreted monolithically; in fact, the experience of 'America' crucially transformed the Puritan religious dogma and increasingly led to conflicts among the Puritans about what their Promised Land should look like.

Illustration 2: Portrait of John Winthrop

Unknown Artist, *John Winthrop* (ca. 1800).

Though they were less radical dissenters than the Pilgrims, the Puritans too accepted neither the Pope nor the English King as religious authorities beside or above the Scriptures. Like the Pilgrims, the Puritans were strongly influenced by Calvinism's doctrine of predestination, which contends that salvation can occur only through the grace of God and that the individual is responsible to God only. As a powerful reformist grassroots movement, Puritanism had been forced underground by the end of the 16th century, as it was considered an affront to England's clergy and king; King James I (after whom Jamestown, Virginia, and the English translation of the Bible commonly referred to as the King James Bible have been named) supposedly threatened: "I will harry them out of the land" (qtd. in Schmidt, *William Bradford* 12), and his successor Charles I (crowned in 1625) was even less tolerant toward the Puritans. Unlike the Pilgrims, however, the Puritans did not consider themselves separatists but reformists; they believed that their New Jerusalem in North America was going to set an example that would be emulated on the other side of the Atlantic, allowing them eventually to return to a fundamentally changed and reformed England. Yet, even if the Puritans may have considered their sojourn in North America to be only temporary (as has been argued most famously by Perry Miller), ultimately only 10 percent of the first settlers of the Great Migration ever went back to England.

John Winthrop, who led the first group of Puritans to North America in 1630 (700 passengers on 11 ships), was a key figure in the founding of Massachusetts with a pronounced sense of self-importance, of which he has left ample evidence himself: "From the time he set foot on the *Arbella* until his death in 1649, he kept a journal, the historical purpose of which is suggested by the fact that after the first few days he refrained from using the first person singular and wrote of himself as 'the governor'" (Morgan, *Founding* 174). Most famously, John Winthrop declared that the Puritans in the 'new world' would be "A Model of Christian Charity" (1630). His famous lay sermon (Winthrop was never ordained officially as a minister) laid out the terms of religious and social coexistence in the colony, a blueprint for the founding of a new community:

For we must consider that we shall be as a city upon a hill. The eyes of all people are upon us, so that if we shall deal falsely with our God in this work we have undertaken, and so cause Him to withdraw His present help from us, we shall be made a story and by-word through the world. We shall open the mouths of enemies to speak evil of the ways of God, and all professors for God's sake. We shall shame the faces of many of God's worthy servants, and cause their prayers to be turned into curses upon us. (216)

Winthrop's use of the biblical topos of the heavenly city evokes the exceptionality of the Puritans as a model for others, if not mankind. He references Jesus's Sermon on the Mount, in which Jesus tells his followers "you are the light of the world" and "the salt of the earth." Whereas Bradford likened himself to Moses leading his people out of bondage to the Promised Land, Winthrop refers to both Jesus and Moses in the closing passage of his sermon. While exhorting the Puritans with words from the Sermon on the Mount, he admonishes them with references to Moses's farewell to the people of Israel "to love the Lord our God and love one another" (*Winthrop Papers* 295), so

that the Lord our God may blesse us in the land whether wee goe to possesse it: But if our heartes shall turne away soe that wee will not obey, but shall be seduced and worship other Gods [...] we shall surely perishe out of the good Land whether wee passe over this vast Sea to possesse it. (ibid.)

Included in Winthrop's vision of the holy community is also a kind of social contract. He likens the Puritans' future civil society to an organism by describing it as "knit together in this worke as one man," and states that its aim is to "partake of each other's strength and infirmity, joy and sorrow, weal and woe." "The care of the public," Winthrop preached, "must oversway all private respects" (ibid.). Winthrop's vision of communal life in the Promised Land of North America is characterized by hope, harmony, and religious freedom as well as by discipline and social control. Similar to Bradford's text, Winthrop's sermon was published rather late:

For two centuries, the sermon circulated in various manuscript versions; upon its first publication, by the Massachusetts Historical Society in 1848, it became known as the classic statement of the Puritans' understanding of their place in history, their mission, and their ideals. (Delbanco, "John Winthrop" 3)

The Exodus and Promised Land rhetoric runs through much of Puritan writing as a kind of "Colonial Puritan hermeneutics" (Bercovitch, *Puritan Origins* 186) throughout the 17th century and well into the 18th century, from Winthrop's sermon to the rather unorthodox and somewhat ironic "New England Canaan" by Thomas Morton of Merrimount. However, on closer inspection, we can detect shifts in the authors' attitude toward the realization of the Promised Land in the colony. At first, many texts equate the Promised Land with America, i.e. New England. John Winthrop initially describes his new home with the following words: "here is sweet air, fair rivers, and plenty of springs, and the water better than in England" (*History* 375). As Puritan scholar Alan Heimert has noted: "America was to be 'the good Land,' [...] a veritable Canaan. The Atlantic, if not the Red, was their 'vast Sea,' and the successful conclusion of their voyage, the end of their tribulations, their emergence from the 'wilderness'" ("Puritanism" 361-62).

This initially positive impression also resonates in Thomas Tillam's eulogy on New England titled "Upon the First Sight," which in the beginning connects the Scriptures to the experiences of the Puritans in New England but soon gives way to less enthusiastic sentiments and at times very different observations. Immediately after their arrival in North America, the Puritans began to experience difficulties which played themselves out internally in communal strife and externally in conflicts with the indigenous population. In fact, "the first decades of settlement were characterised by an ongoing dialogue over the shape that the colony's institutions should take" (Bremer, *Puritan Experiment* 128). As early as the 1630s, theological disputes about the exercise of power over the members of the congregation as well as heavy skirmishes with the Native tribes ensued. Only six years after their arrival in Massachusetts, those conflicts come to a head. In 1636, Thomas Hooker leaves the colony and founds Hartford (in today's

Connecticut); he is followed by Roger Williams, a dissident banned from the Massachusetts Bay Colony for suggesting a more liberal handling of church membership and for approaching the indigenous population with curiosity rather than disdain. Williams authors the first dictionary of Native languages (titled *A Key to the Languages of America*; cf. *Complete Writings*) and founds Providence, Rhode Island, in 1636, where he is joined by Anne Hutchinson, an antinomian who rejected all political and theological authorities in favor of her own version of 'true' Puritanism, which is condemned as heresy by Winthrop, who suppresses Hutchinson and her followers "because she set her private revelation above the public errand" (Bercovitch, *Puritan Origins* 174). In 1638, John Davenport settles the colony of New Haven (later to become part of Connecticut), further diversifying the socio-religious scene of New England.

John Winthrop, who plays a crucial role in policing the Puritans and comes down hard on what he perceives as unauthorized dissent, is commemorated by Puritan historian William Hubbard with the words that he was "a worthy gentleman, who had done good in Israel" (qtd. in Morgan, *Founding* 134). Trying to ban 'difference' outside and inside the community, Winthrop sought to preserve the 'Holy Commonwealth' that had come at such a high cost. As Stephen Foster suggests, the New England clergy were "required to reconcile their movement's conflicting demands" (*Long Argument* 152) at a time when "boatload after boatload brought ashore the refugees" from England's Church, and that they managed to do so is considered by Foster to have been a "masterpiece of ecclesiastical statesmanship" (ibid. 151). As we take a closer look at the early history of the colony, it becomes more and more apparent that the rhetoric of the Promised Land and divine providence on the one hand aims to uphold an ideological construction of the 'new world' which quite obviously was at odds with the actual experiences of the "saints" (as the Puritans called each other), and on the other serves as a legitimization of colonial rule, an instrument of control, and a means to homogenize the colony by defining norms of conduct and marginalizing or excluding those who do not adhere to those norms.

As the population of the colony grew rapidly with the Great Migration, the local tribes, among them the Pequots, fought against the increasing incursions the English settlers made into their land. The Pequot War culminated in the Mystic Massacre in 1637, in which hundreds of women and children were killed. Ultimately the entire tribe was exterminated; survivors were dispersed or sold into slavery. Although victorious, the Puritans themselves experienced this conflict as a major crisis that threatened the existence and future of the colony. The Pequot War shows that the interaction of the Puritans with the indigenous population was far less peaceful than that of the Pilgrims in the first decades, and the ruthlessness with which it was fought reveals the brutality of English colonialism even (or especially) when it is cloaked as religious destiny, as in the case of the Puritans' quest for the Promised Land. Although the war could well have been taken as an indication of God's anger, the victory of the English over the Pequots was readily interpreted as a merciful act of God instead, yet again demonstrating the arbitrariness of ideology.

In sum, the Puritan experience as American experience is characterized by a number of transitions that engendered some paradoxes. The first transition, of course, is their physical movement from England to North America, which entailed events that could not be integrated into the biblical script which they attempted to follow. These discrepancies were initially suppressed, of course, but surfaced time and again over the years. The second transition concerns the Puritans' transformation from an oppressed minority of non-conformist believers into an oppressive ruling elite; yet their efforts to uphold religious orthodoxy in the colony from the beginning were met with heavy resistance. Third and most importantly perhaps, even the firmest of believers became increasingly doubtful whether North America in fact was the Promised Land they had been looking for. How were they to interpret the obstacles and difficulties with which they had to wrestle daily? And why did this Promised Land look like a wilderness? The Puritans' anxieties grew in tandem with internal and external conflicts and led to increased pressure of the Puritan elite on any form of dissent; to them, the violence against the Native tribes seemed both necessary and providential, and thus fully legitimate. Yet, the "Puritan struggle of self-knowledge, relentless introspection, [and] tortured uncertainty" mirrored the tenuousness of their faith and time and again threw into doubt the endeavor of Puritanism, and "[t]he burden of such doubt has never quite lifted from what we once would have called the American soul" (Delbanco and Heimert, "Introduction" xv).

In many texts of the 1630s and 1640s, America figures as an ambiguous force to be reckoned with rather than as a safe haven: "They were [...] uncertain whether New England was to be their Israel or their Wilderness of Sinai – that is, a permanent dwelling place for the elect of God, or a temporary refuge in which their religious affections and institutions would be tried, purged, and perfected" (Slotkin, "Introduction" 11). Patricia Caldwell has identified this ambiguity in many of the early conversion narratives:

For most, it was an America neither of joyous fulfillment nor, on the other hand, of fearsome, howling hideousness, but a strange, foggy limbo of broken promises. [...] [T]he

America encountered by these yearning souls was no visible saint but an invisible, ever-receding, unloving god. (*Puritan Conversion Narrative* 134)

Caldwell's analysis of the ambiguities of North American Puritan conversion narratives evidences that the "specific shift to America," the "motion to New England," reverberates with emotional turmoil and trauma: "[T]he new world is not just a disappointment; it is a positive setback, and one from which many people scarcely recover" (ibid.). Alan Heimert has argued that the colonizing experience so crucially altered Puritan attitudes toward the meaning of their physical surroundings that it was imaginatively transformed from a Promised Land (back) into a wilderness (cf. "Puritanism" 361).

The experience of America shocked the Puritans out of their belief in the Promised Land, so to speak, and left them bewildered in the 'wilderness' of America: "The conditions of life in the colonies did not make for the sort of education that the Puritans had originally conceived. [...] American conditions posed threats to the Puritan system that they could not have anticipated" (Slotkin, "Introduction" 14). And it is from this discrepancy between doctrinaire belief on the one hand and the physical experience of North America on the other that a specifically *American* Puritan culture with its own particular conversion rituals, religious practices, and rhetoric developed, which put the sacred journey as well as the experience of America at the center of both their narrative of the past (genealogy) and their narrative of the future (mission).

After the hardships of the early years (1620-1640), the colony seemed no longer threatened by extinction after the mid-1650s; quite to the contrary: the "Puritan adult of 1670 emerge[d] to a condition of relative ease and prosperity" (ibid. 9). With this prosperity came a decline in church membership, as American-born Puritans no longer wanted to submit to the strict regime of congregational life, and focused more on worldly rather than on religious concerns. In order to keep church membership numbers up, the Puritan elite finally allowed for a half-way covenant (i.e., partial church membership with limited rights) by softening the original membership requirements. This liberalization was the subject of controversial discussions among the Puritan clergy and was also accompanied, once again, by conflicts with other groups living in and on the edges of the colony.

Having reviewed the initial enthusiasm and certainty of the first and second generation of Puritan settlers that was soon followed by anxiety, disappointment, and disorientation, we witness in the rhetoric of the Puritan clergy of the later decades of the 17th century repeated attempts to re-invigorate the early Puritan faith and dogma against the backdrop of a changing American Puritan culture. In this light, we may read sermons such as Samuel Danforth's famous "Errand into the Wilderness," which later gave the title to two seminal works of Puritan scholarship (cf. Miller's book of the same title and Bercovitch, "Rhetoric"). Addressing the assembled delegates on the election day of the Massachusetts General Court, the sermon poses the question of Puritan uniqueness and exceptionality. Danforth quotes Jesus – "What went ye out into the wilderness to see?" (Matthew 11:7) – in order to confront his congregation with the question of why they had come to America. Danforth criticizes those who have of late been more concerned with worldly rather than religious matters. As a direct consequence of the colonists' sins, Danforth identifies God's punitive measures against them. Yet, he also renews the "promise of divine Protection and Preservation," and offers his listeners the opportunity to "choose this for our Portion, To sit at Christ's feet and hear his word; and whosoever complain against us, the Lord Jesus will plead for us [...] and say. They have chosen that good part, which shall not be taken away from them" ("Errand"). By quoting from the Bible, Danforth takes his audience back to their 'new world' beginning, and prophesies in the rhetorical mode of the American jeremiad that by turning away from materialism and worldly pleasures, the Puritans could still transform their environment into the Promised Land. He thus both consolidates and transforms the myth of the Promised Land: Whereas he displaces it into the future and admits that the colony so far has not become the Promised Land, he also affirms the possibility that it may still happen. What we witness in Danforth's text is the transfer of the Promised Land topos from space into time: if the colony falls short of being the realization of God's Promised Land now, it will have to strive harder to attain this status in the future. The discrepancy between what is and what should be propels Danforth's prophecy. Sacvan Bercovitch uses Danforth's sermon to demonstrate the specific structure and formula of the American jeremiad:

Danforth's strategy is characteristic of the American jeremiad throughout the seventeenth century: first, a precedent from Scripture that sets out the communal norms; then, a series of condemnations that detail the actual state of the community (at the same time insinuating the covenantal promises that ensure success); and finally, a prophetic vision that unveils the promises, and explains away the gap between fact and ideal. (*American Jeremiad* 16)

Closing the gap between the wilderness of North America and the Promised Land of the Chosen People, then, Danforth suggests, is the unfinished task of the Puritans that will be achieved in the future.

Whereas Danforth's theological discourse rekindles the idea of turning the American wilderness into God's Promised Land, the events in the colony provide a different kind of closure for the Puritan experiment. In the mid to late 1670s, King Philip's War raged in the American colonies and threatened the survival of the white settlements in an unprecedented manner. This violent confrontation between a coalition of Native tribes led by Metacomet (a.k.a. 'King Philip') and the English settlers spread over the entire territory of the early American frontier, and became one of the most devastating in American history:

For all their suffering, the English fared well compared to New England's Native American peoples. [...] One account estimated that three thousand Native Americans were killed in battle. In a total population of about twenty thousand, this number is staggering. (Schultz and Tougias, *King Philip's War* 15)

At that time, the English settlers face major problems not only in the confrontation with the indigenous population but also within the colony, and with colonial rule. Increasingly, the English monarchy tightened the reigns on the 'new world' dominion of the Pilgrims and the Puritans, paving the way for a final eruption of the inner contradictions and conflicts of interest which culminated in the Salem witch trials and the executions of 19 people in the course of a year. The witchcraft hysteria, which has elicited a whole range of interpretations from social and economic to feminist and psychoanalytic, marks another climax of the inner turmoil of a colony placed under ever tighter control of the English Crown. Soon, the colony was forced to practice religious toleration. In 1692, self-governance was curtailed, and the colony had to accept a royal governor sent from England to North America, whereas before the Massachusetts Bay colonists had appointed this official from their own ranks. "By the end of the seventeenth century," as Ursula Brumm puts it succinctly, "the beginnings of the new world were already history" ("What Went" 1). Faith in the Promised Land was severely shaken, if not quite lost.

Yet, the Puritan elite were neither ready nor willing to concede the shortcomings of their project. In 1702, theologian Cotton Mather (son of Increase Mather, grandson of Richard Mather and John Cotton) published his magnum opus, *Magnalia Christi Americana*, in which he insisted on an affirmative perspective:

I write the Wonders of the Christian Religion, flying from the Depravations of Europe to the American Strand: And, assisted by the Holy Author of the Religion, I do with all the conscience of Truth, required therein by Him, who is the Truth itself, Report the Wonderful Display of his Infinite Power, Wisdom, Goodness and Faithfulness, wherewith his Divine Providence hath irradiated an Indian Wilderness. (*Day* 163)

By that time, the original charter of the colony had been revoked. "These changes meant the end of the society that Winthrop and Cotton had originally envisaged" (Hall, "Introduction" 5). Mather tries to defend the values of the colony's founders against both royal rule and against widening the eligibility for church membership to include those who would not have been considered pious enough by the first and second generation Puritans. Yet, Mather's own exuberant language, "its baroque style" (Brumm, "What Went" 1) and hyperbole reveal that he has come a long way from the sober, understated, and reflective writings of the early Puritans. Mather makes an almost desperate plea for the preservation of the 'New England Way,' reiterating once more the role of the colony in a global scheme of redemption and salvation. He is the first Puritan to call himself 'American' in writing – "I that am an American" – the term having been used until then exclusively to refer to the Native American population (cf. Herget, "Anders" 44). Even if the realization of the Promised Land remained doubtful, the making of Americans in the process of negotiating the terms of (co)existence in a heavenly utopia are explicated in Mather's epic. And, as Alan Heimert has noted, the realization that the New England wilderness was not the Promised Land may have contributed to the continuation of a search in time *and* space: As Danforth's exhortations admonished the Puritans to lead better lives, the "heaven on earth" that the Puritans were looking for could still be imagined by following generations further west in the less populated and 'purer' regions of North America (cf. "Puritanism" 375).

Even though the historical record of the Pilgrims and the Puritans unambiguously shows that the realization of a utopian community on American soil utterly failed, their rhetoric has survived their social experiments in remarkable ways. It is a rhetoric that thrives on the vision of a Promised Land in *this* world, not the next: The Promised Land could be realized – in the near future, and in America. It is this rhetoric of providence that turned those early settlers into forefathers of mythical proportions, even though subsequent conceptualizations of the Promised Land may have diverged greatly. As Christopher Bigsby so succinctly put it:

America has so successfully colonized the future that it has mastered the art of prospective nostalgia. Its natural tense is the future perfect. It looks forward to a time when something will have happened. It is a place, too, where fact and fiction, myth and reality dance a curious gavotte. It is a society born out of its own imaginings. ("Introduction" 1)

The Puritan myth of the Promised Land both generates and displays this dynamism.

5. THE PILGRIMS AND THE PURITANS IN REVOLUTIONARY AMERICA AND THE 19TH CENTURY

> The *Mayflower* cult, the Pilgrim legend, was built up in New England at the end of the eighteenth century and developed in the first half of the nineteenth. It was spreading west into the prairies by the mid-century. [...] The ideas of New England were carried across the continent.
> CRISPIN GILL, *MAYFLOWER REMEMBERED*

Thomas Jefferson, co-author of the Declaration of Independence and third President of the United States of America, early on realized the usefulness of the Exodus narrative for American nation-building. He wanted to place the inscription "the Children of Israel in the Wilderness, led by a Cloud by day, and a Pillar of Fire by night" on the Great Seal of the United States, as John Adams, then delegate to the Second Continental Congress and later second President of the United States, wrote to his wife in 1776 (qtd. in Buckley, "Thomas Jefferson" 46). Time and again, Jefferson returned to the myth of the Promised Land to describe the special relationship of Americans with God. In his second inaugural address, Jefferson refers to "that Being in whose hands we are, who led our fathers, as Israel of old, from their native land; and planted them in a country flowing with all the necessaries and comforts of life" (qtd. in ibid.). In Jefferson's political rhetoric, "the Exodus event in and through which God had formed his chosen people prefigured the formation of the American nation" (ibid.). In the ways that the rhetoric of the Promised Land became partially secularized for the purpose of nation-building, we can observe how the memory of the Pilgrims and Puritans was preserved and adapted into a specific US-American civil religion (to be discussed in detail in the following chapter).

Illustration 3: Plymouth Rock

Photograph by James Freeman and Cindy Freeman (2006).

The memorial culture surrounding the Pilgrim Fathers and the Puritans has both a regional as well as a national tradition. At the site of the founding of Plymouth, a veritable cult of the Pilgrim Fathers started to develop in the second half of the 18th century that continued well into the 19th century. One element of the Pilgrims' story which cannot be found in the 17th-century sources and which is difficult (if not impossible) to authenticate is Plymouth Rock, which became the focus of a narrative of mythical proportions. The rock supposedly marked the spot where the Pilgrims first set foot on American soil and was turned into a fetish of New England beginnings, even though Bradford does not mention it anywhere in his text. It is only in the revolutionary era that promotion of the Rock as "a political icon" sets in (Seelye, *Memory's Nation* 1). By focusing on the physical contact between the feet of the Pilgrim Fathers and a rock at the coastline, this mythology distracts attention away from and displaces the more difficult issue of cultural contact between the indigenous peoples and the Pilgrims – a rock does not speak or fight back, after all. The rock is mentioned for the first time in 1741 and in the following decades is cherished, fenced in, and protected against the weather – especially after 1774. In the 1830s, the famous French traveler Alexis de Tocqueville was struck by the cult around Plymouth Rock, which then was in full swing:

This rock has become an object of veneration in the United States. I have seen bits of it carefully preserved in several towns of the Union. Does not this sufficiently show how all human power and greatness are entirely in the soul? Here is a stone which the feet of a few poor fugitives pressed for an instant, and this stone becomes famous; it is treasured by a great nation, a fragment is prized as a relic. (*Democracy* Vol. 1 34)

The term 'relic,' of course, already connotes the sacral and holy that turns a worldly thing (here a rock) into an object of worship. This symbolic surplus constitutes the mythic quality of lifeless matter in the foundational framework of a nation. Udo Hebel has in great detail chronicled the rise and demise of Plymouth Rock's role in the New England imaginary and in that of the nation. He has pointed out that the "history of the commemoration of the arrival of the May-flower in Plymouth harbour as Forefather's Day dates back to 1769" ("Rise" 142), even as Plymouth Rock's symbolic power diminishes with the rise of Thanksgiving as the more prominent national holiday. To be chosen to compose and to deliver the annual Forefather's Day oratory next to the rock was one of the greatest honors that could be bestowed upon a member of the community. Among the more famous speakers chosen for that occasion was the lawyer, politician, and orator Daniel Webster, who gave an address called "First Settlement of New England" at the bicentenary celebration of the Pilgrims' landing at Plymouth in 1820; the bicentenary was organized by the newly founded Pilgrim Society, which not only took good care of the rock but by 1824 had turned Plymouth into a popular tourist attraction (cf. Uhry Abrams, *Pilgrims* 45). Webster's speech shows how the effort of commemoration is inextricably intertwined with mythmaking, and contains all the elements characteristic of the Pilgrim's myth of origin in New England. First, he delineates the 'new world' as a safe haven for the religious refugees from England, calling New England "the place of our father's refuge" ("First Settlement" 26). Second, he strongly idealizes the Pilgrim Fathers and their "voluntary exile," states that they sought "a higher degree of religious freedom" and "a purer form of religious worship" (ibid. 29), and turns them into victims and quasi-martyrs: theirs "was a humble and peace-able religion, flying from causeless oppression" (ibid. 31). Third, Webster mythologizes the landing and fetishizes the rock by invoking its *spiritus loci*, which "inspires and awes us" at this "memorable spot [...], this Rock [...] on which New England received the feet of the Pilgrims" (ibid. 27). Fourth, Webster emphasizes the distinctness of the Plymouth Colony from all other colonial projects past and present. He even casts the Pilgrims' arrival at the shore as a radical and singular form of a new beginning built upon religious prophecy that made them feel and act 'at home' in the 'new world' immediately (cf. ibid. 36) –

thanks to the Mayflower Compact. Their settlement was not a colonial outpost or a mere extension of the motherland, but marked a radical new beginning "with the very first foundations laid under the divine light of the Christian religion" (ibid. 36) that led to progress and democracy built on "morality and religious sentiment" (ibid. 49). Briefly chastising the slave trade and the institution of slavery, Webster concludes, "let us not forget the religious character of our origin" (ibid. 51). His speech explicitly declares the Pilgrims to be the true founders of the United States of America by inextricably linking the US of 1820 to the New England beginnings of 1620 and assigns this colony an exceptional status. The Pilgrims' endeavor thus figures as an exceptional venture, and the moment of landing is described as a singular temporal constellation, or *kairos*. While Webster explicitly refers to the Pilgrims, the Puritans are also championed in his skilful oratory.

Forefather's Day annually commemorated the landing of the Pilgrims in North America and gave ample opportunity for public addresses to affirm the Pilgrims' importance for the American republic. Among the orators were poet William Cullen Bryant (who could trace both of his parents back to the *Mayflower*), lawyer and politician Rufus Choate, Samuel Davies Baldwin (who gave a speech titled "Armageddon: Or, the Overthrow of Romanism and Monarchy; the Existence of the United States Foretold in the Bible"), as well as Massachusetts politician John Gorham Palfrey, author of a compendious pro-Puritan history of New England (cf. *History*). All in all, these commemorative speech acts were important cultural practices and political rituals that further bolstered the myth of the Pilgrims and the Puritans in the Promised Land.

Other facets of 19th-century American memorial culture reveal the foundational quality attributed to the Pilgrims and the Puritans as mythical figures of the American past. In the same way that the (competing) origin myth of Virginia became part of the national mythical repertoire, the myth of the Pilgrims and Puritans quickly achieved a national dimension. In the United States Capitol, there are three images of Pilgrims and Puritans in and around the rotunda, and additional images of individuals can be found in the Statuary Hall (a statue of Roger Williams) and in the Hall of Columns (a statue of John Winthrop). All of these images attest to the centrality of the Pilgrims and the Puritans for the foundational narratives of the nation and frame them in terms of their religiosity as well as of God's providence. Contrary to the figure of Pocahontas discussed previously, they reference the European, i.e. the English origin of the United States of America.

Illustration 4: The Pilgrims Prepare for the 'New World'

Robert W. Weir, *Embarkation of the Pilgrims* (1843).

Enrico Causici's 1825 relief *Landing of the Pilgrims, 1620* in the Capitol depicts a family in a boat welcomed by a Native offering an ear of corn; the fresco *Landing of Pilgrims at Plymouth, Mass., 1620*, which is part of the Frieze of American History, is a similarly sedate rendering of the landing. The painting *The Embarkation of the Pilgrims at Delft Haven, Holland, July 22nd, 1620* (1843) by Robert W. Weir however is placed even more prominently inside the rotunda of the US Capitol. Weir's painting, like Chapman's Pocahontas painting, highlights the theme of salvation: whereas "Pocahontas saved Virginia for the Anglican Church, the faith of the Pilgrims saved the United States from paganism" (Uhry Abrams, *Pilgrims* 39). The painting suggests that "God willed the transportation of Protestantism to America" (ibid.). Weir focuses on the departure from the 'old world,' not on the arrival in the 'new.' His painting mythologizes the moment of departure and celebrates the trust in God's providence. Geographically, it identifies the founding of Plymouth Colony as an English/European project, by which we can discern a fundamental difference in perspective between the myth of Pocahontas and the myth of the Pilgrims and the Puritans that would continue to fuel controversial discussions.

All of the visual representations of the Pilgrims and Puritans at the meeting place of the national legislature are highly affirmative and work as foundational representations. They are in accordance with contemporaneous historiographies of the United States, most prominently again those by New England historians such as George Bancroft, author of the well-known *History of the United States*:

The pilgrims were Englishmen, Protestants, exiles for conscience, men disciplined by misfortune, cultivated by opportunities of extensive observation, equal in rank as in rights, and bound by no code but that of religion or the public will. (*History* 23)

As a historian of the romantic school, Bancroft sees liberty and God's providence as the defining moments in American history, and thus also accords the Pilgrims a central role.

Yet, the mythologization of the Pilgrims and the Puritans in the 19th century did not only affirm a regional identity and extrapolate from it a national imaginary, but also pursued three major strategic goals in relation to what New Englanders perceived as rival influences coming from three different directions. First, the New England Way is pitted against the genealogy of the South and its foundational mythology. In his oratory, Daniel Webster takes an abolitionist stance and openly opposes the South's system of slavery – an opposition he would later compromise in the so-called Webster-Hayne debate. Within the United States, the North and the South became increasingly polarized. It was in the midst of the sectional conflict that Thanksgiving was pronounced a national holiday in 1863 by President Abraham Lincoln in an act that seemed to proclaim the dominance of the North over the South. Thus here it is against the South's political and cultural aspirations that the myth of the Pilgrims and the Puritans as a foundational American myth is implicitly directed.

Second, the West was perceived by the Protestant elite of New England as a major arena in the cultural battle over dominance with the South and as a fruitful field for missionary activities. Renowned clergyman (and father of Harriet Beecher Stowe) Lyman Beecher for example argues in *Plea for the West* for what Ray Allen Billington refers to as "the Protestant Crusade" (cf. his book of the same title): to spread Puritanism and Protestantism in the West and to contain slavery in the South – an agenda that was shared by many of his contemporaries. In this logic, the West was to become part of the Promised Land of white American Protestants descended from Puritan stock.

Third, we need to consider the narrative that insists on casting the Pilgrims and Puritans as the founders of New England and of the nation as a reaction to the contemporaneous non-English Catholic (and Jewish) immigration from Europe. Mythologizing the Protestant rebels helped to establish a hierarchical contrast to the Catholic newcomers: The "Catholic system is adverse to liberty, and the clergy to a great extent are dependent on foreigners opposed to the principles of our government, for patronage and support," Beecher somewhat self-righteously contends (*Plea* 61). In opposition to other ethnic and religious groups living in and coming to the USA during the second half of the 19th century, the "Plymouth settlers [were cast] as a master race" (Uhry Abrams, *Pilgrims* 145-46).

Throughout the 19th century, the laudatory commemorations of the Pilgrims and Puritans in public and political discourse continued, and "by the end of the century the Puritans were generally regarded as the founders of American democracy" (Hall, "Introduction" 1). This hegemonic discourse is obviously exclusionary – for one thing, because it is profoundly racialized.

6. WHERE IS THE PROMISED LAND?
THE AFRICAN AMERICAN EXPERIENCE

> When Israel was in Egyptland
> Let my People go
> Oppressed so hard they could not stand
> Let my People go
> Go Down, Moses, Way down in Egyptland
> Tell old Pharao let my people go.
> SLAVE SPIRITUAL (JUBILEE SINGERS, 1872)

> We didn't land on Plymouth Rock, brothers and sisters, Plymouth Rock landed on us.
> MALCOLM X

> The fundamental theme of New World African modernity is neither integration nor separation but rather migration and emigration.
> CORNEL WEST, *KEEPING FAITH*

From the perspective of Africans who were brought to North America and forced to work on the cotton fields and in the plantation households, America is obviously not the Land of Freedom but figures as the site of cruel enslavement and bondage, forced labor, cultural destruction, and death. The Middle Passage – the leg of the transatlantic triangle which brought Africans from the coast of West Africa to the Americas – was not a 'sacred journey' but rather a trip to hell, a journey through the underbelly of Western modernity. America was built, at least to a considerable degree, "on the backs of blacks" (cf. Morrison's essay of the same title). The first ship with Africans arrived in Jamestown in 1619, and thus earlier than the Puritans; in fact, slavery was a crucial part of early colonial history. After almost two hundred years of trading and owning slaves, all northern colonies and states abolished slavery between 1777 and 1804 in the wake, it is often suggested, of the American Revolutionary War. Slavery in the southern states continued and intensified until the American Civil War. But before we turn to African American responses to the myth of the Promised Land, we should remind ourselves of racial discourses in the historical context.

Puritan congregations were exclusionary entities that for the most part barred servants and women from membership – not to mention the indigenous population and Africans/African Americans. Slavery in America presented a fact that was camouflaged by an ideologically fraught racial discourse that portrayed America as a land of freedom and deliverance. From the beginning, religious groups such as the Quakers, intellectuals, and politicians wrestled with this conundrum and sought ways to solve this dilemma, but slavery continued to be an integral part of American society well beyond independence; it was sanctioned by the Constitution, and was abolished only after the American Civil War (1861-65). The post-abolition period was characterized by continued and in some ways even worse oppression of African Americans and by the most extreme excesses of racist violence, such as lynching. In the context of his first presidential campaign, Barack Obama even referred to slavery and racism against African Americans as "America's original sin" (qtd. in Leeman, *Teleological Discourse* 55-56).

From the beginning, Protestant evangelical groups argued for the abolition of slavery, and Protestantism is an important factor in the history of abolitionism in the United States; often it is used to distinguish New England (where slavery was abolished in all states by 1804) from Virginia in particular, and the South in general. Many critics contrasted the economic system of the North with the South's exploitation of slave labor, for example Frederick Law Olmsted, designer of the New York Central Park, who contended that Virginians had "never done a real day's work in their lives before they left England" and again refused to do so after the first shipload of Africans had arrived on their shores (qtd. in Uhry Abrams, *Pilgrims* 167).

How can we relate the existence of slavery to the myth of the Promised Land? What position did the religious tradition that had formulated this horizon of expectation take on slavery, and what impact did it have on slavery and the slaves themselves? In order to tackle these questions, we will briefly turn to the antebellum South. Historians of 19th-century American history have for a long time debated the complicated role of the Protestant religion in African American slave culture. Some scholars have claimed that religious indoctrination and conversion were used as an effective instrument of social control. The Christian religion, it is argued, taught the slaves submissiveness, docility, and a negative self-concept based on claims of their unworthiness in the eyes of God; slave-holders frequently drew on the Bible (mostly the Old Testament, and especially the Curse of Ham narrative) to justify slavery to the slaves and to white aboli-tionists (cf. Jordan, *White* 17-20). For many critics, Harriet Beecher Stowe's fictional Uncle Tom – an extremely pious character who does not even try to escape from slavery because of his faith – exemplifies the harmful effects of religious 'education:' even when he is brutalized and finally killed by his master, he suffers without resistance and forgives his tormentor (cf. Stowe's 1852 novel *Uncle Tom's Cabin*).

On the other hand, scholars have insisted that Christianity offered African American slaves access to symbolic resources which they could use for their own purposes and that the relative freedom in which they could gather to prac-tice their faith allowed them to secretly engage in other social, cultural, and political practices. Most importantly, however, the biblical story of the Exodus and the Promised Land – which explicitly addresses the unjust and unjustifiable evil of slavery – provided them with a (religious) narrative model of emancipa-tion, escape, and freedom. This story was as attractive to the African American slaves as it had been to the English Puritans. Stripped of its ideological invest-ment, the story of the Promised Land can be seen (from a structuralist point of view) as a blueprint for collective empowerment, which can thus be appropriated for the purpose of cultural and political critique.

Although the 17th-century Puritan construction of the 'new world' as Prom-ised Land excluded Africans and African Americans, the latter would try to partake in this promise through an appropriation and ideological reconfiguration of the myth. Popular African American spirituals used biblical themes and stories from the Exodus narrative to envision freedom, and turned Moses into an African American hero. To give just one example: Jeremiah A. Wright, Jr., the black theologian who came to fame during Barack Obama's first presidential campaign, wrote his MA thesis on the "Treatment of Biblical Passages in Negro Spirituals" (1969) and discusses biblical narratives (such as the Exodus) as strategies of empowerment for black slaves.

African American intellectual and former slave Frederick Douglass in the 19th century described religious practices already as what later theorists would call 'signifyin' practices' (cf. Smitherman, *Talkin*, and Gates, *Signifying Mon-key*) used as a kind of code by the black slaves:

A keen observer might have detected in our singing of

O Canaan, sweet Canaan,

I am bound for the land of Canaan,

Something more than a hope of reaching heaven. We meant to reach the *North*, and
the North was our Canaan.

"I thought I heard them say,

There were lions in the way;

I don't expect to stay

Much longer here.

Run to Jesus – shun the danger.

I don't expect to stay

Much longer here,"

Was a favourite air, and had a double meaning. On the lips of some it meant the
expectation of a speedy summons to a world of spirits, but on the lips of our company
it simply meant a speedy pilgrimage toward a free state, and deliverance from all the
evils and dangers of slavery. (*Life* 109)

The "double meaning" that Douglass refers to is apparent in many spirituals,
whose lyrics frequently focus on deliverance, salvation, and the topic of mobility. "The escape motif appears in hundreds of songs: the slaves are always
sailing, walking, riding, rowing, climbing, and crossing over into Canaan" (Blassingame, *Slave Community* 142). Most evident was the subversive effect of
religion on a slave in the singular incident that took place in Southampton,
Virginia in 1831 and is often referred to as Nat Turner's Rebellion, in which
Turner and a group of fellow slaves killed most whites they encountered until the
insurrection was squashed. In *The Confessions of Nat Turner*, written down by
Thomas R. Gray before Turner's execution and later used by William Styron in
his 1967 novel of the same title, Turner claims that God appeared to him in a
vision and told him to deliver his people from enslavement and to punish the
whites:

[W]hite spirits and black spirits engaged in battle, and the sun was darkened – the thunder
rolled in the heavens, and blood flowed in streams – and I heard a voice saying, "Such is
your luck, such you are called to see, and let it come rough or smooth, you must surely
bear it." (qtd. in Blassingame, *Slave Community* 219)

Turner, feeling that his actions were in accord with the will of God, set out to kill
whites and to free slaves, deeds for which he was later executed.

The subversive use of the Exodus narrative is not restricted to male fugitives and abolitionists. Most notably, female African American abolitionist activist Harriet Tubman (1820-1913) is referred to as "the Moses of her people" in a book by Sarah H. Bradford (cf. *Harriet*) published under the auspices of Susan B. Anthony. Tubman is compared to Moses because she repeatedly went back to the South after her own escape and led more than 70 slaves to escape to the North. These rescue missions became even more difficult after the passage of the 1850 Fugitive Slave Act, which required the North to cooperate with and assist in the attempts of the South to recapture fugitive slaves. Canada, which no longer had institutionalized slavery in the mid-19th century, then became the 'New Canaan' in place of the North of the United States. The similar spelling of Canada and Canaan further reinforced the notion that the Promised Land for African Americans and fugitive slaves lay beyond the national border. Kathryn Smardz-Frost's *I've Got a Home in Glory Land: A Lost Tale of the Underground Railroad* (2007) picks up this notion in recounting the complicated and paradigmatic escape of Lucy and Thornton Blackwell. Other scholars also affirm the vision of Canada as the Promised Land for African Americans (cf. Winks, *Blacks*). Approximately 60.000 blacks fled to Canada before the outbreak of the Civil War, half of whom supposedly went back after the war was over, the other half staying mostly in small towns in lower Ontario and in Toronto.

The Promised Land topos may thus be seen as a floating signifier that was used by African Americans to refer to various regions or territories. While the foundational national narrative focuses on the arrival of the Pilgrims and Puritans in the Promised Land and thus locates freedom from oppression *in* America, African American appropriations of the biblical story locate freedom from oppression in a Promised Land that is always elsewhere, so to speak, and often outside of the US.

The Great Migration of African Americans to the northern cities at the turn of the 19th to the 20th century is often represented as a 'second exodus,' which is evidenced by such titles as Milton C. Sernett's *Bound for the Promised Land: African American Religion and the Great Migration* (1997), and Nicholas Lemann's *The Promised Land: The Great Black Migration and How It Changed America* (1991). In African American literature addressing the experience of migration, however, there is often an ambivalent evaluation of the Promised Land rhetoric and the expectations with which black characters move from the South to the urban centers of the North. James Baldwin's first novel *Go Tell It on the Mountain* (1952) for example expounds the redemptive quality of migrating from the South to the North, but at the same time addresses the sense of loss, confusion, and displacement of the first generation of African Americans raised in the urban North. African American writing has thus not only promoted but also deconstructed white American versions of the myth of the Promised Land. Along the same lines, Toni Morrison's historical migration novel *Jazz* (1992) "is a portrait of a people in the midst of self-creation, a document of what they created and what they lost along the way" (Griffin, *Who* 197).

A third variation of the African American Exodus narrative reroutes the journey to Africa and can be seen as the most radical and consequential inversion of the Puritan myth of the Promised Land in America. Edwin S. Redkey's *Black Exodus* (1969) discusses Black Nationalism and Back-to-Africa movements since 1890. Many African American intellectuals, among them most prominently Marcus Garvey, proposed in the 1920s a re-migration across the Atlantic; Garveyism became a forceful movement that rested on a radical critique of American society and racist US national discourse. Africa as a place of belonging, as an 'imaginary homeland' and as a site of liberation and cultural and political autonomy has always figured prominently in African American culture. Thus, Black Nationalist discourse is explicitly counter-hegemonic as well as anti-foundational in its repudiation of narratives that idealize the US as the Promised Land.

In the second half of the 20th century, the myth of the Promised Land found resonance in the American civil rights movement and in the rhetoric of emancipation used by religious leaders in anti-racist activism. In April 1968, Martin Luther King, Jr. in his very last speech before his assassination encourages his audience to persevere in the face of often violent resistance to the movement's goals, and emphasizes the worldly and the spiritual dimension connected in the image of a better world:

But it doesn't matter with me now because I've been to the mountaintop. And I don't mind. Like anybody I would like to live a long life. Longevity has its place. But I'm not concerned about that now. I just want to do God's will. And he's allowed me to go up to the mountain, and I've looked over and I've seen the Promised Land. I may not go there with you. But I want you to know tonight that we as a people will get to the Promised Land. So I'm happy tonight. I'm not worried about anything. I'm not fearing any man. Mine eyes have seen the glory of the coming of the Lord. ("I've Been")

In a rhetorical move very similar to that of William Bradford more than 300 years earlier King uses the Exodus narrative to draw a parallel between himself and Moses being led by God to the Promised Land. Only in King's sermon it is the African Americans who are cast as Pilgrims hoping for salvation from racism and oppression – it is they who are God's chosen people.

African American rewritings of the Promised Land narrative adapted and appropriated the biblical story in various ways and for different ideological and counter-hegemonic purposes. At times it may be difficult to ascertain whether these adaptations rest on the Bible directly or rather rewrite the Puritan narrative – or even the semi-secular national narrative into which it evolved. The wide spectrum of interpretations and re-interpretations of the Promised Land myth in any case suggest, first, that it powerfully addresses the human longing for freedom in general, and second, that it lends itself readily to a variety of contradictory evaluations of the project that is America from national, subnational, and transnational perspectives.

7. IMMIGRANT VISIONS: INHERITING THE PROMISED LAND?

> The myth of the promised land is a tale told by strangers. It is the mythology of a people adrift, of a population without location, the rootless and the restless, the displaced, the exiled.
> DAVID F. NOBLE, *BEYOND THE PROMISED LAND*

> The invention of Plymouth (and especially Plymouth Rock) as an exclusivist ethnic symbol replaced earlier ideological readings in revolutionary, religious and abolitionist contexts at the end of the nineteenth and the beginning of the twentieth centuries.
> WERNER SOLLORS, "AMERICANS ALL"

> Every ship that brings your people from Russia and other countries where they are ill-treated is a *Mayflower*.
> MARY ANTIN, "THE LIE"

Despite the fact that the Pilgrim and Puritan myth of origins in the mid-19th century was used by nativists to stoke anti-immigrant sentiment in the face of increased Catholic and other 'foreign' immigration from Europe, many of these immigrants cherished their own version of America as the Promised Land. The Jewish immigrants, for example, clearly recognized in the narrative of the Promised Land their own story of repression, bondage, release, and salvation. The comparison between the Puritans and the Jewish immigrants has often been drawn with regard to typological interpretation, i.e. the collapsing of Holy Scripture and worldly experience. After all, was not William Bradford one of the first immigrants from Europe and his work, *Of Plymouth Plantation*, America's first immigrant narrative?

Illustration 5: Jewish Immigrants as the 'New Pilgrims'

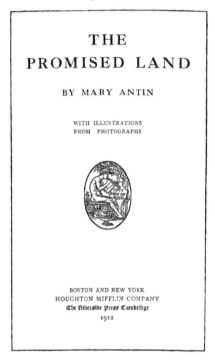

THE PROMISED LAND

BY MARY ANTIN

WITH ILLUSTRATIONS
FROM PHOTOGRAPHS

BOSTON AND NEW YORK
HOUGHTON MIFFLIN COMPANY
The Riverside Press Cambridge
1912

1912 title page of *The Promised Land* by M. Antin.

The most prominent and programmatic author in the field of Jewish immigrant writing is Mary Antin (1881-1949), who immigrated to the United States with her mother and her sisters in 1894 to join her father, who had three years earlier fled the Czarist pogroms. Her autobiographical narrative *The Promised Land* (1912) relates the Puritan topos of the Promised Land to her own exodus from an Eastern European *shtetl* to Boston and New York. In that text she affirms the willingness of immigrants in general and of herself in particular to assimilate into American society, thereby countering nativist claims that immigrants from Southern and Eastern Europe were unwilling or unable to integrate. Repeatedly, Antin refers to the Pilgrim Fathers as "our forefathers" (cf. also *They Who Knock*), thereby claiming a common ancestry of American-born and immigrant citizens. Chapter headings like "The Tree of Knowledge," "The Exodus," "Manna," or "The Burning Bush" evidence that Antin's (spiritual) autobiography strongly references the Old Testament (including the Exodus narrative). *The Promised Land* has become canonical in American studies not only for its topicality but also, as Werner Sollors reminds us, for its subtle aesthetics and versatility: "Antin continued the portraiture of America as a new Canaan from an immigrant's point of view, while leaving no doubt that the metaphor of the promised land was especially suited to Jewish immigrants" (*Beyond Ethnicity* 45). In what was criticized as a "cult of gratitude" (cf. Tumin's article of the same title) "characterized by excessive assimilation and submissiveness," she "claimed the American egalitarian promise defiantly by equating [herself] with George Washington" (Sollors, *Beyond Ethnicity* 45) – and with the Pilgrim Fathers, one might add; the immigrant girl symbolically adopted American foundational figures as her forefathers.

Antin's autobiographical text resonates in the writings of other Jewish American authors, for example in Anzia Yezierska's short story "America and I," which (also) features a female Jewish immigrant protagonist-narrator: "I began to read the American history. I found from the first pages that America started with a band of Courageous Pilgrims. They had left their native country as I had left mine. They had crossed an unknown ocean and landed in an unknown country, as I" (20). This analogy is then used by the narrator for personal empowerment as an immigrant struggling for inclusion: "I saw that it was the glory of America that it was not yet finished. And I, the last comer, had her share to give, small or great, to the making of America, like those Pilgrims who came in the *Mayflower*" (33).

Yezierska, like Antin, rhetorically authorizes her protagonist by establishing a connection between 20th-century Jewish immigrants and the 17th-century Pilgrims. Many authors beside and after Antin and Yezierska have worked with the myth of the Promised Land to make sense of their American experience, as Werner Sollors' enumeration of titles by ethnic and immigrant writers proves:

Lewis E. MacBrayne, "The Promised Land" (1902); Sidney Nyburg, *The Chosen People* (1917); W. Forest Cozart, *The Chosen People* (1924); Rudolph Fisher, "The Promised Land" (1927); Martin Wendell Odland, *The New Canaan* (1933); Margaret Marchand, *Pilgrims on the Earth* (1940); Stoyan Christowe, *My American Pilgrimage* (1947); Robert Laxalt, *Sweet Promised Land* (1957); Mario Puzo, *The Fortunate Pilgrim* (1965); and Claude Brown, *Manchild in the Promised Land* (1965). (*Beyond Ethnicity* 46)

Since Sollors's 1986 study, many more titles have appeared, of which I will brief-ly discuss two contemporary examples in order to demonstrate new and at times ironic turns in the appropriation of the myth. In *Mona in the Promised Land* (1996), Gish Jen takes up Antin's reconfiguration of the myth by portraying a Chinese immigrant family, the Changs, who in the fictional New York neighbor-hood of Scarshill – which is strongly suggestive of Scarsdale, the New York suburb in which Antin had lived at the beginning of the century – are considered the "New Jews" (3). The Changs' new family home is anything but new, as Mona, the Chinese American immigrant protagonist-narrator, quips: "Their house is still of the upstanding-citizen type. *Remember the Mayflower!* It seems to whisper" (ibid. 4). Mona's life is decisively shaped by the old Jewish Ameri-can community her family has moved into, whose members have come a long way from their turn-of-the century ancestors described in Mary Antin's text. As a high school student, Mona has "been to so many bar and bas mitzvahs, she can almost say herself whether the kid chants like an angel or like a train conductor. At Seder, Mona knows to forget the bricks, get a good pile of that mortar. Also she knows what is schmaltz" (ibid. 6). Early on, Mona wishes to become a Jew, and indeed converts to Judaism. To her bewildered and somewhat alarmed parents, Mona explains: "'Jewish is American [...]. American means being whatever you want, and I happened to pick Jewish'" (ibid. 49). She studies the Torah with Rabbi Horowitz, who "assigns so many books that Mona feels like she started on a mud bath, only to end up on a mud swim" (ibid. 35). At the end of the novel, however, the Rabbi also 'converts' and marries a non-Jewish wom-an (cf. ibid. 267). Overall, the novel deftly mocks the Puritan tradition of conversion and offers an ironic, postmodern take on the myth of the Promised Land and the theme of assimilation, which it adjusts to the *zeitgeist* of multiculturalism and to theories of cultural performativity.

Even more recently, the Jordanian American writer Laila Halaby puns on the myth of the Promised Land in her novel *Once in a Promised Land* (2007), in which she chronicles the decline of the marriage of Jassim and Salwa in Tucson, Arizona after the events that occurred in New York and Washington on September 11, 2001. The title, which is suggestive of a fairy tale beginning, already indicates the sense of disillusionment and of things falling apart that per-vades the narrative. Jassim kills a teenage boy in a car accident, and is targeted by the authorities for being an Arab American; Salwa has a miscarriage, and starts an affair with a colleague who turns out to be mentally disturbed and violent. Both Jassim and Salwa are exiles as much as they are immigrants. In this narrative of descent, the Promised Land is no more than a fairy tale – a mere fiction/fantasy. To conclude: immigrant writers have inverted, rejected, mocked, re-arranged and expanded the myth of the Promised Land to fit their own collective experience, to contest dominant regimes of representation, and to call into question the founding myth in its singular historical meaning.

8. MODERNIST REVISIONS: BLAMING THE PURITANS

> But Puritans, as they were called, if they were pure it was more since they had nothing in them of fulfilment than because of positive virtues. By their very emptiness they were the fiercest element in the battle to establish a European life on the New World.
>
> WILLIAM CARLOS WILLIAMS, *IN THE AMERICAN GRAIN*

> Puritanism: The haunting fear that someone somewhere may be happy.
>
> H.L. MENCKEN

> What did the Pilgrim Fathers come for, then, when they came so gruesomely over the black sea? [...] They came largely to get away – that most simple of motives. To get away. Away from what? In the long run, away from themselves.
>
> D.H. LAWRENCE, *STUDIES IN CLASSIC AMERICAN LITERATURE*

After the Pilgrims and Puritans had been mostly celebrated as founding figures of New England since the late 18th century, had acquired mythic proportions during the revolutionary period, and had been idolized in 19th-century national discourse, they came under closer scrutiny in modernist texts. Of course, there had been quite a few critical voices earlier; during the so-called 'American Renaissance' (cf. F.O. Matthiessen's 1941 book of the same title) of the 1850s – which actually was a 'New England Renaissance,' if anything – writers such as Nathaniel Hawthorne, Ralph Waldo Emerson, and Herman Melville among others were quite ambivalent about early Puritan history and mythmaking. Hawthorne most prominently scrutinizes the repressive forces of Puritan doctrine and dogma in his historical romance *The Scarlet Letter* (1850) and in short stories such as "Young Goodman Brown" and "The Maypole of Merrimount." His introduction of the Puritan crowd at the beginning of *The Scarlet Letter* is revealing:

A throng of bearded men, in sad-coloured garments and gray, steeple-crowned hats, intermixed with women, some wearing hoods, and others bareheaded, was assembled in front of a wooden edifice, the door of which was heavily timbered with oak, and studded with iron spikes.

The founders of a new colony, whatever Utopia of human virtue and happiness they might originally project, have invariably recognized it among their earliest practical necessities to allot a portion of the virgin soil as a cemetery, and another portion as the site of a prison. In accordance with this rule, it may safely be assumed that the forefathers of Boston had built the first prison-house somewhere in the vicinity of Cornhill, almost as seasonably as they marked out the first burial-ground, on Isaac Johnson's lot, and round about his grave, which subsequently became the nucleus of all the congregated sepulchres in the old churchyard of King's Chapel. Certain it is, that, some fifteen or twenty years after the settlement of the town, the wooden jail was already marked with weather-stains and other indications of age, which gave a yet darker aspect to its beetle-browed and gloomy front. (45)

Hawthorne casts the new world utopia in a rather "gloomy" and "sad" light and throughout the text maintains an ambiguous stance toward Puritan rigor and American exceptionalism. His protagonist, Hester Prynne, is convicted of adultery and sentenced to wear a scarlet 'A' on her breast as a lasting reminder of her 'crime.' And yet, as Prynne gains the admiration of many community members for the dignity with which she bears her punishment (and also refuses to name her extramarital partner, a hypocritical Puritan clergyman), the narrator concedes that apparently "the scarlet letter had not done its office" (145; cf. Bercovitch, *Office*).

The reluctance of Hawthorne and other writers of the 'American Renaissance' to embrace the foundational myth of the Pilgrims and the Puritans anticipates the skepticism and disillusionment of modernist writers and critics, who thought that Puritanism wielded an immensely detrimental influence on American culture, literature, and intellectuality. From the moderns' point of view, America's early colonial history had been a Dark Age of fanatic religiosity from which Americans had recovered only gradually and to a limited extent, with Puritanism's moralistic and anti-intellectual tendencies continuing to affect American cultural life. With Freudianism en vogue, critics engaged in "blaming the Puritans for the repressive tendencies in American life" (Hall, "Introduction" 1). This "Anti-Puritanism" led some intellectuals to suggest that "the central theme of Massachusetts history was the gradual emancipation of society from the authority of the ministers" (ibid. 2), a sentiment that is shared by George Santayana (cf. *Genteel Tradition*), Waldo Frank (cf. *Our America*), James Truslow Adams (cf. *Epic; Founding*), and Vernon L. Parrington (cf. *Main Currents*). Much of American historiography in the 1920s – in stark contrast to the previous predominance of positive if not idealizing portrayals – is markedly critical of the Pilgrims and Puritans, who it either viewed as religious fanatics or as a sanctimonious plutocracy that camouflaged its interest in maintaining power under a cloak of religiosity. Hence, the Massachusetts Bay Colony was not, as had previously often been suggested, the 'cradle' of American democracy; instead, Puritanism was criticized as inherently anti-democratic. James Truslow Adams quotes John Winthrop describing democracy as "the meanest and worst of all forms of government" (*Epic* 39) and stating that there "was no such government in Israel," which for him meant that to have it in Massachusetts would be "a manifest breach of the 5th Commandment" (*Founding* 143). And G.P. Gooch pointedly quips that democracy may have been a child of the Reformation, yet not of the reformers (cf. *History* 8).

Illustration 6: Lillian Gish as Hester Prynne

The Scarlet Letter (dir. Victor Sjöström, 1926).

James Truslow Adams in his study *The Founding of New England* (1921) approaches the Puritans from yet another revisionist angle. He argues that economic, not religious motives were crucial for emigration to North America. He points out the exclusivist nature of Puritan congregations, which granted church membership to only one out of five men in Massachusetts and barred all others from becoming members. Adams (among others) suggests that people continued to emigrate to America regardless of this exclusionary practice because they simply did not care about religious practice and religious orthodoxy:

They came for the simple reason that they wanted to better their condition. [...] They wanted to own land; and it was this last motive, perhaps, which mainly had attracted those twelve thousand persons out of sixteen thousand who swelled the population of Massachusetts in 1640, but were not church members. (*Founding* 122)

More recently, Uhry Abrams confirms this assessment when she states that "there was far less religious or social conformity than the myths would have one believe" (*Pilgrims* 29).

In the field of literature, William Carlos Williams's 1925 collection *In the American Grain* is a good example of the modernists' tendency to criticize the Puritans and the New England Way as repressive. Intolerance, hypocrisy, and religion are "substitutions for life" for those who with "tight-locked hearts" (63) stressed "the spirit against the flesh" (66): "The jargon of God, which they used, was their dialect by which they kept themselves surrounded as with a palisade" (63). "They must have relied on vigorous hypocrisy to save them – which they did" (67). Williams comments on the Salem witch trials in the colony in 1692 to conclude his argument:

In fear and without guidance, really lost in the world, it is they alone who would later, at Salem, have strayed so far – morbidly seeking the flame, – that terrifying unknown image to which, like savages, they too offered sacrifices of human flesh. [...] And it is still to-day the Puritan who keeps his frightened grip upon the world lest it should prove him – empty. (67)

By likening Puritanism to barbarism ("like savages;" "sacrifices of human flesh"), Williams inverts the hierarchy between Puritans and Native Americans that was established in colonial discourse (civilization vs. savagery) and thus articulates the most radical critique of his time.

Modern writers and essayists thus lamented the harm that the Puritan narrative of origins had done to generations and generations of Americans. They reconfigured the Puritan master narrative of divine liberation and emancipation into one of purposeful oppression both on an individual as well as on a collective level. As a consequence, the Puritans were considered useless if not obnoxious ancestral figures for a modern, 20th-century America, which resulted in a call for disidentification and for the deconstruction of a national narrative obsessed with the Pilgrims and Puritans' Promised Land and some rock on a beach. As early as 1918, Van Wyck Brooks's essay "On Creating a Usable Past" argued for the creation of pasts *other than the Puritan* in the face of a pluralistic America – a timely call that, however, would only be heeded seriously in the second half of the 20th century.

9. PURITAN ORIGIN VERSUS "MESSY BEGINNINGS" IN AMERICAN STUDIES

> The place of the Pilgrim Fathers in American history can best be stated by a paradox. Of slight importance in their own time, they are of great and increasing significance in our time, through the influence of their story on American folklore and tradition. And the key to that story, the vital factor in this little group, is the faith in God that exalted them and their small enterprise to something of lasting value and enduring interest.
> SAMUEL ELIOT MORISON

> Having failed to rivet the eyes of the world upon their city on the hill, they were left alone with America.
> PERRY MILLER, *ERRAND INTO THE WILDERNESS*

During the emergence of American studies as a discipline in the 1930s and '40s, the story of the Pilgrims and the Puritans has often been studied as a foundational narrative of American beginnings in order to explain the cultural specificity of what would later develop into the United States of America. The formation of national identity and national cohesion has repeatedly been delineated as a continuous evolution from the Puritan errand to the 'new world' and from the first generation of English settlers in the Massachusetts Bay Colony to the present. Titles such as *The Puritan Origins of the American Self* by Sacvan Bercovitch indicate the degree to which the concepts of the Puritan errand and covenant with God served as models for accounting for later, specifically US-American, social, cultural and political developments and practices.

Not surprisingly, Harvard University – founded by the Puritans in 1636 as the first institution of higher education in North America – became the center of Puritan scholarship beginning with the long-since canonical work of Samuel Eliot Morison and Perry Miller, among others. It is a remarkable fact that the scholarly reappraisal of the Pilgrims and Puritans took off at the moment when American studies as a new academic discipline was launched in the 1930s. Both Perry Miller and Samuel Eliot Morison found the Puritans to be not dull conformists, but intellectuals who were 'exhilarated' by their faith. Miller's influential studies such as *The New England Mind: The Seventeenth Century*

(1939), *The New England Mind: From Colony to Province* (1953), and *Errand into the Wilderness* (1964) as well as Samuel Eliot Morison's seminal study *Builders of the Bay Colony* (1930) placed the Puritans at the center of a national foundational narrative, which thus also became foundational for American studies. Conservative Puritan scholar Samuel Eliot Morison argues that the Puritans believed what they preached and he sees it as Winthrop's intention "to inspire these new children of Israel with the belief that they were God's chosen people; destined, if they kept their covenant with him, to people and fructify this new Canaan in the western wilderness" (*Builders* 106). It should be noted that Native Americans, however, hardly figure in early Puritan scholarship, which thus contributed to no small degree to popular misconceptions about early North American history.

Sacvan Bercovitch argues in *The Puritan Origins of the American Self* (1975) that "[t]he persistence of the myth is a testament to the visionary and symbolic power of the American Puritan imagination" (186) and that "the Puritan myth prepared for the re-vision of God's country from the 'New England of the type' into the United States of America" (136).

That the (re-)discovery of the Puritans in American history and the establishment of American studies under the arch of American exceptionalism coincide is by no means accidental. Scholars of the so-called Myth and Symbol School turned to the Puritans and Pilgrims and the New England Way in order to identify culturally specific symbols and patterns to bolster the notion that the US was indeed exceptional (there is an astounding amount of Puritan scholarship in the establishment and consolidation of American studies as an academic discipline, of which for the purposes of this chapter I could reference only a fraction). The foundational paradigm of Puritanism embraces the assumption that the origins of American society are exclusively white and European, and credits white Anglo-Saxon Protestants with the formation of the US nation. Not all of the Myth and Symbol scholars shared the same affirmative interpretation of Puritan culture, but the majority placed the Puritan elite center stage and marginalized all other groups – Native Americans, Africans/African Americans, women, indentured servants, etc. – in their work on American beginnings. It is thus unsurprising that this body of work led subsequent generations of Americanists to criticize it for heralding and backing an exclusivist US-American ideology. Philip Fisher's analysis of the first generation of Puritan scholars in American studies points in that direction:

Beginning with the work of Perry Miller in the late thirties, the explanation of America as a long history of Puritan hope and decline resulted from the fact that academic intellectuals, looking into the past to find not necessarily its chief actors but precisely those congenial figures whose analytic and critical stance most resembled their own, discovered in the Puritan writers what was for them the most intelligible feature of the past, the one mirror most filled with familiar features. They too were intellectuals engaged in holding up a mirror of admonition or exhortation to their society. In theocratic New England they found embodied the secret self-image of all intellectual cultures, a society in which the critics and intellectuals were not marginal, but actually in power. ("Introduction" x)

Fisher's statement shows that scholarship is tied as much to the time in which it is practiced as it is about the time that it addresses; if scholars fail to reflect on their own positionality, the outcome of their work may be easily marked by – more or less subtle – ideologically motivated simplifications of their subject matter. Crispin Gill, for instance, sees in the study of Puritanism and, by implication, in the model of the Puritans an effective antidote to the protest movements of the 1960s in America:

In time, youth finds that its new discoveries, like sex, are not really original. There were Harvard students who, during the early days of the 1969 troubles on the campus, realized that there had been a rebellion in America before them. [...] [T]he men and women of the Mayflower have much to say to the young rebels of today. What is more, the Pilgrims were constructive rebels. They were not content with denouncing one form of society, they persevered until they had built another which did give life and reality to their ideals. (*Mayflower* 182)

In a somewhat similar vein, Andrew Delbanco describes the first generation Puritans as follows: "[T]he founders of New England were drop-outs – with all the indignation, idealism and wounded righteousness that the term implies" ("Introduction" xxii). Yet, whereas in 1970, Richard Reinitz could still write that "Puritanism was an English movement which became the single most influential factor in the shaping of American culture and society" ("Introduction" i), such aggrandizement was no longer acceptable in the 1980s and '90s. In 1984, Jan C. Dawson – following the earlier critique of the modernists and Van Wyck Brooks's writings – declares America's Puritan tradition "the unusable past" (cf. her book of the same title). Richard Slotkin, a representative of the Critical Myth and Symbol School, has pointed to the violence at the center of the Puritan experience in the 'new world' (cf. *Regeneration* 5). Other critics look for alternative 'possible pasts,' stressing the fact that the Puritans were not the only residents in North America at that time. Uhry Abrams sees the myth of the Pilgrims and the Puritans as a regional New England narrative that for a long time has erroneously dominated discussions of American beginnings by ignoring for instance the Jamestown colony, which was founded more than a decade before Bradford landed in America and more than two decades before Winthrop's Puritans arrived there, after all (cf. *Pilgrims*); she thus holds that Puritanism as a paradigm in American studies scholarship not only presents a highly idealized version of American beginnings but also marginalizes other stories of American genesis. Whereas Uhry Abrams in her book of the same title rather schematically contrasts "the Pilgrims and Pocahontas," more recent work done on early American history adopts a postcolonial studies approach and operates with the concept of "messy beginnings" (cf. Schueller and Watts's essay collection of the same title) with a three-fold aim: first, to analyze the Puritan project beyond the rhetoric of the Promised Land as colonization, pure and simple – the Pilgrims and Puritans were part of a hierarchical settler colony and acted as colonizers upon the indigenous population; second, to draw attention to other groups in early American history and their versions of the national prehistory; third, to analyze the complicated ways in which these different groups interacted. Approaching early American history and specifically the settlements in New England from the perspective of postcolonial criticism, Schueller and Watts suggest that

the colonization of what became the United States and the formation of the nation involved a complex series of political negotiations, machinations, violent encounters, and legal maneuvers that attempted to define differences among various groups: the Puritan clergy, the emergent bourgeoisie, the white backwoodsmen, the mixed-bloods, American Indians, and African Americans. ("Introduction" 5)

Thus, the earlier scholarship of the Myth and Symbol School in its historical, cultural, and political context must from a postcolonial studies perspective inevitably come into view as part and parcel of the master narrative of white Anglo-Saxon Protestant America.

10. CONCLUSION: BURYING THE ROCK OR PREPARING THE TURKEY?

> The white people made us many promises, more than I can remember. But
> they never kept but one. They promised to take our land, and they took it.
> RED CLOUD

> Finding is the first act
> The second, loss.
> EMILY DICKINSON

Whereas the mythology of the Pilgrims and Puritans, the Promised Land, Plymouth Rock, and Thanksgiving still is firmly embedded in national narratives, iconography, and cultural practices, protest against this WASP version of American beginnings has not abated. Native American organizations have enacted a counter-cultural practice at Plymouth: Burying the rock. On Thanksgiving, November 23, 1995, Moonanum James (Wampanoag), leader of the United American Indians of New England, gathered over 300 Native people and supporters of all nationalities at Plymouth Rock, where "the protesters climbed across a fence to get to the rock and buried it covering it with sand and erecting an indigenous warrior flag on top of it" ("Native People"). This symbolic burial of Plymouth Rock, as the activists explain, "capped the 25th anniversary of the National Day of Mourning speak-out held here in Plymouth. The Day of Mourning is a protest against the U.S. celebration of the mythology of Thanksgiving, and against the racist 'Pilgrim's Progress Parade'" (ibid.). The parade referred to here reenacts Pilgrims walking to church, muskets and bibles in hand. Moonanum James comments that "[t]hey want to act as though we sat down and ate turkey and lived happily ever after. That is simply not true – and we keep coming back year after year in order to give answer to their lies" (qtd. in ibid.). And in regard to the Mayflower Compact, he states:

There was no room in that Compact for women, lesbians and gay men, and the poor, let alone for Native people or our sisters and brothers of African descent. We call on all oppressed people to unite and join the fight against the racist and murderous ruling class, and not glorify the Mayflower Compact but to condemn it and the system it created. (qtd. in ibid.)

Illustration 7: 'Illegal Pilgrims'

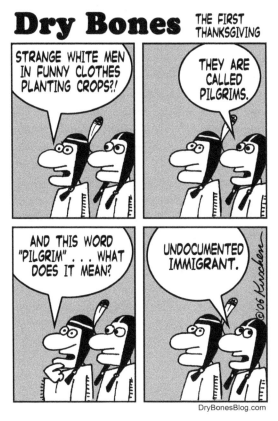

Yaakov Kirschen, *The First Thanksgiving* (2006).

Political protest not only counters sanitized versions of American history in which the Pilgrims and Puritans are painted as victims of an oppressive society rather than as genocidal colonizers, but also other commemorative rituals that are part of the national fantasy of the Puritans which arguably function to suppress the more gruesome aspects of their story. Many aspects of Thanksgiving, "America's most loved holiday" (Dennis, *Red* 81), are by and large later fabrications: The turkey, for one thing, was certainly not part of the Thanksgiving celebration in 1621. Archaeologist James Deetz, who worked at the site of the first settlement of the Pilgrims, points to a long-standing misconception:

We finally found some turkey bone after ten years of digging. The circumstantial evidence is that it wouldn't be likely [that the Pilgrims ate turkey]. Turkeys are very hard to kill and the matchlocks of the period weren't very good for hunting. (qtd. in Dennis, *Red* 100-101)

Dennis elaborates how the American turkey industry has fabricated the traditional Thanksgiving turkey dinner in the latter decades of the 19th century (cf. ibid.). The Thanksgiving turkey turns out to be a fiction – and a market-driven capitalist fiction at that.

And yet, religio-political devotion to the idea that the USA is a (or the) Promised Land and the fantasy of Puritan national origins are still somewhat hegemonic. Many comparisons have been drawn between the Protestant legacy of the Pilgrims and the Puritans and contemporary Evangelicals in the United States, as both groups adhere to Biblical literalism, strive for a theocratic society, and do not allow for a functional differentiation of the social world: in their view, religious doctrine underlies *all* aspects of public and private life. And religious fundamentalism and evangelicalism cannot be neglected as a political force. But even more structural reverberations of Puritan thought can be found in contemporary politics: Kevin R. den Dulk discusses what he refers to as "Evangelical Internationalists" (cf. his article of the same title), and Jeremy Mayer has pointed out the ideological proximity between US-American evangelicals and conservative religio-political groups in Israel, who share, and bond over, an exceptionalist and Promised Land rhetoric: chosen people both (cf. "Christian Fundamentalists"). We may consider this a transnational dimension of the Promised Land myth.

11. STUDY QUESTIONS

1. Relate the Promised Land myth to the biblical Exodus narrative. What kind of correspondences did the Pilgrims and Puritans construct?
2. Discuss William Bradford and John Winthrop as religious leaders in the context of Promised Land mythmaking.
3. Compare the myth of the Promised Land to the myth that has been constructed around Jamestown and Pocahontas. Can you establish similarities and differences between them?
4. Discuss the presence/absence of Native Americans with regard to the myth of the Promised Land.
5. In what way did African Americans appropriate the Promised Land myth? Give examples from the text and from other sources.
6. Discuss Jack Kerouac's novel *On the Road* (1957) as a modern pilgrimage. How does the text make use of the myth of the Promised Land? And how is the myth connected to the genre of the road-narrative/movie in more general terms?
7. Discuss the role of Thanksgiving in the American calendar as a cultural practice of commemoration and the role of Plymouth Rock as a tourist destination.
8. Analyze how selected texts of American popular culture (e.g. lyrics of pop songs such as those mentioned in the text) use the Promised Land rhetoric.
9. Explain the phrase 'messy beginnings.' What kind of vision of early American history does it entail?
10. What are (or could be) the transnational implications of the Promised Land myth?

12. BIBLIOGRAPHY

Works Cited

Adams, James Truslow. *The Epic of America.* New York: Blue Ribbon, 1941.

–. *The Founding of New England.* Boston: Atlantic Monthly, 1921.

Andreae, Johann Valentin. *Christianopolis.* 1619. Introd. and trans. Edward H. Thompson. Dordrecht: Kluver, 1999.

Antin, Mary. "The Lie." *Atlantic Monthly* August 1913: 177-90.

–. *The Promised Land.* Boston: Houghton, 1912.

–. *They Who Knock at Our Gates: A Complete Gospel of Immigration.* Boston: Houghton, 1914.

Bacon, Francis. *The New Atlantis.* 1624. *Project Gutenberg.* http://www.guten berg.org/ebooks/2434. 19 Sept. 2013.

Baldwin, James. *Go Tell It on the Mountain.* New York: Knopf, 1952.

Baldwin, Samuel Davies. *Armageddon: or, The Overthrow of Romanism and Monarchy; the Existence of the United States Foretold in the Bible.* New York: Applegate, 1854.

Bancroft, George. *History of the United States, from the Discovery of the American Continent.* Abridged and ed. Russel B. Nye. Chicago: U of Chicago P, 1966.

Baym, Nina, et al., eds. *The Norton Anthology of American Literature.* 4th ed. Vol. 1. New York: Norton, 1994.

Beecher, Lyman. *Plea for the West.* Cincinnati: Truman and Smith, 1835.

Bercovitch, Sacvan. *The American Jeremiad.* Madison: U of Wisconsin P, 1978.

–. *The Office of the Scarlet Letter.* Baltimore: Johns Hopkins UP, 1991.

–. *The Puritan Origins of the American Self.* New Haven: Yale UP, 1975.

–. "Rhetoric and History in Early New England: The Puritan Errand Reassessed." *Toward a New American Literary History.* Ed. Louis J. Budd. Durham: Duke UP, 1980. 54-86.

Bigsby, Christopher. "Introduction." *The Cambridge Companion to Modern American Culture.* Ed. Christopher Bigsby. Cambridge: Cambridge UP, 2006. 1-32.

Billington, Ray Allen. *The Protestant Crusade, 1800-1860: A Study of the Origins of American Nativism.* New York: Macmillan, 1938.

Blassingame, John. *The Slave Community: Plantation Life in the Antebellum South.* New York: Oxford UP, 1979.

Bradford, Sarah H. *Harriet: The Moses of Her People.* New York: Lookwood and Son, 1886.

Bradford, William. *Of Plymouth Plantation*. Rendered into Modern English and with an Introd. by Harold Paget. Mineola: Dover, 2006.

Breen, Timothy H. *Puritans and Adventurers: Change and Persistence in Early America*. Oxford: Oxford UP, 1980.

Bremer, Francis J. *The Puritan Experiment: New England Society from Bradford to Edwards*. New York: St. Martin's, 1976.

Brooks, Van Wyck. "On Creating a Usable Past." *Dial* 11 April 1918: 337-41.

Brumm, Ursula. "'What Went You Out into the Wilderness to See?' Non-Conformity and Wilderness in Cotton Mather's *Magnalia Christi Americana*." *Prospects* 6 (1981): 1-15.

Buckley, Thomas E. "Thomas Jefferson and the Myth of Separation." *Religion and the American Presidency*. Ed. Mark Rozell and Gleaves Whitney. New York: Palgrave Macmillan, 2007. 39-50.

Caldwell, Patricia. *The Puritan Conversion Narrative: The Beginnings of American Expression*. Cambridge: Cambridge UP, 1983.

Campanella, Tommaso. *The City of the Sun*. 1602. *Project Gutenberg*. http://www.gutenberg.org/ebooks/2816. 19 Sept. 2013.

Clifford, James. "Travelling Cultures." *Roots and Routes: Travel and Translation in the Late Twentieth Century*. Cambridge: Harvard UP, 1997. 17-46.

Danforth, Samuel. "A Brief Recognition of New-Englands Errand into the Wilderness." 1670. *Zea E-Books in American Studies*. Book 6. http://digitalcommons.unl.edu/zeaamericanstudies/6. 19 Sept. 2013.

Dawson, Jan C. *The Unusable Past: America's Puritan Tradition, 1830 to 1930*. Chico: Scholars', 1984.

Delbanco, Andrew. "Introduction." Delbanco, *Writing* i-xxix.

–. "John Winthrop." Delbanco, *Writing* 3.

–, ed. *Writing New England: An Anthology from the Puritans to the Present*. Cambridge: Belknap, 2001.

Delbanco, Andrew, and Alan Heimert. "Introduction." Delbanco and Heimert, *Puritans* i-xviii.

–, eds. *The Puritans in America: A Narrative Anthology*. Cambridge: Harvard UP, 1985.

–. "William Bradford." Delbanco and Heimert, *Puritans* 51-2.

Den Dulk, Kevin R. "Evangelical 'Internationalists' and US Foreign Policy during the Bush Administration." *Religion and the Bush Presidency*. Ed. Mark J. Rozell and Gleaves Whitney. New York: Palgrave Macmillan, 2007. 213-34.

Dennis, Matthew. *Red, White, and Blue Letter Days: An American Calendar*. Ithaca: Cornell UP, 2002.

Douglass, Frederick. *The Life and Times of Frederick Douglass*. Mineola: Courier Dover, 2003.

Fisher, Philip. "Introduction." *The New American Studies: Essays from Representation*. Ed. Philip Fisher. Berkeley: U of California P, 1991. vii-xxii.

Foster, Stephen. *The Long Argument: English Puritanism and the Shaping of New England Culture, 1570-1700*. Chapel Hill: U of North Carolina P, 1991.

Frank, Waldo. *Our America*. New York: Boni and Liveright, 1919.

Gates, Henry Louis, Jr. *The Signifying Monkey: A Theory of African American Literary Criticism*. New York: Oxford UP, 1982.

Gill, Crispin. *Mayflower Remembered: A History of the Plymouth Pilgrims*. New York: Taplinger, 1970.

Gooch, G.P. *The History of English Democratic Ideas in the 17th Century*. Cambridge: Cambridge UP, 1898.

Gray, Thomas R. *The Confessions of Nat Turner*. Baltimore: Gray, 1831.

Greene, Jack P. *The Intellectual Construction of America: Exceptionalism and Identity from 1492 to 1800*. Chapel Hill: U of North Carolina P, 1993.

Griffin, Farah Jasmine. *"Who Set you Flowin?" The African American Migration Narrative*. New York: Oxford UP, 1995.

Halaby, Laila. *Once in a Promised Land*. Boston: Beacon, 2007.

Hall, David D. "Introduction." *Puritanism in Seventeenth-Century Massachusetts*. Ed. David D. Hall. New York: Holt Rinehart and Winston, 1968. 1-6.

Hawthorne, Nathaniel. "The Maypole of Merrimount." 1836. Hawthorne, *Tales* 110-20.

–. *Nathaniel Hawthorne's Tales*. Ed. James McIntosh. New York: Norton, 2013.

–. *The Scarlet Letter: A Romance*. Introd. Nina Baym. Notes by Thomas E. Connolly. New York: Penguin, 1983.

–. "Young Goodman Brown." 1835. Hawthorne, *Tales* 84-96.

Hebel, Udo. "The Rise and Fall of New England Forefather's Day as a Site of National American Memory." *Sites of Memory in American Literatures and Cultures*. Ed. Udo Hebel. Heidelberg: Winter, 2003. 141-92.

Heimert, Alan. "Puritanism, the Wilderness and the Frontier." *New England Quarterly* 26 (1953): 361-82.

Herget, Winfried. "Anders als der Rest der Welt: Die Puritaner in der amerikanischen Wildnis." *Colonial Encounters: Essays in Early American History and Culture*. Ed. Hans-Jürgen Grabbe. Heidelberg: Winter, 2003. 29-50.

Holloway, Mark. *Heavens on Earth: Utopian Communities in America, 1680-1880*. New York: Dover, 1966.

Jen, Gish. *Mona in the Promised Land*. New York: Vintage, 1997.

Jordan, Winthrop. *White Over Black: American Attitudes Toward the Negro, 1550-1812*. Chapel Hill: U of North Carolina P, 1968.

Kerouac, Jack. *On the Road*. New York: Penguin, 1998.

King, Martin Luther, Jr. "I've Been to the Mountaintop." Speech. Memphis, Tennessee, 3 April 1968. *Speeches-USA*. http://www.speeches-usa.com/Transcripts/023_king.html. 10 Sept. 2013.

Lawrence, D.H. *Studies in Classic American Literature*. New York: Penguin, 1990.

Leeman, Richard. *The Teleological Discourse of Barack Obama*. Lanham: Lexington, 2013.

Lemann, Nicholas. *The Promised Land: The Great Black Migration and How It Changed America*. New York: Vintage, 1991.

Mather, Cotton. *Day of Humiliation: Times of Affliction and Disaster, Nine Sermons for Restoring Favor with an Angry God (1669-1727)*. Ed. George Harrison Orians. Gainsville: Scholars' Facsimiles and Reprints, 1970.

Matthiessen, Francis Otto. *American Renaissance: Art and Expression in the Age of Emerson and Whitman*. London: Oxford UP, 1941.

Mazur, Eric Michael, and Kate McCarthy. *God in the Details*. New York: Routledge, 2001.

Mayer, Jeremy. "Christian Fundamentalists and Public Opinion Toward the Middle East: Israel's New Best Friends?" *Social Science Quarterly* 85.3 (2004): 695-712.

Miller, Perry. *Errand into the Wilderness*. Cambridge: Belknap, 1964.

–. *The New England Mind: From Colony to Province*. Boston: Beacon, 1953.

–. *The New England Mind: The Seventeenth Century*. New York: Macmillan, 1939.

More, Thomas. *Utopia*. 1516. *Project Gutenberg*. http://www.gutenberg.org/ebooks/2130. 19 Sept. 2013.

Morgan, Edmund S., ed. *The Founding of Massachusetts: Historians and the Sources*. Indianapolis: Bobbs-Merrill, 1964.

Morison, Samuel Eliot. *Builders of the Bay Colony*. Boston: Houghton, 1930.

Morrison, Toni. *Jazz*. New York: Knopf, 1992.

–. "On the Backs of Blacks." *Arguing Immigration: The Debate Over the Changing Face of America*. Ed. Nicholas Mill. New York: Simon, 1994. 97-100.

Morton, Thomas. "New England Canaan." Baym et al., *Norton Anthology* 206-13.

"Native People Bury Racist Rock." *Worker's World* 1 Dec. 1995. *World History Archives*. http://hartford-hwp.com/archives/41/416.html. 10 Sept. 2013.

New England's First Fruits. 1643. Vaughan, *Puritan Tradition* 65-72.

Noble, David F. *Beyond the Promised Land: The Movement and the Myth*. Toronto: Between the Lines, 2005.

Palfrey, John Gorham. *History of New England*. Boston: Little, 1858.

Parini, Jay. *Promised Land: Thirteen Books That Changed America*. New York: Anchor, 2010.

Parrington, Vernon. *Main Currents in American Thought: An Interpretation of American Literature from the Beginnings to 1920*. 3 vols. New York: Harcourt, 1927-1930.

Redkey, Edwin S. *Black Exodus*. New Haven: Yale UP, 1969.

Reinitz, Richard. "Introduction." *Tensions in American Puritanism*. Ed. Richard Reinitz. New York: Wiley, 1970. i-xiv.

Rosenmeier, Jesper. "'With My Owne Eyes:' William Bradford's *Of Plymouth Plantation*." *The American Puritan Imagination*. Ed. Sacvan Bercovitch. New York: Cambridge UP, 1974. 77-106.

Santayana, George. *The Genteel Tradition: Nine Essays by George Santayana*. Ed. Douglas L. Wilson. Lincoln: U of Nebraska P, 1998.

Schmidt, Gary D. *William Bradford: Plymouth's Faithful Pilgrim*. Grand Rapids: Eerdmans, 1999.

Schueller, Malini Johar, and Edward Watts. "Introduction: Theorizing Early American Studies and Postcoloniality." *Messy Beginnings: Postcoloniality and Early American Studies*. Ed. Malini Johar Schueller and Edward Watts. New Brunswick: Rutgers UP, 2003. 1-25.

Schultz, Eric B., and Michael J. Tougias. *King Philip's War: The History and Legacy of America's Forgotten Conflict*. Woodstock: Countryman, 2000.

Seelye, John. *Memory's Nation: The Place of Plymouth Rock*. Chapel Hill: U of North Carolina P, 1988.

Sernett, Milton C. *Bound for the Promised Land: African American Religion and the Great Migration*. Durham: Duke UP, 1997.

Slotkin, Richard. "Introduction." *"So Dreadfull a Judgment:" Puritan Responses to King Philip's War, 1676-1677*. Ed. Richard Slotkin and James K. Folsom. Hanover: UP of New England, 1978. 3-53.

–. *Regeneration through Violence: The Mythology of the American Frontier, 1600-1860*. Middletown: Wesleyan UP, 1973.

Smardz-Frost, Kathryn. *I've Got a Home in Glory Land: A Lost Tale of the Underground Railroad*. New York: Farrar, 2007.

Smitherman, Geneva. *Talkin and Testifyin: The Language of Black America*. Detroit: Wayne State UP, 1977.

Sollors, Werner. "Americans All! Of Plymouth Rock and Jamestown and Ellis Island; or, Ethnic Literature and Some Redefinitions of 'America.'" *NYU P.* http://www.nyupress.org/americansall/. 15 Sept. 2012.

–. *Beyond Ethnicity: Consent and Descent in American Culture.* New York: Oxford UP, 1986.

Stowe, Harriet Beecher. *Uncle Tom's Cabin.* 1852. New York: Norton, 1994.

Styron, William. *The Confessions of Nat Turner.* New York: Random, 1967.

Tillam, Thomas. "Upon the First Sight of New-England, June 29, 1638." Delbanco and Heimert, *Puritans* 126.

Tocqueville, Alexis de. *Democracy in America.* Vol. 1. Ed. Daniel Boorstein. New York: Vintage, 1990.

Tumin, Melvin. "The Cult of Gratitude." *The Ghetto and Beyond.* Ed. Peter Rose. New York: Random, 1969. 69-82.

Uhry Abrams, Ann. *The Pilgrims and Pocahontas: Rival Myths of American Origin.* Boulder: Westview, 1999.

Vaughan, Alden T., ed. *The Puritan Tradition in America, 1620-1730.* New York: Harper, 1972.

Webster, Daniel. "First Settlement of New England." *The Speeches of Daniel Webster.* Ed. B.F. Tefft. London: Chesterfield Society, 1880. 63-118.

West, Cornel. *Keeping Faith: Philosophy and Race in America.* New York: Routledge, 1993.

Williams, Roger. *The Complete Writings of Roger Williams.* Ed. Perry Miller. New York: Russell and Russell, 1963.

Williams, William Carlos. *In the American Grain.* New York: New Directions, 1925.

Winks, Robin. *Blacks in Canada: A History.* 2nd ed. Montreal: McGill Queens UP, 1997.

Winthrop, John. *The History of New England from 1630 to 1649.* Vol. 1. Boston: Phelps and Farnham, 1825.

–. "A Model of Christian Charity." Baym et al., *Norton Anthology* 214-25.

–. *The Winthrop Papers.* Boston: Massachusetts Historical Society, 1931.

Wright, Jeremiah A., Jr. "Treatment of Biblical Passages in Negro Spirituals." MA thesis Howard University, 1969.

Yezierska, Anzia. "America and I." *In the Open Cage: An Anzia Yezierska Collection.* Ed. Alice Kessler-Harris. New York: Persea, 1979. 20-33.

Young, Alexander. *Chronicles of the Pilgrim Fathers of the Colony of Plymouth from 1602 to 1625.* 1841. Vaughan, Puritan Tradition 50-53.

Further Reading

Alter, Robert, and Frank Kermode, eds. *The Literary Guide to the Bible.* Cambridge: Belknap, 1987.

Axtell, James. *After Columbus: Essays in the Ethnohistory of Colonial North America.* Oxford: Oxford UP, 1988.

–. *The Invasion Within: The Contest of Cultures in Colonial North America.* Oxford: Oxford UP, 1986.

–. *Natives and Newcomers: The Cultural Origins of North America.* Oxford: Oxford UP, 2001.

Baltzell, E. Digby. *Puritan Boston and Quaker Philadelphia: Two Protestant Ethics and the Spirit of Class Authority and Leadership.* New York: Free, 1979.

Bartlett, William H. *The Pilgrim Fathers; or, The Founders of New England in the Reign of James the First.* London: Hall, 1853.

Bercovitch, Sacvan, ed. *The American Puritan Imagination: Essays in Revaluation.* London: Cambridge UP, 1974.

Breen, Timothy H., and Stephen Foster. "Moving to the New World: The Character of Early Massachusetts Migration." *William and Mary Quarterly* 30 (1973): 189-222.

Delbanco, Andrew. *The Puritan Ordeal.* Cambridge: Harvard UP, 1989.

Fluck, Winfried. "A More Natural Union." *A New Literary History of America.* Ed. Greil Marcus and Werner Sollors. Cambridge: Harvard UP, 2009. 292-97.

Fraser, James W. *Pedagogue for God's Kingdom: Lyman Beecher and the Second Great Awakening.* Boston: UP of America, 1985.

Friedman, Lawrence J. *Gregarious Saints: Self and Community in American Abolitionism, 1830-1870.* Cambridge: Cambridge UP, 1982.

–. *Inventors of the Promised Land.* New York: Knopf, 1975.

Geller, L.D., ed. *They Knew They Were Pilgrims: Essays in Plymouth History.* New York: Poseidon, 1971.

Gilmore, Michael T. *The Middle Way: Puritanism and Ideology in American Romantic Fiction.* New Brunswick: Rutgers UP, 1977.

Hebel, Udo. *"Those Images of Jealousie:" Identitäten und Alteritäten im puritanischen Neuengland des 17. Jahrhunderts.* Frankfurt: Lang, 1997. Mainzer Studien zur Amerikanistik 38.

Hill, Christopher. *The World Turned Upside Down: Radical Ideas During the English Revolution.* London: Temple Smith, 1973.

Johnson, Ellwood. *The Pursuit of Power: Studies in the Vocabulary of Puritanism*. New York: Lang, 1995.

Kammen, Michael. *Mystic Chords of Memory: The Transformation of Tradition in American Culture*. New York: Vintage, 1993.

–. *People of Paradox: An Inquiry Concerning the Origins of American Civilization*. New York: Knopf, 1972.

Miller, Perry, and Thomas H. Johnson, eds. *The Puritans*. 2 vols. New York: Harper, 1963.

Morgan, Edmund. *Roger Williams: The Church and the State*. New York: Harcourt, Brace and World, 1967.

–. *The Puritan Dilemma: The Story of John Winthrop*. Boston: Little, 1958.

Nissenbaum, Stephen. *The Battle for Christmas: A Cultural History of America's Most Cherished Holiday*. New York: Vintage, 1996.

Norton, Anne. *Alternative Americas: A Reading of Antebellum Political Culture*. Chicago: U of Chicago P, 1986.

Plumstead, A.W., ed. *The Wall and the Garden: Selected Massachusetts Election Sermons, 1670-1775*. Minneapolis: U of Minnesota P, 1968.

Stowe, Harriet Beecher. *The Mayflower; or, Sketches of Scenes and Characters among the Descendants of the Pilgrims*. New York: Harper, 1843.

Vaughan, Alden T. *New England Frontier: Puritans and Indians, 1620-1675*. Boston: Little, 1965.

Watkins, Owen C. *The Puritan Experience*. London: Routledge, 1972.

Young, Alexander, ed. *Chronicles of the Pilgrim Fathers of the Colony of Plymouth, 1602-1625*. New York: Da Capo, 1971.

Ziff, Larzer. *Puritanism in America: New Culture in a New World*. New York: Viking, 1973.

Chapter IV

American Independence
and the Myth of the Founding Fathers

1. WHY THE FOUNDING FATHERS?

> Who Fathered America?
> TIM LAHAYE, *FAITH OF OUR FOUNDING FATHERS*

> When in doubt, in American politics, left, right, or center, deploy the Founding Fathers.
> JILL LEPORE, *THE WHITES OF THEIR EYES*

The myth of the Founding Fathers constitutes an American master narrative which has enshrined a group of statesmen and politicians of the revolutionary and post-revolutionary period as personifications of the origin of American nationhood, republicanism, and democratic culture. More so than with the previously discussed individuals and groups, the Founding Fathers epitomize a *political* myth of origin that is phrased in a language of kinship. The term 'Fathers' suggests tradition, legitimacy, and paternity and creates an allegory of family and affiliation that affirms the union and the cohesion of the new nation. When the colonists in the revolutionary decade argued that they were no longer subjects of the British King and that they could now govern themselves (cf. Declaration of Independence), they claimed not only the maturity of the colonies and its ruling elite but also their capacity to produce progenitors in their own right. The construction of 'new world' authority and the logic of reproduction went hand in hand.

Second, in contrast to the myths previously discussed, which date back to the era of exploration and colonization, the chronology of the Founding Fathers coincides with the actual founding of the nation, beginning (roughly) with Benjamin Franklin's birth (1706) and ending with James Madison's death (1836). As a myth, founding fatherhood would only be installed firmly much later though – arguably only in the 20th century, as we will see. The Founding Fathers denote a secular myth that in its hegemonic version claims that the US evolved from the Puritans' Mayflower Compact to the political maturity of republicanism. It also constitutes a myth of a new beginning effected through a revolution. Even though this revolution has been interpreted in many different ways, it certainly carries that "specific [...] pathos of the absolutely new, of a beginning which would justify starting to count time in the year of the revolutionary event" (Arendt, *On Revolution* 29-30). In many ways, the American calendar begins with the Declaration of Independence in 1776 and the Revolutionary War, and this new beginning is commemorated each year on the Fourth of July. The myth of the Founding Fathers is also intimately connected to the first explicit articulations of an American civil religion. In his Farewell Address of 1796, George Washington refers to the bonds among the US states as 'sacred ties' to be preserved and cherished on the basis of the Constitution and thus translates the European religious idiom of the 'holy union' into a civil religious framework that would be particularly influential in constructions of the American nation (cf. Spalding and Garrity, *Sacred Union*).

Third, the myth of the Founding Fathers (like that of the Pilgrims and Puritans) focuses on a group of historical actors; it symbolizes cooperation and interdependence by toning down internal conflicts among those actors and by erasing the contingency of their plans and actions, their local and regional (rather than national) interests, and all sorts of major and minor disagreements. Even though members of this group have been heroized individually (George Washington, above all), they still form a collectivity whose military, political, intellectual, and diplomatic talents and efforts have led it to perform what has been referred to in hegemonic versions of the myth as nothing less than "a miracle" (Schachner, *Founding Fathers* vii), or "almost a miracle" (cf. Ferling's book of the same title). It also strongly personalizes the origins of American nationhood, republicanism, and democracy by presenting them as the results of the political genius, virtue, and audacity of extraordinary individuals. The myth has been affirmed by American and European writers, critics, and scholars alike, ranging from Richard Hofstadter to Clinton Rossiter and from Alexis de Tocqueville to Hannah Arendt.

Who exactly is or is not to be included among the Founding Fathers is a matter of scholarly debate, as this term has only been applied retrospectively and inconsistently. Technically, the Founding Fathers were the delegates of the Thirteen Colonies who signed the Declaration of Independence on July 4, 1776, and later the Articles of Confederation, the Constitution, and the Bill of Rights. Some of those "164 Patriots," as Jack Stanfield calls them (cf. *America's Founding Fathers*), are little known today, while others figure prominently in memorial discourses. Richard Brown looks at the "ninety-nine men" – the signers of the Declaration of Independence and the members of the Constitutional Convention (between whom exists some overlap) – and identifies the Founding Fathers as the "uppermost layer of the Revolutionary leadership" ("Founding Fathers" 465). Richard Bernstein even more inclusively describes the Founding Fathers as

those who, by word or deed, helped to found the United States as a nation and a political experiment. Thus, beyond the "seven who shaped our destiny" named by Richard B. Morris, the term includes those who sat in the Congress that declared American independence; it even includes a delegate such as John Dickinson of Pennsylvania, who opposed independence and refused to sign the Declaration but fought for the American cause in the Revolutionary War, and a polemicist such as Thomas Paine, who only briefly held political office but was an extraordinarily effective educator and mobilizer of public opinion. It also encompasses others who fought on the American side in the war, or played important roles (as framers, ratifiers, opponents, or effectuators) in the origins of the Constitution of the United States and the system of government it outlines. (*Founding Fathers* 7-8)

Gore Vidal in contrast singles out Washington, Adams, and Jefferson as the Founding Fathers of the American republic, even though he refers to Alexander Hamilton as often as to the three aforementioned figures, and quite frequently also to John Jay and James Madison (cf. *Inventing*). As Bernstein's reference to Morris's 1976 book *Seven Who Shaped Our Destiny* in the above quotation shows, the epithet 'Founding Fathers' often refers to seven individuals, namely Benjamin Franklin, George Washington, Alexander Hamilton, John Jay, Thomas Jefferson, John Adams, and James Madison; it is by and around these quite iconic figures that the Founding Fathers myth of origin has been predominantly constructed (even if there are other suggestions and additions such as Harlow Giles Unger's rather laudatory appraisal of James Monroe as *The Last Founding Father* [2009]). So whether there were three, seven, ninety-nine, or 164 founding fathers (and some accounts come up with still other numbers) is contentious, and has been subject to processes of canonization and revision time and again.

While we may refer to the American elite of the late 18th century as Founding Fathers (alternatively: framers, founders) and while the group later referred to as the Founding Fathers was already commemorated in early American popular print culture, the phrase 'Founding Fathers' as a label became a fixed expression only in the early 20th century after it was used for the first time in 1916 by Warren G. Harding in a talk at the Republican National Convention (cf. Bernstein, *Founding Fathers* 3; cf. also Lepore, *Whites*). Harding again used this phrase in his 1921 inaugural address:

> Standing in this presence, mindful of the solemnity of this occasion, feeling the emotions which no one may know until he senses the great weight of responsibility for himself, I must utter my belief in the divine inspiration of the founding fathers. Surely there must have been God's intent in the making of this new-world Republic.

Harding's speech may well be considered a founding moment of the Founding Fathers discourse even though group portraits and images of those American politicians and statesmen had, of course, been circulating much earlier.

My aim in this chapter is neither to provide a full-fledged discussion of the merits of American republicanism and constitutionalism as debated and created by the Founding Fathers, nor to present in-depth analyses of the foundational documents, nor to address each of the Founding Fathers as private and public figures, but rather to reconstruct the processes through which the myth of the Founding Fathers developed. In this chapter I will first revisit the historical moment of the American founding; second, trace the affirmative, i.e. foundational memorial culture surrounding the founders in the 19th century; third, consider American slavery in the context of the Founding Fathers myth and the role of Abraham Lincoln as a belated Founding Father, or, more specifically, as the Founding Father for African Americans; fourth, address the long-neglected role women played as 'Founding Mothers' in the metaphorical paradigm of procreation; fifth, direct our attention to the memorial practices of the 20th century, more specifically to the Founding Fathers of Mount Rushmore, a prestigious and very controversial project that, among other things, sheds light on Native American perspectives on the founders; sixth, discuss the latest revisions of the Founding Fathers myth in the context of the Tea Party movement and 'founders chic,' which seem to re-affirm the exclusivity of the Founding Fathers as, again in a civil religious vein, the American 'apostles of freedom;' seventh, and in conclusion, consider the mutable meanings of this myth in the 21st century in national as well as transnational contexts.

2. SEVEN FOUNDING FATHERS – AN OVERVIEW

Politicians are an integral part of "the mysteries of national formations."
ROBERT A. FERGUSON, *READING THE EARLY REPUBLIC*

America's founding fathers, the men who engineered a constitutional convention and drafted a new form of government for the loosely-joined states in 1787, succeeded through the force of personal authority.
JOYCE APPLEBY, *INHERITING THE REVOLUTION*

Despite never-ending debates of who should or should not be considered a member, some definitions of the Founding Fathers have remained more or less constant in American historiography; thus, in order to sketch the dominant version of the myth, let me name and very briefly introduce those who are most often included in the Founding Fathers canon: Benjamin Franklin, George Washington, Thomas Jefferson, James Madison, John Adams, John Jay, and Alexander Hamilton.

Benjamin Franklin (1706-1790) is the oldest member of the Founding Father group and still holds a central place among their ranks as a supposedly multi-talented politician, public educator, and scientist, and as a major representative of the American Enlightenment. In his autobiography, which has issued powerful self-representations of the *homo americanus* and has become a highly canonical text, Franklin fashioned himself as the "good parent" who "treats all Americans as his offspring" (Morgan, *Benjamin Franklin* 127). Due to his participation in the campaign for colonial unity, he was often referred to as "the first American" (cf. H.W. Brands's book of the same title). Benjamin Franklin's self-concocted and self-declared combination of frugality, hard work, community spirit, intellectualism, and democratic participation was highly influential in later mythmaking. He was famously portrayed by Joseph Siffred Duplessis and is commemorated on the one hundred-dollar bill. During his lifetime, the Franklin cult was already international in scope and garnered a substantial transatlantic following. More recently, James Srodes has re-affirmed his centrality by calling him the "essential founding father" (cf. *Benjamin Franklin*).

Somewhat different are the grounds on which *George Washington* (1732-1799), one of the three Virginians in this group, has been elevated as a Founding Father. Washington was commander-in-chief of the Continental Army from 1775-1783 (and as such successful against the British military); he then oversaw the writing of the Constitution in 1787, and was later unanimously voted the first President of the United States (1789-1797). During his presidency many aspects and rituals of the US government were established that are still being practiced today, among them the presidential inaugural address. Washington has often been given the epithet 'Father of his Country' and thus holds a particularly prominent place among the founders. In affirmative versions of the founders myth, he is often referred to as "a modern-day Cincinnatus" (Furstenberg, "Washington's Farewell Address" 122; cf. Wills, *Cincinnatus* 35-37, 248-9) because he allegedly did not strive for political power and planned to return to his plantation after the war for independence was won. As a Virginian, Washington was also "a staunch advocate of American expansion" (Taylor, *Writing* 176) and was among those Founding Fathers who owned slaves. Foundational Washington iconography includes the famous portraits by Charles Willson Peale and Gilbert Stuart, the biographies by John Marshall (cf. *Life*), Washington Irving (cf. *Life*), and Mason Locke Weems (cf. *History*), as well as the sculptures by Jean Antoine Houdon and Horatio Greenough. Washington's Birthday is a federal holiday celebrated on the third Monday of February. Karal Ann Marling has comprehensively documented Washingtonia in her book *George Washington Slept Here* (1988), and François Furstenberg has tried to show that the "freely given," voluntary worship of Washington effectively created a civil religious, national consensus among Americans (*In the Name* 70).

Like Washington, *Thomas Jefferson* (1743-1826) was a member of the Virginia planter elite and thus a slaveholder; he served as delegate from Virginia to the Continental Congress and later on became the third President of the United States (1801-1809). On his gravestone, Jefferson allegedly wished to be remembered for three things: as the author of the Declaration of Independence, as the author of the Virginia Statute for Religious Freedom, and as the founder of the University of Virginia. He purchased the Louisiana territory from Napoleon in 1803, thus doubling the size of the US territory, and supported the Lewis and Clarke expedition (1804-06) to explore it. The ideal of Jeffersonian democracy is often described as an agrarian vision of an imagined "empire of liberty," which is formulated in his *Notes on the State of Virginia* (query 14). The neoclassical Jefferson Memorial on the National Mall in Washington D.C. was completed in 1947, and he is depicted on the rare two-dollar bill. Because of the inconsistencies and contradictions of Jefferson's contribution to the national founding, Joseph Ellis has called him the "American Sphinx" (cf. his book of the same title). In biographical appraisals, he has been given credit for his contribution and successes by Merrill Peterson (cf. *Jefferson Image*) and others, yet he has also been cast quite negatively as "the greatest southern reactionary" (Lind, *Next American Nation* 369) and as an influence on the Ku Klux Klan (cf. O'Brien, *Long Affair*).

James Madison (1751-1836) is the third Virginian plantation owner in the ranks of the Founding Fathers. As a member of Congress (1780-3), he urged the revision of the Articles of Confederation in favor of a stronger national government. As the primary author of the Constitution, he is often called 'Father of the Constitution' and 'Father of the Bill of Rights.' In co-authorship with Alexander Hamilton and John Jay he wrote the *Federalist Papers*. Power must be divided, Madison argued, both between federal and state governments, and within the federal government (checks and balances) to protect individual rights from what he famously called "the tyranny of the majority" ("Advice"). With Jefferson, Madison formed the Republican Party. As the fourth President of the United States (1809-1817), he entered a war against Britain which is often referred to as the War of 1812 (also called 'Mr. Madison's War'); it ended inconclusively but was considered a success by Americans and is thus often also labeled the 'second war for independence.'

Although he is considered one of the key Founding Fathers, *John Adams* (1735-1826) never became the object of any large-scale national individual personality cult, which he seems to have anticipated himself:

The essence of the whole will be that Dr. Franklin's electrical Rod, smote the Earth and out sprung General Washington. That Franklin electrified him with his rod – and henceforth these two conducted all the Policy, Negotiations, Legislatures and War. These underscored lines contain the whole Fable, Plot, and Catastrophe. (qtd. in Ferguson, *Reading* 1)

Adams was a lawyer, a political theorist, and the author of "Thoughts on Government," which early on promoted "a checked, balanced, and separated form of government" (Bernstein, *Founding Fathers* 51) and suggested a bicameral legislature anchored in the Constitution. As delegate for Massachusetts to the Continental Congress he nominated George Washington as commander-in-chief and supposedly prompted Thomas Jefferson to write the Declaration of Independence. He served as Washington's vice president and later became the second President of the United States. Adams is often considered in relation to various famous family members – his wife, Abigail Adams, his son John Quincy Adams, who was the sixth President of the United States, and his great-grandson Henry Adams, a historian and novelist.

Like Franklin and Adams, *John Jay* (1745-1829) was from the North and the delegate to the First Continental Congress from New York; he also drafted New York's first state constitution. At first, Jay was, in John Stahr's view, somewhat of a "reluctant democrat" (*John Jay* xiii) and apparently always favored a strong national government. Next to being one of the authors of the *Federalist Papers*, he wrote the voluminous pamphlet *Address to the People of the State of New York*. As head of the Federalist Party, Jay became Governor of the State of New York (1795-1801), and in this function effected the abolition of slavery in this state. Jay also was involved in what is often referred to as the Jay Treaty (1794), which, for a while, secured peace between the US and Britain. In contrast to other Founding Fathers, Jay has no monument or memorial on the National Mall dedicated to him. It has been repeatedly noted that Jay's legacy has been somewhat overshadowed by that of other Founding Fathers and that he is often "forgotten and sometimes misrepresented" (Stahr, *John Jay* xiii) due in part to his less than exciting lifestyle; Stahr quips somewhat polemically: "He did not die in a duel, like Hamilton, or sleep with a slave, like Jefferson" (ibid. xiv).

Alexander Hamilton (1755/57(?)-1804) is, according to Gore Vidal, "the one true exotic" (*Inventing* 17) among the national founders. Born and raised in the West Indies, Hamilton came to North America for his education (he attended King's College, now Columbia University). He was a delegate to the Congress of the Confederation from New York, a delegate to the 1786 Annapolis Convention to revise the Articles of Confederation, and one of New York's delegates at the Philadelphia Convention that drafted the new constitution in 1787. Hamilton wrote most of the *Federalist Papers* and is often considered a nationalist who emphasized a strong central government. In his political maneuvering, Hamilton has often been cast as authoritarian, even "monarchizing," and has been considered by his political opponents as a "closet Caesar" (Knott, *Alexander Hamilton* 215). Hamilton resigned from office in 1795 but remained influential in politics; he supposedly helped Jefferson defeat Adams in the 1800 presidential elections and had a notorious rivalry with Aaron Burr, who eventually killed Hamilton in a duel. Foreign born, and, we can assume, without the proper habitus of either the Southern planters or the New England intellectuals, Hamilton has often been considered the odd one out among the inner circle of the Founding Fathers – a mere "upstart," an immigrant of illegitimate birth, even "un-American" (ibid. 7; 11). Jefferson once noted that there was a somewhat "faintly alien [...] odor of (his) character and politics" (qtd. in ibid. 230). He has been memorialized in paintings by John Trumbull and Charles Willson Peale, outdoor statues by Carl Conrads (1880), William Ordway (1893 and 1908), and Adolph A. Weinman (1941) in Manhattan as well as a statue in Chicago's Lincoln Park, and, most recently, the PBS production *Rediscovering Alexander Hamilton* (2011).

From these short biographical sketches we can already gather, first, that most sources on the founders have a tendency to affirm the Founding Fathers myth and to contribute to their mythologization (even when they are scholarly publications); and second, that the founders had pronounced differences in background and upbringing, in political vision and experience, in temperament and in career. These differences suggest that their group identity is anything but stable. Benjamin Franklin had a clear sense of the differences among them when he reminded his peers: "We must, indeed, all hang together, or most assuredly we shall all hang separately" (*Works* Vol. 1 408). Franklin's admonishment to "hang together" and to pursue the independence of the colonies as a common cause reveals what was perceived as the danger of factionalism at the time. What many of the elite of the founders indeed had in common is that they were authors – of farewell speeches, pamphlets, constitutions, declarations, bills, essays, autobiographies, letters, etc. – who engaged in at times heated debates and exchange. In the historical context, Robert Ferguson notes:

In the 1770s the Founders are competing propagandists who trade in treason for an uncertain cause and a mixed audience. Confused and divided, they face enormous problems in deciding what to say to whom and when. Neither the British nor the French but factionalism is and remains their clearest enemy. Indeed, the possibility of collapse through internal dissension continues to haunt both political considerations and the literary imagination for generations. ("'We Hold'" 4)

Based on their writings on republicanism and constitutionalism, Hannah Arendt lauds "the thoughtful and erudite political theories of the Founding Fathers" (*On Revolution* 16) and their "deep concern with forms of government" (ibid. 50). This political myth has provided a cohesive national discourse for the United States at a time when it still was characterized by strong local and regional interests. Still, the conflicts among the Founding Fathers and their different political trajectories have led Robert Levine to suggest in hindsight that there was "no single 'American ideology'" or "national narrative" at the time of the founding (*Dislocating* 67).

3. REMEMBERING THE FOUNDERS IN THE 19TH CENTURY: JOHN TRUMBULL'S PAINTING *THE DECLARATION OF INDEPENDENCE*

> [A]n Olympian gathering of wise and virtuous men who stood splendidly
> above all faction, ignored petty self-interest, and concerned themselves only
> with the freedom and well-being of their fellow-countrymen.
> STANLEY ELKINS AND ERIC MCKITRICK, "THE FOUNDING FATHERS"

> [A] staid group of white men, frozen in time.
> RICHARD B. BERNSTEIN, *THE FOUNDING FATHERS RECONSIDERED*

When discussing the iconography of the Founding Fathers, one has to turn once again to the United States Capitol in Washington D.C. and to the rotunda, where crucial scenes from US foundational mythology are exhibited. Whereas George Washington appears in the rotunda in the Trumbull painting *General George Washington Resigning His Commission* (1824) as commander-in-chief, the focus here will be on the representation of the group of founders in *The Declaration of Independence* (1818), also by Trumbull, who painted a series of four rotunda paintings. The painting titled *The Declaration of Independence* is one of the most canonical renderings of the foundational moment of the 'exceptional union' called the United States; its title does not reference the founders' names but their performative act of declaring independence as well as the document confirming that act. It is one among several iconic renderings of foundational moments in US history displayed in the rotunda today, including Howard Chandler Christy's *The Signing of the Constitution* (1940) as well as Barry Faulkner's murals *The Declaration of Independence* and *The Constitution of the United States* (1936, exhibited in the National Archives Building).

John Trumbull, who is referred to by Irma B. Jaffe as the "patriot-artist of the American Revolution" (cf. *John Trumbull*), was well acquainted with Thomas Jefferson (who he also painted), and regularly met with him in Paris in 1786. Clearly, the scene in Trumbull's *The Declaration of Independence* depicts not the July 4 meeting of the founders, but an earlier one – probably the June 28 meeting at which the committee appointed to present a draft of the document offered it up for consideration by the US Congress (cf. Cooper, *John Trumbull* 76). At the center of the composition, Jefferson submits the parchment to John Hancock, then-President of the Continental Congress and the first signer of the Declaration. Jefferson is surrounded by the other members of the drafting committee, some of which are more readily considered Founding Fathers than others: John Adams, Roger Sherman, Robert Livingston, and Benjamin Franklin. In the background, 48 congressmen are clustered in groups of varying size, most of them with their heads turned attentively to the committee. Contemporaneous criticism of this painting held that it was static and repetitive, unoriginal, lacking in refinement, and historically inaccurate. Regardless of these critical responses, the painting has forcefully impacted the way the political founding of the US has been viewed and remembered, even if the Founding Fathers discourse has shifted to include George Washington, James Madison, Alexander Hamilton, and John Jay and to exclude Sherman, Livingston, and Hancock, who are less prominent today.

Illustration 1: Signing the Declaration of Independence

John Trumbull, *The Declaration of Independence* (1818).

And for all the criticism of Trumbull's image, art scholar Irma B. Jaffe has re-minded us that there was no precedent for a painting such as the *Declaration of Independence* at the time:

[H]ow was one to show a large group of ordinary-looking men, dressed not in the glamor-ous costumes of European courts or the crimson robes of English lords, but in everyday American garb; placed in a room undistinguished by any architectural elegance; seated not on crimson and gold but plain wood Windsor chairs; leaning not on marble and ormolu tables but desks covered with dull green baize; watching not the collapse of a national leader but a committee presenting a report to the president of their body. How was one to take these elements and make a painting that would speak to a nation's people as long as that nation survived? (*John Trumbull* 108-109)

Thus, we need to take into account that Trumbull (who had previously painted mostly religious scenes and battle scenes) tried to work out an iconography (and hagiography) of American democracy by focusing on what he considered to be the central aspects of its foundation: the Founding Fathers and the foundational document in a situation of rational contemplation and ceremonial order (cf. Christadler, "Geschichte" 321).

In 1818, Trumbull's iconic painting (still on the back of the US two-dollar bill today), which was recognized to be of "enormous national interest and historical significance" (Cooper, *John Trumbull* 78), was displayed in New York in the American Academy of the Fine Arts, where some 8.000 people came to see it in only one month; it then toured Boston, Philadelphia, and Baltimore before it arrived in Washington in December 1819 and was presented to Congress. "The tour was a tremendous success" and "the high point of Trumbull's career" (ibid.).

That this image, which attempts to balance the "silence and solemnity of the scene" with the wish for a "picturesque and agreeable composition," as Trumbull himself phrased it in the catalogue of an early exhibition (qtd. in Cooper, *John Trumbull* 76), is highly stylized appears to be obvious. Many scholars have emphasized the chaotic state of affairs and the uncertainty of the outcome of any political action at the time. Furthermore, there was a lack of protocol in the constitutional sessions that often led to a less orderly conduct than is portrayed in the Trumbull painting. Here, "the impression prevails that Congress united faces the central group, intent on what is occurring" (Jaffe, *John Trumbull* 105). Asked whether to exclude those delegates from the painting who did not sign the declaration and argued harshly against it, both Jefferson and Adams advised Trumbull not to do so for reasons of accuracy and authenticity. The result is a piece of art that was supposed to start "a great national artistic tradition" (Burns and Davis, *American Art* 102).

Trumbull's iconic image is an example of affirmative 19th-century memorial culture in regard to the US foundational narrative. Even if Trumbull's painting does not visualize all the dimensions of the Founding Fathers myth, it does serve as a classic commemoration of the founding and, in many ways, is an instance of cultural nationalism in a state-dominated memory system (cf. Bodnar, *Public Memory* 251); in what follows, it will serve as a backdrop against which different representations of and perspectives on the Founding Fathers will be discussed. For now, we will take it as a point of departure for discussing questions of legitimacy and authority connected to the foundational moment so powerfully portrayed in this image.

4. EXCURSUS:
THE FOUNDING FATHERS AND THE QUESTION OF LEGITIMACY

> Government requires make-believe. Make believe that the king is divine or that he can do no wrong, make believe that the voice of the people is the voice of God. Make believe that the people *have* a voice or that the representatives of the people *are* the people. Make believe that the governors are the servants of the people. Make believe that all men are equal, or make believe that they are not.
>
> EDMUND S. MORGAN, *AMERICAN HEROES*

I began this chapter by pointing out how the myth of the Founding Fathers partly relies on their authorship of foundational documents and how these documents, in turn, have enhanced, time and again, the fame of the Founding Fathers, particularly when it comes to discussions of original intent. Thus, the Founding Fathers and the founding documents continually reinforce each other's mythical status. Today, a visit at the National Archives on the National Mall in Washington, D.C. easily demonstrates the civil religious dimension of those founding documents. Upon arrival, visitors to the National Archives Building are led through airport-like security to stand in line and slowly work their way forward to the repository in the dimly-lit Rotunda for the Charters of Freedom in which the Declaration of Independence and the Constitution are displayed. Military guards ask the tourists to line up in single-line files and to stand shoulder to shoulder with their feet touching the stairs at the bottom of the last steps one has to climb in order to enter the sacrosanct center. Visitors are also reminded that the chewing of gum is not allowed and that "proper reverence" for the place and the occasion is required. The fact that one can hardly read the documents due to the physical distance visitors have to maintain, the high security vaults, the dim, shadowy lighting, and the constant admonishment from the attending guards to continue moving along, make it clear that it is not the content of the documents one is supposed to take in, but their auratic quality – to imagine being present at the historical moment of founding among those who wrote and signed the Declaration and the Constitution. Pauline Maier has criticized this "imprisonment" of the founding documents "in massive, bronze-framed, bulletproof glass containers filled with inert helium gas" because in her view this ironically contradicts the sense of a "living" constitution that is actually quite "dead" (*American Scripture* ix, xiv). One may argue that this sacralization of beginnings camouflages the absence of authority and legitimacy at the very core of the founding enterprise.

Illustration 2: Signatures on the Declaration of Independence

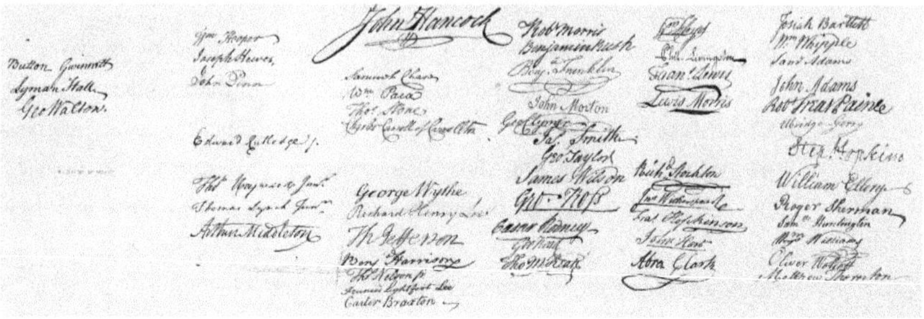

Declaration of Independence (1776).

One of the defining acts of the Founding Fathers certainly is the signing of the Declaration of Independence. It constitutes a moment that has been thoroughly mythologized in spite of (or maybe because of) its in many ways precarious status that is incommensurate with its foundational quality but also presents a particular problem in terms of legitimacy, both overlooked by Trumbull and by the presentation at the National Archives. How did the signers become the Founding Fathers of a new nation? What kind of authority did they have as signers? The various commemorations or presentifications of the signing have been critiqued by revisionists to uncover their ideological investments as well as overall biases in American historiography. The most radical critique has been brought forward by Jacques Derrida, who in his essay "Declarations of Independence" (1986) revisits the scene of the signing and asks:

[W]ho signs, and with what so-called proper name, the declarative act which founds an institution? Such an act does not come back to a constative or descriptive discourse. It performs, it accomplishes, it does what it says it does: that at least would be its intentional structure. (8)

Derrida goes on to ponder the question of authority and of representation in relation to signatures. In the historical drama of the founding, Jefferson is the "draftsman" "drawing up" the declaration (ibid). The representatives of the people of the future state are "the ultimate signers" (9). Of course, contrary to his claims Jefferson was not the sole author of the Declaration of Independence, as he took much from George Mason's Virginia Declaration of Rights and also borrowed freely from other sources (cf. Taylor, *Writing* 197); yet, Derrida follows Jefferson's own version of text production:

But this people does not exist. They do not exist as an entity, it does not exist, before this declaration, not as such. If it gives birth to itself, as free and independent subject, as possible signer, this can hold only in the act of the signature. The signature invents the signer. ("Declarations" 10)

Michael Schudson – in referring to the Constitutional Convention – calls it somewhat less formally "a complex chicken-and-egg problem" (*Good Citizen* 51): The whole event of the Declaration of Independence (along with, following Schudson, the subsequent Constitutional Conventions) thus is in the future perfect. Derrida deconstructs the notion of a foundational moment; he not only addresses the contingency of the historical moment of a/the founding, but in revisiting that moment dis-covers the absence that is gaping at its core and that remains implicit. The declaration is "performative" (not "constative") in nature: it is not the people who create the Declaration, but the Declaration that creates the people (cf. de Ville, "Sovereignty" 89). "Language [and the Signing] in this model is [thus] understood as simply 'supplementing' presence;" there is no "break in presence" but a "continuous, homogenous modification of presence in representation" (ibid. 93). Thus, declarations inevitably have a repetitive or citational structure (cf. ibid. 103). Signatures do not carry with them the legitimacy they claim; it is this slippage, this fundamental uncertainty that is covered up by and transposed into a heroic discourse of paternity, legitimacy, and founding; and it is the very "firstness" of the Founding Fathers (Bernstein, *Founding Fathers* 40) that in precluding any doubt at the same time provokes it.

In the historical context, this doubt was significant. To gain acceptance for the founding documents among the states and their delegates, i.e. the people, Edmund Morgan suggests, it was necessary "to persuade Americans to accept representation on a scale hitherto unknown" (*American Heroes* 240) – namely on a national rather than on a local or regional level. To achieve this goal, the Founding Fathers created a "new fiction" (ibid. 239) – i.e., an "American people capable of empowering an American national government" (ibid). It seemed uncertain for quite some time whether Americans would accept this new fiction arguing for a national union of the individual colonies as a matter of survival. How can a small group of individuals speak for "the people"? How could the delegates claim to be "at the point of origin?" (Schudson, *Good Citizen* 52). Numerous pamphlets as well as the *Federalist Papers* were written to produce the much needed consent among the 'American' people and to encourage them to consider themselves as such: American.

The founders themselves, I should add, were well aware at least of the *legal* problem of their actions and procedures, even though many historians of the founding and worshippers of the Founding Fathers were not. Derrida's text provides a perspective from which to explore the 'foundational momentum' of US democracy/democratic culture in terms of authority, legitimacy, and genealogy, and the problem of an absence retroactively occluded and tacitly installed as a presence. It is this sense of crisis and this struggle for legitimacy that provide a point of entry for reviewing the narratives and counter-narratives of the foundational moment of the Declaration.

To see the Founding Fathers as having little legitimacy to begin with and as being propelled by their own political, social, and economic interests rather than by abstract ideals is now part of a tradition of revisionism that includes Charles Beard's *Economic Interpretation of the Constitution* (1913) and John Franklin Jameson's *The American Revolution* (1926), in which the author considers "the American Revolution as a social movement" (8); much of Progressivist historiography until 1945 and the new social history of the 1970s and 1980s has focused on that claim with varying results (cf. Herbert Aptheker's study of slave revolts). Class, race, and gender, as we will see, have been the variables in revisionist, critical readings of the political founding by scholars such as Gary Nash (*The Forgotten Fifth*), Linda Kerber (*Women of the Republic*), and Woody Holton (*Forced Founders*), who reconsider "the radicalism of the American revolution" (cf. Wood's book of the same title) and inquire about alternative narratives of American beginnings. Even as it has been affirmed and reinvigorated time and again, the myth of the framers has come under scrutiny (particularly in the 20th century) for its omissions, falsifications, and one-sidedness, and for celebrating slavery along with the national beginning. Thus, we find very different interpretations of the historical events commemorated by Trumbull and others in counter-narratives that include individuals and groups left out of conventional representations of the founding (Black Founding Fathers, Founding Mothers, as well as forgotten founders of all kinds). We will consider some of these revisionist perspectives in the following sections.

5. CONTRADICTIONS AND OPPOSITION:
BLACK SLAVES AND BLACK PROTEST VS. THE FOUNDING FATHERS

> The simultaneous development of slavery and freedom is the central paradox of American history. [...] George Washington led Americans in battle against British oppression. Thomas Jefferson led them in declaring independence. Virginians drafted not only the Declaration, but the Constitution and its first ten amendments as well. *They were all slaveholders.*
> EDMUND S. MORGAN, *AMERICAN SLAVERY, AMERICAN FREEDOM*

> There is a painting in Philadelphia of the men who signed it. These men are relaxed; they are enjoying the activity of thinking, the luxury of it. They have the time to examine this thing called their conscience and to act on it. They need not feel compromised because they do not need to compromise. They are wonderful to look at. Some keep their hair in an unkempt style (Jefferson, Washington), and others keep their hair well groomed (Franklin). Their clothes are pressed, their shoes polished; nothing about their appearance is shameful. Can they buy as much land as they like? Can they cross the street in a manner that they would like? Can their children cleave to their breasts until death, or until the children simply grow up and leave home? The answer is yes.
> JAMAICA KINCAID, "THE LITTLE REVENGE"

Even if in the context of the American Revolution, 'slavery' often referred metaphorically to the political situation of being colonized (cf. Foner, *Story* 29), the continued existence of *real* slavery in the young republic has to be seen as one of the most glaring contradictions at the heart of the new political system created by the Founding Fathers. Despite the anti-slavery imperative of the Declaration of Independence, the founding documents not only do not abolish slavery, but the Constitution ultimately affirms it by way of the Fugitive Slave Clause and further regulations concerning the representation of the slave states in the federal government (such as the Three-Fifths Compromise), which has led Paul Finkelman in his *Slavery and the Founders* to refer to the Constitution as a "proslavery compact" (34); even if "the word 'slavery' is never mentioned in the Constitution," "its presence was felt everywhere" (ibid). Thus, the articulations of independence, freedom, and liberty in the founding documents cast a dubious light on some of the Founding Fathers and their status as slaveholders. As mentioned previously, Jefferson, Madison, and Washington were among those Founding Fathers who owned slaves, i.e. they held human beings as property, like chattel.

Edmund Morgan has analyzed the "ordeal" of Virginia regarding its racial politics (cf. *American Slavery*). To be sure, many Founding Fathers (defined in a broad sense) owned slaves, including practically all of the Virginia delegates. Whereas we have little or no information about most of these slaves, individual slaves have become modestly well-known in the context of the American Revolution: these include Jefferson's slave Sally Hemings and her brother James, both of whom accompanied Jefferson as servants to Paris (Sally was also Jefferson's mistress); Washington's slave and groom Henry/Harry Washington, who later escaped from slavery; Hercules, who was Washington's chef at the White House; and James Madison's manservant and 'factotum' Paul Jennings (cf. Dowling Taylor, *Slave* xx), who gained his freedom many years after Madison's death with the help of then-senator Daniel Webster at the age of 48 (cf. ibid. xxi). Jennings composed what became known as the first White House memoir, in which he recounts his time in the White House with the Madisons and which has recently been reprinted in Elizabeth Dowling Taylor's careful study of Jennings's life and career within the larger context of politics, abolitionism, and African American culture.

It is also recorded that Harry Washington, who was born around 1740 in Africa, after repeated attempts to escape from slavery eventually managed to do so and became part of the group of black loyalists who sided with Britain in order to gain their freedom and boarded a ship to Nova Scotia; his name (along with those of many other fugitive slaves of the Founding Fathers) is recorded in the "Book of Negroes" that lists all of those who escaped to the North. Jill Lepore records Harry Washington's path to Nova Scotia and back to Africa in 1792, where he was one of many to build a colony in Sierra Leone and thus became a founding father of sorts in his own right. By 1799, the colony was plagued by disease und unrest; after Harry Washington briefly became the leader of a group of exile rebels, he ultimately died not far from where he had been born (cf. Lepore, "Goodbye Columbus"). The histories of those black American fugitives who tried to gain their freedom at the same time yet in dramatically different ways than the American colonies have long been neglected. For many slaves, "the vaunted war for liberty was [...] a war for the perpetuation of servitude" (Schama qdt. in Davis, *America's Hidden History* 159). Cassandra Pybus and Simon Schama have traced the fugitive slaves' paths to many places, including Africa and Australia (cf. Pybus, *Epic Journeys*; Schama, *Rough Crossings*). Lepore suggests that we may want to think about those fugitives as "honorary Founding Fathers" (cf. "Goodbye Columbus").

Hercules, Washington's cook, was more than a mere provider of warm meals; historical sources refer to him as "a celebrated artiste" and "as highly accomplished a proficient in the culinary art as could be found in the United States" (Custis, *Recollections* 422). He earned money on the side by selling left-overs from his kitchen. Given the freedom to walk the city by himself, he eventually failed to return and made the black community of Philadelphia his new home. His former owner, George Washington, assumed that it would discredit him as President of the US in the North to aggressively try to recapture one of his slaves, an estimation that worked to Hercules's advantage – he was never caught.

Singularly prominent by now is the story of Sally Hemings and her family at Jefferson's Monticello estate. Recent scholarship, such as Annette Gordon-Reed's study *The Hemingses of Monticello: An American Family* (2009), as well as popular cultural productions have dealt with the relationship between Jefferson and his slave Sally Hemings; her descendants, proven to be indeed descendants of Jefferson by DNA tests in 1996, may now also be interred on the burying ground of the Jefferson family at Monticello. The fate of their children was already the topic of William Wells Brown's sentimental novel *Clotel, Or the President's Daughter* (1853), published in London and considered to be the first novel by an African American; Clotel, the protagonist, time and again escapes enslavement, yet ultimately cannot protect herself or her daughter, who becomes Clotel's former white lover's servant and commits suicide by jumping into the Potomac River near the White House, where her father had once lived. The 2012 exhibition *Slavery at Jefferson's Monticello: Paradox of Liberty*, held at the National Museum of American History (which is part of the Smithsonian Institution), detailed the lives of six slave families (among them the Hemingses) living at Monticello as slaves of Jefferson. Of all the slaves he owned, Jefferson only ever freed four: Sally Hemings, and three children he had with her.

The stories of Paul Jennings, Harry Washington, and Sally Hemings not only evidence the complicated and close relationships some of the Founding Fathers had with some of their slaves who yet did not figure in their scheme of independence and emancipation, but also what canonical historiography has ignored for a long time and what has only recently been addressed: the symbolic significance and cultural authority of the slaves' and fugitives' stories for creating newly foundational and anti-foundational narratives regarding the myth of the Founding Fathers. American fugitives like Harry Washington not only left America, they also disappeared from American historiography, as Jill Lepore notes (cf. "Goodbye Columbus"), and need to be put back into the picture. And Saidiya Hartman contends that whereas "assertions of free will, singularity, autonomy and consent necessarily obscure relations of power and domination," any "genealogy of freedom, to the contrary, discloses the intimacy of liberty, domination, and subjection" (*Scenes* 123). Thus, a genealogy of the myth of the Founding Fathers reveals the dialectic of free and unfree, of master and slave that is at the core of that myth. The mixed-race heritage explicated by Clarence E. Walker in his study *Mongrel Nation: The America Begotten by Thomas Jefferson and Sally Hemings* (2009) renders Hemings a black founding mother, and Jefferson and Hemings "founding parents" (29) of an (albeit often unacknowledged) American "mixed-race state" (17). Of course, we must not romanticize the Jefferson-Hemings union, as it took place in a context of glaring asymmetries between a master and a slave, i.e. a person considered property and used for profit (cf. e.g. Henry Wiencek's 2012 study *The Master of the Mountain: Thomas Jefferson and His Slaves*). The stories of the slaves of the Founding Fathers serve to disqualify once and for all statements such as Arthur Schlesinger's that "to deny the essentially European origins of American culture is to falsify history" ("When Ethnic" A14).

The African American revolutionary experience has often been left out of history books, from which "it would appear that the British and the Americans fought for seven years as if half a million African Americans had been magically whisked off the continent" (Nash, *Forgotten Fifth* 4). Important contributions to black revolutionary historiography were made by Herbert Aptheker, Benjamin Quarles, and, most recently, Gary Nash, who chronicles, among other things, the many "freedom suits" in which African American individuals sued successfully for their freedom from slavery in the courts of New England in the revolutionary era (cf. *Forgotten Fifth* 18), as well as the repercussions of the Haitian Revolution (1791-1804) that led to Haitian independence from the French colonial empire and to the first black republic in the Americas. In particular, Nash stresses the very different conditions that black Americans faced in the revolutionary moment:

[T]he black American people, who composed one-fifth of the population, had to begin the world anew with only the rudimentary education and often with only the scantiest necessities of life. [...] They [their emerging black leaders] could not write state constitutions or transform the political system under which white revolutionaries intended to live as an independent people. But the black founding fathers embarked on a project to accomplish what is almost always part of modern revolutionary agendas – to recast the social system. (*Forgotten Fifth* 50)

Slavery has repeatedly been referred to as the unfinished business of the American Revolution by which a system of bondage was continued that ran counter to the ideals of liberty and freedom supposedly at the core of American independence, even as a substantial number of slave-owning Southerners freed their slaves "to the extent that one of every eight black Virginians was free by the year of Washington's death, 1799" (ibid. 105). It has also to be noted that the Northern states, one after the other, legislated for the gradual emancipation of slaves. Northern abolition came into increasingly stark contrast with Southern slaveholding and plantation life. By 1810, 75% of all blacks in the North were free, and in 1840 virtually all of them had been emancipated (cf. Kolchin, *American Slavery* 81). Of course, abolition in the North did not imply racial equality, quite the contrary – free black people were subjected to racism in all matters of daily private and public life.

The paradoxes, contradictions, and (negative) dialectics in the Founding Fathers' political vision revealed by slavery and racial inequality did not remain uncommented on by those who suffered from exclusion on the basis of race. Black protest continually addressed the grievances of disenfranchised African Americans, slaves and free, in the US, and the rise of the black press in the 19th century created new platforms for these articulations. Among the early, most vocal voices of opposition is David Walker (1785-1830), the author of *David Walker's Appeal* (published in 1826), which Robert Levine considers "one of the most influential and explosive black-nationalist documents authored by an African American" (*Dislocating* 70). Walker was the son of a free black mother and an enslaved father; born in Wilmington, North Carolina, he apparently traveled quite a bit before he went to live in Boston in the 1820s. He was a member of the Methodist Church and an active abolitionist. In 1827, he became an agent and writer for the newly founded *Freedom's Journal*. In 1829, one year before his death, he published his famous *Appeal*, which expresses as much anger and despair about racial hatred in the North than about the system of slavery in the South, and articulates an open attack on American society and the founders. Many in the South wanted him dead, and in fact Walker did die shortly after the publication of his *Appeal* under somewhat mysterious circumstances.

It is particularly Thomas Jefferson whom Walker takes to task for his views on race and for what Walker sees as his feeble attempts to justify slavery and racism; the *Appeal* elaborately chides him for his writings on race, African Americans, and slavery, particularly in his *Notes on the State of Virginia*, and offers a harsh and biting critique of Jefferson's pseudo-scientific findings, abstractions, and generalizations concerning black people. Walker claims natural rights for African Americans – "nothing but the rights of man" (qtd. in Levine, *Dislocating* 66) – and repeatedly accuses slaveholders of cruelty and barbarity. Walker ends the four articles of his *Appeal* by quoting from the Declaration of

Independence's list of grievances addressed to the British King, and challenges his white readers:

Do you understand your own language? [...] Compare your own language above, extracted from your Declaration of Independence, with your cruelties and murders inflicted by your cruel and unmerciful fathers and yourselves on our fathers and on us [...]. Now, Americans! I ask you candidly, was your suffering under Great Britain, one hundredth part as cruel and tyrannical as you have rendered ours under you? (75)

Walker's strategy is twofold: on the one hand, he identifies the gap between the vision of freedom and the reality of black people in the republic in no uncertain terms; on the other hand, he uses the Declaration as a model of resistance and empowerment for African Americans by enlisting Jefferson's revolutionary and liberatory rhetoric for his own cause (cf. Levine, *Dislocating* 96f.).

Clearly, David Walker is one of the more militant voices of black opposition and nationalism, particularly by early 19th-century standards. Another rhetorical masterpiece which engages the political legacy of the Founding Fathers from the perspective of a former African American slave is Frederick Douglass's famous text "What to the Slave Is the Fourth of July?" (1841). In this text, Douglass debunks the myth of the American founding by addressing his white audience as "you" (celebrating "your National Independence" and "your political freedom") and as "fellow citizens" at the same time, which marks the paradox that he is invited to give a speech at an event commemorating American independence while at the same time being excluded from what is celebrated on the Fourth of July:

What, to the American slave, is your 4th of July? I answer: a day that reveals to him, more than all other days in the year, the gross injustice and cruelty to which he is the constant victim. To him, your celebration is a sham; your boasted liberty, an unholy license; your national greatness, swelling vanity; your sounds of rejoicing are empty and heartless; your denunciations of tyrants, brass fronted impudence; your shouts of liberty and equality, hollow mockery; your prayers and hymns, your sermons and thanksgivings, with all your religious parade, and solemnity, are, to him, mere bombast, fraud, deception, impiety, and hypocrisy – a thin veil to cover up crimes which would disgrace a nation of savages. There is not a nation on the earth guilty of practices, more shocking and bloody, than are the people of these United States, at this very hour. ("What")

The myth of American 'independence' crumbles under Douglass's harsh criticism. What indeed is there to be celebrated for African Americans on July 4, 1841? For Douglass, the patriotic rhetoric of Fourth-of-July festivities mocks

African Americans in their continued plight by "veiling" the injustices perpetrated in the name of American independence and democracy, and he describes slavery as a singularly barbaric aspect of American exceptionalism. With Douglass, we may consider the slaveholding Founding Fathers as savages who led a nation of savages into independence on the backs of enslaved blacks who cooked their meals, groomed their horses, and took care of all aspects of their physical wellbeing. The sentimentality of the festivities appalls Douglass, who considers them hollow and hypocritical.

The texts of both Walker and Douglass thus hold the founders up to the egalitarian ideals articulated in the founding documents and present a stark contrast to the image of sober reflection and cultural refinement attached to the Founding Fathers in many representations; John Trumbull for instance certainly did not represent "savages" or "barbarians" in his painting. Yet, from the perspective of African Americans, the founding of the US with its continued tolerance of and acquiescence to the system of slavery may very well be considered a barbaric act, as it consolidated some people's freedom at the expense of the freedom of others.

In many ways, the Emancipation Proclamation issued by President Abraham Lincoln on January 1, 1863, has been viewed as the founding document for African Americans. The Proclamation along with the defeat of the Confederacy and the end of the Civil War is often called a "second founding" or a "re-founding" (cf. Quigley, *Second Founding*; Kantrowitz, "Abraham Lincoln") with regard to the preservation of the national union, the abolition of slavery, and the granting of citizenship to blacks, whereby nearly four million people were freed from lifelong bondage. Quigley introduces the term "Second Founding" in his 2004 study and suggests that "[b]ack in 1787, America's first founding had produced a constitution profoundly skeptical of democracy. James Madison and his co-authors in Philadelphia left undecided fundamental questions of slavery and freedom. All that would change in the 1860s and 1870s" (*Second Founding* ix). For many scholars "the 'Second Founding' marked the beginning of constitutional reforms that aimed at establishing an interracial democracy" (Twelbeck, "New Rules" 179). Much of the discourse on these efforts at reform still crystallizes in the figure of Abraham Lincoln as a symbol of integration, even if the historical accuracy of this assessment is debatable. Lincoln has been referred to as the founding father for African Americans, particularly in the context of civil rights in the 20th century. Stephen Kantrowitz even calls him "the only, the lonely founding father of the modern United States that emerged from the ashes of the civil war" also (but not only) with regard to racial politics ("Abraham Lincoln") and also regards him as the author of a "New American Testament" (with reference to Pauline Maier's "American Scripture" metaphor for the founding documents of the 18th century; cf. her book of the same title) (ibid.).

Illustration 3: Barack Obama as Founding Father

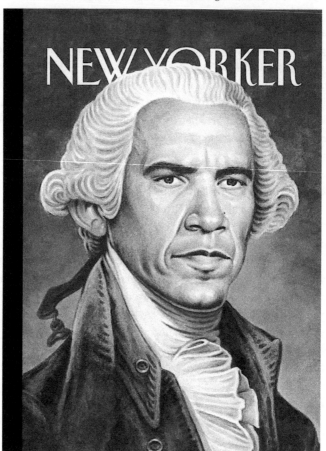

Drew Friedman, cover ill. for *The New Yorker* (Jan. 26, 2009).
© Condé Nast

Barack Obama has invoked Lincoln's presidency and his legacy for African American political culture both as presidential candidate and as elected president. Like Martin Luther King and Jesse Jackson before him, Obama takes up Lincoln's place in a collective black imagination and affirms the great role of the Thirteenth, Fourteenth, and Fifteenth Amendments to the United States Constitution passed during and after the Civil War. Obama's 2008 speech "A

More Perfect Union" has been compared to Lincoln's Cooper Union Speech of 1860 and his Gettysburg Address of 1863. Lincoln and Obama have also been compared because of their shared background in law and Illinois politics. Probing the visual iconography of the election of the first non-white American president, *The New Yorker* featured a picture of Obama on the cover dressed up like George Washington, i.e., a founding father; this anachronistic fashioning draws attention both to the perceived 'whiteness' of the US presidency and the Founding Fathers and to the fact that this whiteness may itself have become as anachronistic as a wig.

Within the national paradigm, the various contestations of the Founding Fathers myth discussed in this section call into question the narrow canon of (white) Founding Fathers by recognizing and reflecting upon the different roles of African Americans in the context of independence, revolution, and nation-building.

6. FOUNDING MOTHERS:
GENDER, NATURAL RIGHTS, AND REPUBLICAN MOTHERHOOD

> All Men Are Created Equal – But What About the Women?
> SLOGAN OF THE 20TH-CENTURY WOMEN'S MOVEMENT

> When you hear of a family with two brothers who fought heroically in the Revolutionary War, served their state in high office, and emerged as key figures in the new American nation, don't you immediately think, "They must have had a remarkable mother"?
> COKIE ROBERTS, *FOUNDING MOTHERS*

> [I]ndeed, I think you ladies are in the number of the best patriots America can boast.
> GEORGE WASHINGTON

To identify a core group of Founding Mothers may be even harder than to identify a core group of Founding Fathers. Whereas the Founding Fathers are usually considered in light of their political activism during and after the American Revolution, the concept of 'Founding Mothers' is an attempt to come to a gender-specific correlation by way of analogy that may be skewed in a historical context in which women were not considered political actors at all and in which a private-public distinction was firmly in place. This may be one of the reasons why

Mary Beth Norton's study *Founding Mothers and Fathers: Gendered Power and the Forming of American Society* goes back to colonial New England's gender discourse, in which structures of family and community were not yet clearly defined by a private-public dichotomy, and focuses on such foundational figures as Anne Hutchinson and Anne Hibbins, whose initiatives, deeds, and statements indeed have to be considered as a form of political participation, and a transgressive one at that. Closer to the revolutionary moment, white women of privilege were bound to their "small circle of domestic concerns" (Norton, *Liberty's Daughters* 3) even as they may have shared political ideas with their male contemporaries. In the historical context of the Revolution, women were mostly excluded from the political realm; New Jersey was the only state that permitted women to vote after the Revolutionary War, and this right was revoked in 1806 (cf. Collins, *America's Women* 83-4). Women only slowly (re)gained the right to vote in local elections (first and predominantly in New England by the end of the 19th century) and were only granted full suffrage with the ratification of the Nineteenth Amendment to the United States Constitution in 1920. Even though women were barred from the constitutional debates and none ever attended a single constitutional meeting, we can index their role as Founding Mothers in the revolutionary age and in the early republic and look at their contributions to the revolutionary political discourse of the time. Abigail Adams (1744-1818) for instance, the wife of John Adams, is often considered a Founding Mother in her own right. Her letters to her husband have become canonized in the *Norton Anthology of American Literature* for their political radicalism as well as for their rhetorical beauty. Most famously, in March 1776, she admonished her husband with the following words:

I long to hear that you have declared an Independency and by the way in the new Code of Laws which I suppose it will be necessary for you to make I desire you would Remember the Ladies, and be more generous and favourable to them than your ancestors. Do not put such unlimited power in the hands of the Husbands. Remember all Men would be tyrants if they could. (*Quotable Abigail Adams* 356)

Illustration 4: Portrait of Abigail Adams

Gilbert Stuart, *Abigail Smith Adams* (1815).

Abigail Adams used "Portia" as her penname (in reference to Roman senator Marcus Junius Brutus's wife), by which she implied that she was "the obscure wife of a great politician" (Gelles, *Portia* 47). Contrary to this image of submissiveness, modesty, and domesticity, Adams's writings exhibit a proto-feminist streak; she is commonly considered a radical in regard to women's rights at a time when "[m]ost founders could not imagine a society where women were free and equal, and were governed by their own consent [...]. Generally, the founders took patriarchy for granted and forgot the ladies" (Kann, *Gendering* 7). John Adams outright dismissed his wife's request: "As to your extraordinary code of laws, I cannot but laugh" (qtd. in ibid. 8).

Yet, "the ladies" – at least some of them – articulated their own views, and thus we can identify female participation in the revolutionary effort on many levels and in many forms. First of all, women were authors and publicists who wrote letters, diaries, pamphlets, and commentaries; second, they were caretakers, farmers, and entrepreneurs who through their work enabled their husbands to go off to war and to conduct politics in often far-away places; third, women were considerably involved and depended upon as fundraisers for the war effort, founded associations to develop the needed infrastructure (e.g. the Ladies Association of Philadelphia), called meetings, and gave speeches; fourth, they contributed in many other minor and major ways to the war effort, e.g. by sewing uniforms or by joining the military cross-dressed as men (cf. Roberts, *Founding Mothers* 125ff.). All of the individuals involved in these revolutionary activities may be considered Founding Mothers of some sort.

The different dimensions of women's activities for the new republic both affirm and contest the ideological constructions of women at the time of the political founding of the US, and reveal the ambivalences women had to navigate in their social roles. In fact, the term 'Founding Mothers' may be read, in view of biological essentialism, as a form of containment that links women to their reproductive function and not so much to some sort of authority in the public sphere. The five justifications for the exclusion of women from political life rooted in stereotypes of women in the late 18th century are reminiscent of the cult of True Womanhood that would dominate much of the 19th century: women's domesticity, women's dependency, women's passions, women's disorders, and women's consent to patriarchy (cf. Kann, *Gendering* 23). And yet, the new republic also created a new ideology of gender roles and gender relations. The discourse of Republican Motherhood (cf. Kerber, *Women*) has been particularly useful to grasp the contradictions of a doctrine that both consolidates and expands women's domestic realm. Linda Kerber and Mary Beth Norton have pointed out how, in the name of the republic, women were esteemed as mothers of future citizens, and how their education, as teachers of the next generation, became more relevant and more acceptable. New educational opportunities opened up, and formal schooling for women improved immensely. As Republican Mothers, women were to raise the citizens and leaders of the republic while remaining firmly confined to the domestic sphere without any direct political participation in a kind of domestic patriotism. In fact, by granting women these educational opportunities, one could claim "that women needed no further political involvement, since they already possessed the power to mold their husbands' and sons' virtuous citizenship" (Scobell, "Judith Sargent Murray" 12). In historical and feminist scholarship, the Republican Mother has alternately been considered a figure of empowerment or of confinement, and clearly remains an ambivalent role model.

At the time that this discourse is forming in the soon-to-be-independent colonies, we can find women who actively engaged in political activities despite the fact that revolutionary womanhood and Republican Motherhood often may not have been easily reconcilable. For the sake of briefly reviewing the revolutionary activism of American women, I want to turn to Judith Sargent Murray (1751-1820) and Mercy Otis Warren (1728-1814). In her essay "On the Equality of the Sexes" (1790), Judith Sargent Murray proposes the idea of a companionate marriage (such as the one she led with her second husband, John Murray), and argues for the inherent rationality of women and for women's political partici-pation. She pleads for women's education on the basis of a subversive reinter-pretation of the biblical story of Adam and Eve, in which she casts Eve as being thirsty for knowledge rather than content and complacent in the Garden of Eden (cf. Scobell, "Judith Sargent Murray" 11). Further, she criticizes women's do-mestic role within the patriarchal household, through which women "should at present be so degraded, as to be allowed no other ideas, than those which are suggested by the mechanism of a pudding, or the sewing the seams of a gar-ment" (Murray, "Equality" 7). Murray further suggests that "from the com-mencement of time to the present day, there hath been as many females, as males, who, by the *mere force of natural powers*, have merited the crown of applause; who, *thus unassisted*, have seized the wreath of fame" (ibid. 134, 135). Murray was somewhat of a public figure of her time, and was portrayed by John Singleton Copley in 1763 (who would later paint political figures such as Samuel Adams and Paul Revere) and by Gilbert Stuart, who also famously portrayed George Washington. Murray's writings, in particular her contributions to the *Massachusetts Magazine*, were very popular and in 1798 appeared in a three-volume collection titled *The Gleaner* under the pen name Constantia. The collection has been reissued in 1992.

Along with Judith Sargent Murray, Mercy Otis Warren (1728-1814), who self-identified as a "politician" (Kerber, *Women* 84), has become recognized for her contribution to American revolutionary thought, which she articulated in poems, plays, and pamphlets. Like Murray, Warren frequently adopts a satirical, farcical tone in her writings, which include very prominently female protagonists who struggle within their 'domestic economy' in much the same way the author did. Warren also sought "to live in both the world of intellect and the world of domesticity" (ibid. 256). Warren (just as Murray) did not completely reject the traditional roles of wife and mother, quite the contrary; this resulted in an ambivalence exemplified by her outstanding *History of the Rise, Progress, and Termination of the American Revolution* (1805), the first history of the American Revolution and for a long time the only female-authored one, in which Warren perhaps somewhat self-consciously and defensively pays almost no attention to women's revolutionary experiences and efforts but instead focuses on the deeds of the 'great men,' i.e. the Founding Fathers (in 1848, Elizabeth Ellet's *The Women of the American Revolution* would remedy Warren's omissions). In her lifetime, Warren was a highly esteemed publicist and, like Murray, was por-trayed by John Copley; memorials in her honor were erected in many New England towns, and a US cargo ship launched during World War II, the SS

Mercy Warren, was named after her, perhaps somewhat ironically affirming her (rhetorical) power.

It is thus in the prose and dramas by early republican women writers such as Murray and Warren as well as Eliza Foster Cushing, Susan Sedgwick, and others that we find female protagonists and characters who defy women's exclusion from politics. As women were not included in the political discourse of the founding, they "were left to invent their own political character" (ibid. 269) and fought for full citizenship by creating their own foundational discourse on the basis of a natural-rights rhetoric:

The founding fathers had used the language of natural rights to argue for the protection and preservation of their prerogatives of citizens. Women could not start from the same place. While no one was likely to deny that they were citizens, it was clear that female citizenship was not the same as male citizenship and that men and women in practice had very different civic duties and prerogatives. Woman's rights advocates, therefore, had to use Locke not to argue for the preservation of their rights but to gain their rights in the first place. (Hoffert, *When Hens Crow* 40)

American women arrived at a full-fledged feminist agenda with the Declaration of Sentiments, a document prepared for the 1848 Seneca Falls Convention, which was the first convention of a national women's movement; in contemporary newspapers, it was ridiculed as "the hen convention" of "divorced wives, childless women, and some old maids" (qtd. in Clift, *Founding Sisters* 13). More than 300 people gathered on July 19, a regular weekday, in the small town of Seneca Falls in Upstate New York. With their Declaration of Sentiments, which was rhetorically modeled after the Declaration of Independence, women's rights activists fashioned themselves as Founding Mothers:

By their act of mirroring, the signers of the Declaration of Sentiments generated a critique of the Declaration of Independence that made it impossible to read the original text in the same way ever again. The Seneca Falls Convention took aim at the Founding Fathers' ambivalence toward their own "high ideals" with the weapon Homi Bhabha describes as "the displacing gaze of the disciplined [...] that liberates marginal elements and shatters the unity of man's being through which he extends his sovereignty." (Wexler, "All Men" 352)

The small canon of revolutionary Founding Mothers that Cokie Roberts identifies for the 18th century, which includes next to Abigail Adams, Judith Sargent Murray, and Mercy Otis Warren also Deborah Read Franklin, Eliza Pinckney, and Betsy Ross, seems as exclusive and elitist as the ranks of the canonical

Founding Fathers. When considering the contributions and achievements of the women under consideration, we have to acknowledge their privileged positions in colonial and postcolonial US society. Somewhat in contrast, we have already discussed the symbolic power of Sally Hemings as a Founding Mother, and we may also note that many African American women were active in the women's movement. Most famously, Sojourner Truth delivered her speech "Ain't I a Woman" at the Ohio Women's Rights Convention in Akron in 1851, in which she demanded equality not only between whites and blacks, but specifically between white and black women.

Beyond the founding phase and the early 19th-century initiatives to organize and institutionalize women's political participation, Elizabeth Cady Stanton, Lucretia Mott, Susan B. Anthony, Isabella Hooker, and many others, all of whom Eleanor Clift refers to as "founding sisters," worked successfully toward the passage of Amendment XIX, which they considered their victory at the end of a "seventy-two year battle" (*Founding Sisters* 4). The slogan of the feminist movement of the 1960s and 1970s opening this section brings us to the question of gender in our discussion of the Founding Fathers, as they appear to be a paternal if not a patriarchal construction. A feminist revision of the myth of the Founding Fathers not only implies adding women to the canon of male founders, but also points to the Founding Fathers as a patriarchal and paternalistic invention that claimed to speak for women and that denied their natural rights, which – according to Lockean principle – should have been acknowledged. For more than one hundred years after the founding, Motherhood had trumped women's humanity in philosophical discourse; 'Founding Mothers' therefore remains a precarious concept.

7. DISPOSSESSION AND EMPIRE:
THE FOUNDING FATHERS OF MOUNT RUSHMORE (AND BEYOND)

> Why are those four men up there?
> WILLIAM ZINSSER, *AMERICAN PLACES*

Beyond discussions of who in the context of the War of Independence and the early republic is and should be commemorated as a founder of the US, there have also been discussions of which more recent historical figures should be added to the canon of the most important founders and preservers of the nation. One of the most extraordinary examples concerning these ongoing discussions is the controversial Mount Rushmore National Memorial in South Dakota. While

South Dakota's state historian Doane Robinson originally planned to boost state tourism by having figures from local history carved into the Black Hills, sculptor Gutzon Borglum gave the project a national rather than regional focus and turned it into "a colossal undertaking commemorating the idea of union" (Borglum qtd. in Bergman, "Can Patriotism" 92). Construction began in the 1920s and was concluded in 1941 by Borglum's son, aptly named Lincoln. The sculpture consists of the faces of four presidents carved into Mount Rushmore: George Washington, Thomas Jefferson, Abraham Lincoln, and Theodore Roosevelt, who signify the "founding, growing, preservation, and development" (ibid.) of the United States of America; Washington clearly symbolizes the nation's founding, Jefferson its expansion (via the Louisiana Purchase), Lincoln the 'preservation' of the Union, and Roosevelt, again, expansion of American hegemony. Thus, each in his own way contributed to the existence and expansion of the US as empire. Simon Schama refers to Mount Rushmore as a "landscape myth" (*Landscape* 15) which in sheer scale suggests the "sculptor's ambition to proclaim the continental magnitude of America as the bulwark of its democracy" (ibid. 15-16), and many other scholars have also described the monument more or less critically along those lines: as a patriotic icon and "a site of national symbolism" (Bergman, "Can Patriotism" 89), as "patriarchy fixed in stone" (cf. Boime's article of the same title), or as a "commemoration of US expansionism" and "a monument to imperialism" (Bergman, "Can Patriotism" 94). Tom Saya considers Mount Rushmore a "glittering billboard of imperial supremacy" ("Whiteness" 145). Blair and Michel regard Mount Rushmore as a "shorthand for patriotism" ("Rushmore Effect" 156) and "as constituting a dwelling place of national character, a construction of the national *ethos*" (ibid. 159). Alfred Runte sees US national parks as compensating for the absence of castles, ancient ruins, and cathedrals in the US, and Mount Rushmore seems to be a particularly grand example of this kind of compensation (cf. *National Parks*). Along those lines, William Zinsser refers to Mount Rushmore as "four pharaohs in the sky" (*American Places* 6). Many scholars note that it is the sheer size that creates the quasi-sublime character and aesthetic experience of the monument while diverting attention from its political implications:

Like Disneyland, Mount Rushmore transformed history into theatre, something only a megalomaniacal actor with boundless energy and confidence could have pulled off. [...] Mount Rushmore, like the Statue of Liberty, succeeds primarily through the impact of scale rather than through its aesthetic quality. (Boime, "Patriarchy" 149)

Illustration 5: The Mount Rushmore National Memorial

Photograph by Jim Bowen (2005).

Perhaps not surprisingly, for the entire duration of the construction (1927-41) and even after its completion, the monument has been a matter of contention. The logic of empire resides in its scope as much as in its location, as it is built on land belonging to and considered holy by the Lakota:

It seems difficult to imagine now [...] that there was not substantial negative reaction to the memorial's theme [...]. It is especially astonishing when we take into consideration the irony of location. Here was a planned monument honouring "continental expansion," sited in a territory that, by treaty, still belonged to the Lakota, and that the local Native people considered consecrated ground. (Blair and Michel, "Rushmore Effect" 169)

The Lakota referred to the Black Hills into which Borglum carved the 'White Fathers' as the 'Six Grandfathers,' and the site for them clearly had a spiritual connection. When dedicating the monument in 1927, President Calvin Coolidge wore an Indian headdress to symbolically give credit to and appease indigenous protest and resentment. In hindsight, this form of 'playing Indian' seems to mock the protesters.

The 1868 Treaty of Fort Laramie limited the land ownership of the Sioux to the Great Sioux Reservation, a region west of the Missouri River which included the Black Hills. This treaty was violated during the years of the gold rush by settlers whose presence was validated by new treaties and forced requisitions of Native land through legislation enacted by the US Congress in 1877, 1889, and 1890. The 1877 usurpation of the Black Hills is still considered by the Lakota an illegal act for which they have refused compensation in the amount of $106 million in 1980, and they continue to demand the return of the land (cf. Lazarus, *Black Hills/White Justice* 38).

Thus, from its very inception, the monument has been viewed by the Lakota and other tribes as a symbol of dispossession and oppression. Throughout its construction and again with new urgency since the 1970s, Native Americans have challenged the rightfulness, validity, and legitimacy of the memorial. To Franklin Roosevelt's calling Mount Rushmore the "shrine of democracy," Dennis Bank, leader of the American Indian Movement, has responded by calling it a "hoax of democracy" (qtd. in Fleming, "Mount Rushmore;" cf. also Bergman, "Can Patriotism" 99); the sculpted faces have also been labeled "faces of killers" and "national graffiti" desecrating Native sacred ground as well the "white faces" of "the founding terrorists" (Perrottet, "Mt. Rushmore").

The resistance to the transformation of Native sacred ground into an American civil religious monument opens up a discussion of indigenous history and its presence and role in the processes of founding. In *Forced Founders*, Woody Holton has argued that indigenous peoples, usually marginalized in canonical accounts of the American Revolution, were in fact instrumental for bringing about the events of 1775. According to Holton, the revolutionary effort itself was a strategy of the white gentry to contain the pressures of Native claims. He thus holds that the catalyst of the Revolution was Native action and sees the Founding Fathers as reacting to their pressures rather than taking a "confident step" toward independence (*Forced Founders* 164). Clearly, the revolutionary events were not beneficial for the indigenous population, as its claims and pressures were contained and repelled after the founding even as it had been involved in the process: it is still little known today (and the object of controversy) that representatives of the so-called Five Civilized Tribes were asked to attend the constitutional meetings and that the Iroquois longhouse served as a model for the framing of the US Constitution (cf. Grinde and Johansen, *Exemplar*; Starna and Hamell, "History;" Johansen, *Forgotten Founders*).

In this light, the Mount Rushmore National Memorial may appear as a celebration of the (white) American triumph over the native population of North

America. Symbolically, the monument has been the "battleground for defining the very nature of American society" (Jacobson, *Place* 23).

As controversial as the Mount Rushmore National Memorial is the initiative of eight chiefs of the Lakota tribe to counter the monument by a Crazy Horse Memorial to display Native heroism in similar fashion to Borglum's project (cf. Crazy Horse Memorial website). The work on this counter-monument, which is to even exceed the Mount Rushmore monument in size and scope, began in 1948 and is ongoing. This project has been criticized by Native representatives as imitating the megalomania of white memorial culture and as giving a distorted sense of 'Indianness.'

To this day, information and orientation films at Mount Rushmore do not acknowledge Native land rights, ongoing legal disputes, and the larger history of empire and dispossession paradigmatically revealed in the monument. Instead, the self-representations in the expository material at the visiting center have moved in a mildly revisionist manner from championing Borglum and his notion of American greatness to stressing the hardships of those workers who labored in the mountain (cf. Bergman, "Can Patriotism" 104). This more recent bottom-up perspective may present a more ambiguous view of the monument by acknowledging the plight and death toll of the workers, yet it does not pose a radical critique of the foundational character of the monument itself, as it still focuses on its genesis rather than on its legitimacy. Today, Mount Rushmore still draws millions of visitors each year. In many ways, tourism of this sort – visiting this monument or any other of the numerous Founding Fathers heritage sites – is a cultural, even civil religious practice that thrives on national myths such as that of the Founding Fathers creating tourist destinations, and thus is also a form of nationalist consumerism.

Another controversy surrounding Mount Rushmore concerns the question of its patriarchal bias. Rose Arnold Powell for example campaigned for the inclusion of women's rights activist Susan B. Anthony on Mount Rushmore: "I protest with all my being against the exclusion of a woman from the Mount Rushmore group of Great Americans. [...] Future generations will ask why she was left out of the memorial [...] if this blunder is not rectified" (qtd. in Schama, *Landscape* 385). Even though Powell spent much of her life lobbying for Anthony's inclusion in the sculpture and was able to enlist considerable public support for her cause, she was put off time and again by Borglum and others (Borglum's compromise proposal to have Anthony's head carved into the *back* of the mountain, of course, was unsatisfactory). The inclusion of Anthony as a Founding Mother would certainly have given the monument a decidedly different twist –

so radically different, in fact, that in hindsight it seems obvious that Powell's plea had no chance of success. The Mount Rushmore National Memorial thus personifies the patriarchal myth of American genesis and continued American greatness as a group of white men, although some early visitors to the monument actually thought that a female figure was included: "[Jefferson] appears younger and more feminine than the other Presidents, partly because of his wig. Many early visitors were disappointed. They said it wasn't a good likeness of Martha Washington" (Zinsser, *American Places* 11).

The Mount Rushmore National Memorial may easily be considered the most spectacular and controversial project of commemoration in the 20th century. Its popularity was further enhanced by being included in many cultural productions, for example in the climactic finale of Alfred Hitchcock's thriller *North by Northwest* (1959). But it has also frequently become the object of caricature, parody, and ridicule, for instance in the films *Mars Attacks!* (1996) and *Team America: World Police* (2004).

Way beyond Mount Rushmore, the Founding Fathers continued to figure in narratives, plays, and films throughout the 20th century. Just to mention one more example: the musical libretto *1776* (1969) by Peter Stone and Sherman Edwards is a semi-comical and quasi-campy rendering of the events leading to the Declaration of Independence. After a steady trickle of popular commemoration in the 20th century, a new popular Founding Fathers 'cult' sets in at the beginning of the 21st century: founders chic.

8. FOUNDERS CHIC AND THE CONSUMPTION OF AN AMERICAN MYTH

> What would the Founding Fathers think?
> CAROL BERKIN, *A BRILLIANT SOLUTION*

Even though a number of critics have suggested moving "beyond the founders" (cf. e.g. Pasley, Robertson, and Waldstreicher's essay collection of the same title) in the writing of (political) history, the Founding Fathers have had a comeback in the new millennium. Of course, elite revisionism does not rule out the public commemoration and commodification of national history; ideology critique and revisionist projects to some degree have always co-existed with affirmative modes and rituals of commemoration, as was shown in the preceding chapters of this book. Still, we can observe that elite and popular discourses converge in an unprecedented way in the phenomenon of founders chic, and we may wonder whether the recent popularity boost that the Founding Fathers myth has experienced has implications for and connections to the multicultural re-writings of 'new world' beginnings resulting from the canon debates and 'culture wars' of the post-civil rights era.

Against the backdrop of the above-referenced revisionism, the renewed interest in the myth of the Founding Fathers seems ill-timed and awkward. But what exactly is the so-called founders chic in relation to this renewed interest? Founders chic is often said to begin in 2001 with David McCullough's best-selling biography of John Adams and the HBO series based on it. The term itself was coined by a *Newsweek* journalist, Evan Thomas, in an article titled "Founders Chic: Live from Philadelphia" (July 9, 2001), and was subsequently picked up by scholars. It has been described as "an excessive fascination with the thoughts and actions of a small group of elite men at the expense of other political actors and social groups" (Cogliano, *Thomas Jefferson* 8). After decades of social history and multicultural and bottom-up approaches to the American Revolution, founders chic directs our attention back to the founders and to a "Founder-based beginning" (Nobles, "Historians" 141). The 'biographical bang' diagnosed by some historians at the beginning of the 21st century led to an upsurge in historical and fictional narratives about the founders: Adams, Washington, Franklin, Jefferson, and Hamilton all became the subject of new biographies often written by scholars with little (or no) scholarly inclinations. Sean Wilentz in a review for instance harshly criticizes McCullough's biography of Adams for being adulatory ("the essential goodness of John Adams is the central theme of this long book"), for its lack of intellectual rigor – implying McCullough himself may have understood little of Adams's systematic political theory –, for its focus on domestic details, and for its lurid prose ("America Made Easy"). Wilentz furthermore sees McCullough's *John Adams* as characteristic of "the current condition of popular history in America," which he views as mere "gossip about the past" that makes history appear as a kind of "valentine" (ibid.). Wilentz is not alone in his critique of what he calls "crossover professors" who in their new biographies of the founders have left some of the standards of their profession behind; others have also severely criticized Joseph Ellis for his book *Founding Brothers*, H.W. Brands for his Franklin-biography *The First American*, which was described as "light on analysis but rich in the description of settings, personalities, and action" (Nobles, "Historians" 141), and even Edmund Morgan for his *Benjamin Franklin*.

Apart from new individual and collective biographies of the Founding Fathers, we encounter a whole range of founders-chic products on the post-millennial literary market that often lack historical veracity and clearly are predominantly fictional: these include historical novels as well as books dealing with the private lives, families, love interests, and even the hobbies of the Founding Fathers. When we survey the phenomenon of founders chic, we cannot but concede that the Founding Fathers have become a best-selling brand: The founders are marketed as Founding Gardeners (cf. Andrea Wulf's book of the same title), architects (as in Hugh Howard and Roger Straus's *Houses of the Founding Fathers*), and anglers (as in Bill Mares's *Fishing with the Presidents*). For children, there is the Jr. Graphic Founding Fathers series, whereas Thomas Fleming delves into *The Intimate Lives of the Founding Fathers*, and books such as Dennis J. Pogue's *Founding Spirits: George Washington and the Beginnings of the American Whiskey Industry* show that there is hardly a thing to which the founders are not linked (more or less facetiously) in founders chic literature.

Beneath all the human interest, these products revitalize the notion of individual heroism that had already largely been dismissed in critical work on the founders. Reiterating the purposefulness and telos of the founding and reinstating the Founding Fathers as authority figures and role models at the beginning of the 21st century may be considered as an indication of some sort of crisis; founders chic, then, on one level, registers and is symptomatic of that crisis, whereas, on another level, it is an attempt to overcome that crisis.

Most of the manifestations of the founders chic phenomenon are utterly nostalgic; they pretend to return us to "an earlier era of genuine statesmen" in both private and political life (Thomas, "Founders Chic 48). Thus, they have been read as reinforcing moral standards (for instance, McCullough's comparison of John and Abigail Adams's marital union with Bill Clinton's "extramarital exploits" (Nobles, "Historians" 139). In another commentary we find references to a "post 9/11 crisis" that would endear Americans to the founders once again (ibid.). Founders chic writer Edith Gelles finds comfort in these texts herself: "Perhaps because our times are so complex and out of control it is nice to recall as well that there were dangerous times in our past, more dangerous probably, where great people were needed and rose to the occasion" (qtd. in Nobles, "Historians" 139). Gelles's wording clearly returns us to the 19th-century Bancroftian romantic-historicist approach and does away with 150 years of critical reinterpretation.

Illustration 6: Founding Father Cuisine

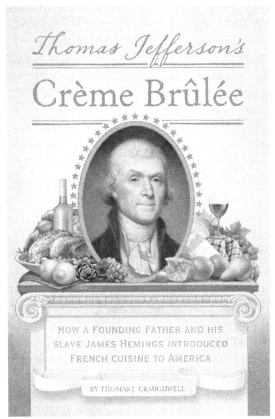

Cover of *Thomas Jefferson's Crème Brûlée* (2012) by T. Craughwell.

One realm in which the branding of the Founding Fathers has recently flourished particularly is the cookbook market, which in and of itself is one of the largest segments of the US publishing industry, with annual revenues of $780 million. Recent culinary publications on the Founding Fathers include Dave DeWitt's 2010 *The Founding Foodies: How Washington, Jefferson, and Franklin Revolutionized American Cuisine* (note the somewhat unconventional usage of 'revolution'); Pelton W. Pelton's 2004 *Baking Recipes of Our Founding Fathers*; and Thomas J. Craughwell's 2012 *Thomas Jefferson's Crème Brûlée: How a Founding Father and His Slave James Hemings Introduced French Cuisine to America*. Not only are there a plethora of new cookbooks such as these, but also reprints of older ones, for instance of the famed cookbook by Martha Washington, and of early American recipe collections which also invoke the Founding Fathers as a frame of reference. The list of examples is sheer endless.

For a closer inspection of cookbook founders chic I will exemplarily look at DeWitt's *The Founding Foodies*. This book offers historical trivia and recipes of dishes such as terrapin soup and salted cod; it falsely suggests that Benjamin Franklin was the inventor of popcorn, then referred to as parched corn (DeWitt fails to mention its indigenous source), and that we find the first description of grits and polenta in Franklin's papers. We learn about Paul Revere's rum punch and rum flip, Philadelphia pepper pot soup, and Thomas Jefferson's French connection; in the subchapter titled "America's First French Chef: The Culinary Education of the Slave James Hemings" (104-26), we learn that apparently "Jefferson was charged twelve francs a day" for Hemings's culinary education and lodging in Paris "in extravagant circumstances with a member of the French royal family" (ibid. 106). DeWitt suggests that "[i]ndeed, Hemings lived a charmed life," while Jefferson was apparently doing all the hard work (ibid.). We also learn that Jefferson was obsessed with maple sugar, imported waffle irons from Amsterdam to Virginia, introduced deep-fried potatoes (French fries) to America, and wrote recipes himself (one for ice cream, for example; cf. ibid. 123). Similarly edifying information is provided on George Washington, whose culinary culture according to DeWitt owed much to his slave Hercules, who made "presidential fruitcake" and lots of meat dishes before disappearing from sight when Washington relocated to Mount Vernon after his presidency. Even though many of the recipes in DeWitt's book are in fact taken from Mary Randolph's 1824 cookbook *The Virginia Housewife* (reissued in 1984 by Karen Hess), the alleged link to the Founding Fathers is always affirmed. And the author also distances himself from the so-called "fakelore" (cf. Smith, "False Memories") by which the heritage of certain dishes is falsely attributed – after all, Jefferson did *not* introduce vanilla and macaroni to the US (cf. DeWitt, *Founding Foodies* 121).

The Founding Foodies is mostly anecdotal and provides a mixed bag of insights into the Founding Fathers' culinary inventiveness, yet the author opens his collection on a pseudo-conceptual note which is worth quoting at length:

In their never-ending attempts to fully understand American history, historians began using the phrase "Founding Fathers" to designate the men and women, mostly early politicians, who founded the United States or were influential in its founding. At first, the phrase referred to three superstar fathers, George Washington, Thomas Jefferson, and John Adams. That list was later expanded to include James Madison, Alexander Hamilton, Benjamin Franklin, and John Jay. Eventually, the list of the Founding Fathers was expand-

ed further to include many of the lesser-known signers of the Declaration of Independence, members of the Constitutional Convention, and others.

Given the number of Founding Fathers, it should not come as any surprise that some of
them had a very profound interest in food and drink. Some might think that by calling
these people, some of the most famous and talented people in American history, foodies I
am trivializing them. I don't think so. To the contrary, I am elevating them into a new dimension of humanity, one that transcends politics. Today, the Founding Fathers would be
superstars of sustainable farming and ranching, exotic imported foods, brewing, distilling,
and wine appreciation. In other words, they would be foodies. (ibid. xv)

Never mind that it was not historians who coined the term 'Founding Fathers,'
that the women somehow disappear after the first lines of this passage, and that it
contains several non sequiturs; the relevant part comes at the end, where DeWitt
elevates the Founding Fathers in a way that transcends politics. How to transcend politics, one may ask, but DeWitt's logic can be succinctly analyzed with
reference to Lauren Berlant's critical assessment of the sentimental nation: sentimentalism of the kind we see at work here "develops *within political thought* [or
within what should be primarily a political discourse] a discourse of ethics that,
paradoxically, denigrates the political and claims superiority to it" (*Female
Complaint* 34); at the same time it camouflages "the fundamental terms that
organize power," which remain unaddressed (ibid). The function of the cookbook in the discourse of founders chic more clearly than many other texts and
practices turns the political into the domestic and the revolutionary kitchen into a
"post-public public sphere" (ibid. 223) with a "displacement of politics to the
realm of feeling" (ibid. xii). DeWitt and others enact a culinary white reconstruction on the backs of blacks and other nonwhites in an essentially nostalgic mode
and thus re-install an image of a predominantly white nation. The "sentimental
cultural politics" (Berlant, *Queen* 4) of DeWitt in particular, and of founders chic
in general, separate the political from politics. Berlant argues that the political
public sphere thus has become an intimate public sphere which produces a "new
nostalgia-based fantasy nation" (ibid. 5), and it is in this sense that we may talk
about the consumption of American democracy.

What is striking about this "fantasy nation" envisioned in *The Founding
Foodies* and similar founders chic publications in which the Founding Fathers
once more reign supreme, is that (1) it re-inscribes social hierarchies; (2) it re-
erects and legitimates discursive systems of oppression and exclusion (it
definitely flirts with past injustices such as slavery, etc.); (3) it re-establishes a
European genealogy of American national culture by way of French cuisine (obviously the black slave would not be able to cook if he had not been trained to do

so in France); (4) it romanticizes consumption and obscures the conditions of production, i.e. slave labor – after all, it is slaves who put into practice all of the glorious ideas about composting, fermenting, wine-growing etc.; (5) it (re)sacralizes the Founding Fathers by giving them celebrity status – visiting Monticello or Mount Vernon in person or through the consumption of founders chic products may qualify as a kind of civil religious 'pilgrimage' as much as visiting Washington, D.C.; (6) it operates in a discourse of 'cultivating' and 'civilizing' the 'new world' palate, adding culinary refinement to statesmanship and republicanism; (7) it condones an "utterly privatized model of citizenship and the good life" (Giroux, *Public Spheres* 56) with the Founding Fathers as exemplary entrepreneurs and private agents in a public sphere (in fact, they would have thrived in any neoliberal market economy); and (8) it re-organizes a national memorial culture and re-installs the myth of a 'domestic' nation in a double sense (cf. Berlant, *Queen*). At the same time, the sentimental discourse of the "intimate public sphere" in which we find "nostalgic images of a normal, familial America" (ibid. 3-4) infantilizes and trivializes this displacement of political critique: from the perspective of a nostalgic cookbook, the Founding Fathers hardly seem controversial. Who would argue over old recipes? In getting into the kitchen with Jefferson, Washington, and Franklin, we follow and condone their immunization from political critique as well as the immunization of those who so often use them for their own political ends.

Founders chic thus clearly is part of a broader marketing of nostalgic images of a "normal," "familial" America: "Sentimental politics are being performed whenever putatively suprapolitical affects or affect-saturated institutions (like the nation and the family) are proposed as universal solutions to structural [...] antagonism" (Berlant, *Female Complaint* 294). This is also reflected in the way that the Founding Fathers mythology is used for instance by the activists and advocates of the Tea Party movement.

9. CONCLUSION: THE FOUNDING FATHERS AS NATIONAL FANTASY IN TRANSNATIONAL CONTEXTS

> When I first saw a painting of George Washington framed by a toilet seat, hanging on the walls of a local junior college, I realized that the history revisionists had gone too far.
> TIM LAHAYE, *FAITH OF OUR FOUNDING FATHERS*

> At a resonant 1,776 feet tall, the Freedom Tower — in my master plan, second in importance only to the 9/11 memorial itself — will rise above its predecessors, reasserting the preeminence of freedom and beauty, restoring the spiritual peak to the city and proclaiming America's resilience even in the face of profound danger, of our optimism even in the aftermath of tragedy. Life, victorious.
> DANIEL LIBESKIND, "GROUND ZERO MASTER PLAN"

The Liberty Tower at Ground Zero symbolizes a national fantasy that refers, by way of its height of 1,776 feet, to the year of the Declaration of Independence. This new architectural symbol also reinforces and re-invigorates the myth of the founding and the Founding Fathers. Particularly in the wake of 9/11, we can observe a political climate in which many Americans were protective of the Founding Fathers again. Thus, we may relate the comeback of the founders in founders chic to other political developments and movements which affirm their role for the national founding; as Jill Lepore has pointed out, the new historical revisionism initiated by the Tea Party movement and religious groups alike presents a confused discursive conglomerate that is "conflating originalism, evangelicalism, and heritage tourism" and which "amounts to fundamentalism" (*Whites* 16). In this fundamentalist discourse, the Founding Fathers serve as the historical authority for neoconservative and evangelical agendas; this imagined alliance highlights the activists' lack of historical knowledge or their willingness to purposefully misrepresent history to further their own ends. It is well-known that, in an interview with Glenn Beck on January 13, 2010, former Governor of Alaska Sarah Palin (R) invoked the "sincerity of the Founding Fathers" and yet was at first unable to name even one of them (cf. "Sarah Palin"). Similarly, Congresswoman Michele Bachmann (R-Min) falsely claimed that "the very founders that wrote those [founding] documents worked tirelessly until slavery was no more in the United States [...]," and went on to say that John Quincy Adams "would not rest until slavery was extinguished in the country" (Amira, "Michele Bachmann; cf. McCarthy, "John Quincy Adams"). Adams, who died in 1848, did rest before slavery was abolished. This skewed and counterfactual version of history shows that the Founding Fathers are used here as a projection screen for the present which enables a fantasy of the nation through a retrospectively imagined original, primary moment.

The Tea Party movement has been considered by many commentators and scholars to advocate an extremist political agenda based on anti-elitism and anti-statism, even as it lacks a consistent common ideology (cf. Greven, "Die Tea-Party-Bewegung" 147). Thomas Greven refers to a "tea party-brand" (ibid. 145) that includes 'Don't tread on me' merchandize and a rhetoric of 're-founding' and 'taking back' the country that seems as regressively nostalgic as founders chic memorabilia.

In the context of evangelical popular culture, Tim LaHaye, co-author of the phenomenally successful *Left Behind* series of books, is one of the most prom-inent evangelical Christian ministers and speakers to have contributed to the debates around the Founding Fathers. In *Faith of Our Founding Fathers*, he champions the evangelical origins of the US, which he is able to do only by offering an alternative set of Founding Fathers: James Madison, Robert Morris, Roger Sherman, Alexander Hamilton, and George Mason. Argumentatively, LaHaye employs a revisionist rhetoric when he refers to the "untold story" of the Christian origin of the country and to the "debt owed to the Founding Fathers;" he bemoans "the distortion of history in the state-approved textbooks" and "the total absence of the Christian religion in them," whereby in his view "a whole generation of schoolchildren is robbed of its country's religious heritage" (1). Much can be said about LaHaye's claim regarding the foundational quality of Christianity as opposed to secularism (he hardly ever takes into account the American Enlightenment). According to him, "secular humanists" in the US have produced a "moral holocaust" (note the metaphor) by blindly attacking "Christianity and its moral values" (ibid. 4) and by engaging in a "deliberate rape of history" (ibid. 5). LaHaye suggests in his culture war on US-American paternity that "evangelical Protestants who founded this nation" (qtd. in Lepore, *Whites* 121) should be reinstalled whereas both Jefferson (who "had nothing to do with the founding of our nation" [ibid]) and Franklin (who in LaHaye's view was not a Christian) should be discounted. LaHaye's hagiographic fashioning of the Christian Founding Fathers explains historical events through individual achievement and character rather than through systemic forces and contingency (cf. ibid. 36). In many ways, LaHaye offers a counter-narrative to secularization and the Enlightenment by (mis)reading a civil religious discourse as religious (more specifically, Christian) and thus by projecting religion back onto the newly emergent revolutionary civil religion.

The so-called "teavangelicals," as David Brody calls them appreciatively (cf. his book of the same title), even as they present two distinct groups (i.e., Tea Party movement activists and evangelical Christians), can be considered aligned on a variety of issues. For one thing, both converge in a new embrace of the myth of the Founding Fathers under political and religious considerations, re-spectively, and share a unilateral, patriotic discourse that identifies outside, 'foreign' influences and US international involvement as harmful to the US. These anxieties come to the fore in discussions of Obama's birth certificate (revolving around the question of whether he is a foreigner, i.e. 'un-American'), in blaming foreign (European) influence for the secularization of the US, as well as in post-9/11 discussions of the 'terrorist threat.' LaHaye is forcefully anti-French and anti-European in general, complaining in his book that at the revolu-tionary moment, 'old world' forces already attempted to secularize and corrupt the American Founding Fathers. Thus, the discussion of the Founding Fathers continues to be deeply polarized, and the founders' original intent is time and again debated in political arguments that are still often quite divisive. In order to describe the social, cultural, and political chasm within American society that these debates seem to reveal, John Sperling and Suzanne Wiggins Helburn have used the framework of a conservative "retro America" vs. a liberal "metro America" (cf. *Great Divide*), and Stanley B. Greenberg similarly identifies "two Americas" (cf. his 2004 book) divided along the lines of religion and politics.

In stark contrast to the reinvigoration of the Founding Fathers myth as a national fantasy, we find much historical evidence corroborating the transnational di-mension of the political experiences of men like Franklin, Jefferson, Adams, Jay, Hamilton, and Madison. From a transnational perspective, the Founding Fathers, of course, were retrospectively contained in a national paradigm that was non-existent at the time of the American Revolution and has more recently become an anachronism. A number of recent studies have addressed this conundrum: Gordon S. Wood in his *The Americanization of Benjamin Franklin* (2004) re-opens a discussion of the founders outside the nationalist paradigm by looking at Franklin as "the principal American abroad" (*Americanization* 201), who en-joyed life in France. At a time when "[c]ultural nationalism had not yet devel-oped enough to disrupt the cosmopolitan republic of letters that made learned men like Franklin 'citizens of the world'" (Bender, *Nation* 89), many of the Founding Fathers would have defined themselves as part of a broader inter-national culture. Similarly, Francis Cogliano has pointed out that for Jefferson "the spread of liberty was, and must be, an international movement" (*Thomas Jefferson* 264) that may have begun in the Thirteen Colonies yet should expand to other parts of the world. It was a "global republicanism" (ibid. 265) that he had in mind: reading him as an American statesman misses "the international outlook at the heart of Jefferson's beliefs" (ibid). Similarly reading back a cosmopolitan internationalism into the founding phase of the republic, Thomas Bender has elaborated on the many ways in which the American past is not "a linear story of progress or a self-contained history" (*Nation* 60). He considers the American Revolution as, among other things, part of "a global war between European great powers" (France and England more specifically) in which the colonies in North America were caught up and in which they constituted one actor among many (ibid. 61). Any account of the American Revolution should thus also consider the French Revolution as well as the Haitian Revolution, which for Bender clearly was the most radical in the Americas in the 18th century. Regarding Jefferson, Adams, and Franklin, Gore Vidal notes that "[i]t is a triple irony that three of the principal inventors of the United States should have been abroad in Europe during the Constitution-making period" (*Inventing* 62). Heroizing the Founding Fathers has always been an attempt at keeping contingency at bay, as "[t]here is very little about the events of 1776 that, on close examination, suggests inevitability" (ibid. 33). And Thomas Bender further notes that

[t]he new nation was independent, but very limited in its freedom of action. Far from being isolated, it was perhaps more deeply entangled in world affairs, more clearly a participant in histories larger than itself, than at any other time in its history. (*Nation* 103)

Thus, scrutinizing the complexity of the Founding Fathers myth may necessitate looking beyond the national context. The American Revolution also bespeaks a *transnational* moment, and recent scholarship has begun to reconstruct just that.

While the Founding Fathers as a collective myth have come into being relatively late, their symbolic capital in American public life and political culture today clearly exceeds that of Columbus, Pocahontas, and perhaps even that of the Pilgrims and Puritans; in fact, the status of the Founding Fathers is quite elevated among the foundational mythological personnel. It is therefore important to note the various processes in which the making, remaking and (partial) unmaking of this myth has unfolded.

10. STUDY QUESTIONS

1. Define the 'Founding Fathers' 1) in a narrow and 2) in a broader sense.
2. In retrospect, what unites the Founding Fathers as a group and what differences can we discern between them in the historical context?
3. Discuss the notion of a "second founding" of the US. What does it refer to?
4. Give an interpretation of the *New Yorker* cover showing Barack Obama as a Founding Father.
5. Crispus Attuck, Richard Allen, Barzillai Lew, Peter Salem, Prince Whipple, Jenny Slew, Mum Bett, Harry Hosier, Daniel Coker, and James Forten have been to varying degrees referred to as Black Founding Fathers and Mothers. Research and discuss their stories!
6. Eliza Pinckney, Deborah Sampson, Lydia Darragh, Emily Geiger, Sybil Luddington, Catherine Littlefield Greene, Margaret Beekman Livingston, and Annis Boudinot Stockton have been to varying degrees referred to as Founding Mothers. Research and discuss their stories!
7. In her book *On Revolution*, Hannah Arendt argues that "[n]o revolution has ever taken place in America" (17). Daniel Boorstin in *The Genius of American Politics* (1953) refers to the historical event as a "revolution without dogma." Discuss!
8. When Horatio Greenough's statue of George Washington (modelled after a statue of Zeus) was displayed in the rotunda of the US Capitol in 1841, responses were quite mixed. Discuss the role of Classicism in the depiction and self-fashioning of the Founding Fathers.
9. Watch and discuss the HBO miniseries *John Adams*. How are the Founding Fathers represented?
10. What does a transnational perspective on the Founding Fathers entail and why is it useful?

11. BIBLIOGRAPHY

Works Cited

Adams, Abigail. *The Quotable Abigail Adams*. Ed. John P. Kaminski. Cambridge: Harvard UP, 2009.

Adams, John. "Thoughts on Government." 1776. *Papers* 4. Ed. Robert J. Taylor, et al. Cambridge: Harvard UP, 1977. 86-93.

Amira, Dan. "Michele Bachmann Stands By Ridiculous Thing She Said about Slavery." *New York* 28 June 2011. http://nymag.com/daily/intelligencer/2011/06/michele_bachmann_stands_by_rid.html. 30 Sept. 2013.

Appleby, Joyce. *Inheriting the Revolution: The First Generation of Americans*. Cambridge: Harvard UP, 1991.

Aptheker, Herbert. *American Negro Slave Revolts*. New York: Columbia UP, 1943.

Arendt, Hannah. *On Revolution*. London: Faber, 1963.

Beard, Charles. *An Economic Interpretation of the Constitution of the United States*. 1913. New York: Macmillan, 1962.

Bender, Thomas. *A Nation among Nations: America's Place in World History*. New York: Hill, 2006.

Bergman, Teresa. "Can Patriotism Be Carved in Stone? A Critical Analysis of Mt. Rushmore's Orientation Films." *Rhetoric and Public Affairs* 11.1 (2008): 89-112.

Berkin, Carol. *A Brilliant Solution: Inventing the American Constitution*. Orlando: Harvest, 2002.

Berlant, Lauren. *The Female Complaint: The Unfinished Business of Sentimentality in American Culture*. Durham: Duke UP, 2008.

–. *The Queen of America Goes to Washington City: Essays on Sex and Citizenship*. Durham: Duke UP, 1997.

Bernstein, Richard B. *The Founding Fathers Reconsidered*. Oxford: Oxford UP, 2009.

Blair, Carole, and Neil Michel. "The Rushmore Effect: Ethos and National Collective Identity." *The Ethos of Rhetoric*. Ed. Michael J. Hyde. Columbia: U of South Carolina P, 2004. 156-96.

Bodnar, John E. *Public Memory, Commemoration, and Patriotism in the Twentieth Century*. Princeton: Princeton UP, 1994.

Boime, Alfred. "Patriarchy Fixed in Stone." *American Art* 5 (1991): 142-60.

Boorstin, Daniel J. *The Genius of American Politics*. Chicago: U of Chicago P, 1953.

Brands, H.W. *The First American: The Life and Times of Benjamin Franklin.* New York: Anchor, 2002.

Brody, David. *The Teavangelicals: The Inside Story of How the Evangelicals and the Tea Party Are Taking Back America.* Grand Rapids: Zondervan, 2012.

Brown, Richard D. "The Founding Fathers of 1776 and 1787: A Collective View." *William and Mary Quarterly.* Third Series. 33.3 (1976): 465-80.

Brown, William Wells. *Clotel, Or the President's Daughter.* London: Partridge and Oakley, 1853.

Burns, Sarah, and John Davis. *American Art to 1900: A Documentary History.* Berkeley: U of California P, 2009.

Christadler, Martin. "Geschichte in der amerikanischen Malerei zwischen Revolution und Bürgerkrieg." *Metaphors of America: Metaphern der Neuen Welt. Selected Essays by Martin Christadler.* Ed. Olaf Hansen, et al. Trieste: Edizioni Parnaso, 2003. 319-25.

Clift, Eleanor. *Founding Sisters and the Nineteenth Amendment.* New York: Wiley, 2003.

Cogliano, Francis D. *Thomas Jefferson: Reputation and Legacy.* Charlottesville: U of Virginia P, 2006.

Collins, Gail. *America's Women.* New York: Harper, 2003.

Cooper, Helen A. *John Trumbull: The Hand and Spirit of a Painter.* New Haven: Yale U Art Gallery and Yale UP, 1982.

Craughwell, Thomas J. *Thomas Jefferson's Creme Brûlée: How a Founding Father and His Slave James Hemings Introduced French Cuisine to America.* Philadelphia: Quirk, 2012.

Crazy Horse Memorial. http://crazyhorsememorial.org. 27 Oct. 2013.

Custis, G.W.P. *Recollections and Private Memoirs of Washington.* Philadelphia: J.W. Bradley, 1861.

Davis, Kenneth C. *America's Hidden History: Untold Tales of the First Pilgrims, Fighting Women, and Forgotten Founders Who Shaped a Nation.* New York: Smithsonian, 2008.

Declaration of Independence. *Library of Congress.* http://www.loc.gov/rr/program/bib/ourdocs/DeclarInd.html. 30 Aug. 2013.

Declaration of Sentiments. *The Heath Anthology of American Literature.* 3rd ed. Vol. 1. Ed. Paul Lauter, et al. Boston: Houghton, 1998. 2035-37.

Derrida, Jacques. "Declarations of Independence." *New Political Science* 7.1 (1986): 7-15.

DeWitt, Dave. *The Founding Foodies: How Washington, Jefferson, and Franklin Revolutionized American Cuisine.* Naperville: Sourcebooks, 2010.

de Ville, Jacques. "Sovereignty Without Sovereignty: Derrida's Declarations of Independence." *Law and Critique* 19 (2008): 87-114.

Douglass, Frederick. "What to the Slave Is the Fourth of July?" *Frederick Douglass: Selected Speeches and Writings*. Ed. Philip S. Foner. Chicago: Lawrence Hill, 1999. 188-206. *Teaching American History*. http://teaching americanhistory.org/library/document/what-to-the-slave-is-the-fourth-of-july/. 30 Sept. 2013.

Dowling Taylor, Elizabeth. *A Slave in the White House: Paul Jennings and the Madisons*. New York: Palgrave MacMillan, 2012.

Elkins, Stanley, and Eric McKitrick. "The Founding Fathers: Young Men of the Revolution." *Political Science Quarterly* 76.2 (1961): 181-216.

Ellet, Elizabeth. *The Women of the American Revolution*. 3 vols. New York: Baker and Scribner, 1848-50.

Ellis, Joseph. *American Sphinx: The Character of Thomas Jefferson*. New York: Vintage, 1998.

–. *Founding Brothers: The Revolutionary Generation*. New York: Vintage, 2002.

Ferguson, Robert A. *Reading the Early Republic*. Cambridge: Harvard UP, 2004.

–. "'We Hold These Truths:' Strategies of Control in the Literature of the Founders." *Reconstructing American Literary History*. Ed. Sacvan Berco-vitch. Cambridge: Harvard UP, 1986. 1-28.

Ferling, John. *Almost a Miracle: The American Victory in the War of Indepen-dence*. Oxford: Oxford UP, 2007.

Finkelman, Paul. *Slavery and the Founders: Race and Liberty in the Age of Jefferson*. 2nd ed. Armonk: M.E. Sharpe, 2001.

Fleming, Annette. "Mount Rushmore, the Fulfillment of a Dream?" *TIE – Technology & Innovation in Education*. http://moh.tie.net/content/docs/MountRushmore.pdf. 30 Sept. 2013.

Fleming, Thomas. *The Intimate Lives of the Founding Fathers*. New York: Smithsonian, 2009.

Foner, Eric. *The Story of American Freedom*. New York: Norton, 1998.

Franklin, Benjamin. *The Works*. Vol. 1. Ed. Jared Sparks. Boston: Tappan and Whittemore, 1840.

Furstenberg, François. *In the Name of the Father: Washington's Legacy, Sla-very, and the Making of a Nation*. New York: Penguin, 2006.

–. "Washington's Farewell Address." Marcus and Sollors, *New Literary History* 122-26.

Gelles, Edith B. *Portia: The World of Abigail Adams*. Bloomington: Indiana UP, 1992.

Giroux, Henry. *Public Spheres, Private Lives: Beyond the Culture of Cynicism.* New York: Rowman and Littlefield, 2003.

Gordon-Reed, Annette. *The Hemingses of Monticello: An American Family.* New York: Norton, 2008.

Greenberg, Stanley B. *The Two Americas: Our Current Political Deadlock and How to Break It.* New York: Thomas Dunne, 2004.

Greven, Thomas. "Die Tea-Party-Bewegung und die Krise der amerikanischen Demokratie." *American Dream? Eine Weltmacht in der Krise.* Ed. Andreas Etges and Winfried Fluck. Frankfurt/Main: Campus, 2011. 137-57.

Grinde, Donald A., Jr., and Bruce E. Johansen. *Exemplar of Liberty: Native America and the Evolution of Democracy.* Los Angeles: American Indian Studies Center, 1991.

Hamilton, Alexander, James Madison, and John Jay. *The Federalist Papers.* 1788. Ed. Lawrence Goldman. Oxford: Oxford UP, 2008.

Harding, Warren G. "Inaugural Address, March 4, 1921." *AMDOCS.* http://www.vlib.us/amdocs/texts/34hard1.htm. 30 Sept. 2013.

Hartman, Saidiya V. *Scenes of Subjection: Terror, Slavery, and Self-Making in Nineteenth Century America.* Oxford: Oxford UP, 1997.

Hoffert, Sylvia D. *When Hens Crow: The Women's Rights Movement in Antebellum America.* Bloomington: Indiana UP, 1995.

Holton, Woody. *Forced Founders: Indians, Debtors, Slaves, and the Making of the American Revolution in Colonial Virginia.* Chapel Hill: U of North Carolina P, 1999.

Howard, Hugh, and Roger Straus. *Houses of the Founding Fathers.* New York: Artisan, 2007.

Irving, Washington. *The Life of George Washington.* 5 vols. New York: Putnam, 1856-59.

Jacobson, David. *Place and Belonging in America.* Baltimore: Johns Hopkins UP, 2001.

Jaffe, Irma B. *John Trumbull: Patriot-Artist of the American Revolution.* Boston: New York Graphic Society, 1975.

Jameson, John Franklin. *The American Revolution Considered as a Social Movement.* 1926. Princeton: Princeton UP, 1967.

Jay, John. "Address to the People of New York, Urging the Adoption of the New Federal Constitution." *The Correspondence and Public Papers of John Jay.* Ed. Henry P. Johnston. Vol. 3. New York: G.P. Putnam's Sons, 1890-93. 294-320.

Jefferson, Thomas. "Notes on the State of Virginia." 1787. *The Selected Writings of Thomas Jefferson.* Ed. Wayne Franklin. New York: Norton, 2010. 24-177.

Johansen, Bruce E. *Forgotten Founders: How the American Indian Helped Shape Democracy*. Cambridge: Harvard Common, 1987.

John Adams. Dir. Tom Hopper. HBO, 2008.

Kann, Mark E. *The Gendering of American Politics: Founding Mothers, Founding Fathers, and Political Patriarchy*. Westport: Praeger, 1999.

Kantrowitz, Stephen. "Abraham Lincoln and the Second Founding of the American Nation." Public Lecture. *WPT*. http://video.wpt.org/video/1538548487/. 30 Sept. 2013.

Kerber, Linda K. *Women of the Republic: Intellect and Ideology in Revolutionary America*. Chapel Hill: U of North Carolina P, 1980.

Kincaid, Jamaica. "The Little Revenge from the Periphery." *Transition* 73 (1997): 68-73.

Knott, Stephen F. *Alexander Hamilton and the Persistence of Myth*. Lawrence: UP of Kansas, 2002.

Kolchin, Peter. *American Slavery: 1619-1877*. New York: Farrar, 1994.

LaHaye, Tim. *Faith of Our Founding Fathers*. Brentwood: Wolgemuth and Hyatt, 1987.

Lazarus, Edward. *Black Hills/White Justice: The Sioux Nation versus the United States, 1775 to the Present*. New York: Harper, 1991.

Lepore, Jill. "Goodbye, Columbus: When America Won Its Independence, What Became of the Slaves Who Fled for Theirs?" *The New Yorker* 8 May 2006. Online ed. http://newyorker.com/archive/2006/05/08/060508crat_atlarge. 20 Aug. 2013.

–. *The Whites of Their Eyes: The Tea Party's Revolution and the Battle Over American History*. Princeton: Princeton UP, 2010.

Levine, Robert. *Dislocating Race and Nation: Episodes in Nineteenth-Century American Literary Nationalism*. Chapel Hill: U of North Carolina P, 2008.

Libeskind, Daniel. "Ground Zero Master Plan." 2003. *Studio Daniel Libeskind* http://daniel-libeskind.com/projects/ground-zero-master-plan. 30 Sept. 2013.

Lind, Michael. *The Next American Nation: The New Nationalism and the Fourth American Revolution*. New York: Free, 1995.

Madison, James. "Advice to My Country." 1836. *Constitution Society*. http://www.constitution.org/jm/18340000_advice.txt. 30 Sept. 2013.

Maier, Pauline. *American Scripture: Making the Declaration of Independence*. New York: Vintage, 1997.

Marcus, Greil, and Werner Sollors, eds. *New Literary History of America*. Cambridge: Harvard UP, 2009.

Mares, Bill. *Fishing with the Presidents: An Anecdotal History*. Mechanicsburg: Stackpole, 1999.

Marling, Karal Ann. *George Washington Slept Here: Colonial Revivals and American Culture, 1876-1986*. Cambridge: Harvard UP, 1988.

Mars Attacks! Dir. Tim Burton. Warner Bros., 1996.

Marshall, John. *The Life of George Washington*. New York: Derby and Jackson, 1857.

McCarthy, Kate. "John Quincy Adams a Founding Father? Michele Bachman Says Yes." *ABC News* 28 June 2011. http://abcnews.go.com/blogs/politics/2011/06/john-quincy-adams-a-founding-father-michele-bachmann-says-yes/. 30 Sept. 2013.

McCullough, David. *John Adams*. New York: Simon, 2001.

Morgan, Edmund S. *American Heroes*. New York: Norton, 2009.

–. *American Slavery, American Freedom: The Ordeal of Colonial Virginia*. New York: Norton, 1965.

–. *Benjamin Franklin*. New Haven: Yale UP, 2002.

Morris, Richard B. *Seven Who Shaped Our Destiny: The Founding Fathers as Revolutionaries*. New York: Harper, 1976.

Murray, Judith Sargent. "On the Equality of the Sexes." *Selected Writings of Judith Sargent Murray*. Ed. Sharon M. Harris. New York: Oxford UP, 1995. 3-14.

–. *The Gleaner*. Introd. Nina Baym. Schenectady: Union College, 1992.

Nash, Gary B. *The Forgotten Fifth: African Americans in the Age of Revolution*. Cambridge: Harvard UP, 2006.

Nobles, Gregory H. "Historians Extend the Reach of the American Revolution." *Whose American Revolution Was It? Historians Interpret the Founding*. Ed. Alfred F. Young and Gregory H. Nobles. New York: New York UP, 2011. 135-256.

North by Northwest. Dir. Alfred Hitchcock. Metro-Goldwyn-Mayer, 1959.

Norton, Mary Beth. *Founding Mothers and Fathers: Gendered Power and the Forming of American Society*. New York: Vintage, 1997.

–. *Liberty's Daughters: The Revolutionary Experience of American Women, 1750-1800*. 1980. Ithaca: Cornell UP, 1996.

Obama, Barack. "A More Perfect Union." *Washington Wire – WSJ*. http://blogs.wsj.com/washwire/2008/03/18/text-of-obamas-speech-a-more-perfect-union/. 30 Sept. 2013.

O'Brien, Conor Cruise. *The Long Affair: Thomas Jefferson and the French Revolution, 1785-1800*. Chicago: U of Chicago P, 1996.

Pasley, Jeffrey L., Andrew W. Robertson, and David Waldstreicher, eds. *Beyond the Founders: New Approaches to the Political History of the Early American Republic*. Chapel Hill: U of North Carolina P, 2004.

Pelton, Pelton W. *Baking Recipes of Our Founding Fathers*. West Conshohocken: Infinity, 2004.

Perrottet, Tony. "Mt. Rushmore." *Smithsonian Magazine* May 2006. http://www.smithsonianmag.com/travel/da_rushmore.html. 30 Sept. 2013.

Peterson, Merrill. *The Jefferson Image in the American Mind*. New York: Oxford UP, 1960.

Pogue, Dennis J. *Founding Spirits: George Washington and the Beginnings of the American Whiskey Industry*. Madeira Park: Harbour, 2011.

Pybus, Cassandra. *Epic Journeys of Freedom: Runaway Slaves of the American Revolution and Their Global Quest for Liberty*. Boston: Beacon, 2007.

Quarles, Benjamin. *The Negro in the American Revolution*. Chapel Hill: U of North Carolina P, 1961.

Quigley, David. *Second Founding: New York City, Reconstruction, and the Making of American Democracy*. New York: Hill, 2005.

Randolph, Mary. *The Virginia Housewife*. 1824. Facsimile edition with historical notes and commentaries. Ed. Karen Hess. Columbia: U of South Carolina P, 1984.

Roberts, Cokie. *Founding Mothers: The Women Who Raised Our Nation*. New York: Harper, 2004.

Runte, Alfred. *National Parks: The American Experience*. Lanham: Taylor Trade, 2010.

"Sarah Palin on 'Glenn Beck.'" *Fox News* 14 Jan. 2010. Transcript of 13 Jan. 2010 interview. http://www.foxnews.com/story/2010/01/14/sarah-palin-on-glenn-beck/. 27 Oct. 2013.

Saya, Tom. "The Whiteness of Mount Rushmore." *The Midwest Quarterly* 47.2 (2006): 144-54.

Schachner, Nathan. *The Founding Fathers*. South Brunswick: A.S. Barnes, 1954.

Schama, Simon. *Landscape and Memory*. New York: Vintage, 1995.

–. *Rough Crossings: Britain, the Slaves and the American Revolution*. New York: Vintage, 2009.

Schlesinger, Arthur, Jr. "When *Ethnic* Studies Are *Un-American*." *Wall Street Journal* 23 April 1990: A14.

Schudson, Michael. *The Good Citizen: A History of American Civic Life*. New York: Free, 1998.

Scobell, Sara. "Judith Sargent Murray: The 'So-Called' Feminist." *Constructing the Past* 1.1 (2000): 4-21.

Smith, Andrew F. "False Memories: The Invention of Culinary Fakelore and Food Fallacies." *Proceedings of the Oxford Symposium on Food and Cookery, 2000.* Ed. Harlan Walker. Devon: Prospect, 2001. 254-60.

Spalding, Matthew, and Patrick J. Garrity. *A Sacred Union of Citizens: George Washington's Farewell Address and the American Character.* New York: Rowman and Littlefield, 1998.

Sperling, John, and Suzanne Wiggins Helburn. *The Great Divide: Retro vs. Metro America.* Sausalito: PoliPoint, 2004.

Srodes, James. *Benjamin Frankin: The Essential Founding Father.* Washington, D.C.: Regnery/Gateway, 2003.

Stahr, Walter. *John Jay: Founding Father.* New York: Hambledon and Continuum, 2006.

Stanfield, Jack. *America's Founding Fathers: Who Are They? Thumbnail Sketches of 164 Patriots.* Universal, 2001.

Starna, William, and George R. Hamell. "History and the Burden of Proof: The Case of Iroquois Influence on the U.S. Constitution." *New York History* 77 (1996): 427-52.

Stone, Peter, and Sherman Edwards. *1776: A Musical Play.* New York: Penguin, 1969.

Taylor, Alan. *Writing Early American History.* Philadelphia: U of Pennsylvania P, 2005.

Team America: World Police. Dir. Trey Parker. Paramount, 2004.

Thomas, Evan. "Founders Chic: Live from Philadelphia." *Newsweek* 9 July 2001: 48-51.

Truth, Sojourner. "Ain't I a Woman." 1851. *The Norton Anthology of Literature by Women: The Tradition in English.* Ed. Sandra M. Gilbert and Susan Gubar. New York: Norton, 1985. 253.

Twelbeck, Kirsten. "The New Rules of the Democratic Game: Emancipation, Self-Regulation, and the 'Second Founding' of the United States." *Civilizing and Decivilizing Processes: Figurational Approaches to American Culture.* Ed. Christa Buschendorf, Astrid Franke, and Johannes Voelz. Newcastle upon Tyne: Cambridge Scholars, 2011. 175-208.

Unger, Harlow Giles. *The Last Founding Father: James Monroe and a Nation's Call to Greatness.* Cambridge: Da Capo, 2009.

Vidal, Gore. *Inventing a Nation: Washington, Adams, Jefferson.* New Haven: Yale UP, 2003.

Walker, Clarence E. *Mongrel Nation: The America Begotten by Thomas Jefferson and Sally Hemings.* Charlottesville: U of Virginia P, 2009.

Walker, David. *David Walker's Appeal, in Four Articles; Together with a Preamble, to the Coloured Citizens of the World, But in Particular, and Very Expressly, to Those of the United States of America.* 1829; 1830. Ed. Sean Wilentz. New York: Hill, 1995.

Warren, Mercy Otis. *History of the Rise, Progress, and Termination of the American Revolution.* Boston: Manning and Loring, 1805.

Washington, George. "Washington's Farewell Address 1796." *The Avalon Project.* http://avalon.law.yale.edu/18th_century/washing.asp. 27 Oct. 2013.

Weems, Mason Locke. *A History of the Life and Death, Virtues and Exploits of General George Washington.* Philadelphia: J.B. Lippincott, 1918.

Wexler, Laura. "All Men and Women Are Created Equal." Marcus and Sollors, *New Literary History* 349-53.

Wiencek, Henry. *The Master of the Mountain: Thomas Jefferson and His Slaves.* New York: Farrar, 2012.

Wilentz, Sean. "America Made Easy: McCullough, Adams, and the Decline of Popular History." Rev. of *John Adams*, by David McCullough. *The New Republic* 2 July 2001. http://www.newrepublic.com/article/books-and-arts/90636/david-mccullough-john-adams-book-review. 30 Sept. 2013.

Wills, Garry. *Cincinnatus: George Washington and the Enlightenment.* London: Hale, 1984.

Wood, Gordon S. *The Americanization of Benjamin Franklin.* New York: Penguin, 2004.

–. *The Radicalism of the American Revolution.* New York: Knopf, 1992.

Wulf, Andrea. *Founding Gardeners: The Revolutionary Generation, Nature, and the Shaping of the American Nation.* New York: Knopf, 2011.

Zinsser, William. *American Places: A Writer's Pilgrimage to Sixteen of This Country's Most Visited and Cherished Sites.* Philadelphia: Paul Dry, 2007.

Further Reading

Ackerman, Bruce. *The Failures of the Founding Fathers: Jefferson, Marshall, and the Rise of Presidential Democracy.* Cambridge: Belknap, 2005.

Adair, Douglass. *Fame and the Founding Fathers: Essays by Douglass Adair.* Ed. Trevor Colbourn. New York: Norton, 1974.

Appleby, Joyce. *Liberalism and Republicanism in the Historical Imagination.* Cambridge: Harvard UP, 1992.

Bailyn, Bernard. *To Begin the World Anew: The Genius and Ambiguities of the American Founders.* New York: Vintage, 2003.

Berkin, Carol. *First Generations: Women in Colonial America*. New York: Hill, 1999.

–. *Revolutionary Mothers: Women in the Struggle for America's Independence*. New York: Knopf, 2005.

Bernstein, Richard B. *Are We to Be a Nation? The Making of the Constitution*. With Kym S. Rice. Cambridge: Harvard UP, 1987.

Burns, Eric. *Infamous Scribblers: The Founding Fathers and the Rowdy Beginnings of American Journalism*. New York: Public Affairs, 2006.

Burstein, Andrew. *America's Jubilee*. New York: Knopf, 2001.

Chaplin, Joyce. *The First Scientific American: Benjamin Franklin and the Pursuit of Genius*. New York: Basic, 2006.

Clough, Wilson Ober, ed. *Intellectual Origins of American National Thought: Pages from the Books Our Founding Fathers Read*. 2nd rev. ed. New York: Corinth, 1961.

Cohen, Bernard I. *Science and the Founding Fathers: Science in the Political Thought of Jefferson, Franklin, Adams, and Madison*. New York: Norton, 1995.

Combs, Jerald A. *The Jay Treaty: Political Battlegrounds of the Founding Fathers*. Berkeley: U of California P, 1970.

Cornell, Saul. *The Other Founders: Anti-Federalism and the Dissenting Tradition in America, 1788-1828*. Chapel Hill: U of North Carolina P, 2002.

Craven, Wesley Frank. *The Legend of the Founding Fathers*. Ithaca: Cornell UP, 1956.

Cunliffe, Marcus. *George Washington: Man and Monument*. Revised ed. New York: Mentor, 1982.

Farquhar, Michael. *A Treasury of Great American Scandals: Tantalizing True Tales of Historic Misbehavior by the Founding Fathers and Others Who Let Freedom Swing*. New York: Penguin, 2003.

Gelles, Edith B. *Abigail and John: Portrait of a Marriage*. New York: Harper, 2009.

Gerber, Scott Douglas, ed. *The Declaration of Independence: Origins and Impact*. Washington: CQ, 2002.

Gibson, Alan. *Interpreting the Founding: Guide to the Enduring Debates Over the Origins and Foundations of the American Republic*. Lawrence: UP of Kansas, 2006.

Goldford, Dennis J. *The American Constitution and the Debate Over Originalism*. Cambridge: Cambridge UP, 2005.

Grant, James. *John Adams: Party of One*. New York: Farrar, 2005.

Hamilton, Alexander. *A Full Vindication of the Measures of Congress.* New York: James Rivington, 1774.

Hofstadter, Richard. *The American Political Tradition and the Men Who Made It.* New York: Knopf, 1951.

Homberger, Eric. "Image-Making and the Circulation of Images: Peale, Trumbull, and the Founding Fathers." *European Journal of American Culture* 24.1 (2006): 11-38.

Kaminski, John P., ed. *The Founders of the Founders: Word Portraits from the American Revolutionary Era.* Charlottesville: U of Virginia P, 2008.

Kammen, Michael. *A Season of Youth: The American Revolution and the Historical Imagination.* New York: Knopf, 1978.

Kersch, Rogan. *Dreams of a More Perfect Union.* Ithaca: Cornell UP, 2001.

Lambert, Frank. *The Founding Fathers and the Place of Religion in America.* Princeton: Princeton UP, 2003.

–. *Religion in American Politics: A Short History.* Princeton: Princeton UP, 2008.

Lepore, Jill. *The Story of America: Essays on Origins.* Princeton: Princeton UP, 2012.

Lhotta, Roland, ed. *Die hybride Republik: Die* Federalist Papers *und die politische Moderne.* Baden-Baden: Nomos, 2010.

Lipset, Seymour Martin. *The First New Nation: The United States in Historical and Comparative Perspective.* New York: Norton, 1979.

Lowenthal, David. *The Past Is a Foreign Country.* Cambridge: Cambridge UP, 1985.

Maier, Pauline. *From Resistance to Revolution.* New York: Knopf, 1972.

McGuire, Robert A. *To Form a More Perfect Union: A New Economic Interpretation of the United States Constitution.* Oxford: Oxford UP, 2003.

Meacham, Jon. *American Gospel: God, the Founding Fathers, and the Making of a Nation.* New York: Random, 2006.

Meister, Charles W. *The Founding Fathers.* Jefferson: McFarland, 1987.

Middlekauff, Robert. *Benjamin Franklin and His Enemies.* Berkeley: U of California P, 1996.

Morgan, Edmund S. *The Birth of the Republic 1763-89.* Chicago: U of Chicago P, 1956.

Morgan, Jeff. "The Founding Father: Benjamin Franklin and His Autobiography." *Romanticism and Parenting: Image, Instruction and Ideology.* Ed. Carolyn A. Weber. Newcastle: Cambridge Scholars, 2007.

Morris, Richard B. *The American Revolution Reconsidered.* New York: Harper Torchbooks, 1967.

–. *The Emerging Nations of the American Revolution*. New York: Harper, 1970.

Nell, William C. *The Colored Patriots of the American Revolution*. New York: Arno, 1968.

Pole, J.R. *The Pursuit of Equality in American History*. Berkeley: U of California P, 1978.

Rakove, Jack. *The Beginnings of National Politics*. New York: Knopf, 1979.

Roberts, Kenneth. *Rabble in Arms*. Garden City: Doubleday, 1950.

Rossiter, Clinton. *1787: The Grand Convention*. New York: Norton, 1966.

Savage, John. *Monument Wars: Washington, D.C., the National Mall, and the Transformation of the Memorial Landscape*. Berkeley: U of California P, 2005.

Shuffelton, Frank, ed. *The Cambridge Companion to Thomas Jefferson*. Cambridge: Cambridge UP, 2009.

Smith, Rex Alan. *The Carving of Mount Rushmore*. New York: Abbeville, 1985.

Spragens, William C., ed. *Popular Images of American Presidents*. New York: Greenwood, 1988.

Spurlin, Paul Merrill. *The French Enlightenment in America: Essays on the Times of the Founding Fathers*. Athens: U of Georgia P, 1984.

Taliaferro, John. *Great White Fathers: The Story of the Obsessive Quest to Create Mount Rushmore*. New York: Public Affairs, 2002.

Trees, Andrew S. *The Founding Fathers and the Politics of Character*. Princeton: Princeton UP, 2004.

Varg, Paul A. *Foreign Policies of the Founding Fathers*. East Lansing: Michigan State UP, 1963.

Waldman, Steven. *Founding Faith: Providence, Politics, and the Birth of Religious Freedom in America*. New York: Random, 2008.

Warren, Charles. *The Making of the Constitution*. Boston: Little, 1928.

Wright, Louis B. *Tradition and the Founding Fathers*. Charlottesville: UP of Virginia, 1975.

Chapter V

E Pluribus Unum? The Myth of the Melting Pot

1. WHY THE MELTING POT?

> Imagine if you can, my dear friend, a society comprising all the nations of the world: English, French, German. [...] All people having different languages, beliefs, and opinions. In short, a society without roots, without memories, without prejudices, without routines, without common ideas, without national character. [...] What ties these very diverse elements together? What makes a people of all this?
>
> ALEXIS DE TOCQUEVILLE TO ERNEST DE CHABROL, JUNE 9, 1831

> Was it not possible, then, to think of the evolving American society not simply as a slightly modified England but rather as a totally new blend, culturally and biologically, in which the stocks and folkways of Europe were, figuratively speaking, indiscriminately mixed in the political pot of the emerging nation and melted together by the fires of American influence and interaction into a distinctly new type?
>
> MILTON GORDON, *ASSIMILATION IN AMERICAN LIFE*

A widely known rendering of the melting pot idea is the phrase *E Pluribus Unum*, on which the US Department of the Treasury provides the following information:

The motto "E Pluribus Unum" was first used on our coinage in 1795, when the reverse of the half-eagle ($5 gold) coin presented the main features of the Great Seal of the United States. "E Pluribus Unum" is inscribed on the Great Seal's scroll. The motto was added to certain silver coins in 1798, and soon appeared on all of the coins made out of precious metals (gold and silver). In 1834, it was dropped from most of the gold coins to mark the change in the standard fineness of the coins. In 1837, it was dropped from the silver coins, marking the era of the Revised Mint Code. An Act of February 12, 1873 made the inscription a requirement of law upon the coins of the United States.

"E Pluribus Unum" does appear on all coins currently being manufactured. The motto means "Out of Many, One," and probably refers to the unity of the early States. (US Department of the Treasury website; cf. also below)

Illustration 1: Great Seal of the United States

Wikimedia Commons (Web, 4 May 2014).

E Pluribus Unum is also engraved on the globe at the feet of the Statue of Freedom, the classical female allegorical figure at the top of the US Capitol dome. It can be regarded as an unofficial motto of the United States, and has become a standard manifestation of the melting pot myth, which more than any other foundational myth evokes a vision of national unity and cohesion through participation in a harmonious, quasi-organic community that offers prospective members a second chance and a new beginning and molds them into a new 'race,' a new people. Whereas the myths discussed in the preceding chapters (Columbus, Pocahontas, the Pilgrims and Puritans, and the Founding Fathers) established a 'usable past' for the nation and commemorated heroic figures of 'new world' beginnings, the melting pot, just as the myths discussed in the remaining chapters (the West and the self-made man), is a myth about the making of American society. In its dominant version, it envisions the US in a state of perpetual change and transformation that is partly assimilation, partly regeneration, and

partly emergence, and emphasizes the continuous integration of difference experienced by both immigrant and longer-established sections of the population.
As imagined communities (cf. Benedict Anderson's book of the same title),
nations not only need narratives of origin, but also narratives of their future – in
the case of the US, which looked upon itself as a nation of immigrants, such a
forward-looking narrative needed to address how differences of origin and
descent could be transcended, and the melting pot seemed to be the perfect
model to describe the particular composition of US society:

In general, the cluster of ideas [surrounding the melting pot] included the belief that a new
nation, a new national character, and a new nationality were forming in the United States
and that the most heterogeneous human materials could be taken in and absorbed into this
nationality. (Gleason, *Speaking* 5)

Of course, from the beginning, the melting pot has been seen as an ambiguous
symbol of American unity; it has been looked upon as a myth providing
cohesion and a sense of evolving Americanness on the one hand, and as an instrument of forced acculturation and violent assimilation on the other. Several
questions suggest themselves when assessing this myth: Who is in the 'pot' and
who is doing the 'melting'? What exactly is melted down? Which elements
would prove to be resilient or dominant in the process, and with what result? In
my discussion of the melting pot myth, I will point to narrative variations, iconic
symbolizations, and ritualistic practices that have shaped it across time. This
reconstruction reveals, as we will see, that the melting pot myth emerges from a
rather confused discourse: the melting pot has been used, first, as a phrase with
which historical developments in the US have been described and projected into
the future; it has been used, second, as a normative concept in order to affirm the
melting pot at various moments in American history; and it has been used, third,
as an analytic term in order to study cultural, social, and demographic processes
in American society. These three different modes (descriptive, normative, and
analytical) are usually not properly distinguished, which at times makes it difficult to keep them apart; normative frameworks in particular often appropriate a
descriptive mode and/or immunize themselves against criticism by pretending to
be analytical. The melting pot in all three modes (as history, program, and
analytical category) appears to be infused with an exceptionalist logic and a civil
religious dimension that invariably reinforce its mythic quality. Melting pot
rhetoric often describes the overcoming of cultural and national differences in
general, but at times it more specifically is about racial, religious, or class differences. These oscillations and variations contribute to the elasticity of the myth

even as they often render discussions of the melting pot quite ambiguous and contradictory.

In what follows, I will sketch several phases in the making, remaking, and unmaking of the myth of the melting pot. First, I will trace melting pot myth-making from the foundational phase of the United States in the second half of the 18th century, during which a number of now canonical texts articulated this myth in powerful ways, all the way through the 19th century. Second, I will address Israel Zangwill's play *The Melting Pot* (1908) in some detail, as it is a singularly important narrative of melting pot rhetoric and aesthetic and as such will serve as a touchstone for subsequent discussions of the myth of the melting pot. Third, I will reconstruct responses to the myth in the late 19th and early 20th centuries, a period in which it became a central reference point for discussions of immigration and America's future and a highly contested metaphor of Progressivist thinking that was attacked from different positions on the political spectrum – from advocates of cultural pluralism on the left as well as from advocates of eugenics on the right. Fourth, I will look at sections of the population that have been regularly excluded by melting pot rhetoric: minority groups such as Native Americans, African Americans, and Asian Americans. If nation-building is intricately intertwined with racialization (cf. Weinbaum, "Nation"), then the melting pot metaphor – despite its ostensibly inclusivist orientation – implies exclusionary practices, just as any other model that constructs a homogenous national body from a racially diverse population. Debates around forms of "American Apartheid" (cf. Massey and Denton's book of the same title), taboos on miscegenation, and a new emphasis on religious difference within the melting pot discourse also need to be addressed in this section. Fifth, I will turn to the post-World War II period in order to show how the melting pot controversies were continued and renewed in the wake of the social protest movements and new immigration legislation in the 1960s and 1970s, particularly in discussions of Nathan Glazer and Patrick Moynihan's by now classic study *Beyond the Melting Pot* (1963). I will then outline how more recent discussions of the melting pot have been informed by notions of multiculturalism and ethnic diversity. In recent years, we have also seen a (re)turn to models of assimilation (cf. e.g. Salins, *Assimilation*) which often affirm and rehash older, rather conservative positions; at the same time, alternatives to the melting pot such as the mosaic, the salad bowl, cultural hybridity, etc. have been discussed in American studies and postcolonial studies scholarship.

The melting pot myth thus has been used in very different ways and for different political purposes. It has been the subject of sociological discussions as well as of immigrant love stories; it is a model of literary aesthetics as well as a metaphor for change and hybridity, and it is also at the core of some strands of utopian thinking. Above all, one might say that it is a myth of cultural mobility and cultural sharing. Despite having lost mainstream popularity in recent years, melting pot rhetoric still enjoys some currency, as the issues that the melting pot myth tackles – i.e., processes of voluntary or coerced political, social, and/or cultural integration – are still on the agenda. In fact, recent scholarship stresses the "ideological variability of the melting pot" (Wilson, *Melting-Pot Modernism* 7) and identifies it with the first cultural turn in American history (cf. ibid. 198). However, the notion of culture and society that the metaphor of the melting pot conjures up remains problematic and does not lend itself easily to ideological rearticulations: alloying, the metaphor's source, always involves a primary constituent into which the other constituents are dissolved. Literalizing the melting pot metaphor thus points to built-in asymmetries, limitations, and pitfalls of the concept which the foundational and exceptionalist version of the myth has often successfully managed to camouflage.

2. "What Then Is The American, This New Man?"

> The bosom of America is open to the oppressed and persecuted of all Nations and Religions. [...] Whereas by an intermixture with our people, they, or their descendants, get assimilated to our customs, measures and laws: in a word, soon become one people.
> George Washington

> The time [...] is anticipated when the language, manners, customs, political and religious sentiments of the mixed mass of the people who inhabit the United States, shall have become so assimilated, as that all nominal distinctions shall be lost in the general and honourable name of Americans.
> Jedidiah Morse, *The American Universal Geography*

The first author to be credited with describing American society as a melting pot is John Hector St. John de Crèvecoeur (1735-1813) (cf. Sollors, *Beyond Ethnicity* 75), a French aristocrat who emigrated to North America in 1755. While back in Europe in 1782, he arranged for the publication of his *Letters from an American Farmer* in London, which is *the* key text for tracing the history and origin of the melting pot myth and may very well be looked upon as "the first sustained attempt by a European-born writer to define Americanness" (Moore,

Introduction ix). The *Letters* consist of semi-autobiographical accounts of rural life in 18th-century America, American flora and fauna, politics, family life, and culture; but most noteworthy in the context of my discussion of the melting pot myth is Crèvecoeur's description of the 'American' in the third letter:

What then is the American, this new man? He is either an European, or the descendant of an European, hence that strange mixture of blood, which you will find in no other country. I could point out to you a family whose grandfather was an Englishman, whose wife was Dutch, whose son married a French woman, and whose present four sons have now four wives of different nations. *He* is an American, who leaving behind him all his ancient prejudices and manners, receives new ones from the new mode of life he has embraced, the new government he obeys, and the new rank he holds. He becomes an American by being received in the broad lap of our great *Alma Mater*. Here individuals of all nations are melted into a new race of men, whose labours and posterity will one day cause great changes in the world. (43)

Crèvecoeur envisions the 'melting' of distinct Western and Northern European 'races' (French, German, Dutch, and Scandinavian) into a new American one. He "uses the word 'new' seventeen times in letter 3, often in company with such words as *metamorphosis*, *regeneration* and *resurrection*" (Sollors, *Beyond Ethnicity* 75; cf. Nye, *American Literary History* 157). At various points in his letters, Crèvecoeur also includes Native Americans in his melting pot, a fact that has often been omitted in standard interpretations of the *Letters*. In a recent edition of Crèvecoeur's writings, we find the following description (rendered in the original version in which he wrote it):

the Sweed the low the high dutch the French the English the scotch the Irish, Leaving behind them their National Prejudices soon Imbibe those of the new country they are come to Inhabit, they mix with Eachother or with the Natives as conveniency or chance may direct. (*More Letters* 137)

Whereas Native Americans became more and more identified in public discourses of the 18th and 19th centuries with savagery (in contradistinction to the 'civilized' white Europeans) and were thus increasingly excluded from white-authored melting pot visions of the future American (along with African Americans and Asian Americans), in Crèvecoeur's account of America/nization they are (still) included (albeit in a homogenized fashion). 'Mixing with each other and with the Natives,' Europeans are transformed into Americans by a process of biological hybridization that is invested in a heteronormative ideology of reproduction. Concerning the relations between Europeans and Native Americans, Thomas Jefferson (1743-1826) in a similar vein and around the same time proposes "to let our settlements and theirs meet and blend together, to intermix, and become one people [i]ncorporating themselves with us as citizens of the U.S." (To Benjamin Hawkins Washington). Jefferson's semantics of 'blending' comes close to 'melting' and indicates the potential he sees for a kind of 'new race,' a potential that is also expounded by other founding fathers (George Washington, for instance; cf. this section's first epigraph). In fact, "several prominent southerners in the eighteenth century proclaimed intermarriage the solution to the Indian problem" (Dippie, *Vanishing* 260). However, Jefferson's utopian "vision of interracial nationhood" (Onuf, *Jefferson's Empire* 52) is ambivalent as it also prefigures and accepts the dissolution of the Native Americans and their cultures through racial mixing; ultimately, he did not favor the melting pot as an all-embracing model but instead argued for "the separation, or elimination, of disparate ethnic groups – Indians and blacks – who refused to disappear through civilization and assimilation, or were, in his view, incapable of participating as citizens in the republic" (Anthony Wallace, *Jefferson* 338). Today, Jefferson is seen as both "the scholarly admirer of Indian character, archaeology, and language and as the planner of cultural genocide, the architect of the removal policy, the surveyor of the Trail of Tears" (ibid. vii). When he tells the chiefs of the Upper Cherokee that "your blood will mix with ours" (qtd. in Roger Kennedy, "Jefferson" 105), it is not quite clear whether this is meant as a promise or a threat. In later scholarship, this vision will be explicitly connected to Anglo-American plans to annihilate the Native population *through* racial mixing. According to the phrenologist Charles Caldwell (1772-1853), the "only efficient scheme to civilize the Indians is to *cross the breed*" (qtd. in Haskins, *History* 111). This view was also shared by Lewis Henry Morgan (1818-1881), the founding figure of American anthropology, who noted that "the only way to tame him [the Indian] is to put in the white blood" (qtd. in Bieder, *Science* 225; cf. also Eggan, "Lewis H. Morgan"), and by cartographer and geologist John Wesley Powell, who thought that "mixing blood" was a way to avoid "spilling blood" and spoke out in favor of "rapid amalgamation" (qtd. in Dippie, *Vanishing* 248). As Brian Dippie points out, amalgamation fit very well with the larger programmatic notion of the 'vanishing Indian:' "Assimilation would effect the same end as extermination and more insidiously and more surely because it annihilates without raising a sword or a murmur of protest" (*Vanishing* 244). The notions of 'melting' and miscegenation in this melting pot design thus point to and justify what amounts to extermination policies – or what Matthew Jacobson in a different context has termed "malevolent assimilation" (cf. his essay of the same title, esp. 154) – that were part of what white colonizers liked to call their 'civilizing mission' (cf. Bieder, *Science* 226, 231-33).

Echoes of the melting pot myth as a foundational narrative of the American experience and as an American ideal reverberate beyond Crèvecoeur's articulation of the idea of the melting pot and Jefferson's half-hearted (or even disingenuous) embrace of a mixed-race future America in essays, poetry, and historical works by a number of writers in 19th-century North America. These texts prefigure the immigration debate that was to gain momentum in the late 19th and early 20th centuries through melting pot imagery – referred to by this or any other name – that is often ambiguous, idiosyncratic, and impressionistic. Most of these articulations of the melting pot take a top-down rather than a bottom-up perspective and display the same kind of inherent tension and volatility that we have found in Jefferson and, to a lesser extent, in Crèvecoeur, especially as to questions of inclusion and exclusion and the potential or problems anticipated in the process of mixing. Whereas we can note that "[b]y the middle of the nineteenth century it was widely accepted in America that the nation had a cosmopolitan origin and that the unifying element of American nationalism for the time being was neither a common past, nor common blood, but the American Idea" and that "[t]he motto of American nationalism – *E Pluribus Unum* – stresses the ideal of unity that will arise out of diversity" (Lissak, *Pluralism* 2), the perspectives on just how this ideal was to be achieved varied greatly and were mostly inconclusive.

Philosopher and poet Ralph Waldo Emerson (1803-1882) is among the American writers of the 19th century who are often considered to be proponents of the melting pot. References to Emerson's usage of the (s)melting pot metaphor are linked to the following passage from a journal entry:

Man is the most composite of all creatures. [...] Well, as in the old burning of the Temple at Corinth, by the melting and intermixture of silver and gold and other metals a new compound more precious than any, called Corinthian brass, was formed; so in this continent, – asylum of all nations, the energy of Irish, Germans, Swedes, Poles, and Cosacks, and all the European tribes, – of the Africans, and of the Polynesians, – will construct a new race, a new religion, a new state, a new literature, which will be as vigorous as the new Europe which came out of the smelting pot of the Dark Ages, or that which earlier emerged from the Pelasgic and Etruscan barbarism. *La Nature aime les croisements.* (Entry 119, *Journals* Vol. 9, 299-300)

Emerson includes Europeans, Africans, and even Polynesians, but no Native Americans in his version of the melting pot. Although he seems to champion racial and cultural amalgamation and thus to contest notions of racial and cultural purity, as with Crèveceour and Jefferson, we need to look beyond the canonized passage quoted above to get a fuller sense of Emerson's 'smelting pot;' his American 'Corinthian brass' is informed as much by cultural exchange as by processes (and theories) of natural selection. Emerson's conceptualization of the "genius of the American race" is referred to by Luther Luedtke in an overall assessment of his oeuvre as harboring a "eugenics of American nationhood" ("Ralph Waldo Emerson" 7). While Emerson clearly speaks out against nativist and anti-immigration polemics, he also writes in a Darwinist spirit that "the Atlantic is a sieve" (qtd. in ibid. 10) through which immigrants on their passage to America are filtered to sort out the 'unfit.' Even though he refers to "the legend of pure races" (Emerson, "Race" 49) and to the fact that "all our experience is of the gradation and resolution of races" (ibid. 50), he still clings to a strict racial hierarchy: in reference to the chapter titled "Race" in his *English Traits*, Luedtke holds that for Emerson, "the emergence of higher forms of human life entailed not only the hybridization of races but also the extinction of existentially inferior forms" ("Ralph Waldo Emerson" 8; cf. also Nicoloff, *Emerson* 46-47), and John Carlos Rowe has pointed to Emerson's complicity in mid-19th-century discourses of race as well (cf. *At Emerson's Tomb*). Reading Emerson with Jefferson thus may shed light on why Native Americans are not mentioned in his smelting pot vision: Even though Emerson's metaphor of (s)melting is often placed in a smooth continuum between Crèvecoeur in the late 18th and Zangwill in the early 20th century, it reveals on closer inspection that it is based as much on processes of cultural transformation as on the discourses of biological determinism increasingly popular and accepted at that time.

In many ways, Emerson's vision is reflected in the works of Walt Whitman (1819-1892), whose writing has been credited as exemplifying the American melting pot by way of a "a new language" and "a new literary idiom appropriate to what Whitman saw as uniquely American experiences" (Archambeau, "Immigrant Languages" 79). In his preface to the 1855 edition of his magnum opus *Leaves of Grass*, Whitman refers to "the Americans of all nations" as a "race of races" and to the United States as not merely a nation but "the nation of many nations" (22). However, Whitman employs different melting pot metaphors in the various versions of *Leaves of Grass*: in the 1855 version, the speaker addresses the American "[o]f every hue and trade and rank, of every caste and religion, [n]ot merely of the New World but of Africa Europe or Asia" (23), while in the last version, now titled "Song of Myself" and newly organized in sections, the speaker describes himself as an American "[o]f every hue and caste [...], [o]f every rank and religion, [a] farmer, mechanic, artist, gentleman, sailor, quaker, [p]risoner, fancy-man, rowdy, lawyer, physician, priest" (87). Clearly, the 1855 text is more open and inclusive than the 1881 version, to which Whitman added a somewhat nativist streak: "Born here of parents born here from parents the same, and their parents the same" (71). The melting pot rhetoric is less radical in this final version, which stresses American sameness rather than immigrant difference. This change can be read as an indication of the larger ideological shift toward nativism in the period of mass immigration from Europe. Whitman's final version of his famous poem, then, appears to partially turn away from the melting pot idea and to emphasize an Ur-American genealogy.

Toward the end of the 19th century several historians offered various models of national amalgamation, all of which relied to some degree on melting pot imagery for conceptualizing the transformation of immigrants from Europe. The historian Francis Parkman (1823-1893) contended that

[s]ome races of men seem moulded in wax, soft and melting, at once plastic and feeble. Some races, like some metals, combine the greatest flexibility with the greatest strength. But the Indian is hewn out of a rock. You can rarely change the form without destruction of the substance. (*Conspiracy* 45)

Racial difference thus figured prominently in Parkman's explanation of the failure of the "wilderness melting pot" (Saveth, *American Historians* 102); in addition to the supposedly unchangeable Natives, Parkman also dismissed in no uncertain terms as not fit for progress Catholic groups, especially North Americans of French descent.

The jurist, historian, and statesman James Bryce (1838-1922), who served as British Ambassador to the United States from 1907 to 1913, states in his voluminous treatise on the US titled *The American Commonwealth* (1888):

What strikes the traveller, and what the Americans themselves are delighted to point out, is the amazing solvent power which American institutions, habits, and ideas exercise upon newcomers of all races. [...] On the whole we may conclude that the intellectual and moral atmosphere into which the settlers from Europe come has more power to assimilate them than their race qualities have power to change it. (Vol. 2 922-23)

The image of America's "solvent power" affirms once more the idea of 'melting down' racial difference, even if race here (as in many 19th-century texts) refers to European groups such as the Nordic, Iberic, Anglo-Saxon, Celtic, Slavic, or

Teutonic races (cf. Jacobson, *Whiteness* 7) rather than to 'whites,' African Americans, Native Americans, or Asian Americans. Over all, the 19th century largely consolidated a racialized version of the melting pot idea and with it "the institutionalization of a racial order that drew the color line around, rather than within, Europe" (Omi and Winant, *Racial Formation* 65). The melting pot myth thus seemingly describes but actually produces an implicit and highly normative conception of whiteness that has become more inclusive over time but at the same time also continued to be profoundly exclusivist.

Following up on Bryce at the very end of the 19th century, historian Frederick Jackson Turner (1861-1932) used the melting pot metaphor to describe processes of Americanization at what he refers to as the 'frontier.' In his lecture on "The Significance of the Frontier in American History," Turner suggests:

The frontier promoted the formation of a composite nationality for the American people [...]. In the crucible of the frontier the immigrants were Americanized, liberated, and fused into a mixed race, English in neither nationality nor characteristics.

The claim that this "amalgamation is destined to produce a new national stock" (ibid.) here is obviously used to assert US distinctness from England and to bolster the notion of American exceptionalism. This new national stock, in which "no element remained isolated," again relates mostly to European immigrants, even if Turner refers to "immigrants from all nations of the world." Turner's frontier thesis – to be addressed in more detail in the following chapter – echoes Crèvecoeur's melting pot, yet Turner never mentions his name or quotes from his writings. By describing the frontier melting pot as a specifically rural phenomenon, Turner programmatically shifts the site of Americanization from the Eastern Seaboard to the Midwest and thus positions the West at the center of the nation (later critics would turn to the American city as the major arena of assimilation processes).

While historians, essayists, politicians, and poets in the 18th and 19th centuries, as we have seen, referred in their appraisals and critiques of the melting pot idea to the mixing, (s)melting, and blending of differences in America in very different ways and often quite unspecifically, in the late 19th and early 20th centuries, the melting pot emerged as a particularly prominent yet controversial and often very differently accentuated model to describe the potential effects of mass immigration. Turner (among others) was skeptical about the 'melting' of one immigrant group in particular: the Eastern European and, specifically, Jewish immigrants, since he saw them as a 'city people' who did not experience the transforming effects of the frontier in the same beneficial way as other immigrant groups. In view of this assessment, it may seem ironic that it is a dramatic text by a Jewish (and British) author that at the beginning of the 20th century fuelled public debates on US national identity with its rendering of an urban melting pot scenario of mythic proportions.

3. ISRAEL ZANGWILL'S *THE MELTING POT*: JEWISH IMMIGRANTS AND AMERICAN ALCHEMY

> [T]he real American has not yet arrived. He is only in the Crucible, I tell you
> – he will be the fusion of all races, perhaps the coming superman.
> ISRAEL ZANGWILL, *THE MELTING POT*

In the passage quoted above, the protagonist of Israel Zangwill's play *The Melting Pot* portrays the American experience as a process of amelioration through amalgamation out of which the future American will arise like a "superman." Zangwill's play widely popularized the idea of the melting pot and was "[a]dvertised as a 'Drama of the Amalgamation of Races'" (Goldstein, *Price* 99); it opened in Washington, D.C. on October 5, 1908 in front of an audience that included then-president Theodore Roosevelt and his family. It ran for six months in Chicago and ran for 136 performances in New York in 1908 and 1909. Whereas theater critics at first had little enthusiasm for the play due to its sentimentalism, the audience flocked to it: "[T]he public crowded the performances [...]. It is a play of the people, touched with the fire of democracy, and lighted radiantly with the national vision" (review qtd. in Gleason, *Speaking* 7). From 1909 until the US entered World War I in 1917, it was republished yearly and widely read in schools and colleges (cf. Browder, *Slippery Characters* 149).

Israel Zangwill (1864-1926), the author of this huge success, was a playwright, journalist, essayist, and activist whose family emigrated from Czarist Russia and Poland to England. He was a central figure of Anglo-Jewish intellectualism and politics and was considered by many as "an interpreter of Jewish life" (Nahshon, Prologue 3) but was also seen as a somewhat controversial figure within the Jewish community because of his marriage with non-Jewish British writer and feminist Edith Ayrton. When his play *The Melting Pot* premiered in Washington, Zangwill traveled to the US to be in the audience.

Illustration 2: Celebrating Assimilation?

Cover of *The Melting Pot: The Great American Drama*
by Israel Zangwill (1916).

The Melting Pot, Zangwill's best-known play, is a melodrama whose plot revolves around David Quixano, a Jewish-Russian musician who immigrates to the
United States after his family has been killed in the Kishinev pogrom. In New
York, he meets Vera Revendal, the daughter of wealthy Russian immigrants,
who does charity work in a housing project; as their relationship progresses and
they fall in love with each other, they learn that it was Vera's father who had
been responsible for the brutal murder of David's family. At this point in the
play, a shocked David leaves Vera, and it seems as if their budding relationship
cannot overcome the trauma of the past:

David *(In low, icy tones)*: You cannot come to me. There is a river of blood between us.
Vera: Were it seven seas, our love must cross them. [...]
David: Love! Christian love! For this I gave up my people – darkened the home that
sheltered me – there was always a still, small voice at my heart calling me back, but I

heeded nothing – only the voice of the butcher's daughter. Let me go home, let me go home. (347-9)

Later on, David acknowledges that he has been wrong in rejecting Vera's love and embraces the redemptive influence of melting pot America, which in the play acquires the aura of the Redeemer Nation so cherished in exceptionalist rhetoric:

I preached of God's Crucible, this great new continent that could melt up all race differences and vendettas, that could purge and recreate, and God tried me with his supremest test. He gave me a heritage from the Old World, hatred and vengeance and blood, and said, "Cast it all into my Crucible." And I said, "Even thy Crucible cannot melt this hate, cannot drink up this blood." And so I sat crooning over the dead past, gloating over the old bloodstains – I, the apostle of America, the prophet of the God of our children. (360)

David interprets his tragic family history (Vera's father having murdered his parents) as a trial used by God to put his faith to the test. By mastering this religious crisis, repenting his skepticism, and converting once more, and firmly, to the American creed, David's faith in the melting pot is not only reassured but strengthened. In the last part of the play, David and Vera overcome the painful history of 'old world' anti-Semitism and make a new start in America; David creates a musical vision of melting pot America that moves the hearts of his immigrant audience, while Vera is "[m]elting at his touch" (315). The second chance offered to them by the American crucible does away with all past suffering and guilt and makes them literally new (cf. Browder, *Slippery Characters*).

In discussions of the play, it is mostly its happy ending that is quoted as evidence for its endorsement of melting pot ideology. The play concludes with the following lines:

It is the fires of God round His Crucible. There she lies, the great Melting-Pot – listen! Can't you hear the roaring and the bubbling? There gapes her mouth [...] Yes, East and West, and North and South, the palm and the pine, the pole and the equator, the crescent and the cross – how the great Alchemist melts and fuses them with his purging flame! Here shall they all unite to build the Republic of Man and the Kingdom of God. Ah, Vera, what is the glory of Rome and Jerusalem where all nations and races come to worship and look back, compared with the glory of America, where all the races and nations come to labour and look forward! Peace, peace, to all ye unborn millions, fated to fill this giant continent – the God of our *children* give you Peace. (362-63)

With these words, which echo Promised Land rhetoric, the doctrine of Manifest Destiny, American exceptionalism, and American civil religion, the play fades out after allowing a final glimpse of the torch of the Statue of Liberty in the background while a patriotic song is played. Thus, the final scene calls for unconditional identification with the US, reaching out to the audience on all available channels.

Zangwill's play thus has been read and canonized as a programmatic illustration and optimistic confirmation of the workings of the melting pot in American society which dramatizes the 'new world' as a place of new beginnings that discounts the individual's past and affirms that "old ethnic loyalties would diminish in the face of an inexorable process which emphasised those values that Americans held in common rather than those which kept them apart" (Campbell and Kean, *American Cultural Studies* 54). Rather than focusing merely on the assimilation of immigrants, "*The Melting Pot* made an explicit bid for a more expansive sense of U.S. nationhood" (Browder, *Slippery Characters* 150) and was seen as an affirmation of a universal ideology of cultural mixing and cultural change.

Yet in contrast to this canonical reading of the play, it has been argued by some scholars that its conflict may be resolved a little too nicely at the end. Neil Shumsky for example finds the play's rendering of the melting pot myth more complex than is generally acknowledged, and more ambivalent than the final scene suggests; he points out that the play "does not merely present the melting pot theory" ("Zangwill's *The Melting Pot*" 36) but structurally calls into question the message of its ending. Shumsky sees the anti-climactic moment of the play in David's ultimate moment of crisis when he finds out about the murder of his parents at the hands of Vera's father and his belief in the melting pot is shaken. Vera affirms her love, but he cannot accept it; he is unable to eradicate the past and wants to go home. The melting pot is 'only a dream:'

One could logically argue that *The Melting Pot* should end at this point. Its hero has admitted the futility of his dream and recognized that it cannot come true; but the play continues. It has a second conclusion which seems contrived and appears to contradict much of the play's development. In this anticlimax, David and Vera have finally realized that their futures lie apart and seem reconciled to that fact. Then suddenly, and for no apparent reason, David begs her to stay. (Shumsky, "Zangwill's *The Melting Pot*" 35)

Shumsky's reasoning that the play has two endings throws into doubt its ending's unequivocal affirmation of the melting pot myth: what if the myth *is* a dream? Who is dreaming it? And whose agency and interest propel the dream-like vision?

Scholars have further complicated the picture by pointing to the role of Judaism in Zangwill's *The Melting Pot* and have argued that the play is not so much about Americanization but about the future of the Jewish people in the diaspora. The question then is: Do the characters become Americanized or do they become Judaized? According to Biale, all Americans in *The Melting Pot* become "crypto-Jews" ("Melting Pot" 20); Vera Revendal in the beginning holds anti-Semitic attitudes but sheds her prejudices as the play continues – ultimately, she even wants to convert to Judaism for David's sake. In so far as Vera feels that she should assume David's cultural heritage, Zangwill's play is a narrative of conversion rather than an affirmation of melting pot ideology. In discussing David with her father, she says that

[I was] never absolutely sure of my love for him – perhaps that was why I doubted his love for me – often after our enchanted moments there would come a nameless uneasiness, some vague instinct, relic of the long centuries of Jew-loathing, some strange shirking from his Christless creed – [...] But now, now, David, I come to you, and I say in the words of Ruth, thy people shall be my people and thy God my God! (347)

Like Vera, the Quixano's Irish Catholic maid Kathleen overcomes her prejudices against Jews, develops an appreciation for Jewish rituals, and even participates in them herself. Vera and Kathleen may serve as examples that the play prominently engages with anti-Semitic prejudices and turns them around. Non-Jewish characters in *The Melting Pot* want to become (like) Jews rather than Americans, it has been argued: "Zangwill's cosmopolitanism turned out to be something like a form of Jewish particularism" (Biale, "Melting Pot" 19). This way of reading the play would have been more acceptable to those Jewish American contemporaries of Zangwill who felt compelled to embrace the melting pot as a political strategy while in fact being opposed to intermarriage as a form of assimilation (cf. Goldstein, *Price* 101).

The influence of *The Melting Pot* cannot be overstated: "[m]ore than any social or political theory, the rhetoric of Zangwill's play shaped American discourse on immigration and ethnicity, including most notably the language of self-declared opponents of the melting-pot concept" (Sollors, *Beyond Ethnicity* 66). The melting pot concept echoed in ethnic and immigrant literature of the 1910s and 1920s, a period in which nativist sentiments were on the rise as a reaction to mass immigration from Europe. Yet, the concept was neither uncontested, nor did its appropriation always occur in the melodramatic mode of Zangwill's play. Quite the contrary: we find a number of attempts to critique the metaphor by taking it more or less literally. Orm Øverland has shown how the melting pot as a symbol of assimilation was contested rather than whole-heartedly embraced in Scandinavian immigrant fiction (cf. *Immigrant Minds*), for example by Waldemar Ager (1869-1941), Norwegian immigrant and author of *On the Way to the Melting Pot* (1917), who describes the road toward assimilation as a process of loss, not of gain or liberation. Lars, the protagonist of the novel, is portrayed as assimilated and as culturally and socially impoverished at the same time; the process leading to that condition is described by another character in the book as follows:

First they stripped away their love for their parents, then they sacrificed their love for the one they held most dear, then the language they had learned from mother, then their love for their childhood upbringing, for God and man, then the sounds they learned as children, then their memories, then the ideals of their youth – tore their heritage asunder little by little – and when one had hurled from his heart and mind everything which he had been fond of earlier, then there was a great empty void to be filled with love of self, selfishness, greed, and the like. [...] Thus they readied themselves for the melting pot's last great test. (197)

And Lars's employer, a factory manager, muses not without irony that "[h]e could not recall having seen a single typewriter, an electric motor, a usable sewing machine or piece of farm machinery wander into the melting pot" (173): obviously, valuable and fully functioning things would not be melted down. Perhaps it is not accidental that Ager's critique of the melting pot was originally published in the Norwegian language for the thriving Norwegian American community and was translated into English only in 1995. In Ager's view, "[t]he melting pot [...] was primarily a metaphor of destruction, more about the killing of the old man than the creation of the new" (Øverland, "From Melting Pot" 53), a metaphor used "to denationalize those who are not of English descent" (ibid).

Almost two decades later, another immigrant writer includes a very unusual melting pot image in his work: In the climactic scene of Henry Roth's (1906-1995) novel *Call It Sleep* (1934), the protagonist, a young Jewish immigrant by the name of David Schearl (another David), touches the electrified rail of the trolley tracks on Avenue D in New York's East Village with a milk ladle, which results in "a surrealistic melting pot melange" (Sollors, *Ethnic Modernism* 140) accompanied by "lightning" and "radiance" (Roth, *Call It Sleep* 571). In literalizing the melting pot metaphor, David's experience with electricity is cast as an epiphany in the Joycean sense, as a moment of total presence: "[h]e views the electric current as if it were a divine power" (Sollors, *Ethnic Modernism* 141); David's almost-fatal 'melting' however can be read more fruitfully as a personal *rite de passage* that gives his life another turn rather than as a ritual of Americanization.

Ager and Roth are only two exemplary cases that show how the melting pot myth is criticized, perhaps even ridiculed, in the writings of first generation immigrants to the US; far beyond the realm of fiction, however, the melting pot becomes fiercely contested in debates on the future of US society in the Progressive Era, which will be discussed in the next section.

4. CONTESTING THE MELTING POT: CULTURAL PLURALISM VS. RACIAL HYGIENE?

> America has believed that in differentiation, not in uniformity, lies the path of progress.
> LOUIS DEMBITZ BRANDEIS, "TRUE AMERICANISM"

> We in this country have been so imbued with the idea of democracy, or the equality of all men, that we have left out of consideration the matter of blood or natural inborn hereditary mental and moral differences. No man who breeds pedigreed plants and animals can afford to neglect this thing, as you know.
> HARRY H. LAUGHLIN

In the face of more than 18 million immigrants entering the US between 1891 and 1920, the idea of racial and cultural amalgamation was discussed controversially by intellectuals as well as the public at large at that time. In these discussions, the melting pot concept provided a kind of middle ground between irreconcilable perspectives on the left and on the right: while liberals such as Horace Kallen and Randolph Bourne criticized the melting pot idea as a model of assimilation that led to homogenization and suggested alternative models geared toward ethno-cultural plurality and diversity instead, nativist anti-immigration critics and specifically eugenicists such as Madison Grant and Theodore Lothrop Stoddard perceived the melting pot as an imminent threat to (Anglo-) American society, welcomed the restrictive immigration legislation that curtailed large-scale immigration in 1924, and called for measures to secure the 'national health' on overtly racist grounds – proto-fascist notions of racial hygiene and racial purity are of central concern in their writings about American society.

Kallen, Bourne, and others perceived the melting pot as a repressive concept rather than as "genuine assimilation to one another," as John Dewey called it (qtd. in Wilson, *Melting-Pot Modernism* 14). Their critique of the melting pot as an ideology of Americanization grounded in coercive homogenization narrowly defined the melting pot as full assimilation to Anglo-Saxon culture. Horace Kallen (1882-1974), a Jewish American philosopher who had emigrated to the US as a child, proposed in his influential essay "Democracy versus the Melting-Pot" (1915) a democracy of various nationalities, a nation of nations, rather than a melting pot America:

Thus "American civilization" may come to mean the perfection of the cooperative harmonies of "European civilization" – the waste, the squalor, and the distress of Europe being eliminated – a multiplicity in a unity, an orchestration of mankind. As in an orchestra, every type of instrument has its specific *timbre* and *tonality*, founded in its substance and form; as every type has its appropriate theme and melody in the whole symphony, so in society each ethnic group is the natural instrument, its temper and culture may be its theme and melody, and the harmony and dissonances and discords of them all make the symphony of civilization. (116-17)

Kallen argues that cultural pluralism (a term he has been credited with coining), ethnic affiliation, and national pride are indeed compatible; he envisions America as a "nation of discrete nationalisms" and identifies ethnic diversity as "a national asset" (Hansen, *Lost Promise* 95) rather than seeing immigrants' loyalties to their countries of origin as an obstacle to the national coherence of the US. To illustrate his position, Kallen repeatedly uses musical metaphors that he seems to have borrowed from Jane Addams's 1892 essay "The Subjective Necessity for Social Settlements:"

If you have heard a thousand voices singing in the Hallelujah Chorus in Handel's "Messiah," you have found that the leading voices could still be distinguished, but that the differences of training and cultivation between them and the voices of the chorus were lost in the unity of purpose and the fact that they were all human voices lifted by a high motive. This is a weak illustration of what a Settlement attempts to do. (25)

Addams's use of Händel's oratorio to describe her settlement project Hull House is similar to the function of David's American symphony in Zangwill's *The Melting Pot* (which in fact has a non-fictional counterpart in Antonín Dvořák's

Symphony No. 9, which he composed in the US in 1893 – popularly known as the *New World Symphony*, it has since become one of the most popular symphonies in the romantic repertoire). That both advocates of cultural pluralism as well as melting pot advocates have used musical metaphors to stress the harmonious result of their respective approaches may be taken as indicative of how difficult it is at times to distinguish between the two positions.

In a similar vein to Kallen, writer and intellectual Randolph Bourne (1886-1918) argues in his essay "Trans-National America" (published in the *Atlantic Monthly* in July 1916) that Americanism should not be equated with Anglo-Saxonism and that immigrants should retain their languages and customs: "What we emphatically do not want is that these distinctive qualities should be washed out into a tasteless, colorless fluid of uniformity," he writes; immigrants "merge but they do not fuse." Bourne holds that US society consists of "a unique sociological fabric" which would allow it to become a "federation of cultures." Thus Bourne, like Kallen, criticizes the Anglo-Saxon elite for pushing their own culture as an American *leitkultur* and strictly opposes assimilation, which he deems undemocratic and even inhumane. He affirms the ethnic diversity of the US and defends the tendency of immigrants to maintain ties to their countries of origin against xenophobic and nationalist sentiments that in the context of World War I (which the US would formally enter in April 1917) had been on the rise. The pressure exerted on immigrants to conform and to assimilate in these years is enormous, but many of them do not bow to these pressures. While conservative critics lament this "failure of the melting-pot," Bourne, who values cultural difference and abhors uniformity, views it positively:

The failure of the melting-pot, far from closing the great American democratic experiment, means that it has only just begun. Whatever American nationalism turns out to be, we see already that it will have color richer and more exciting than our ideal has hitherto encompassed. In a world which has dreamed of internationalism, we find that we have all unawares been building up the first international nation. The voices which have cried for a tight and jealous nationalism of the European pattern are failing. From that ideal, however valiantly and disinterestedly it has been set for us, time and tendency have moved us further and further away. What we have achieved has been rather a cosmopolitan federation of national colonies, of foreign cultures, from whom the sting of devastating competition has been removed. America is already the world-federation in miniature, the continent where for the first time in history has been achieved that miracle of hope, the peaceful living side by side, with character substantially preserved, of the most heterogeneous peoples under the sun. Nowhere else has such contiguity been anything but the breeder of misery. Here, notwithstanding our tragic failures of adjustment, the outlines are already too clear not to give us a new vision and a new-orientation [sic] of the American mind in the world. ("Trans-National America")

Bourne advocates an American internationalism that leaves behind European factionalism and violent conflict; he is convinced that within the democratic framework of the US, all the cultures of the world could peacefully coexist. Bourne's views are articulated in the context of American Progressivism, a reform movement consisting "of shifting, ideologically fluid, issue-focused co-alitions, all competing for the reshaping of American society" (Rodgers, "In Search" 114), and stand in stark contrast to more conservative positions that finally won the day.

Illustration 3: The Mortar of Assimilation

PUCK.

THE MORTAR OF ASSIMILATION — AND THE ONE ELEMENT THAT WON'T MIX.

Ill. by C.J. Taylor (*Puck*, 26 June 1889).

Contrary to the reformist positions of Kallen, Bourne, and other leading intellectual progressive figures such as John Dewey, Jane Addams, Robert Park, and Franz Boas, conservative critics were opposed to the melting pot idea for quite different reasons. Kallen for example expressly attacked one of them, the American sociologist and eugenicist E.A. Ross (1866-1951), for his Anglo-American conservatism:

Kallen broke with Ross by interpreting America as a work in progress rather than a nation in the grip of cultural decline. Whereas Ross regarded the United States as the province of an Anglo-American cultural majority, Kallen advanced an ideal of cultural diversity. Where Ross delineated a program for cultural renewal that combined immigration restriction with assimilation to Anglo-American norms, Kallen discarded the metaphor of America-as-melting-pot in favour of the symbol of orchestral harmony. (Hansen, *Lost Promise* 92)

Kallen even addresses Ross in his essay "Democracy versus the Melting Pot" directly: "Hence, what troubles Mr. Ross and so many other Anglo-Saxon Americans is not really inequality; what troubles them is *difference*" (107). While the cultural pluralists Kallen and Bourne criticized the melting pot as assimilationist and homogenizing, conservative critics of the melting pot such as Ross found both pluralism and assimilation equally problematic and repulsive; their strict anti-immigration stance was motivated by a nationalist outlook based on the notions of white supremacy and racial purity, a position that denigrated all racial mixing as 'mongrelization.' Drawing on widespread xenophobic resentments, their message met with a lot of approval and became politically influential: After the Chinese Exclusion Act of 1882 and the so-called Gentleman's Agreement of 1907 (severely restricting Chinese and Japanese immigration, respectively), the likewise overtly racist Immigration Acts of 1917 and 1924 further restricted immigration, which reflects the then widespread acceptance of racist ideologies (cf. Gerstle, *American Crucible*).

Among the proponents of 'scientific' racism was Harry H. Laughlin (1880-1953), who as an "expert eugenics agent" delivered a report to Congress in 1922 in which he correlated so-called forms of social degeneracy (feeblemindedness, insanity, criminality, epilepsy, tuberculosis, alcoholism, dependency) with "racial degeneracy;" Laughlin "purported to find much higher levels of degeneracy among the new immigrants than among the old, and this finding became a central weapon in the restrictionists' arsenal" (ibid. 105). Laughlin's conjoining of the racist ideology of white supremacy with eugenicist principles enjoyed strong support from politicians: Calvin Coolidge himself, US president from 1923 to 1929, contended that "Nordics deteriorate when mixed with other races" (qtd. in Browder, *Slippery Characters* 146). It has been quite effectively erased from public memory that there was a strong eugenics movement in the US which propagated what Daylanne English refers to as "a central national ideology" (*Unnatural Selections* 14). This movement, in which American scientists and intellectuals played a vanguard role, pushed for 'perfecting' the human 'gene pool' by controlling the process of reproduction (cf. ibid.). American biologists like Harry H. Laughlin and Charles B. Davenport claimed that most 'ailments,' including social problems such as poverty and criminality, were genetically programmed and thus hereditary in nature – therefore persons with a 'good genetic makeup' should be encouraged to have families, while 'inferior' people of allegedly poor genetic stock should be prevented from reproducing. Among those people regarded as inferior were epileptics, manic-depressives, prostitutes, alcoholics, the homeless, criminals, as well as non-white residents and immigrants. Under the eugenics laws, people who came to the negative attention of the social authorities could be branded as 'feeble-minded' by court order and were then forcibly sterilized. By the early 1930s, some 30 American states had adopted such eugenics laws. Most of them were modelled after the law which Laughlin had drafted for the state of Virginia in 1924, which also served Germany's National Socialists as a model for their 1933 Law for the Prevention of Genetically Diseased Offspring, on the basis of which at least 400,000 men and women were forcibly sterilized. The University of Heidelberg was apparently so grateful to Laughlin that it awarded him an honorary doctorate for his 'services on behalf of racial hygiene' in 1936. The influence of American eugenics on Nazism goes even further: The notorious term 'Untermensch,' a core concept in Nazi ideology, is a translation from the English term 'Underman,' which, as unidiomatic as it may sound today, was coined by the American journalist and historian Theodore Lothrop Stoddard (1883-1950) in his 1922 study *The Revolt against Civilization: The Menace of the Under Man* (Stoddard, who held a PhD from Harvard University, was extremely popular during the heyday of 'Pop-Darwinism' and the so-called 'eugenics fad' in the 1920s). The equally notorious term 'aufnorden,' which also relates to an integral concept of Nazi ideology, similarly is a translation of Madison Grant's term 'to nordicize,' which he used in his 1916 *The Passing of the Great Race*. Obviously neither Laughlin nor Grant nor Stoddard found the melting pot idea appealing, as to them it signified the downfall of the American nation through the 'degeneration' of the Anglo-Saxon 'race.'

Today Stoddard is very much forgotten, as are Grant and Laughlin; in canonical American literature however, we find a clue as to his enormous popularity in the 1920s:

"Civilization's going to pieces," broke out Tom violently. "I've gotten to be a terrible pessimist about things. Have you read 'The Rise of the Colored Empires' by this man Goddard?"

"Why, no," I answered, rather surprised by his tone.

"Well, it's a fine book, and everybody ought to read it. The idea is if we don't look out the white race will be – will be utterly submerged. It's all scientific stuff; it's been proved."

(Fitzgerald, *Great Gatsby* 14)

Henry Fairchild (1880-1956) is another influential figure who makes a case against what he calls "unrestricted immigration" in his influential study *The Melting-Pot Mistake* (1926), in which he argues that "the consequence of non-assimilation [to Anglo-Saxon conformity] is the destruction of nationality" (253). Fairchild refers to the melting pot as an illusion and as dangerous wishful thinking: "The figure was a clever one – picturesque, expressive, familiar, just the sort of thing to catch the popular fancy and lend itself to a thousand uses" (ibid. 10). Like many of his contemporaries with similar political views, he metaphorically equates the American nation with a tree, and immigrants with parasites, "foreign forces," and "minute hostile organisms" that "sap the very vitality of their host" (ibid. 255):

In so doing the immigrants may be merely following out their natural and defensible impulses without any hostility toward the receiving nation, any more than parasites upon a tree may be considered to have any hostility to the tree. [...] The simple fact is that they are alien particles, not assimilated, and therefore wholly different from the foreign particles which the tree rakes in the form of blood, and transforms into cells of its own body. (ibid.)

This kind of crude and simplistic organicist imagery together with racist rhetoric that draws on biology in general has lastingly influenced the discourse on immigration until today.

Illustration 4: The Melting Pot, Inc.

The Ford English School Graduation Ceremony of 1916 (The Henry Ford Collections).

As has been shown, the melting pot myth became a prime target of criticism by intellectuals on the left and on the right for contradictory reasons: the pluralists argued that it was too repressive, while for the nativists, it was too inclusive. Still, the melting pot myth is a singular vision in the way that it *de*-emphasizes difference while holding the middle ground between total assimilation on the one hand and racist exclusion on the other. American journalist, novelist, and cultural critic Ernest Poole (1880-1950) describes the city of Chicago in 1910 as a "mixing-bowl for the nations" (*Voice* 554) and hails the urban melting pot as the "Tower of Babel's drama reversed" (ibid. 555). Whereas the biblical story dramatizes the production of difference as tragic dispersal, the melting pot narrative promises unification through the creation of "a new race of men upon the earth" (ibid.). Socialist writer Michael Gold (1894-1967) argues in his essay "Towards Proletarian Art" that mass immigration could fuel a melting pot of new internationalist radicalism that he describes as a "cauldron of the Revolution" (62). Yet, as much as the melting pot myth could be used to critique white Anglo-Saxon social and political dominance, it was also used to enforce the conformity of immigrants entering the American workforce. Melting pot rituals performed for example at the Ford English School for immigrant automobile factory workers in Highland Park, Michigan reveal that the melting pot myth could also serve as an instrument of corporate self-fashioning and of Americanization in the corporate interest with a clearly *anti*-revolutionary impetus. More recently, Jeffrey Eugenides's novel *Middlesex* (2002) offers a literary re-telling of this kind of ritual (cf. 103-05).

In the period between the 1880s and the 1920s, discussions of the melting pot as a societal model thus became increasingly polarized, and the concept lost much of its "original elasticity" (Wilson, *Melting-Pot Modernism* 15) and critical appeal. Yet reconstructing the melting pot myth of that time allows us to see how race and racial difference gained prominence in debates on national, social, and cultural cohesion, as Gary Gerstle writes:

We do not usually think of the 1920s, the easygoing Jazz Age, as a time when the racialized character of the American nation intensified, reinforcing the barriers separating blacks and Asians from whites, eastern and southern Europeans from "Nordics," and immigrants from natives. Yet these developments were central to the age. That the proponents of these changes frequently justified their aims in the name of science underscores the modern character of the racial regime they implemented. Indeed this regime, backed by an edifice of race law, would remain in place for forty years, persisting through the Great Depression, World War II, the affluent 1950s, and John F. Kennedy's 1960 election. It must be seen for what it was: a defining feature of modern America. (*American Crucible* 114-15)

The melting pot myth in its hegemonic version has often obscured the role of racism in American society by projecting a colorblind vision of social harmony and by obscuring ongoing inequality. For the longest time, the democratic potential of the melting pot has clearly not been realized in American society.

5. MULTIPLE MELTING POTS AND MISCEGENATION

> When push came to shove, the color line between "the Negro" and everyone
> else mattered far more to patrician Americans than the markers within white-
> ness.
>
> MATTHEW PRATT GUTERL, *THE COLOR OF RACE IN AMERICA*

> There is a new race in America. I am a member of this new race. It is neither
> white nor black nor in-between. It is the American race, differing as much
> from white and black as white and black differ from each other. It is possible
> that there are Negro and Indian bloods in my descent along with English,
> Spanish, Welsh, Scotch, French, Dutch, and German. This is common in
> America; and it is from all these strains that the American race is being born.
> But the old divisions into white, black, brown, red, are outworn in this
> country. They have had their day. Now is the time of the birth of a new order,
> a new vision, a new ideal of man. I proclaim this new order.
>
> JEAN TOOMER, "A NEW RACE IN AMERICA"

Long after its heyday in the early 20th century, the melting pot concept continued
to shape public and academic debates. Ruby Kennedy's research into patterns of
intermarriage led her in 1952 to propose a triple rather than single melting pot
theory, as she found that in American society, Protestant, Catholic, and Jewish
"pool[s]" (in other words, 'pots') functioned as "fundamental bulwarks" into
which different nationalities and ethnicities 'melted' ("Single" 56). These findings were corroborated by Will Herberg's study *Protestant – Catholic – Jew*
(1955), in which religion also figures as a crucial sociological factor in processes
of group identity formation in American society. George Stewart's concept of
the "transmuting pot" (*American Ways* 23) on the other hand is more conformist,
as it assumes that "as the foreign elements, a little at a time, were added to the
pot, they were not merely melted but were largely transmuted, and so did not affect the original material as strikingly as might be expected" (ibid.). Building on
the research of Kennedy, Herberg, and Stewart, Milton Gordon in 1964 reviewed
the divergent positions on assimilation promoting Anglo-Saxon conformity, the
melting pot, and cultural pluralism, respectively, with the intent to establish an
empirical approach to processes of assimilation that would not rely on a normative ideal, a political doctrine, or a vague metaphor. He dismissed the "single
melting pot" as an idealistic "illusion" (*Assimilation* 129), which led him to
develop it into a theory of multiple melting pots or "subsocieties" that are com-

prised not only of different religious identities (Protestant, Catholic, Jewish) but also for example (and somewhat surprisingly) of "intellectuals:"

All these containers, as they bubble along in the fires of American life and experience are tending to produce, with somewhat differing speeds, products which are culturally very similar, while at the same time they remain structurally separate. The entire picture is one which, with the cultural qualifications already noted, may be called a "multiple melting pot." And so we arrive at the "pluralism" which characterizes the contemporary American scene. (ibid. 131)

As this quotation shows, Gordon focuses primarily on structural divisions in the composition of American society, and in that context also points out that "Negroes, Orientals, Mexican-Americans, and some Puerto Ricans are prevented by racial discrimination from participating meaningfully in either the white Protestant or the white Catholic communities" (ibid. 129). Gordon thus explicitly addresses the exclusion of African American communities from white society at a time when marriage between African Americans and whites was still legally prohibited in 22 (mostly Western and Southern) states (cf. ibid. 165) – these and other Jim Crow laws regulating racial segregation were only abolished by the Civil Rights Act of 1964 (it should be noted, however, that recently several state legislatures announced their intention to pass what would amount to neo-segregationist laws after the Supreme Court decided in *Shelby County v. Holder* on June 25 2013 that important anti-discrimination measures provided by the Voting Rights Act of 1965 were unconstitutional). Yet, somewhat symptomatically, the categories 'black' and 'negro' are not further problematized in Milton's study. Due to the one-drop rule in US cultural and legal history, an example of hypodescent that classifies as black individuals with *any* African ancestry, African American communities are racially mixed in unacknowledged ways, which led some scholars to state that the 'black' segment of the US population constitutes the only genuine melting pot in American society:

The melting pot is hardly a suitable metaphor for a system characterized by an unstable pluralism. But – bitter irony – isn't there a sense in which the melting pot notion is more applicable within the black American nation than within the white? There was great diversity in the African origins of American Negroes: regional, linguistic, and tribal differences, as well as in their prior condition of freedom. [...] Despite this diversity, however, Africans were forcibly homogenized after several generations into a fairly singular Afro-American mold with common folkways. Thus, the only American melting pot has perhaps been a black one, though in this case the putative pot has been reluctant to call the kettle black. (Kammen, *People* 82)

It is ironic, if not outright cynical that the exclusion of those considered 'black' from the national melting pot has led to the creation of this social category of the 'black' melting pot. The horrendous violence that fuelled this particular melting pot and created this 'new' identity by eradicating all prior cultural markers from forcibly uprooted individuals makes one wonder whether the melting pot is not, after all, a metaphor of destruction. At the very least it appears as a symbol of "renouncing – often in clearly public ways – one's subjectivity, who one literally was: in name, in culture, and, as far as possible, in color" (Goldberg, "Introduction" 5).

Historically, African Americans thus were excluded from the melting pot; participants in the envisioned amalgamation process have mostly been European groups (e.g. in Zangwill's *The Melting Pot*), and even as Crèvecoeur includes Native Americans in his account of racial and cultural mixing, Natives (as well as African Americans and Asian Americans) have been mostly absent from melting pot rhetoric. In a speech held in 1919, then-president Woodrow Wilson (1856-1924) "appealed for the extension of the melting pot principle to all the nations of the world" (Saveth, *American Historians* 147) "even as he segregated government employees by race" (Browder, *Slippery Characters* 146). The policing and prohibition of racial mixing in America has amounted to what some scholars have termed "American Apartheid" (cf. Massey and Denton's book of the same title) through Jim Crow legislation, segregation based on racial discrimination, and black ghettoization across the country – which is why subnational perspectives on the melting pot myth unsurprisingly have found it exclusive rather than inclusive. 'Racial' mixing (i.e., social/sexual relations between whites and blacks) was commonly referred to as miscegenation and as such was illegal in many parts of the US for most of its history. The term 'miscegenation' was first used in 1863 in a pamphlet titled *Miscegenation: The Theory of the Blending of the Races, Applied to the American White Man and Negro* (cf. Croly), which advocated the mixing of the races; supposedly published by the Republican Party, it turned out to have been an attempt by Democrats to discredit their political opponents. Before the term miscegenation was coined, the term 'amalgamation' was in common use, but whereas 'amalgamation' could also refer to the intermixing between non-racially defined groups (e.g. Irish Catholics and Protestants), 'miscegenation' has always referred specifically to black-white relations and can be considered to be part of a particular kind of American exceptionalism:

One theme that has been pervasive in US history and literature and that has been accompanied by a 300-year long tradition of legislation, jurisdiction, protest and defiance is the deep concern about, and the attempt to prohibit, contain, or deny, the presence of black-white sexual interracial relations, interracial marriage, interracial descent, and other family relations across the powerful black-white divide. Even the term "miscegenation" is an American invention. (Sollors, "Introduction" 3)

Laws prohibiting racial mixing were passed in the colonies as early as 1664 in Maryland and 1691 in Virginia. In 1883, the US Supreme Court upheld the constitutionality of anti-miscegenation laws in *Pace v. Alabama*, a decision that was overturned only in *McLaughlin v. Florida* (1964) and *Loving v. Virginia* (1967). The latter case involved Richard and Mildred Loving, who in 1958 went to Washington, D.C. to get married because interracial marriages at that time were still illegal in their home state of Virginia, where they were prosecuted for and convicted of violating the state's anti-miscegenation laws in 1959. Their sentence of one year in prison was suspended after they agreed to leave the state. Forced to leave their home and families, the Lovings decided to challenge the constitutionality of Virginia's anti-miscegenation statutes in court; after the Virginia Supreme Court of Appeals affirmed the legality of the statutes, they were finally ruled unconstitutional by the US Supreme Court in 1967 (cf. Newbeck, *Virginia*). Barack Obama reflects on this history in his memoir, *Dreams from My Father*:

Miscegenation. The word is humpbacked, ugly, portending a monstrous outcome: like *antebellum* or *octoroon*, it evokes images of another era, a distant world of horsewhips and flames, dead magnolias and crumbling porticos. [...] In 1960, the year that my parents were married, *miscegenation* still described a felony in over half the states in the Union. In many parts of the South, my father could have been strung up from a tree for merely looking at my mother the wrong way; in the most sophisticated of northern cities, the hostile stares, the whispers, might have driven a woman in my mother's predicament into a back-alley abortion. [...] Their very image together would have been considered lurid and perverse, a handy retort to the handful of softheaded liberals who supported a civil rights agenda.
Sure – but would you let your daughter marry one?
The fact that my grandparents had answered yes to this question, no matter how grudgingly, remains an enduring puzzle to me. (11-12)

In the history of these legal statutes, the melting pot myth becomes undone. Throughout American literature, interracial figures appear as 'tragic mulatta/os,' i.e. stereotypical characters who decide to 'pass' as white in order to evade being subjected to an exclusionary and frequently violent racism; passing in American literature is variably interpreted as loss or treason and as a tragic metamorphosis that destabilizes one's identity and oftentimes ends in death. Troping mixed-race individuals as tragic mulatta/os who do not fully belong to any group in American society went along with the notion that unions between blacks and whites should be prohibited, or in any case avoided. When the film *Guess Who's Coming to Dinner* (1967) featured Hollywood's first interracial kiss, it could only be shown in the mirror of a taxi, with the taxi driver gazing through the mirror at the couple in the backseat as the only (shocked and dismayed) eyewitness. Mary Dearborn has pointed out that the taboo on miscegenation furthermore has been coded in American cultural and literary history in a way that likens racial mixing to incest (cf. *Pocahontas's Daughters* 158).

Throughout American intellectual history, writers and activists have voiced opposition to segregationist laws and practices. 19th-century writer and activist Lydia Maria Child (1802-1880) and 20th-century philosopher Hannah Arendt (1906-1975) both advocated racial mixing as a means to overcome social and racial divisions in American society. Writing on the eve of the American Civil War, Child developed plots of miscegenation in which whites and non-whites could no longer be told apart, and racial conflicts were resolved through infinite racial mixing; she thus fictionally realized "a truly egalitarian society, one in which blacks and whites in all walks of life could mingle freely and easily" (Clifford, *Crusader* 280), even though her writings, like many abolitionist texts of the 19th century, clearly reflect a white middle class ideology (cf. Karcher, "Lydia Maria Child's" 81). In the decades after the Civil War, it was particularly African American writers like Charles Chesnutt who took up the notion of a 'new race' and questioned constructions of the color line (cf. Chesnutt, "Future American" and "What Is a White Man?;" McWilliams, *Charles W. Chesnutt*). In her famous essay "Reflections on Little Rock," published about one hundred years later, Hannah Arendt provocatively remarked that school desegregation could never bring about integration and social change as long as white and black adults were not allowed to marry each other, which at that time was still legally prohibited in 29 states by laws that Arendt considered "a much more flagrant breach of letter and spirit of the Constitution than segregation of schools" (231). Werner Sollors has reconstructed the uproar this essay caused among contemporary audiences for explicitly addressing a widely accepted taboo (cf. "Introduction"), and for criticizing

[t]he reluctance of American liberals to touch the issue of the marriage laws, their readiness to invoke practicality and shift the ground of the argument by insisting that the Negroes themselves have no interest in this matter, their embarrassment when they are reminded of what the whole world knows to be the most outrageous piece of legislation in the whole western hemisphere. (Arendt, "Reflections" 246)

Both Child and Arendt each in her own way were advocates of a melting pot that included African Americans, yet their voices have been marginalized by sancti-monious segregationists who have been in denial about the realities of human relations – as the protagonist of Warren Beatty's *Bulworth* (1998) bluntly asserts: "Everybody's fuckin' everybody else till you can't tell the difference" (qtd. in Elam, *Souls* 9).

Within the African American community, we can trace different reactions to the melting pot myth over time: accommodation with racial segregation and ac-ceptance of restricted access to the American melting pot; harsh criticism of the melting pot ideology and its mechanisms of exclusion; a clear rejection of racial mixing with whites in an inverted discourse of racial supremacy (for instance in many publications of representatives of the Nation of Islam) based on racial pride; and, last but not least, an affirmation of a more inclusive melting pot that is explicitly multiracial and moves past the tormenting "double-consciousness" and its "two unreconciled strivings" which W.E.B. Du Bois has diagnosed for African Americans in the US (*Souls* 2).

The first position – accommodation with segregation and African Amer-icans' exclusion from the melting pot after the Civil War – has often been associated with former slave and black intellectual Booker T. Washington (1856-1915). In the so-called Atlanta Compromise Speech given by Washington on September 18, 1895, he stated in regard to black and white interaction and coexistence that "[i]n all things that are purely social we can be as separate as the fingers, yet one as the hand in all things essential to mutual progress" (*Up from* 100). This analogy accepts and affirms the cultural logic of racial segregation and opts for a strategy of gradualism for which Washington was sharply criti-cized by some of his African American contemporaries, because they considered his position to be submissive to whites and accepting of racial discrimination.

Melvin Steinfield similarly criticizes the hypocrisy of the melting pot myth in the context of the continued exclusion of African Americans from national models of cohesion and belonging in the mid-20th century by asserting that "[e]very instance of racism or discrimination was a vivid contradiction of the myth of the Melting Pot [...]," or what he calls "cracks in the Melting Pot" in his book of the same title (xvii, xx). In his well-known poem "The Melting Pot," Dudley Randall (1914-2000) contrasts the experience of European immigrants to the US with the experience of African Americans:

> There is a magic melting pot
> where any girl or man
> can step in Czech or Greek or Scot,
> step out American.
>
> **Johann** and **Jan** and **Jean** and **Juan**,
> **Giovanni** and **Ivan**
> step in and then step out again
> all freshly christened **John**.
>
> Sam, watching, said, "Why, I was here
> even before they came,"
> and stepped in too, but was tossed out
> before he passed the brim.
>
> And every time Sam tried that pot
> they threw him out again.
> "Keep out. This is our private pot.
> We don't want your black stain."
>
> At last, thrown out a thousand times,
> Sam said, "I don't give a damn.
> Shove your old pot. You can like it or not,
> but I'll be just what I am."
> (167, emphasis in the original)

In Randall's poem, the melting pot signifies assimilation to the dominant culture (as it commonly does in modern day usage) rather than a form of hybridity: all European immigrants regardless of their ethnic backgrounds become "Johns," i.e., their Americanization amounts to Anglicization. The African American's reaction to being rejected – "But I'll be just what I am" – anticipates the development of modern Black nationalism, whose proponents responded to racial discrimination and exclusion by programmatically rejecting racial fusion with whites and thus by rejecting the melting pot logic on their own terms. African American intellectuals in the Black Power movement of the 1960s and 1970s thus negated and ridiculed notions of racial and cultural mixing. Malcolm X for example used black coffee as a symbol for racial purity and integrity:

It's just like when you've got some coffee that's too black, which means it's too strong. What do you do? You integrate it with cream, you make it weak. But if you pour too much cream in it, you won't even know you ever had coffee. It used to be hot, it becomes cool. It used to be strong, it becomes weak. It used to wake you up, now it puts you to sleep. ("Message" 16)

In the last decades, in which American society has been labeled "post-racial" or "post-ethnic" by critics such as David Hollinger – who has also (half-seriously) suggested that American society may be described as a "quintuple melting pot" (*Postethnic America* 24) differentiated into Euro-Americans, Asian Americans, African Americans, Hispanics, and Indigenous peoples (cf. ibid. 23) – more inclusive versions of the melting pot have been articulated that attempt to bridge the divide between blacks and whites (cf. Randall Kennedy, *Interracial Intimacies*; Elam, *Souls*). Upon the founding of the Association of MultiEthnic Americans (AMEA) in 1988, activist Carlos Fernandez quipped:

We who embody the melting pot [...] stand up [...] as intolerant participants against racism from whatever quarter it may come [...]. We are the faces of the future. Against the travails of regressive interethnic division and strife, we can be a solid core of unity bonding peoples together in the common course of human progress. (qtd. in Kennedy, *Interracial Intimacies* 141)

Currently, the AMEA is one of the most influential mixed race organizations; it prompted the reform that in 2000 allowed census respondents for the first time to check more than one box for racial self-identification. Activists campaigning for the recognition of multiraciality assert that they are the outcome of the 'true melting pot:' "This then is my claim: I am in all America. All America is in me" (Taylor Haizlip, *Sweeter*, epigraph). The oftentimes uncritical celebration of multi-raciality in the new mixed race literature prompts Michelle Elam to ask what the much-touted "New Amalgamationism" and the "Mulatto Millennium" (Senna qtd. in Elam, *Souls* 12) imply for *black* people in US society; the arrival of this new melting pot 'in black and white' to her is a hollow emblem of *faux* cultural and racial hybridity that invokes an 'American multiracial democracy' which seems to be serving various ideological interests: the 'multiracial American' appears to be vested with a precarious domestic exoticism more than slightly at odds with the identity politics of its representatives.

Besides European immigrants and African Americans, whose ambivalent reactions toward the melting pot myth have so far been at the center of my discussion, other groups of course have also dealt with the topic: Native American, Asian American, and Mexican American critics and writers have articulated alternative models to the melting pot such as "mestizaje" (cf. Anzaldúa, *Borderlands/La Frontera*) and "crossblood" (cf. Vizenor, *Manifest Manners*), which emphasize the hybridity, fluidity, and multidimensionality of American identities. Owing much to theories of cultural and racial difference that had been gaining ground since the 1960s, these more recent models have strongly influenced public debates around collective identity, especially in regard to American multiculturalism, which has been hotly debated in particular during the 1980s.

6. OUT OF MANY, MANY – AMERICAN MULTICULTURALISM

> The luck so far of the American experiment has been due in large part to the vision of the melting pot.
> ARTHUR M. SCHLESINGER, *THE DISUNITING OF AMERICA*

> The point about the melting pot [...] is that it did not happen.
> NATHAN GLAZER AND DANIEL PATRICK MOYNIHAN, *BEYOND THE MELTING POT*

> Hyphen: Nation
> MATTHEW FRYE JACOBSON, *ROOTS TOO*

It is in the 1960s that the (multi)cultural turn marks a shift in the perception of the melting pot myth that subsequently tends to be lumped together with models of assimilation of all kinds, in the process of which the melting pot loses all of its utopian appeal because it has since been primarily seen as a form of standardization implying the destruction of cultural variety, and has been falsely equated with assimilation. The advent of multiculturalism thus precluded any further discussion of the melting pot among the cultural left. When Gordon suggests that the multiple melting pots in American society point to cultural pluralism rather than to homogeneous Americanness (cf. *Assimilation*), he is articulating the *zeitgeist* of the 1960s, which celebrated pluralism under the banner of 'multiculturalism.' The "dawn of the new pluralism" (Feldstein and Costello, *Ordeal* 415) and the beginning of the new "age of pluralism in American public discussion" (Landsman and Katkin, "Introduction" 2) are often dated back to the publication of Nathan Glazer and Daniel Patrick Moynihan's influential study *Beyond the Melting Pot* in 1963. Using the melting pot concept as a shortcut to refer to various processes of assimilation, its authors contend that there never was a melting pot in the history of the US, but only distinct and diverse groups and group identities. Focussing in their study on New York City's socio-cultural composition, Glazer and Moynihan argue that even though New York City cannot be equated with the United States at large because of its "extreme" heterogeneity (*Beyond the Melting Pot* 9), it can nevertheless be regarded as the country's cultural epicenter (cf. ibid. 6). The authors find that "the negroes, Puerto Ricans, Jews, Italians and Irish of New York City" are all *distinct* ethnic groups with identifiable characteristics and life patterns; even though the melting pot may have been "an idea close to the heart of an American self-image" (ibid. 288), according to Glazer and Moynihan, it has neither been realized in New York City, nor elsewhere in the US: instead, it is the "pattern of ethnicity" (ibid. 310) that they consider to be at the heart of urban politics and institutions, which is why they suggest moving "beyond the melting pot" to account for the complexities of affiliation and loyalties in the ongoing formation of a US national identity. Glazer and Moynihan's study clearly constituted a paradigm shift in the discussion of the melting pot and paved the way for the discourse of multiculturalism, i.e. the explication of the "multicultural condition" (Goldberg, "Introduction" 1) on the one hand, and the political debate on the cultural heterogeneity of the US on the other. Multiculturalism, in its programmatic version, is positioned in clear opposition to the melting pot myth: First, like cultural pluralism, multiculturalism as a political program recognizes and seeks to retain cultural difference within the US as valuable and characteristic of a collective/ national American identity; second, it considers "monoculturalism" (ibid. 3) and ethnocentrism as repressive and coercive; third, multiculturalism engages in identity politics and calls for the representation and recognition of individuals and groups formerly underrepresented; fourth, it formulates a clear political agenda in terms of citizenship and access to society's resources (such as education) through, for instance, affirmative action programs. Multiculturalism calls for a pluralism based on an "ethic of toleration" (Landsman and Katkin, "Introduction" 4) and the primacy of "recognition" (cf. Gutmann, *Multiculturalism*). In the 1980s and beyond, discussions around multiculturalism were so polarized – especially in regard to canon debates and controversies around school curricula – that they have often been called veritable 'culture wars.' Rick Simonson and Scott Walker's *The Graywolf Annual Five: Multi-Cultural Literacy* (1988) for example explicitly sought to challenge E.D. Hirsch's *Cultural Literacy: What Every American Needs to Know* (1987), which the authors found "alarmingly deficient in its male and European bias" (Simonson and Scott, *Graywolf* 191), as well as Allan Bloom's *The Closing of the American Mind* (1987), which claimed that American education was in decline. Hirsch's selection of what he thinks an American needs to know about – for instance, act of God, Adam and Eve, John Adams, John Quincy Adams, adultery, Adonis, and *The Aeneid* – is based on a very different (humanist/universalist) notion of cultural literacy than the multi-cultural literacy of Simonson and Walker, who think that an American should also be knowledgeable about, for instance, the Asian Exclusion Act, action painting, Agent Orange, Alcoholics Anonymous, and Chinua Achebe.

Conservatives have denounced initiatives such as Simonson and Walker's as an "attack on the common American identity" and as an "ethnic revolt against the melting pot" (Schlesinger, *Disuniting* 119, 133); they thought that multi-culturalism was overcritical of the US and its history and bred a "culture of complaint" (cf. Hughes's book of the same title) defined by intolerance and political correctness. Other critics in contrast suggested that "we are all multi-culturalists now" (cf. Glazer's book of the same title), since sensibilities do have changed, and quite ubiquitously, we find the rejection of the melting pot myth and assimilation policies in favor of a celebration of the diverse cultures of America's many racial and ethnic groups (cf. Gerstle, *American Crucible* 348). As the debates around multiculturalism in American academia have ebbed, the term itself seems to have done its part: recent American studies glossaries frequently even fail to include an entry for the term multiculturalism. Moreover, a re-evaluation and critical assessment of multiculturalism has been offered by scholars such as those of the Chicago Cultural Studies Group, who critique what they call "the flattening effect typical of corporate multiculturalism" ("Critical Multiculturalism" 540); Terence Turner, who engages with "difference multi-culturalism" as an impoverished version of multiculturalism (cf. "Anthropol-ogy"); Michelle Wallace, who views multiculturalism as a new institutional logic that preserves the status quo (cf. *Invisibility Blues*); Ella Shohat and Robert Stam, who argue for a "polycentric multiculturalism" that takes into account "all cultural history in relation to social power" (*Unthinking* 48); and Richard Sennett, who suggests that diversity may eventually discourage solidarity and in fact breed indifference rather than tolerance (cf. *Conscience*). Sennett reflects on this matter in his description of a walk through a New York City neighborhood; whereas Glazer and Moynihan described New York City as a space differ-entiated along ethnic lines, Sennett holds that the city should be a space of interaction, of *civitas* and engagement rather than what he perceives as "[a] city of differences and of fragments of life that do not connect" (ibid. 125). In Sennett's story "of the races, who live segregated lives close together, and of social classes, who mix but do not socialize" (ibid. 128), tolerance has turned into indifference, and multiculturalism into disengagement. Sennett's account of his New York City neighborhood points to the potential problems of multiculturalism and critically re-interprets the meaning of living "in the presence of difference" (ibid. 121).

The affirmation of ethnic, often hyphenated identities has also led to an ethnic revival among those groups in American society commonly categorized as 'white' or 'non-ethnic.' Thus, it almost seems as if the melting pot not only failed to 'melt' non-white ethnic groups, but also managed to 'melt' white immigrant groups only superficially, as their third or fourth generation descendants have been coming forward to identify themselves as ethnic Americans. Early on philosopher and journalist Michael Novak in *The Rise of the Unmeltable Ethnics* (1972) anticipated a (re)turn to ethnicity among the lower-middle-class whites of Irish, Polish, Italian, etc. descent that had no longer been perceived as ethnic. Yet, this book about the ethnic revival among white (Catholic) Americans had – much to the discomfort of its author – a curious career: As Novak had written his book in 1972 "to divert attention from 'blacks, women, and the poor'" (Novak, *Rise* xiii), he felt uneasy about the enlistment of his study by scholars and advocates of multiculturalism in the 1970s and 1980s – so uneasy, in fact, that he felt compelled to re-issue his book in 1996 with a new introduction in which he disclaimed any affiliation with the "multiculturalists," listed what he called the "Nine Perversions of 'Multiculturalism'" (e.g. "Anti-Americanism," "Tactical Relativism," "Censorship," and "Double Standards") (Novak, *Rise* xvi-xvii), and related his conversion from the cultural left to the cultural right and to a whole-hearted embrace of capitalism.

Novak's unease notwithstanding, the discussion of those white ethnics who had only seemingly melted into American society continued in the context of multiculturalism and critical whiteness studies, which analyzed the power and the limits of white privilege. Sociologist Mary Waters points in her study *Ethnic Options* to the flexibility of the category of whiteness, which may accommodate Jewish Americans, Polish Americans, or Italian Americans (to name but a few groups), but may also lead them "to misconstrue the experience of their counterparts across the color line" (36; cf. also Jacobson, *Roots*) by over-emphasizing the voluntary character of ethnic identification. The latter also resonates in David Hollinger's idealistic vision of a "post-ethnic America" that has at its basis the notion that "the identities people assume are acquired largely through affiliation, however prescribed or chosen" (*Postethnic America* 7, 12).

The new popularity and acceptance of hyphenated identities in the context of multiculturalism encompass African American, Asian American, Hispanic American, Native American, as well as European American groups (e.g. Irish Americans, Italian Americans, and Norwegian Americans). Matthew Jacobson relates an episode in which members of an anti-racism workshop, one by one, disown their status as white ("'I'm not white; I'm Italian;' 'I'm not white; I'm Jewish,'" etc.), leaving the teacher to wonder: "'What happened to all the white people who were here just a minute ago?'" (*Roots* 1-2). Whether in the context of immigrant genealogies or mixed race identities, at the end of the 20th and the beginning of the 21st century, ethnicity is seen largely as a way of distinction and distinctiveness, as "a distinguishing from" rather than as a "merging with" (ibid. 36). However, subnational melting pot myth revisionism is somewhat polarized: For the multiculturalists on the left, the melting pot model is unattractive because it is perceived as "the cover for the domination of one [group]" over others (Appiah, "Limits" 52), whereas cultural critics on the right have ironically become its most outspoken defenders, and have celebrated it as a genuinely American invention. Yet, contemporary critics as well as defenders of the melting pot myth operate with a very simplistic notion that equates the melting pot with assimilation and Anglo-Saxon conformity rather than with a creative, continuous, and democratic process of hybridization – i.e., both strip the idea of its transformative power. On a somewhat different note, Richard Alba and Victor Nee have recently considered the "remaking [of] the American mainstream" through processes of migration and cultural change by applying the term "assimilation" to the mainstream rather than to minorities:

Assimilation has reshaped the American mainstream in the past, and it will do so again, culturally, institutionally, and demographically. [...] Through assimilation, the mainstream has become diverse in ethnic origins of those who participate in it; and the ethnic majority group, which dominates the mainstream population, has been reconstituted. (*Remaking* 282, 284)

In their "new assimilation theory" Alba and Nee stress that the incorporation of immigrant groups in the long run always involves a transformation of the mainstream, which as a result becomes increasingly heterogeneous itself; thus, they come close to a re-interpretation of melting pot dynamics which presupposes that cultural contact leaves no one unchanged.

7. CONCLUSION

> No modern state has been constituted by a single, coherent cultural group; all
> have incorporated disparate and even hostile ethnicities, each with its special
> history, some with their own language.
> RICHARD SLOTKIN, "UNIT PRIDE"

Even if Arthur M. Schlesinger in an attempt to identify the cornerstones of
American exceptionalism has listed the melting pot among America's ten great
contributions to civilization (cf. *Disuniting*), the melting pot myth was not an
American invention: Israel Zangwill, who popularized the concept in the US and
abroad, was a British Jew whose play *The Melting Pot* entails a transnational
vision that negotiates Jewish identity in the diaspora and the role of Judaism in
America.

In a scholarly context, a transnational perspective on the melting pot was articulated as early as 1911 in the writings of anthropologist Franz Boas, who did
not question the American melting pot as such, yet doubted its exceptionality:

It is often claimed that the phenomenon of mixture presented in the United States is
unique; that a similar intermixture has never occurred before in the world's history; and
that our nation is destined to become what some writers choose to term a "mongrel" nation
in a sense that has never been equalled anywhere. When we try to analyze the phenomenon in greater detail, and in the light of our knowledge of conditions in Europe as well as
in other continents, this view does not seem to me tenable. ("Race Problems" 320)

Boas points to historical evidence of intermixture as the rule rather than the
exception in the European context, which could be traced as far back as the
Migration Period (*Völkerwanderung*). In historical perspective, nation-building
is quite a recent phenomenon, while intermarriage seems to be quite an old one.

On a transnational, i.e. comparative note, again, we may conclude that
whereas the melting pot myth has been central to American self-representations
throughout the centuries and into the present, it is by no means a concept that
can only be found in the US; melting pot rhetoric has for example also been used
in Russian and in Israeli political culture in the context of current immigration
debates (cf. Nahshon, Introductory Essay 211). In Israel, "Mizug Galuyot," i.e.
the integration of different communities of immigrants from the Jewish diaspora
into Israeli society, can be considered to be the Israeli equivalent of the melting
pot model, and the national policy of the "ingathering of exiles" has led to political and sociological discussions about cultural pluralism and ethnic separatism

in modern Israeli society with at times explicit reference to Zangwill's work (cf. Krausz, *Studies*).

Even if the melting pot already seemed to be "a closed story, an unfashionable concept, a version of repressive assimilation in the service of cultural homogenization" (Wilson, *Melting-Pot Modernism* 14), it has once again been revitalized in political and scholarly debates following 9/11. *Reinventing the Melting Pot*, an essay collection published in 2004, may serve as an example that relates the events of 9/11 directly to problems of American identity, society, politics, and culture; 9/11, according to the collection's editor, triggered intensified "soul-searching" about "what it meant to be American" (Jacoby, "What It Means" 293). Critics such as Peter Salins refer to "the need [post 9/11] to reaffirm our commitment to the American concept of assimilation" (*Assimilation* 103) and call for "a more forthright discussion of what needs to be done to sustain e pluribus unum for the generations to come" (ibid. 107). In Jacoby's strange collection, we also find the continued conflation of melting pot logic with assimilation to Americanism. Developments since 9/11 have clearly shown that US "racial nationalism" has not been laid to rest (cf. Gerstle, *American Crucible* 368-371) but has been merely reconfigured to create new patterns of exclusion (cf. Bakalian and Bozorgmehr, *Backlash 9/11*; Peek, *Behind the Backlash*). Post-9/11 racism and xenophobia clearly touch on the melting pot myth: In 2001, Gary Gerstle predicted that "tensions with [...] Islamic fundamentalist groups abroad, could easily generate antagonism toward [...] Muslim Americans living in the United States, thus aiding those seeking to sharpen the sense of American national identity" (*American Crucible* 371). A comment by rock musician and activist Ted Nugent titled "Multicultural Rot in the Melting Pot," which was printed in the *Washington Post* on March 4, 2011, confirms Gerstle's prediction, as Nugent claims that Islam seeks to dominate the West and warns that the "culture war is on, whether they [i.e. politicians] like it or not." Nugent rehashes some of the arguments brought forward by Samuel Huntington in his *The Clash of Civilizations*, a book which amounts to an antithetical configuration to the melting pot myth on a global scale. Huntington challenges and modifies the melting pot myth both for the US and for a transnational context as he declares the end, i.e. the failure of the melting pot with regard to Islam and Muslims in American society; Huntington's ideas, which "more closely resemble nativist ravings than scholarly assessment" (Glenn, "Critics"), uncannily return us to the discussions around cultural, racial, and religious differences that had already accompanied immigration processes one hundred years prior to Huntington's polemic.

The visions of the melting pot as a model for American society were radical at the time they were first articulated; as limited as they may have been in other ways, they put into question fixed and static notions of collective American identity as well as notions of Anglo-Saxon dominance and conformity. Presently, the critical potential of the melting pot needs to be reassessed as a model into which both subnational and transnational perspectives are inscribed. The melting pot is a myth that rejects narratives of purity and potentially also simplistic and one-sided notions of assimilation. As I have pointed out, the melting pot has become "the standard metaphor for cultural hybridization" (Hansen, *Lost Promise* 98); in postcolonial studies (cf. e.g. Bhabha, *Location*), the preoccupation with hybridity can be seen as a return to melting pot theories under the arch of poststructuralism. Over all, as a somewhat skewed metaphor for processes of individual and collective identity formation that are understood as dynamic, provisional, and without closure or final result, the melting pot seems to echo less in theories of assimilation than in theories of hybridization and creolization in an increasingly globalized world (cf. Hannerz, *Transnational Connections*; Appadurai, *Modernity*; Pieterse, "Globalisation").

To end on a lighter note: Philip Gleason lists many culinary manifestations and replacements of the melting pot, like stew, soup, salad, and salad bowl (*Speaking* 14), as well as Karl E. Meyer's "pressure cooker" (*New America* 119). The Melting Pot is now also a chain of franchised fondue restaurants which by picking that name literalized the metaphor and recharged the melting pot's culinary dimension that it has had all along. The melting pot as a corporate brand projects its name as a euphemistic symbol of a shared culinary feast engaged in by those who can afford to consume in rather than be consumed by a globalized world.

8. STUDY QUESTIONS

1. What are the key differences between the melting pot myth and foundational myths that focus on historical personae? Why should we consider the melting pot as a foundational myth of the US?
2. Describe different versions of the melting pot myth and contextualize them historically. Who is included and who is excluded when and why?
3. How does melting pot rhetoric describe the interaction between whites and indigenous populations in North America in the early republic, and how does it refer to the interaction between the American-born population and immigrants in the Progressive Era? Discuss similarities and differences.
4. Contrast the melting pot as a national model with notions of assimilation and ideas of cultural pluralism.
5. Zangwill's play *The Melting Pot* uses a romance plot to overcome 'old world' histories and differences. Discuss the suitability of romantic discourse for the affirmation of the melting pot myth.
6. What role does religion play in melting pot rhetoric, past and present?
7. Discuss the notion of a 'black' melting pot in the US in light of the one-drop rule, notions of 'passing,' and mixed-race discourses. Check and discuss the following websites: Eurasiannation.com, Mixedfolks.com.
8. Discuss the metaphors of musicality that have been used to evoke the melting pot idea. What are the implications of music, singing, orchestra, and symphony for the way a new collective is imagined? Listen to Dvořák's *New World Symphony* and reflect on its structure and instrumentation. Does it convey the idea of a 'melting' of differences?
9. How does the melting pot myth connect to postcolonial theories of hybridity with regard to its approach to difference?
10. Can you identify transnational dimensions of the melting pot myth and/or comparable concepts in other national and international contexts? Explore, for instance, the notion of "the cosmic race" envisioned by José Vasconcelos for the Americas in his "La Raza Cósmica" (1925). How can we relate it to the melting pot myth?

9. BIBLIOGRAPHY

Works Cited

Addams, Jane. "The Subjective Necessity for Social Settlements." 1892. *The Jane Addams Reader*. Ed. Jean Bethke Elshtain. New York: Basic, 2002. 14-28.

Ager, Waldemar. *On the Way to the Melting Pot*. 1917. Trans. Harry T. Cleven. Madison: Prairie Oak, 1995.

Alba, Richard, and Victor Nee. *Remaking the American Mainstream: Assimilation and Contemporary Immigration*. Cambridge: Harvard UP, 2003.

Anderson, Benedict. *Imagined Communities: Reflections on the Origin and Spread of Nationalism*. 1983. London: Verso, 2006.

Anzaldúa, Gloria. *Borderlands/La Frontera: The New Mestiza*. San Francisco: Aunt Lute, 1987.

Appadurai, Arjun. *Modernity at Large: Cultural Dimensions of Globalization*. Minneapolis: U of Minnesota P, 1998.

Appiah, Anthony Kwame. "The Limits of Pluralism." *Multiculturalism and American Democracy*. Ed. Arthur Melzer, et al. Lawrence: UP of Kansas, 1998. 37-54.

Archambeau, Robert. "Immigrant Languages: Dialogism and the Poetry of North American Migration." *English Literature and the Other Languages*. Ed. Ton Hoenselaars and Marius Buning. Amsterdam: Rodopi, 1999. 75-86.

Arendt, Hannah. "Reflections on Little Rock." 1959. *The Portable Hannah Arendt*. Ed. Peter Baehr. New York: Penguin, 2000. 231-46.

Bakalian, Anny, and Mehdi Bozorgmehr, eds. *Backlash 9/11: Middle Eastern and Muslim Americans Respond*. Berkeley: U of California P, 2009.

Bhabha, Homi K. *The Location of Culture*. London: Routledge, 1994.

Biale, David. "The Melting Pot and Beyond: Jews and the Politics of American Identity." *Insider/Outsider: American Jews and Multiculturalism*. Ed. David Biale, Michael Galchinsky, and Susannah Heschel. Berkeley: U of California P, 1998. 17-33.

Bieder, Robert E. *Science Encounters the Indian, 1820-1880: The Early Years of American Ethnology*. Norman: U of Oklahoma P, 1986.

Bloom, Allan. *The Closing of the American Mind*. New York: Simon, 1987.

Boas, Franz. "Race Problems in America." *The Shaping of American Anthropology, 1883-1911: A Franz Boas Reader*. Ed. George W. Stocking, Jr. New York: Basic, 1974. 318-30.

Bourne, Randolph. "Trans-National America." *Atlantic Monthly* 118 (1916). http://www.swarthmore.edu/SocSci/rbannis1/AIH19th/Bourne.html. 3 Dec. 2013.

Brandeis, Louis Dembitz. "True Americanism." *Brandeis on Zionism: A Collection of Addresses and Statements by Louis D. Brandeis.* Union: The Lawbook Exchange, 1999. 3-11.

Browder, Laura. *Slippery Characters: Ethnic Impersonators and American Identity.* Chapel Hill: U of North Carolina P, 2000.

Bryce, James. *The American Commonwealth.* Vol. 2. Completely rev. ed. New York: Macmillan, 1923.

Bulworth. Dir. Warren Beatty. 20th Century Fox, 1998.

Campbell, Neil, and Alasdair Kean. *American Cultural Studies: An Introduction to American Culture.* London: Routledge, 1997.

Chesnutt, Charles W. "The Future American." *Theories of Ethnicity: A Classical Reader.* Ed. Werner Sollors. Basingstoke: MacMillan, 1995. 17-33.

–. "What Is a White Man?" Sollors, *Interracialism* 37-42.

Chicago Cultural Studies Group. "Critical Multiculturalism." *Critical Inquiry* 18.3 (1992): 530-55.

Clifford, Deborah P. *Crusader for Freedom: A Life of Lydia Maria Child.* Boston: Beacon, 1992.

Crèvecoeur, Hector St. John de. *Letters from an American Farmer.* New York: E.P. Dutton, 1912.

–. *More Letters from an American Farmer.* Ed. Brian Moore. Athens: U of Georgia P, 1995.

Croly, David. *Miscegenation; The Theory of the Blending of the Races, Applied to the American White Man and Negro.* New York: Dexter, 1864.

Dearborn, Mary. *Pocahontas's Daughters: Gender and Ethnicity in American Culture.* New York: Oxford UP, 1986.

Dippie, Brian. *The Vanishing American.* Middletown: Wesleyan UP, 1982.

Du Bois, W.E.B. *The Souls of Black Folk.* Mineola: Dover, 1994.

Eggan, Fred. "Lewis H. Morgan and the Future of the American Indian." *Proceedings of the American Philosophical Society* 109.5 (1965): 272-76.

Elam, Michelle. *The Souls of Mixed Folk: Race, Politics, and Aesthetics in the New Millennium.* Stanford: Stanford UP, 2011.

Emerson, Ralph Waldo. "Race." *English Traits: The Complete Works of Ralph Waldo Emerson.* Centenary ed. Vol. 5. Boston: Houghton, 1876. 28-47.

–. Entry 119. *The Journals and Miscellaneous Notebooks of Ralph Waldo Emerson.* Ed. Ralph H. Orth and Alfred K. Ferguson. Vol. 9, 1843-47. Cambridge: Belknap, 1971. 299-300.

English, Daylanne. *Unnatural Selections: Eugenics in American Modernism and the Harlem Renaissance.* Chapel Hill: U of North Carolina P, 2004.

Eugenides, Jeffrey. *Middlesex.* London: Bloomsbury, 2002.

Fairchild, Henry Pratt. *The Melting-Pot Mistake.* Boston: Little, 1926.

Feldstein, Stanley, and Lawrence Costello. *The Ordeal of Assimilation: A Documentary History of the White Working Class.* Garden City: Anchor/Doubleday, 1974.

Fitzgerald, F. Scott. *The Great Gatsby.* 1925. Cambridge: Cambridge UP, 1991.

Gerstle, Gary. *American Crucible: Race and Nation in the Twentieth Century.* Princeton: Princeton UP, 2001.

Glazer, Nathan. *We Are All Multiculturalists Now.* Cambridge: Harvard UP, 1998.

Glazer, Nathan, and Daniel Patrick Moynihan. *Beyond the Melting Pot: The Negroes, Puerto Ricans, Jews, Italians, and Irish of New York.* Cambridge: MIT P/Harvard UP, 1963.

Gleason, Philip. *Speaking of Diversity: Language and Ethnicity in Twentieth-Century America.* Baltimore: Johns Hopkins UP, 1992.

Glenn, David. "Critics Assail Scholar's Article Arguing That Hispanic Immigration Threatens U.S." *Chronicle of Higher Education* 24 Feb. 2004. http://chronicle.com/article/Critics-Assail-Scholars/102472. 3 Dec. 2013.

Gold, Michael. "Towards Proletarian Art." *Mike Gold: A Literary Anthology.* Ed. Michael Folsom. New York: International, 1972. 62-70.

Goldberg, David Theo. "Introduction: Multicultural Conditions." *Multiculturalism: A Critical Reader.* Ed. David Theo Goldberg. Oxford: Blackwell, 1994. 1-44.

Goldstein, Eric L. *The Price of Whiteness: Jews, Race, and American Identity.* Princeton: Princeton UP, 2006.

Gordon, Milton. *Assimilation in American Life: The Role of Race, Religion, and National Origins.* New York: Oxford UP, 1964.

Grant, Madison. *The Passing of the Great Race: Or, the Racial Basis of European History.* New York: Scribner's, 1916.

Guess Who's Coming to Dinner. Dir. Stanley Kramer. Columbia, 1967.

Guterl, Matthew Pratt. *The Color of Race in America, 1900-1940.* Cambridge: Harvard UP, 2001.

Gutmann, Amy, ed. *Multiculturalism: Examining the Politics of Recognition.* Princeton: Princeton UP, 1994.

Hannerz, Ulf. *Transnational Connections – Culture, People, Places.* London: Routledge, 1996.

Hansen, Jonathan. *The Lost Promise of Patriotism: Debating American Identity, 1890-1920*. Chicago: U of Chicago P, 2003.

Haskins, R.W. *History and Progress of Phrenology*. Buffalo: Steele and Peck, 1839.

Herberg, Will. *Protestant – Catholic – Jew: An Essay in American Religious Sociology*. Garden City: Doubleday, 1955.

Hirsch, E.D. *Cultural Literacy: What Every American Needs to Know*. Boston: Houghton, 1987.

Hollinger, David. *Postethnic America: Beyond Multiculturalism*. New York: Basic, 1995.

Hughes, Robert. *Culture of Complaint: The Fraying of America*. New York: Oxford UP, 1993.

Huntington, Samuel P. *The Clash of Civilizations and the Remaking of World Order*. New York: Simon, 1996.

Jacobson, Matthew Frye. "Malevolent Assimilation: Immigrants and the Question of American Empire." Katkin, Landsman, and Tyree, *Beyond Pluralism* 154-81.

–. *Roots Too: White Ethnic Revival in Post-Civil Rights America*. Cambridge: Harvard UP, 2006.

–. *Whiteness of a Different Color: European Immigrants and the Alchemy of Race*. Cambridge: Harvard UP, 1999.

Jacoby, Tamar. "What It Means to Be American in the 21st Century." *Reinventing the Melting Pot: The New Immigrants and What It Means to Be American*. Ed. Tamar Jacoby. New York: Basic, 2004. 293-314.

Jefferson, Thomas. To Benjamin Hawkins Washington. *American History: From Revolution to Reconstruction and Beyond*. http://www.let.rug.nl/usa/presidents/thomas-jefferson/letters-of-thomas-jefferson/jefl150.php. 10 Oct. 2013.

Kallen, Horace. "Democracy versus the Melting Pot." 1915. *Culture and Democracy in the United States: Studies in the Group Psychology of the American Peoples*. Introd. Stephen Whitfield. New Brunswick: Transactions, 1998. 59-117.

Kammen, Michael. *People of Paradox: An Inquiry Concerning the Origins of American Civilization*. New York: Knopf, 1975.

Karcher, Carolyn. "Lydia Maria Child's *A Romance of the Republic*: An Abolitionist Vision of America's Racial Destiny." *Slavery and the Literary Imagination*. Ed. Arnold Rampersad and Deborah E. McDowell. Baltimore: Johns Hopkins UP, 1989. 81-103.

Katkin, Wendy F., Ned Landsman, and Andrea Tyree, eds. *Beyond Pluralism: The Conception of Groups and Group Identity in America*. Urbana: U of Illinois P, 1998.

Kennedy, Randall. *Interracial Intimacies: Sex, Marriage, Identity, and Adoption*. New York: Pantheon, 2003.

Kennedy, Roger. "Jefferson and the Indians." *Winterthur Portfolio* 27.2/3 (1992): 105-21.

Kennedy, Ruby Jo Reeves. "Single or Triple Melting-Pot? Intermarriage in New Haven, 1870-1950." *American Journal of Sociology* 58.1 (1952): 56-59.

Krausz, Ernest, ed. *Studies of Israeli Society*. Vol. 1. New Brunswick: Transaction, 1980.

Landsman, Ned, and Wendy F. Katkin. "Introduction: The Construction of American Pluralism." Katkin, Landsman, and Tyree, *Beyond Pluralism* 1-10.

Lissak, Rivka Shpak. *Pluralism and Progressives: Hull House and New Immigrants, 1890-1919*. Chicago: U of Chicago P, 1989.

Luedtke, Luther. "Ralph Waldo Emerson Envisions the 'Smelting Pot.'" *MELUS* 6.2 (1979): 3-14.

Massey, Douglas, and Nancy Denton. *American Apartheid: Segregation and the Making of the Underclass*. Cambridge: Harvard UP, 1993.

McWilliams, Dean. *Charles W. Chesnutt and the Fictions of Race*. Athens: U of Georgia P, 2002.

Meyer, Karl E. *The New America: Politics and Society in the Age of the Smooth Deal*. New York: Basic, 1961.

Moore, Dennis. Introduction. Crèvecoeur, *More Letters* i-xci.

Morse, Jedidiah. *The American Universal Geography*. 1789. Boston: Thomas and Andreas, 1802.

Nahshon, Edna, ed. *From the Ghetto to the Melting Pot: Israel Zangwill's Jewish Plays*. Detroit: Wayne State UP, 2006.

–. Introductory Essay: *The Melting Pot*. Nahshon, *From the Ghetto* 211-63.

–. Prologue. Nahshon, *From the Ghetto* 1-3.

Newbeck, Phyl. *Virginia Hasn't Always Been for Lovers: Interracial Marriage Bans and the Case of Richard and Mildred Loving*. Carbondale: Southern Illinois UP, 2004.

Nicoloff, Philip L. *Emerson on Race and History: An Examination of* English Traits. New York: Columbia UP, 1961.

Novak, Michael. *Unmeltable Ethnics: Politics and Culture in American Life*. Rev. ed of *The Rise of the Unmeltable Ethnics*. New Brunswick: Transaction, 1996.

Nugent, Ted. "Multicultural Rot in the Melting Pot: The West Awakens to Islam's Intent to Dominate, Not Assimilate." *Washington Post* March 4, 2011. B 3.

Nye, Russel. *American Literary History: 1607-1830.* New York: Knopf, 1970.

Obama, Barack. *Dreams from My Father: A Story of Race and Inheritance.* 1995. New York: Three Rivers, 2004.

Omi, Michael, and Howard Winant. *Racial Formation in the United States: From the 1960s to the 1980s.* New York: Routledge, 1986.

Onuf, Peter S. *Jefferson's Empire: The Language of American Nationhood.* Charlottesville: UP of Virginia, 2001.

Øverland, Orm. "From Melting Pot to Copper Kettles: Assimilation and Norwegian-American Literature." *Multilingual America: Transnationalism, Ethnicity, and the Languages of American Literature.* Ed. Werner Sollors. New York: New York UP, 1998. 50-63.

–. *Immigrant Minds, American Identities: Making the United States Home, 1870-1930.* Urbana: U of Illinois P, 2000.

Parkman, Francis. *The Conspiracy of Pontiac and the Indian War after the Conquest of Canada.* 1851. Lincoln: U of Nebraska P, 1994.

Peek, Lori. *Behind the Backlash: Muslim Americans after 9/11.* Philadelphia: Temple UP, 2011.

Pieterse, Jan Nederveen. "Globalisation and Hybridisation." *International Sociology* 9.2 (1994): 161-84.

Poole, Ernest. *The Voice of the Street.* New York: A.S. Barnes, 1906.

Randall, Dudley. "The Melting Pot." *Roses and Revolutions: The Selected Writings of Dudley Randall.* Ed. Melba J. Boyd. Detroit: Wayne State UP, 2009. 167.

Rodgers, Daniel. "In Search of Progressivism." *Reviews in American History* 10.4 (1982): 113-32.

Roth, Henry. *Call It Sleep.* New York: Ballou, 1934.

Rowe, John Carlos. *At Emerson's Tomb: The Politics of Classic American Literature.* New York: Columbia UP, 1997.

Salins, Peter. *Assimilation, American Style.* New York: Basic, 1997.

Saveth, Edward N. *American Historians and European Immigrants 1875-1925.* New York: Russel and Russel, 1965.

Schlesinger, Arthur M., Jr. *The Disuniting of America: Reflections on a Multicultural Society.* New York: Norton, 1992.

Sennett, Richard. *The Conscience of the Eye: The Design and Social Life of Cities.* New York: Norton, 1992.

Shohat, Ella, and Robert Stam. *Unthinking Eurocentrism: Multiculturalism and the Media*. London: Routledge, 2001.

Shumsky, Neil Larry. "Zangwill's *The Melting Pot*: Ethnic Tensions on Stage." *American Quarterly* 27.1 (1975): 29-41.

Simonson, Rick, and Scott Walker, eds. *The Graywolf Annual Five: Multi-Cultural Literacy*. St. Paul: Graywolf, 1988.

Slotkin, Richard. "Unit Pride: Ethnic Platoons and the Myths of American Nationality." *American Literary History* 13.3 (2001): 469-98.

Sollors, Werner. *Beyond Ethnicity: Consent and Descent in American Culture*. New York: Oxford UP, 1986.

–. *Ethnic Modernism*. Cambridge: Harvard UP, 2008.

–, ed. *Interracialism: Black-White Intermarriage in American History, Literature, and Law*. New York: Oxford UP, 2000.

–. "Introduction." Sollors, *Interracialism* 3-16.

Steinfield, Melvin. *Cracks in the Melting Pot: Racism and Discrimination in American History*. 2nd ed. Beverly Hills: Glencoe, 1974.

Stewart, George R. *American Ways of Life*. Garden City: Doubleday, 1954.

Stoddard, Theodore Lothrop. *The Revolt against Civilization: The Menace of the Under Man*. New York: Scribner, 1922.

Taylor Haizlip, Shirlee. *The Sweeter the Juice: A Family Memoir in Black and White*. New York: Touchstone, 1994.

Toomer, Jean. "A New Race in America." *A Jean Toomer Reader*. Ed. Frederik Rusch. New York: Oxford UP, 1993. 105.

Turner, Frederick Jackson. "The Significance of the Frontier in American History." 1893. *American Studies at the University of Virginia*. http://xroads.virginia.edu/~hyper/turner/chapter1.html. 3 Oct. 2013.

Turner, Terence. "Anthropology and Multiculturalism: What Is Anthropology That Multiculturalists Should Be Mindful of It?" *Cultural Anthropology* 8.4 (1993): 411-29.

US Department of the Treasury. http://www.treasury.gov/resource-center/faqs/Coins/Pages/edu_faq_coins_portraits.aspx. 3 Oct. 2013.

Vasconcelos, José. *The Cosmic Race: A Bilingual Edition*. Transl. and annot. Didier T. Jaén. Baltimore: Johns Hopkins UP, 1979. 28-40.

Vizenor, Gerald. *Manifest Manners: Narratives on Postindian Survivance*. Lincoln: U of Nebraska P, 1999.

Wallace, Anthony. *Jefferson and the Indians: The Tragic Fate of the First Americans*. Cambridge: Belknap P of Harvard UP, 1999.

Wallace, Michelle. *Invisibility Blues: From Pop to Theory*. New York: Verso, 1990.

Washington, Booker T. *Up from Slavery*. New York: Norton, 1996.

Waters, Mary. *Ethnic Options: Choosing Identities in America*. Berkeley: U of California P, 1990.

Weinbaum, Alys Eve. "Nation." *Keywords for American Cultural Studies*. Ed. Bruce Burgett and Glenn Hendler. New York: New York UP, 2007. 164-69.

Whitman, Walt. *Song of Myself and Other Poems*. Selected and introd. Robert Hass. Berkeley: Counterpoint, 2010.

Wilson, Sarah. *Melting-Pot Modernism*. Ithaca: Cornell UP, 2010.

X, Malcolm. "Message to the Grass Roots." Detroit. 10 Nov. 1963. *Malcolm X Speaks: Selected Speeches and Statements*. Ed. George Breitman. New York: Grove Weidenfeld, 1965. 3-17.

Zangwill, Israel. *The Melting Pot: A Drama in Four Acts*. 1909. New York: Macmillan, 1910.

Further Reading

Addams, Jane. *Twenty Years at Hull House*. New York: Macmillan, 1910.

Appiah, K. Anthony, and Amy Gutmann. *Color Conscious: The Political Morality of Race*. Princeton: Princeton UP, 1996.

Bender, Thomas. *Toward an Urban Vision: Ideas and Institutions in Nineteenth-Century America*. Lexington: U of Kentucky P, 1975.

Birkle, Carmen. *Migration – Miscegenation – Transculturation*. Heidelberg: Winter, 2004.

Boelhower, William, and Alfred Hornung, eds. *Multiculturalism and the American Self*. Heidelberg: Winter, 2000.

Bramen, Carrie Tirado. *The Uses of Variety: Modern Americanism and the Quest for National Distinctiveness*. Cambridge: Harvard UP, 2000.

Brodkin, Karen. *How Jews Became White Folks and What That Says About Race in America*. New Brunswick: Rutgers UP, 1999.

Buenker, John D., and Lorman A. Ratner, eds. *Multiculturalism in the United States: A Comparative Guide to Acculturation and Ethnicity*. New York: Greenwood, 1992.

Dewey, John. "The Principle of Nationality." 1917. *The Middle Works. 1899-1924*. Vol. 10: 1916-1917. Ed. Jo Ann Boydston. Carbondale: Southern Illinois UP, 1980. 285-95.

Douglas, Ann. *Terrible Honesty: Mongrel Manhattan in the 1920s*. New York: Farrar, 1995.

Drachsler, Julius. *Democracy and Assimilation*. New York: Macmillan, 1920.

Du Bois, W.E.B. "The Conservation of Race." 1897. *On Sociology and the Black Community*. Ed. Dan S. Green and Edwin D. Driver. Chicago: U of Chicago P, 1978. 238-49.

Eisenach, Eldon J. *The Lost Promise of Progressivism*. Lawrence: UP of Kansas, 1994.

Gleason, Philip. "The Melting Pot: Symbol of Fusion or Confusion?" *American Quarterly* 16.1 (1964): 20-46.

Harper, Richard Conant. *The Course of the Melting Pot Idea to 1910*. New York: Arno, 1980.

Hegeman, Susan. *Patterns for America: Modernism and the Concept of Culture*. Princeton: Princeton UP, 1999.

Hirsch, E.D. *The Making of Americans: Democracy and Our Schools*. New Haven: Yale UP, 2009.

Ignatieff, Michael. *Blood and Belonging: Journeys into the New Nationalism*. New York: Farrar, 1993.

King, Desmond. *The Color of Race in America: Immigration, Race, and the Origins of the Diverse Democracy*. Cambridge: Harvard UP, 2000.

Livingston, James. *Pragmatism and Democracy: Rethinking the Politics of American History*. New York: Routledge, 2001.

Mann, Arthur. *The One and the Many: Reflections on the American Identity*. Chicago: U of Chicago P, 1979.

Michaels, Walter Benn. *Our America: Nativism, Modernism, and Pluralism*. Durham: Duke UP, 1995.

Myrdal, Gunnar. *An American Dilemma: The Negro Problem and Modern Democracy*. New York: Harper, 1944.

Palumbo-Liu, David. *Asian/American: Historical Crossings of a Racial Frontier*. Stanford: Stanford UP, 1999.

Ravitch, Diane. "Multiculturalism: E Pluribus Plures." *Race and Ethnicity in the United States: Issues and Debates*. Ed. Stephen Steinberg. Malden: Blackwell, 2000. 267-76.

Riis, Jacob A. *The Making of an American*. 1901. New York: Macmillan, 1943.

Rogin, Michael. *Blackface, White Noise: Jewish Immigrants in the Hollywood Melting Pot*. Berkeley: U of California P, 1996.

Ross, Edward Alsworth. *The Old World in the New: The Significance of Past and Present Immigration to the American People*. 1913. *The Early Sociology of Race and Ethnicity*. Ed. Kenneth Thompson. London: Routledge, 2005.

Sollors, Werner. "The Rebirth of All Americans in the Great American Melting Pot: Notes toward the Vindication of a Rejected Popular Symbol; or: An Ethnic Variety of a Religious Experience." *Prospects* 5 (1980): 79-110.

–. *Theories of Ethnicity: A Classical Reader*. Basingstoke: MacMillan, 1996.

Westbrook, Robert B. *John Dewey and American Democracy*. Ithaca: Cornell UP, 1991.

Willett, Cynthia, ed. *Theorizing Multiculturalism: A Guide to the Current Debate*. Malden: Blackwell, 1998.

Yuchtman-Yaar, Ephraim. "Continuity and Change in Israeli Society: The Test of the Melting Pot." *Israel Studies* 10.2 (2005): 91-128.

Zeidel, Robert F. *Immigrants, Progressives, and Exclusion Politics: The Dillingham Comission, 1900-1927*. DeKalb: Northern Illinois UP, 2004.

Chapter VI

Agrarianism, Expansionism,

and the Myth of the American West

---

1. WHY THE WEST?

> America only more so.
> NEIL CAMPBELL, *THE RHIZOMATIC WEST*

> [The] West is a country in the mind, and so eternal.
> ARCHIBALD MACLEISH

> Can the West be heard?
> WALTER PRESCOTT WEBB

The American West has captured the imagination of Americans and Americanists alike. It has been foundational for multi-disciplinary American studies scholarship since Frederick Jackson Turner in 1893 identified the frontier as the most decisive factor in shaping American political and social institutions and in creating a specifically American national character (cf. "Significance"). Shifting the focus away from America's European heritage and divisions between the North and the South, Turner's frontier thesis argued for studying America from an East/West perspective that inaugurated an exceptionalist discourse based on experiences of and with the land. At the time it was not entirely well received by his fellow historians and has been contested from various perspectives and by various groups throughout the 20th and 21st centuries, yet it has provided a host of resonant images for the American cultural imaginary, and has been highly influential in the study of American history, culture, and literature. It is thus no coincidence that one of the earliest classics of American studies scholarship, Henry Nash Smith's *Virgin Land: The American West as Symbol and Myth*, has lent its name to the first generation of Americanists: the Myth and Symbol School (cf. the introduction to this book). The construction and affirmation of the West in Turner and Smith already conveys many of the aspects of the myth of the West to be considered in this chapter: first of all, the American West is often viewed not so much as a region or an area than as a space of transition that does not necessarily have a precise geographical location, but rather changes with Euro-American settlement expanding westward. Second, the West as a transformative space has often been considered as a *pars pro toto* for the nation and as a special place from which its future could be built, making "the discovery, conquest, and settlement of the West [...] the dominant theme of American history" (Slotkin, "Unit Pride" 472). As part of a "homogenized national geography" (Lopez, "American Geographies" 136) and as a "nationalist West" (Dorman, *Hell* xii), it has been a locus, however vaguely defined, for developing epic cultural scripts of Americanness. Third, the West as a region – defined e.g. as the "17 coterminous states located on and westward of the 100th meridian" (ibid. xii) – is connected to visions of an agrarian ideal that for a long time has been seen as standing for authentic Americanness, but also, from a more critical perspective, for an "enduring provincial mentality" (Von Frank, *Sacred Game* 5). Pitting the rural West against the newly emerging urban centers in the East in the 19th century has shaped a whole range of dichotomies that are still at work today and that have been described as the country vs. the city (cf. Williams, *Country*) or the frontier vs. the metropolis (cf. Slotkin, *Fatal Environment* 35). Thus, the myth of the West also reflects a rural ideal that grows out of a conception of the United States as predominantly rural or as having a distinct rural past. Fourth, the attributes often given to the West reflect a number of implications regarding a particular way of life, which may be associated with notions of the pre- or anti-modern, traditionalism, folk culture, and specific cultural codes and idioms: "The West, at bottom, is a form of society rather than an area," Hofstadter notes quoting Turner ("Thesis Disputed" 102). Lastly, the myth of the West includes a pastoral dimension; by adapting a much older European pastoral discourse to the US-American context, Leo Marx has theorized the pastoral as the middle ground between the city and the 'wilderness' and as a vehicle for social critique (cf. *Machine*). Even if the myth of the West is organized around certain recurring (stock) characters (farmers, cowboys, 'Indians'), it is not focused on people, but on "[t]he land itself" (Fox, *Void* 130).

Illustration 1: The West as Symbol and Myth

Ben Shahn, cover design for *Virgin Land* (1957; Harvard
Art Museums/Fogg Museum, Imaging Department). ©
President and Fellows of Harvard College

The agrarian myth of the West and the myth of the frontier can be traced back to
the beginning of European settlement in North America in the 17th and 18th centuries, and connects to narratives of chosenness (cf. chapter 3) and the melting
pot (cf. chapter 5). The frontier may well be considered "the longest-lived of
American myths" (Slotkin, *Fatal Environment* 15); its scholarly treatment by
Turner followed the so-called second founding of the US during Reconstruction,
when "the unitary American nation became a primary focus of ideology and
power" (Slotkin, "Unit Pride" 472), and the US Census Bureau's declaration in
1890 that there no longer was a frontier. The rise of the US to world power went
along with the interpretation of westward expansion and settlement as an integral
part of that process and as "a westward creation story" (Campbell, *Rhizomatic
West* 2). As the hub of this national cosmology, the frontier myth has been the
object of much critical attention – most notably from Richard Slotkin, who is the
author of three singularly important critical monographs on the frontier myth
(*Regeneration through Violence, The Fatal Environment*, and *Gunfighter Nation*).

My discussion of the American West will focus on agrarianism and expansionism as two basic tenets in cultural history and the cultural imaginary. For one thing, I will address the West as a space of residence and settlement that is often imagined as a kind of garden or even Edenic paradise symbolizing pastoral simplicity and economic independence based on subsistence farming. This semi-'civilized,' "domesticated West" (Smith, *Virgin Land* 138) is imagined in popular culture, for instance, in Laura Ingalls Wilder's book *Little House on the Prairie* and the television series of the same title that was adapted from it, and in the lyrics of contemporary country music. Second, the American West is constructed as a site of individual and collective quests for land and dominance. Violent conflict between settlers and Native Americans often is the focus of narratives that represent the West as a still 'uncivilized' space yet to be conquered and controlled, as is the case e.g. in classical Westerns. It is useful to distinguish between the two versions of the West as peaceful garden (agrarianism) and as conflicted frontier (expansionism), even if, of course, both versions overlap in most representations: a Western may e.g. tell the story of a farmer and his family (agrarian version of the West) but may for their protection enlist the masculinist, individualist, classical Western hero (expansionist version). The Western may also present the second as a precondition for the first, or use images of the agrarian West to legitimize the violence that is at the heart of expansionism. We may thus think of them as sequentially connected, yet not in any straightforward way. As David Wrobel has pointed out, "[t]he two sentiments, the hope for a postfrontier future in the West, followed later by a longing for the frontier past, have played an important part in the formation of western identities" (*Promised Lands* 1) – and of US national identity, one should add. It is the cultural work of the myth that apparently has neutralized these contradictions and paradoxes of the West.

In this chapter, I will address both versions of the mythical West separately, but also show how they interconnect. The figure of the American farmer as 'American Adam' and the rural, agrarian myth as found in the canonical writings of Thomas Jefferson and J. Hector St. John de Crèvecoeur will serve as my point of departure. Second, I will focus on the concept of the frontier and notions of expansionism and manifest destiny. Revisionist approaches have contested the rather idyllic and often one-sided images in these two conceptualizations of the West, third, from a gender perspective, and fourth, from an ethnic (more specifically, Japanese American) perspective. Fifth, I will look at popular culture that has represented and affirmed the myth of the West by developing and using the formula of the Western. Sixth, using the war in Southeast Asia popularly known as the Vietnam War as an example, I will point to the role and symbolic power of the frontier myth in political rhetoric and political culture. Last but not least, I will point to the West in discourses of transnationalism and globalization, as the American West has become a preeminent symbol of exceptionalist 'American-ness' around the world.

2. THE AGRARIAN WEST: THE AMERICAN FARMER AND THE GARDEN MYTH IN THE EARLY REPUBLIC AND BEYOND

> The United States was born in the country.
> RICHARD HOFSTADTER

> No Easterner, born forlornly within the sphere of New York, Boston, or Philadelphia, can pass very far beyond the Alleghenies without feeling that American civilization is here found in the full tide of believing in itself. The flat countryside looks more ordered, more farmlike; the Main Streets that flash by the car-windows somehow look more robust and communal.
> RANDOLPH S. BOURNE, "A MIRROR OF THE MIDDLE WEST"

One of the most canonical definitions of the agrarian myth can be found in Richard Hofstadter's *The Age of Reform*:

> The American mind was raised upon a sentimental attachment to rural living and upon a series of notions about rural people and rural life that I have chosen to designate as the agrarian myth. The agrarian myth represents a kind of homage that Americans have paid to the fancied innocence of their origins. Like any complex of ideas, the agrarian myth cannot be defined in a phrase, but its component themes form a clear pattern. Its hero was the yeoman farmer, its central conception the notion that he is the ideal man and the ideal citizen. (23)

Hofstadter identifies this myth as an initially "elitist," "literary notion" (expressed, for instance, in Walt Whitman's "O Pioneers") which later turned into a "mass creed" (ibid. 25, 28). We find manifestations of it in writings of the early republic and the 19th century, and increasingly nostalgic ones in 20th-century and contemporary literature and popular culture. Among the early proponents of this myth were a Virginian slaveholder and a French immigrant: Thomas Jefferson and Hector St. John de Crèvecoeur. In *Notes on the State of Virginia* (1785), Jefferson envisions the United States as a republic of self-determined, autonomous, and virtuous farmer-citizens, who he juxtaposes as "the chosen people of God" (135) with the tradesmen and merchants of mercantilist, predominantly urban Europe, which for Jefferson signifies corruption, alienation, and immorality.

Crèvecoeur's writings on the American farmer collectively are more ambivalent than Jefferson's, yet in the passages that have been selectively canonized over the centuries, Crèvecoeur shows a similar enthusiasm for the farmer as a new North American type, and includes himself among this group of husbandmen:

Some few towns excepted, we are tillers of the earth, from Nova Scotia to West Florida. We are a people of cultivators scattered over an immense territory communicating with each other by means of good roads and navigable rivers, united by the silken bands of mild government, all respecting the laws, without dreading their power, because they are equitable [...]. [T]hat of a farmer is the only appellation of the rural inhabitants of our country. (*Letters* 40)

Crèvecoeur's description of European settlers in North America as "farmers" here figures as a democratic form of address ("appellation") that signifies equality and the absence of rank and hierarchy among men in rural America, or what Perry Miller called "nature's nation" (cf. his book of the same title). The logic of the interdependence of land ownership, equality, and republicanism that underlies both Jefferson's as well as Crèvecoeur's version of the agrarian myth is described by Christopher Curtis as follows:

Grounding republican citizenship in the allodial freehold expressed a belief that the absolute ownership of a tangible piece of property would reconcile the indulgent characteristics of economic individualism with a vested social attachment to a particular local community and, accordingly, foster civic virtue through self-interest. (*Jefferson's Freeholders* 8)

Correlating self-interest, self-sufficiency, and the bond with and loyalty to a local collectivity appears to be rather idealistic of course, and glosses over the by no means inclusive dynamics at work within such communities.

Contextualizing Jefferson and Crèvecoeur as proponents of the agrarian myth necessitates inspecting a number of aspects more closely. As Henry Nash Smith and, more recently, Christopher Curtis have pointed out, Jefferson and Crèvecoeur did not invent this agrarian myth, and were not even all that original in articulating it in late 18th-century America: for one thing, because this kind of rural, pastoral vision dates back to the work of Virgil (70-19 BC) and other writers of antiquity, and had been part of the colonial imaginary of the 'new world' since the early 17th century (cf. Michael Drayton's "To the Virginian Voyage"); and secondly, because many contemporaries of Jefferson and Crève-coeur were sharing similar sentiments, as agrarianism was a dominant discourse in the foundational phase of the republic – Jefferson's and Crèvecoeur's texts at the time were by far not the only ones to imagine the US along those lines. Thirdly, with regard to the intended audiences of their writings, we can add that both clearly write in a promotional vein and seek to advertise the United States to a European readership: Their self-fashioning as inhabitants of a new Garden of Eden is part of efforts to legitimize the new republic and to entice more prospective settlers to cross the Atlantic. Jefferson addresses his *Notes* to François Barbé-Marbois, secretary of the French legation to the United States; Crèvecoeur, whose letters were first published in London in 1782, more broadly addresses a wider European readership. In promoting America as the 'Garden of the World,' they thus gave a nationalistic, civil religious dimension to (much) older utopian visions of which they presented North America and more specifi-cally the West as a concrete realization:

The image of this vast and constantly growing agricultural society in the interior of the continent became one of the dominant symbols of nineteenth-century American society – a collective representation, a poetic idea [...] that defined the promise of American life. (Smith, *Virgin Land* 138)

Whereas in texts of the early republic, the agrarian myth is employed to envision America's future as a rural democracy, later references turn increasingly nos-talgic regarding a rural social order and way of life. As a fourth aspect, then, rurality in the Jefferson-Crèvecoeur tradition can be considered as increasingly turning into a cherished anachronism. Raymond Williams identifies a similar dynamic of increasing nostalgia for the "rural" as a form of community in Britain (cf. *Country* 102). "Oddly enough," Hofstadter notes, "the agrarian myth came to be believed more widely and tenaciously as it became more fictional" (*Age* 30). In the US, the farmer has remained the emblem of an ethic of hard work, a lifestyle close to nature, and egalitarianism. However, fifthly, Jefferson and Crèvecoeur also reflect different versions of the myth of the West, which can be distinguished into a Northern and Southern version. The Southern imagi-nary of the West casts the farmer as a plantation owner, and for that reason alone is a far cry from egalitarian dreams; Smith has shown that the literature of the early republic "did not always readily embrace the democratic principles" on which the US was founded by pointing to, among other texts, James Kirke

Paulding's work and the "ingrained class feeling" of his protagonists (*Virgin Land* 160). In the Northern version of the myth on the other hand, the West is usually conceived of as free and as holding the promise of land ownership for everyone, which however does not necessarily mean that it was not exclusivist in regard to class, race, or gender.

While Lincoln's signing into law of the Homestead Act on May 20, 1862 suggested that indeed "the dream of free land had become law" (Hine and Faragher, *American West* 334), the Homestead Act has also been read as nothing more than "a tribute to the high ideal of the yeoman farmer" in the context of a corrupt and inefficient system that facilitated land speculation rather than free settlement and small-scale land acquisition (Limerick, *Legacy* 62). The consequences of the Homestead Act, thus, were not democratic land ownership:

A further analysis of the data reveals that only 3.653.000 farms in 1900 were operated, even in part, by their owners. But at the same time at least 21.000.000 farm people were tenants and wage laborers and their families on the total of 5.737.000 farms in the nation. These laborers were rarely any better off financially (often worse) than the toiling multitudes in the cities. (Shannon, "Not Even" 44)

Yet, empirical findings can hardly ever successfully contest the validity of myth, as its foundational quality and emotional appeal tend to override minor and major contradictions. Despite the dire consequences that the Homestead Act had for many settlers, the myth of the West remained alive, even if it has not gone uncontested in rural vernacular culture and folklore, as the following folk song from Kansas shows:

A chattel mortgage in the West
Is like a cancer on your breast;
It slowly takes your life away,
And eats your vitals day by day. (qtd. in Hine and Faragher, *American West* 348)

The song describes the mortgage system not as the promise but as the pathology of the West – a pathology whose effects are like that of a lethal disease for which there is no cure.

Even though the American farm was in many ways not a locus of autonomy and self-sufficiency, as many scholars of the early republic and the 19th century have pointed out (cf. Appleby, *Capitalism*; Limerick, *Legacy* 68; Trachtenberg, *Incorporation* 22-23), the iconography of the farmer and of the farm in the West has been part of national mythmaking that embraces the West as a pastoral idyll, a democratic space, and as a land of opportunity; to this day, we find notions of America as garden-like and of the American Adam as farmer in cultural productions ranging from historical novels to tobacco commercials. It is mostly the perspective of non-Westerners on the West, as regionalist scholars have noted, from which we perceive the West in terms of harmony, intact communities, and a simple way of life; in many such representations of the West, "we view the region from inside the window of a railroad car" – i.e., as "voyeurs" rather than as residents (Goldman, *Continental Divides* ix). Among others, Randolph Bourne (cf. this section's second epigraph) also attests to the appropriation of the West as a region and as a specific locality and culture for a hegemonic discourse of wholesome Americanness.

In the third decade of the 20th century, however, the agrarian myth of the West underwent an important crisis: in the context of the Great Depression, the American farm was turned into an icon of the rural population's collective suffering in the social documentary photography sponsored by the Resettlement Administration and later the Farm Security Administration; artists such as Walker Evans, Dorothea Lange, and Arthur Rothstein in their photographic representations pointedly critiqued the agrarian myth and pastoral projections on the rural West (cf. Lange, *American Exodus*). More recently, this sense of crisis has prevailed and coexists with discourses that continue to idealize farm life and heroize the farmer. Organizations and initiatives such as the American Farmland Trust, which was founded in 1980, and Farm Aid (inaugurated by Willie Nelson, John Mellencamp, and Neil Young), which since 1985 has raised funds for the preservation and support of family farms in the US through benefit concerts, indicate that the farmer still holds a prominent place in the cultural imaginary. Farm Aid's political engagement also led to the passage by Congress of the Agricultural Credit Act of 1987, which was intended to help small farmers in financial distress. It should be noted, however, that organizations such as Farm Aid "sell authenticity as much as they sell sound land-use policies" (Cook, "Romance" 228), as the lyrics of many singers and bands show (cf. e.g. John Mellencamp's "Rain on the Scarecrow," Shannon Brown's "Corn Fed," or Kenny Chesney's "She Thinks My Tractor's Sexy").

Illustration 2: Against the Agrarian Myth

Arthur Rothstein, *Potato Pickers, Rio Grande County, Colorado* (1939).

In the history of the American West, settlement policies were certainly less invested in egalitarianism than popular representations of pioneers and homesteaders would have us believe, as agrarianism relied on the cheap labor of migrant workers from Asia, slaves and former slaves, poor immigrants from Europe, and, not least, on the expropriation of Native Americans. Thus, popular visions of farming and gardening in the early republic and the 19th century are not as 'innocent' as they may appear at first. For Jefferson, agrarianism and expansionism clearly went hand in hand, as his notion of an "empire of liberty" (cf. Onuf, *Jefferson's Empire*) was based on landownership. The purchase by the Jefferson administration of French Louisiana in 1803, which doubled the size of the US and in the logic of the Jeffersonians created new opportunities for yeoman farmers out West, must be seen in this context. Official rhetoric emphasized that the 1804-06 expedition of the (tellingly named) Corps of Discovery under Meriwether Lewis (1774-1809) and William Clark (1770-1838), which was sent to explore the newly acquired territory, was "destined" to extend the "discovery" of Christopher Columbus and to

explore the Missouri River, and such principal stream of it, as, by its course and communication with the waters of the Pacific Ocean; whether the Columbia, Oregon, Colorado or any other river may offer the most direct and practicable communication across the continent for the purposes of commerce. (*Cong. Rec.* 22 Sept. 1998 to 26 Sept. 1998: 21532)

This expedition provided mappings of and, more generally, data on the West through which its systematic conquest became possible. Most importantly, the members of the expedition employed an evocative literary language in their journals with lasting effect:

[t]he importance of the Lewis and Clark expedition lay on the level of imagination: it was drama, it was the enactment of a myth that embodied the future. It gave tangible substance to what had been merely an idea, and established the image of a highway across the continent so firmly in the minds of Americans that repeated failures could not shake it. (Smith, *Virgin Land* 17)

The expedition account was later even called "our national epic of exploration" (Coues qtd. in Lawlor, *Recalling* 29).

Despite all the fanciful depictions, the winning of the West was above all a process of taking possession. Jeffersonian (and later Jacksonian) visions of the yeoman going west helped build not a "virtuous republic," but a "violent empire," as Carol Smith-Rosenberg puts it in her study of American national identity, in which many sections of American society (including academics) were complicit; for instance, the history of American geography and cartography not only has us think about Lewis and Clark and those 'explorers' who followed in their footsteps, e.g. Francis Parkman or John C. Frémont (cf. Parkman, *Oregon Trail*; Frémont, *Report*), but also reminds us of the "cartographic imperative" of the Jeffersonian grid system, which we still today connect to visions of the West as vast and monotonous: as "a direct corollary to the doctrine of Manifest Destiny [...] the grid exercises authority over space by applying a ruler to it in all senses of the word," as William Fox points out (*Void* 129). Similarly, cultural geographer John Brinckerhoff Jackson noted with regard to foundational American iconography that "it is the grid, not the eagle, not the stars and stripes, which is our true national emblem" (*Sense* 153). The grid, in that it overwrites prior meanings and symbolic structures of the land, is a massively effective instrument of colonization. We may relate this to the beginning of this section and argue that the cultural work of the garden myth is to camouflage this violence by glossing over conflicts and contradictions through its configuration of the American West as an American pastoral that is suggestive of an organic, smooth, and well-measured sense of the (growth of the) nation – in rectangular squares and green fields.

3. "CROSSING A CONTINENT" AND "WINNING A WILDERNESS" – 19TH-CENTURY EXPANSIONISM, THE FRONTIER, AND THE 'WILD' WEST

> Give me land, lots of land
> Under starry skies above,
> Don't fence me in.
> Let me ride through the wide
> Open country that I love,
> Don't fence me in.
> COLE PORTER/ROBERT FLETCHER, "DON'T FENCE ME IN"

The ideology of US expansionism and empire was resonantly articulated by John L. O'Sullivan (1813-1895) in an article published in the *Democratic Review* in 1845 that advocated the annexation of Texas, which indeed came to pass later in the same year; in this editorial, O'Sullivan most notably coined the phrase "manifest destiny:" "The American claim is by right of our manifest destiny to overspread and to possess the whole of the continent which Providence has given us for the development of the great experiment of liberty and federative self government entrusted to us" ("Annexation" 6). O'Sullivan was a journalist, lawyer, and a leading propagandist for the Democratic Party; he also was a key member of the so-called Young America Movement, a group of intellectuals and politicians "who concocted a new ideology of American expansion in the 1840s" (Hine and Faragher, *American West* 199; cf. Eyal, *Young America Movement*). In neo-Jeffersonian fashion, they saw in westward expansion the opportunity for an "agrarian counterrevolution" against industrialization and urbanization in Europe and the Eastern United States (Hietala, *Manifest Design* 105). O'Sullivan's claim that US-Americans by right of their manifest destiny could and should spread over the whole American continent connected the myth of the West to notions of Puritan chosenness and "destinarian thought" (Stephanson, *Manifest Destiny* 55) by rhetorically linking west- and southward expansion to notions of the Promised Land (cf. chapter 3) and *translatio imperii*, and thus expressed an idea that "held currency long before it was sloganized" (Fresonke, *West* 7). Expansionism was a key issue in the presidential elections of 1844, which pitted expansionists such as Democratic candidate James K. Polk, who called for "the reoccupation of Oregon and the reannexation of Texas at the earliest practical period" (insinuating the recovery of territories that had never been 'occupied' or had not even been part of the US in the first place), against anti-expansionists such as then-member of the Illinois General Assembly Abraham Lincoln, who was intent on "keeping our fences where they are and cultivating our present possession, making it a garden, improving the morals and education of the people" (qtd. in Hine and Faragher, *American West* 201). Polk won the election by a slim margin; yet, the above-quoted statements once again show how the West was used as a kind of empty signifier that could be variously ideologically charged as either a (foreign) space to be conquered or as a (domestic) space to be contained and protected as a (national) garden.

In 1893, Frederick Jackson Turner turned O'Sullivan's and many of his contemporaries' claims into a scholarly argument by putting US territorial expansion in the West in the context of geographical determinism and building around it a genuine US-American evolutionary theory in his lecture on "The Significance of the Frontier in American History," a text that would firmly lodge the frontier concept in scholarly discourse and everyday speech. Arguing that "[t]he existence of an area of free land, its continuous recession, and the advance of American settlement westward, explain American development," Turner uses the frontier concept to write a Eurocentric history of settlement in North America that paradoxically tries to downplay America's European roots:

Thus American development has exhibited not merely advance along a single line, but a return to primitive conditions on a continually advancing frontier line, and a new development for that area. American social development has been continually beginning over again on the frontier. This perennial rebirth, this fluidity of American life, this expansion westward with its new opportunities, its continuous touch with the simplicity of primitive society, furnish the forces dominating American character. The true point of view in the history of this nation is not the Atlantic coast, it is the Great West. ("Significance")

The West is conceived by Turner not as a specific region or place but as the dynamic space of the frontier, which according to Turner is "the meeting point between savagery and civilization;" he goes on to say that "[t]he most significant thing about it is, that it lies at the hither edge of free land" (ibid.). In that Turner's definition of the frontier remains analytically underdetermined as well as imaginatively evocative, it serves as an "elastic" term (ibid.) describing the experience which Turner believed captures best the ambivalent and partially regressive process of Americanization:

The frontier is the line of most rapid and effective Americanization. The wilderness masters the colonist. It finds him a European in dress, industries, tools, modes of travel, and thought. It takes him from the railroad car and puts him in the birch canoe. It strips off the garments of civilization and arrays him in the hunting shirt and the moccasin. It puts him in the log cabin of the Cherokee and Iroquois and runs an Indian palisade around him. Before long he has gone to planting Indian corn and plowing with a sharp stick; he shouts the war cry and takes the scalp in orthodox Indian fashion. In short, at the frontier the environment is at first too strong for the man. He must accept the conditions which it furnishes, or perish, and so he fits himself into the Indian clearings and follows the Indian trails. Little by little, he transforms the wilderness, but the outcome is not the old Europe, not simply the development of Germanic germs, any more than the first phenomenon was a case of reversion to the Germanic mark. The fact is, that here is a new product that is American. At first, the frontier was the Atlantic coast. It was the frontier of Europe in a very real sense. Moving westward, the frontier became more and more American. (ibid.)

Turner held that the frontier as the prime locus of Americanization generated a "composite nationality" in its "crucible" (ibid.), which has been identified as a specifically American trope in the previous chapter on the melting pot myth. In Turner's view, the frontier also promoted "individualism, democracy, and nationalism […]" (ibid.), which he thus connected to the westward expansion of the US, and served as a kind of safety valve for potential social unrest. His essay concludes with an affirmation of the frontier's importance in shaping the American nation and character by linking it to well-known foundational figures and events such as Christopher Columbus and American independence: "And now, four centuries from the discovery of America, at the end of a hundred years of life under the Constitution, the frontier has gone, and with its going has closed the first period of American history" (ibid.).

Discussions of Turner's frontier thesis have been highly controversial and fill whole libraries. Initially, many scholars still favored Herbert Baxter Adams's thesis about the Germanic origins of America, but Turner's argument soon became widely accepted and by the 1920s had turned into the dominant scholarly opinion on American national history, rendering the American Historical Association, as one critic has it, "One Big Turner *Verein*" (Billington, "Introduction" 3). The persuasiveness of Turner's argument had been amplified in the previous decades by semi- or pseudo-scholarly works such as Theodore Roosevelt's multi-volume *The Winning of the West* (1889-96), which identifies "race expansion" and "Western conquest" as foundational for American nation-building and as a monumental and successful effort at "carv[ing] states out of the forest and the prairie" (*Works* Vol. 9, 527). Throughout the Great Depression and especially after Turner's death in 1932, critical assessments of Turner's work came to the fore in regard to the (a) speculative, (b) hyperbolic, and (c) entirely unempirical character of his argument, which to many no longer seemed convincing:

"How could a frontier environment, which persisted only briefly before the settlement process was completed exert such an enduring influence over [...] the nation as a whole?" (Billington, "Introduction" 4). More fundamentally, the Great Depression led to a reconsideration of the frontier myth in general. For one thing, Turner's safety valve argument was reversed in the sense that cities on the Eastern Seaboard rather than the rural West were attributed the function of containing and defusing social turmoil (cf. Shannon, "Not Even"). In a broader framework, George Pierson argued that Turner's thesis had replaced "the God of the Puritans," who had until then vouched for American superiority, with a seemingly "natural force" – the frontier – "as source and justification" of American exceptionalism ("Turner's Views" 39). Rather than supporting this reformulation of exceptionalist designs, Pierson early on argues for a comparative perspective on US history and settlement (cf. ibid. 40). In the 1950s in the context of the 'Cold War,' the Turner Thesis once more was widely praised only to be yet again radically critiqued in the 1970s by revisionist scholars such as Richard Slotkin, Annette Kolodny, and Patricia Nelson Limerick, who have emphasized the violence of colonization and expansionism, the masculinist matrix of discourses about the West and empire-building, and the Eurocentric and ethnocentric biases involved in the frontier logic. Slotkin in particular has addressed the ways in which "the inanimate world of nature" is "humanized" in the appreciation and appropriation of the West, while the Native Americans at the same time are "dehumanized" (*Fatal Environment* 53). The Native American genocide can be considered the gaping absence in Turner's thesis as well as in much of its early revisions; it has only been addressed more fully in the past decades in alternative histories of "how the West was lost," not won by Native Americans (cf. Calloway, *Our Hearts*), of which Dee Brown's *Bury My Heart at Wounded Knee: An Indian History of the American West* (1970) is perhaps the best-known example. In contemporary scholarship of the so-called New Western Historians, the frontier has become the "f-word," as Patricia Limerick quips ("Adventures" 72). But even if many scholars have found Turner's argument utterly problematic, if not ridiculous, it has not lost its powerful grip on the popular imagination.

Both images of the American West as mythic rural Arcadia and as a site of historic conflict and conquest of mythic proportions remain entangled with each other and are central elements in discourses of nation-building and American exceptionalism in its crudest form, as both agrarians and expansionists ignore or dismiss the indigenous population as inhabitants of the land they seek to conquer and/or 'cultivate:' "The divisibility of the native and the land permitted the formulation of a myth and ideology of expansion in which racial warfare complements the processes of agrarian development" (Slotkin, *Fatal Environment* 53). We can see this complicity perhaps most clearly in writings of authors who are critical of the American empire yet at the same time remain attracted to its expansionist logic. Henry David Thoreau for example, one of the central figures in early American nature writing, wrote that "[t]he nation may go their way to their manifest destiny which I trust is not mine" (qtd. in Fresonke, *West* 128), yet at the same time was fascinated by the West: "Eastward I go only by force; westward I go free" (Thoreau, "Walking" 268). Thoreau, it seems, wanted "a nation of Walden Ponds, just as Jefferson, equally at odds with his own political impetus, wanted a nation of yeoman Monticellos" (Fresonke, *West* 15). Both Thoreau and Jefferson thus are caught in – and perpetuate – the mythical, exceptionalist "frontier magic" (Slotkin, *Fatal Environment* 40).

4. ENGENDERING THE AMERICAN WEST AND MANIFEST DOMESTICITY

> There is a region of America that I have come to call Hisland. In a magnificent western landscape, under perpetually cloudless western skies, a cast of heroic characters engage in dramatic combat, sometimes with nature, sometimes with each other. Occupationally, these heroes are diverse: they are mountain men, cowboys, Indians, soldiers, farmers, miners, and desperadoes, but they share one distinguishing characteristic – they are all men. It seems that all rational demography has ended at the Mississippi River; all the land west of it is occupied only by men. This mythical land is America's most enduring contribution to folklore: the legendary Wild West.
> SUSAN ARMITAGE, "THROUGH WOMEN'S EYES"

Susan Armitage, a feminist scholar of the West, in the above passage defines her field in terms of the absence of women in classical accounts of the West and the westering experience, and via reference to Charlotte Perkins Gilman's feminist utopian classic *Herland*; recuperating and ascertaining the presence of women in the West has been one crucial dimension of engendering (the study of) the West. One of the earliest attempts to document the lives of women in the West is certainly Elizabeth Ellet's *Pioneer Women of the West* (1901), which is based on private sources and biographical material. Dee Brown in his 1958 study of women in the West titled *The Gentle Tamers* clearly relates notions of the 'Wild West' to the 'civilizing' female touch of the "petticoated pioneers" (297), yet refutes historian Emerson Hough's "sunbonnet myth" (*Passing* 93), which implied that women's presence in the West was merely passive and decorative. Even if

Brown documents the female experience in the West as varied by pointing to its oppressive as well as emancipatory dimensions, he still remains largely stuck in a pre-feminist rhetoric, and with the then-common racial bias refers to white women only. Brown's study shows the very limited presence women were granted in the classical discourse on the West, in which two images prevail: on the one hand, the "weary and forlorn frontier wife, a sort of helpless heroine" who is generically derived from the captivity narrative and is often described as a 'Prairie Madonna,' and on the other hand, "the westering woman as sturdy helpmate and civilizer of the frontier" (Myres, *Westering Women* 2); additional stock characters include "the good woman, the schoolmarm, [and] the kindhearted prostitute" (Riley, *Female Frontier* 10). All of these characters have limited agency and are circumscribed by roles which mostly keep them indoors. Additionally, hardly any mention is made in these early studies of Native American, Mexican American, and other non-white women.

An early and noteworthy instance of US memorial culture dedicated to the role of women in the history of the West is the Madonna of the Trail series of twelve statues, which commemorates the endurance of pioneer women in the US. Commissioned by The National Society of Daughters of the American Revolution and created by sculptor August Leimbach, the statues were dedicated in 1928 and 1929, and today are still placed in each of the twelve states along the National Old Trails Road, which led from Cumberland, Maryland, to Upland, California. In the Ohio dedication ceremony, Harry S. Truman stated that the women "were just as brave or braver than their men because, in many cases, they went with sad hearts and trembling bodies. They went, however, and endured every hardship that befalls a pioneer" (qtd. in Algeo, *Harry Truman's* 50). The monuments are placed mostly in small towns in Maryland, Pennsylvania, West Virginia, Ohio, Indiana, Illinois, Missouri, Kansas, Colorado, New Mexico, Arizona, and California. Even if the monuments seek to remind us of the hardships undergone by women in the West, their representation of women as mother and nurturing presence in the West affirms traditional gender roles and once again asserts woman's out-of-placeness in the West.

Critical engagement with representations of the West in regard to race and gender and the reconstruction of 'other,' non-hegemonic voices in the West has been more prominently on the agenda of historians and other scholars in the past decades. Women's diaries of their westward journeys have become a valuable source for writing a bottom-up social history of women in the West, to which many scholars have contributed important studies and anthologies such as Julie Roy Jeffrey's *Frontier Women: "Civilizing" the West? 1840-1880* (1979); Lillian Schlissel's *Women's Diaries of the Westward Journey* (1982); Lillian

Schlissel, Vicki Ruíz, and Janice Monk's *Western Women: Their Land, Their Lives* (1988); Glenda Riley's studies *Women and Indians on the Frontier, 1825-1915* (1984) and *The Female Frontier: A Comparative View of Women on the Prairie and the Plains* (1988); Elizabeth Jameson and Susan Armitage's *Writing the Range: Race, Class, and Culture in the Women's West* (1997); and Susan Cummins Miller's *A Sweet, Separate Intimacy: Women Writers of the American Frontier, 1800-1922* (2000). All of these studies contributed to complicating our sense of women's presences and roles in the American West, as a result of which also fictional representations of women in the West have changed over time, as can be seen, for instance, in Kelly Reichardt's *Meek's Cutoff* (2010), Ethan and Joel Coen's *True Grit* (2010), or Logan Miller's *Sweetwater* (2013).

Illustration 3: The Frontier Woman as Madonna

W.H.D. Koerner, *The Madonna of the Prairie* (1921).

A second dimension of gender scholarship has been to investigate the particular logic of female absence in conventional accounts and representations of the West. In a Freudian spirit, Leslie Fiedler has defined the American West as symbolizing a male homosocial and at times interracial space "to which White male

Americans flee from their own women into the arms of Indian males, but which those White women, in their inexorable advance from coast to coast, destroy" (*Return* 50). In the context of westward expansion, women have been commonly portrayed as "obstacles to the male hero's freedom" (Georgi-Findlay, *Frontiers* 6) in popular culture, which is why they are often left behind – in the East, in the domestic space of the house or the log cabin, or in the garden.

Yet, processes of gendering do not only relate to women but work in a dialectical dynamic that co-constructs femininity and masculinity, as Annette Kolodny's work on the American West shows. Kolodny points out in *The Lay of the Land* (1975) that women were absented and excluded from conventional accounts of settlement and westward expansion, whereas the land itself was coded in overtly feminine terms in

what is probably America's oldest and most cherished fantasy: a daily reality of harmony between man and nature based on an experience of the land as essentially feminine – that is, not simply the land as mother, but the land as woman, the total female principle of gratification – enclosing the individual in an environment of receptivity, repose, and painless and integral satisfaction. (4)

It is the symbolic capital of the feminine, so to speak, that is appropriated to signify metaphorically on the male experience of settlement in a patriarchal fantasy of 'exploring' the 'virgin land.'

This particular form of engendering the American West is not only evident in the 17th-, 18th-, and 19th-century primary sources which Kolodny analyzes, but also in earlier Americanist scholarship such as Smith's *Virgin Land*, whose guiding metaphor of a feminized landscape by implication affirms the male figure as colonist, settler, and cultivator. Kolodny's account of this gendered discourse is nuanced and quite explicit: by taking the metaphors of discovery, expansion, and possession literally and seriously in a reading that is both feminist and ecocritical, she views the conquest of the West as "rape" (*Lay* 4).

Among the newly canonized writings on the West by women, we find European women's travel accounts, for example by Frances Trollope, Ida Pfeiffer, and Frederika Bremer, as well as white American writers' fictional and often semi-autobiographical representations of life in the West, for example Caroline Kirkland's *A New Home, Who'll Follow? Or, Glimpses of Western Life* (1839), Eliza Farnham's *Life in Prairie Land* (1846), Catherine Stewart's *New Homes in the West* (1843), or, much later, Willa Cather's *My Ántonia* (1918) and *O Pioneers!* (1913). I will exemplarily single out for closer analysis Caroline Kirkland's text, which after once having been dismissed by Henry Nash Smith as "extremely simple" (*Virgin Land* 263) has seen a feminist reappraisal over the last decades. Published under the pseudonym "Mrs. Mary Clavers, An Actual Settler," Kirkland in this novel wrote back to male-authored works (by James Fenimore Cooper or John Filson, for instance) that prominently featured romanticized representations of the West by describing

the very ordinary scenes, manners and customs of Western Life. No wild adventure, – no blood curdling hazards, – no romantic incidents, – could occur within my limited and sober sphere. No new lights have appeared above my narrow horizon. Commonplace all, yet I must tell it. (*New Home* 10)

The irony of Kirkland's "pioneer realism" and early local color writing (Zagarell, Introduction xiv) is often quite biting; by resorting to the conventional topos of modesty often used by female authors, she presents as mere "gossip" (Kirkland, *New Home* 3) what clearly constitutes a critique of patriarchal norms and especially of Jacksonian ideals of manhood. The text unfolds in satirical sketches that depict the settlement of the protagonist in Western Michigan in 1837 and often ridicules male efforts at empire-building, the 'frontier democracy,' and the garden myth (cf. Georgi-Findlay, *Frontiers* 28; Gebhardt, "Comic Displacement" 157). Kirkland also "exposes pastoral conventions as inadequate for writing a western narrative, especially from a woman's viewpoint" (Georgi-Findlay, *Frontiers* 31); her female characters are often isolated, lonely, and dependent on husbands who are abusive alcoholics, utterly inept farmers, or both. At the same time, Kirkland articulates a classist, 'civilized' ideal that connects femininity, domesticity, material culture, and consumerism to a rural setting that quite obviously still lacks proper refinement (cf. Merish, "Hand").

The ideology of domesticity by Kirkland and other 19th-century women writers has also been critically examined with regard to the dominant discourses of expansionism and empire; a third aspect to be addressed in relation to the gendering of the West in terms of space and agency thus concerns the ways in which white women were not only the objects and victims of patriarchal expansionism, but were also complicit in affirming the ideologies of manifest destiny and exceptionalism. Moving beyond a simplistic and binary feminist critique of the frontier myth, Brigitte Georgi-Findlay has shown that women's writing reveals that "the cultural domestication of an eccentric West" does not simply present

a female countervision to male fantasies of conquest and possession, but is in fact complementary to them: the ideal of domesticity, read in a context of empire building, also functions as an instrument for imposing cultural and social control and order upon the "disorderly" classes of the West. (*Frontiers* 29-30)

Amy Kaplan's concept of "manifest domesticity" similarly describes the "spatial and political interdependence of home and empire" (*Anarchy* 25) as a kind of "imperial domesticity" (ibid. 29) that can be found in white women's writing of the time: "'Manifest Domesticity' turns an imperial nation into a home by producing and colonizing spectres of the foreign that lurk inside and outside its ever-shifting borders" (ibid. 50). (White) women in the West or moving to the West thus sided with white patriarchy in affirming the civilizing project and its accompanying violence instead of critiquing it.

If, as Kathleen Neils Conzen has suggested, the West is "a family story" negotiating the "insistent themes of family, kinship, and community" ("Saga" 315), the family in the West also figures as national allegory. As Richard Slotkin and others have argued, the ideology of US domestic expansion (particularly after the Louisiana Purchase) has always obscured processes of empire-building and conquest that were anything but a domestic affair by presenting them as family matters, so to speak. On the whole, 19th-century white female perspectives both affirmed and appropriated the myth of the West and its "moral authority" (Slotkin, *Fatal Environment* 126), as recasting the West as a domestic space only reinforced the ostensibly intra-national quality of expansion.

In conclusion of this section, I would like to briefly discuss Nebraskan writer Willa Cather as an outstanding figure of a generation of women writers who addressed the West in the early 20th century. According to critics of her time, Cather's depictions of the West in *O Pioneers!* and *My Ántonia* are regionalist without being provincial, and nostalgic yet modern (cf. Reynolds, "Willa Cather's"). Cather shows her protagonists to share a deep mythic connection to the land that evolves from the ultimately redemptive and rewarding hardships of farm life; narrator Jim Burden for example muses on the transformations of the Nebraska of his childhood in *My Ántonia*: "[A]ll the human effort that had gone into it was coming back in long, sweeping lines of fertility. The changes seemed beautiful and harmonious to me; it was like watching the growth of a great man or of a great idea" (97). Jim projects the "heartland's vitality" and seemingly organic growth (another aspect of the geographic determinism we are already familiar with from Turner's works) onto Àntonia, who thus "embodies the ideological fantasy [...] of national development" (Matthews, "What Was" 294) along the lines of a much older – and deeply problematic – agrarian vision.

5. A VIEW *FROM* THE WEST: JAPANESE AMERICANS AND THE WEST AS A LANDSCAPE OF CONFINEMENT

> The barbed fence
> protected us
> from wildly twisted
> sagebrush.
> MITSUYE YAMADA, "BLOCK 4 BARRACK 4 'APT' C"

The critique of Turner's Eurocentrism has led to correcting a tacit assumption that underlies many representations of the West, namely, that one arrives there from the east – arguably, North America was settled from west to east as well. The history of Asian immigration to America provides a view from the West on the West as East, so to speak, and thus the basis for a forceful rebuttal of the mythical West. Asian immigration to the US and to the 'West' was restricted by a series of exclusionary acts (e.g. the Chinese Exclusion Act of 1882; the Asiatic Barred Zone Act of 1917; the Asian Exclusion Act of 1924; and the Tydings-McDuffie Act of 1934) until the Immigration and Nationality Act of 1965, which marked the end of the National Origins quota system. Lisa Lowe and Mae Ngai, among others, have traced the way in which "Asian *immigrants*" have been defined in legal, racial, economic, and cultural terms in opposition and contradistinction to "American *citizens*" (Lowe, *Immigrant Acts* 4). The Asian American experience of the West is marked by "legal exclusions, political disenfranchisement, labor exploitation, and internment" (ibid. 9), which time and again affirmed Asian Americans' status as 'other' and as 'alien' (cf. Ngai, *Impossible Subjects*). Against the backdrop of this history, the American West is, not surprisingly, often portrayed by Asian Americans as a space of restriction and confinement rather than of freedom.

I cannot provide a detailed history of Asians' experience of the West here (for example as laborers in the mines and on the transcontinental railroad in the 19th century), but I would like to single out the experience of Japanese Americans during World War II as one of many examples that is at odds with and thoroughly challenges the hegemonic discourse of the West on the West. After the Japanese attack on Pearl Harbor on December 7, 1941, the Japanese American population of about 120,000 – of whom about 80,000 were American citizens – came to be seen as a threat to national security by the US government, and was forcibly relocated from the Pacific coast to inland internment camps, or 'War Relocation Centers' (Gila River and Poston, Arizona; Jerome and Rohwer, Arkansas; Manzanar and Tule Lake, California; Amache, Colorado; Minidoka,

Idaho; Topaz, Utah; and Heart Mountain, Wyoming). The 'westering' experience of Japanese immigrants (*Issei*) as well as second and third generation Japanese Americans (*Nisei* and *Sansei*) thus stood in stark contrast to the mythologized one that was propagated by Hollywood and American popular culture at large on an unprecedented scale in the 1940s (close to 100 Western movies were produced in 1942 alone). Yet, Japanese American internment was couched by the US government in terms of exploration, individualism, and mobility: "[T]he language of America's frontier myth [...] frame[d] the relocation program. In their information material, government agencies referred to the Japanese Americans as 'pioneers' and to the camps as their 'frontier'" (Streamas, "Frontier Mythology" 175). Alternatively, Japanese Americans were described as "colonists," and the camps as "colonies" (ibid.). In a 1942 pamphlet titled *The War Relocation Work Corps*, a relocation center is defined as a "pioneer community with basic housing and protective services provided by the Federal Government, for occupancy by evacuees for the duration of the war" (qtd. in ibid.). In uncanny ways, this euphemistic rhetoric whitewashes the forced displacement and incarceration of the Japanese American population by "forcing concentration camps into the frontier myth" (ibid. 183).

It is perhaps somewhat surprising that texts by Japanese Americans about the internment experience also use the rhetoric of the frontier, albeit not without irony. In her autobiography *Nisei Daughter* (1953), Monica Sone relates that she was born in Seattle's Pioneer Square neighborhood, the very site of the city's founding, from where she was relocated at age 22 with her family to Camp Harmony in Idaho. When permitted to leave the camp, Sone has to go east, as the internees were at first not allowed to return to the West Coast. The narrator inverts and appropriates slogans like 'Westward, Ho' and 'Go West, Young Man' in chapter titles such as "Eastward, Nisei" (216) and "Deeper into the Land" (226). Throughout her narrative, Sone appropriates American myths in order to describe her experiences, and thereby connects the internment of Japanese Americans to the racist and imperialist logic that underlies the ideology of manifest destiny (cf. Paul, *Mapping* 98); yet, the actual trauma of internment in her text remains an "articulate silence" (cf. Cheung's book on Asian American and Asian Canadian women's writing).

Whereas the desert is addressed in a variety of texts about internment (c.f. e.g. Yoshiko Uchida's memoir *Desert Exile: The Uprooting of a Japanese American Family* and Mitsuye Yamada's poems and stories in *Desert Run*), there is also a strong focus on gardens and gardening in camp memoirs that documents a particular reaction to the arid landscape which has been read by Patricia Nelson Limerick as a form of resistance to internment, as the (traditional Japanese) gardens that the internees were cultivating in the camps under adverse circumstances added a new dimension to the Jeffersonian agrarian ideal and to the garden myth of the American West (cf. *Something* 209) – gardening for the internees thus may have been more than a way to improve their bleak living conditions.

Illustration 4: The West as Prison

Anselm Adams, *Manzanar Relocation Center from Tower* (1943).

Not only in the context of internment have Japanese American writers addressed the West as a place of confinement. Hisaye Yamamoto's short fiction (most famously "Seventeen Syllables"), or the plays by Wakako Yamauchi (cf. *Songs*) and Velina Hasu Houston for example often deal with the alienation, loneliness, and melancholia of Japanese American women in the post-World War II rural West. Houston's play *Tea* for instance, which references Susan Glaspell's *Trifles* (1916), focuses on Japanese women who live as "war brides" in Kansas in the 1950s and 1960s; these women's "feeling of lingering exile is a far cry from the sense of boundless opportunity so often associated with immigration to the American West in our national mythology" (Berson, "Fighting" 266). The counter-image of the West as a traumatic and "grief-haunted place" (Proulx, "Dangerous Ground" 15) that is here articulated in subtle, culturally specific ways is also addressed in many other revisionist and more recent fictional and non-fictional texts and images which comprise what has been identified as "frontier gothic" (cf. Mogen, Sanders and Karpinski's book of the same title).

6. COWBOYS (AND 'INDIANS'): THE AMERICAN WEST IN POPULAR CULTURE

> People from all levels of society read Westerns: presidents, truck drivers, librarians, soldiers, college students, businessmen, homeless people. They are read by women as well as men, rich and poor, young and old. In one way or another, Westerns – novels and films – have touched the lives of virtually everyone who lived during the first three-quarters of this century. The arch-images of the genre – the gunfight, the fistfight, the chase on horseback, the figure of the mounted horseman outlined against the sky, the saloon girl, the lonely landscape itself, are culturally pervasive and overpowering.
>
> JANE TOMPKINS, *WEST OF EVERYTHING*

Violence in the hegemonic discourse on the 'Wild' West has been largely imagined as regenerative and cathartic (cf. Slotkin, *Regeneration*); the various elements of the frontier myth "center on the conception of American history as a heroic-scale Indian war, pitting race against race" (Slotkin, *Fatal Environment* 32). This fantasy of the West as a site of necessary quasi-mythical violence can be found in print media, performance culture, film, and television, which I will exemplarily address in my discussion of the West in popular culture (and the West's popular culture) in order to uncover the ideological manoeuvres that have contained and controlled violence in the West along with Native American presences and absences and that have belittled or even completely disavowed the Native American genocide. For an analysis of print culture's role in the making of heroes and villains of the West in the late 18th and early 19th centuries, we can turn to pioneer Daniel Boone's (1734-1820) elevation to the status of national hero in John Filson's pamphlet *The Discovery, Settlement and Present State of Kentucke* (1784) and to the heroes of James Fenimore Cooper's historical romances. Both authors popularized the binary stereotypes of the noble and the ignoble savage, whose most prominent exemplars are perhaps the heroic and 'noble' Chingachgook and Uncas, and the villainous, 'ignoble' Magua in Cooper's *The Last of the Mohicans* (1826); whereas the former correspond to the image of the 'vanishing Indian' and support Euro-American westward expansion as they conveniently seem to anticipate their own extinction, the latter is representative of depictions of Natives as barbaric and primitive peoples who need to be vanquished in order for the West to be 'won,' settled, and 'civilized.' Cooper's dichotomous stereotypes have been extremely influential and to this day inform the majority of representations of the West and its indigenous inhabitants. In the logic of Cooper's Native presences, the very existence of the noble savage justifies the racist depiction of Natives in that it ostensibly counterbalances (but actually reinforces) their otherwise more overtly negative characterization.

Even more widely read than Cooper's highly successful novels were the dime novel Westerns, which became an unprecedented phenomenon in publishing and consumer culture in the second half of the 19th century (cf. Bill Brown, "Introduction" 6). Sold at very cheap prices (five to twenty-five cents), these pocketsize 'novels' were put out in series that ensured the recognizability of their title heroes (such as Deadwood Dick or Seth Jones), and prominently included dramatic scenes of violence as a major part of their attraction (cf. ibid. 2). Somewhat paradoxically, these texts projected rugged individualism and outstanding heroism in a format that relied to a large extent on standardization, serialization, and mass consumption:

If we suppose that the mass-produced myth effected some degree of national cohesion, then we should also suppose that both cohesion and alienation lay in the shared reading practice, the shared relation to consumer culture, and the newly shared pace and privacy of reading as an act of consumption. The material facts of the dime novel's production and distribution help us to appreciate the Western as a rationalization of the West that synchronized the realm of leisure in the rhythms of work and industry. (ibid. 30)

Picking up Adorno and Horkheimer's critique of mass culture in "The Culture Industry: Enlightenment as Mass Deception," Brown points to the anachronism at the heart of the popularity of the Western: while the success of dime novel Westerns hinged on mass production and thus on the industrialization of the US, the texts depicted pre-industrial frontier life. With the so-called Indian Wars still going on, the dime Westerns time and again staged and re-staged conflicts with the Native population as wars against 'savages' to which there was no alternative. Borrowing selectively from the racist "Cooperian mythology" (Slotkin, *Fatal Environment* 106), these Westerns focused on the ignoble savage and indulged in and legitimized white violence against the indigenous population of the American West (it is only after it had been drastically reduced due to warfare and 'removal' policies that they began to stage conflicts between white men). A closer look at Edward S. Ellis's *Seth Jones; or, The Captives of the Frontier* (1860), one of the most successful early dime novel Westerns – we could sample randomly from many others to find similar constellations, though – reveals how Native Americans are demonized in stereotypical descriptions such as the following one:

Behind were a half-dozen savages, their gleaming visages distorted with the passions of exultation, vengeance, and doubt, their garments flying in the wind, and their strength pressed to its utmost bounds. They were scattered at different distances from each other, and were spreading over the prairie, so as to cut off the fugitive's escape in every direction. (197)

The Natives' dehumanizing representation as evil, animalistic, and dangerous puts them into stark opposition to the white characters, whose sense of entitlement to land and power is unquestioned and whose extreme brutality is condoned and legitimated by the narrative. White violence is described almost gleefully and in disturbing graphic detail, and is obviously supposed to be pleasurable for the (white) audience. The text continues with Seth Jones beginning to take revenge for the capture of whites by the Natives:

So sudden, so unexpected, so astonishing was the crash of Seth's tomahawk through the head of the doomed savage, that, for a moment after, not an Indian moved or spoke. The head was nearly cleft in twain (for an arm fired by consuming passion had driven it), and the brains were spattered over numbers of those seated around. Seth himself stood a second to satisfy himself the work was complete, and when he turned, walked to his seat, sat down, coolly folded his arms and *commenced whistling*. (212, emphasis in the original)

The slaughtering of the Native in this passage is described in hyperbolic yet at the same time realist fashion; whereas many other cultural productions (including Cooper's) would disavow or at least camouflage violence against Native Americans, in scenes such as this one – which abound in dime novel Westerns, and qualify in some instances as a precursor to what in contemporary jargon is labelled 'torture porn' – even the most 'savage' white violence is represented as acceptable and legitimate in an unequivocal assertion of white superiority. The dime novel Westerns do not claim national allegorical status, which is perhaps why their implication in the construction and affirmation of white supremacy is more overt than in other, more subtle cultural productions. The fact that these mass-produced and mass-consumed fantasies do not hide or feel the need to explain the white violence that they describe points us to the tacit dimension of the myth of the West in hegemonic discourse: "This is how the Western produces what we might call its 'mythology effect' – with the presumption that the West already exists as shared knowledge, with an absence of detail that insists on familiarity" (Bill Brown, "Introduction" 33). This "familiarity" is grounded in the unquestioned acceptance and successful naturalization of the fundamental ideological premises of frontier discourse, which above all include the assumption that white people's usurpatory presence in North America is justified at all.

Illustration 5: Popular Stereotypes of the West

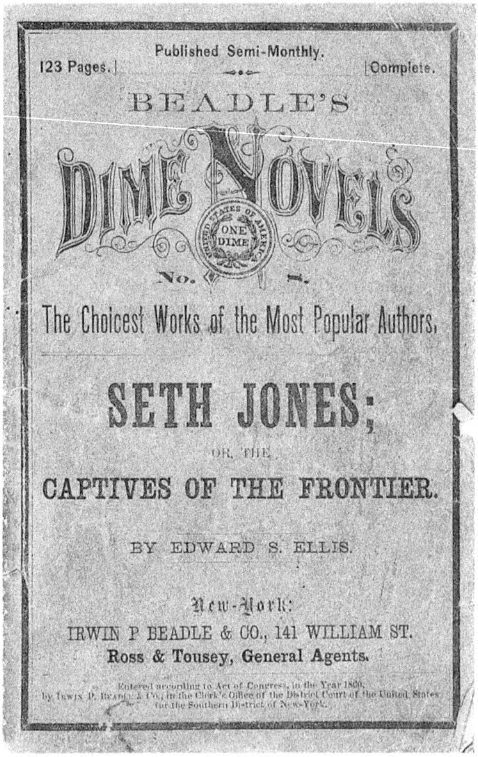

Cover of *Seth Jones: Or, the Captives of the Frontier*
by Edward S. Ellis (New York: Beadle, 1860).

None of these dime novel Westerns have been canonized; in fact, they have often been overlooked despite having constituted a large-scale phenomenon that connects to the earlier texts by James Fenimore Cooper as well as to later writers such as Owen Wister, whose novel *The Virginian* (1902) is often considered the first literary Western. This neglect has perhaps been motivated more by political rather than by aesthetic considerations in that their explicit descriptions of raw violence in contrast to other texts' more sanitized representations of westward expansion inconveniently point to – rather than obscure or rationalize – the brutality of the 'Indian Wars.'

That the Western is to a large degree "a matter of geography and costume" (Cawelti, *Six-Gun Mystique* 35) is also in evidence in my second example of how the West figures in popular culture: Buffalo Bill's Wild West, a national as well as international phenomenon that evolved out of the 19th-century print culture on the West. This Wild West Show was founded in Nebraska in 1883 by William Frederick Cody (1846-1917), a veteran of the Civil War and former bison hunter who created Buffalo Bill as his alter ego. For roughly 30 years (1883-1916), this show was one of the largest and most popular entertainment businesses in the world; it toured in the US and throughout Europe, and in addition to Buffalo Bill featured other prominent western figures such as James Butler "Wild Bill" Hickok, Annie Oakley, and Calamity Jane. Cody a.k.a. Buffalo Bill became a "national icon" – Larry McMurtry suggests that in his day he was probably "the most recognizable celebrity on earth" (*Colonel* 5) – and a figure that embodied and continued the tradition of earlier well-known fictional and semi-fictional figures of the West such as Natty Bumppo a.k.a. Leatherstocking/Hawkeye, and Daniel Boone; Buffalo Bill carried on the legacy of an ethnically white man who had partially 'gone native' and incorporated aspects of both the white and the Native world yet for the same reason was also an outstanding 'Indian fighter' and buffalo hunter, and was never in doubt about his cultural loyalties and allegiances: the gist of many of Cody's Buffalo Bill sketches is that the white man, time and again, outperforms the Native by using the latter's techniques.

The persuasiveness of these shows can be glimpsed in the following eyewitness account by Dan Muller, who lived and worked with Cody:

The show started. The band played a lively opening number. The Grand Entry was on. A group of riders appeared in the swinging spotlight at the scenic entrance. They loped around the arena and pulled up at the far end. [...] A spotlight now picked up a single rider loping toward the head of the assembled group of riding battalions. "LADEEZ AND GENTLEMEN," shouted the announcer. "ALLOW ME TO PRE-SENT THE GREAT-EST SCOUT OF THE OLD WEST: BUF-FA-LO B-I-I-I-L-L-L." The trumpets of the band burst into a loud blare of sound. By now Uncle Bill had brought his prancing horse to a theatrical stop that set him up on his hind feet. The crowd roared approval. [...] The program was action-packed from the first announcement to the grand closing. [...] There was a buffalo chase, and Uncle Bill, riding a horse at the buffalo's flank, blazed away with a rifle. [...] There were trick ropers the climax of whose act was dropping a loop over four running horses. [...] But the one I liked best was the stagecoach chase. In this act the stagecoach, drawn by six wildly galloping horses, its top crowded with men with rifles and with riflemen poking their weapons through the windows, tore around the arena with Indians mounted bareback in chase. And all the while the stagecoach blazed with the fire of the rifles and the Indians fired back. It sure was exciting. (*My Life* 113-17)

Illustration 6:
Buffalo Bill Stamp

US Postal Service, *Buffalo Bill Cody 15¢* (1988).

Native Americans figured prominently in Cody's shows; for one thing, because they included re-enactments of 'Custer's Last Stand,' i.e. the defeat of the 7th Cavalry Regiment of the US Army in the Battle of the Little Bighorn in 1876 by a coalition of Native tribes. This battle re-enactment was performed with Sitting Bull, military leader of the Lakota, who actually led the fateful attack against Custer. Knowing that the Natives' military success had only been temporary, white audiences apparently did not feel threatened by this performance; at the same time, it provided a great deal of spectacle. The collaboration between Cody and Native American leaders has been considered quite remarkable and somewhat puzzling: "Over the years Buffalo Bill managed to engage such figures as Sitting Bull and Geronimo as performers, and a great number of Indians who had fought against the cavalry less than a year before, as well as the services of regular units of the US Cavalry to perform opposite them" (Slotkin, *Gunfighter Nation* 68). Besides Native celebrities, Cody also needed Native actors for the 'typical scenes' and tableaux vivants his troupe staged. The ambivalence of their appearance can be grasped when weighing the worldwide reception and (apparently equal) pay they received during the tours against the fact that it helped freeze the image of Natives – by way of the show's content – into that of stereo-

typical, archaic warriors whose resistance to a superior Euro-American civilization had to be overcome, and indeed was by and large overcome by the time the
performances took place. At the height of the show's success in the 1890s,
Cody's troupe included one hundred Native men, women, and children among a
total staff of 500. Bringing the 'Wild West' to Americans throughout the US and
to Europe required a logistical effort that was impressive: "In 1899, Buffalo Bill's
Wild West covered over 11.000 miles in 200 days giving 341 performances in
132 cities and towns across the United States" (Fees, "Wild West Shows").
Buffalo Bill's Wild West became an international trademark whose successful
branding of the American West many performers sought to emulate. The show
produced, enhanced, and affirmed the myth of the West and of the frontier for
national and international audiences. The decline of the show coincides with the
rise of another medium that would become dedicated to representing and mythologizing the West: film. Toward the end of his life and career, Buffalo Bill's
show no longer convinced audiences, who sometimes even considered his enact-
ments of the 'Wild West' laughable (cf. Muller, *My Life* 256).

In the 20th century, the Western can be considered the American film genre par
excellence; it has been an important object of scholarship in American popular
culture studies, and will be my third and final example of cultural productions on
the West in this section. From Edwin S. Porter's *The Great Train Robbery*
(1903) onwards, the Western's negotiation of questions of individualism and
community, masculinity, alterity, and violence as well as national and racial
supremacy has codified the West as a formative space of US national identity.
Visually, it is a genre that can easily be identified: "[W]hen we see a couple of
characters dressed in ten-gallon hats and riding horses, we know we are in a
Western" (Cawelti, *Six-Gun Mystique* 34). The so-called Golden Age of the
Western is often dated from John Ford's *Stagecoach* (1939) to Sam Peckinpah's
The Wild Bunch (1969), with the latter already operating at quite a distance from
the classical Western; Neo-Westerns that have partially absorbed revisionist
historiography include Kevin Costner's *Dances with Wolves* (1990), Clint Eastwood's *Unforgiven* (1992), Jim Jarmusch's *Dead Man* (1995), Ang Lee's *Brokeback Mountain* (2005), and Quentin Tarantino's *Django Unchained* (2012).

The Western's long-time popularity, once more, corroborates Robert Dorman's argument that the frontier is "the prime commodity of the *Old West
culture industry*" (*Hell* 11). John Cawelti – whose work is closely related to that
of Leslie Fiedler and Richard Slotkin – has identified a particular formula of the
Western: its setting is the West, i.e a locale that existed in a very brief period of
time which is turned into the central "epic moment" (*Six-Gun Mystique* 39); its

cast of characters usually includes settlers and outlaws (who are sometimes Native Americans but, somewhat surprisingly perhaps, more often are white); its hero, who has a horse and a gun, intervenes on behalf of the "agents of civilization" (ibid. 46) while sometimes taking recourse to the same methods as the outlaws in order to win over them, and thus remains ambivalently 'in the middle' as he is at the same 'advancing' and escaping from 'civilization' (cf. ibid. 52); its plots usually revolve around capture, flight, and pursuit (cf. ibid. 67). Cawelti's typology links the Western to the archetypal narrative structure and patterns of the hero myth; the Western thus dramatizes a "foundation ritual" (ibid. 73) in the sense that

it presents for our renewed contemplation that epic moment when the frontier passed from the old way of life into social and cultural forms directly connected with the present. By dramatising this moment, and associating it with the hero's agency, the Western affirms the act of foundation. In this sense, the Western is like a Fourth of July ceremony. (ibid.)

Cawelti's relevance for discussing the West as a foundational myth is obvious, as in his view the function of the Western is to ritualistically affirm the hero's integrity and innocence despite his acts of violence against what hegemonic discourse represents as 'savages' or 'outlaws;' while some Westerns explore the moral dilemma of innocence and aggression in more ambiguous terms, Westerns by and large still are "fantasies of legitimated violence" and "moralistic aggression" (ibid. 85).

In many ways the Western films seem to transform the 'virgin land' of Henry Nash Smith into a 'crowded prairie' (cf. Coyne's book of the same title) from which, however, one part of the North American population is increasingly and symptomatically absent: In reconstructing the history of the Western, Jane Tompkins observes how Native Americans appear to disappear from a genre for which they actually were foundational (cf. *West*); the topos of the "vanishing race" (Fiedler, *Return*) and the "romance of disappearing" (Lawlor, *Recalling* 41) have been widely noted. In Frank Gruber's typology of basic Western plots, Native Americans appear only in one out of seven: "Custer's Land Stand, or the Cavalry and Indian Story" (qtd. in Cawelti, *Six-Gun Mystique* 35). In line with the pernicious notion of the 'Vanishing Indian,' the West in the Western becomes a stage for white (male) fantasies: "Westerns marginalized the Indian because they were only marginally *about* the Indian" (Coyne, *Crowded Prairie* 5). The white hero's 'just' fight against his enemies instead has a redemptive function in that it provides "regeneration through violence" (cf. Slotkin's book of the same title); the hero's *rite de passage* takes center stage and pushes the

Native genocide to the sidelines, or leaves it completely out of the picture. Roy Harvey Pearce has suggested that in the 19th century, the stereotype of the Native as either evil or noble savage slowly gave way to a white view on Natives as an inferior 'race' that belonged to an earlier (and thus doomed) stage of civilization (cf. *Savagism*). When looking at more contemporary productions, we may wonder if the Neo-Western has managed to challenge or alter the classical Western formula all that much in regard to its deeply problematical ideological underpinnings.

7. THE FRONTIER MYTH AND POLITICAL RHETORIC: THE CASE OF THE 'VIETNAM WAR'

> Vietnam was where the Trail of Tears was headed all along.
> MICHAEL HERR, *DISPATCHES*

> We use the term "Indian country" to describe Vietnam.
> AIRBORNE RANGER INFANTRY VETERAN ROBERT B. JOHNSON

> All I remember is that I was with Custer's Seventh Cavalry riding toward the Little Big Horn and we were struck by the Indians. After we crossed the Rosebud, we made it to Ridge Red Boy and then we were hit. No. I must have my wars confused. That was another time, another place. Other Indians.
> WILLIAM EASTLAKE, *THE BAMBOO BED*

As a public myth and "structure of feeling" (cf. Williams's text of the same title), the West has not only been expressed in mass culture but has also been used in political culture; presidents, presidential candidates, and others seeking or holding office have often fashioned themselves as farmers, cowboys, or pioneers, and employed the rhetoric of the frontier myth. The first 'cowboy president' was probably Andrew Jackson (cf. Lepore, *Story*), a former US Army general who embodied a heady mix of frontierism, militarism, and expansionism. In the context of the 20th and 21st centuries, we may think for example of Lyndon B. Johnson, who wore a Stetson and rode on horseback in his 1964 presidential campaign; Richard Nixon, who exploited his friendship with John Wayne and James Stewart for political gain (cf. Coyne, *Crowded Prairie* 1); Ronald Reagan, who made political use of the cowboy image even if among his 54 films only six were Westerns (cf. ibid.; Rogin, *Ronald Reagan*; Jeffords, *Hard Bodies*); or George W. Bush, who liked to pose on his Texas ranch dressed in a cowboy outfit. All of them used these references to the West in order to convey a sense of rugged masculinity and strong leadership. By the 20th century, the frontier myth had become engrained in political discourse and campaign rhetoric through a set of tacit references that were understood by all Americans.

One of the best-known examples of an appropriation of the American West in political rhetoric by way of the frontier myth is certainly John F. Kennedy's acceptance speech at the 1960 Democratic National Convention in Los Angeles. While Kennedy did not fashion himself as a cowboy during his candidacy and later as president but rather displayed the habitus of an East Coast urbanite, he did use the myth of the West in this so-called "New Frontier" speech, and invested it with new meanings:

I stand here tonight facing west on what was once the last frontier. From the lands that stretch 3000 miles behind us, the pioneers gave up their safety, their comfort, and sometimes their lives to build our new West. [...] [T]he problems are not all solved and the battles are not all won, and we stand today on the edge of a new frontier – the frontier of the 1960s, the frontier of unknown opportunities and perils, the frontier of unfilled hopes and unfilled threats. [...] I'm asking each of you to be pioneers towards that new frontier. [...] For the harsh facts of the matter are that we stand at this frontier at a turning point of history.

Kennedy's 'new frontier' rhetoric, which helped him win the presidential election, was fuelled by a 'Cold War' logic that would also provide the rationale for the US military involvement in Cambodia, Laos, and Vietnam. The latter's descriptions in official rhetoric, fiction, film, and memoirs likewise often reference the frontier and the 'Indian Wars,' and draw analogies between Native Americans and the Vietnamese (cf. Bates, *Wars* 10):

The invocation of the Indian war and Custer's Last Stand as models for the Vietnam war was a mythological way of answering the question, *Why are we in Vietnam?* The answer implicit in the myth is, "We are there because our ancestors were heroes who fought the Indians, and died (rightly or wrongly) as sacrifices for the nation." There is no logic to the connection, only the powerful force of tradition and habits of feeling and thought. (Slotkin, *Fatal Environment* 19)

These attempts at making the war in Southeast Asia intelligible and comprehensible through the familiar language of the frontier myth cannot be considered a simple, successful transference; they also challenged American self-perceptions

in new and unprecedented ways, and tested the myth's elasticity and, more profoundly, its validity:

> Vietnam is an experience that severely called into question American myth. Americans
> entered Vietnam with certain expectations that a story, a distinctly American story, would
> unfold. When the story of America in Vietnam turned into something unexpected, the true
> nature of the larger story of America itself became the subject of intense cultural dispute.
> On the deepest level, the legacy of Vietnam is the disruption of our story, of our explana-
> tion of the past and vision of the future. (Hellmann, *American Myth* x)

The interdependency of the myth of the West and the interpretation of the war in
Southeast Asia as well as the "Vietnamization" of the West (Coyne, *Crowded
Prairie* 120) can be identified on several levels; we can for instance analyze how
representations of the 'Vietnam War' use the Western formula in order to describe individual and collective war experiences. The convergence of the West
and the East is most clearly evident in the Pentagon-sponsored *The Green Berets*
(1968), which was one of the first Vietnam War films; based on Robin Moore's
bestselling novel of the same title which had been published three years earlier,
it starred and was co-directed by John Wayne, the prototypical Western hero.
Hoping to "make the old magic work" (Adair, *Hollywood's Vietnam* 38), this
film is quite overtly anti-communist propaganda cloaked in Western imagery:
the film's depiction of a base camp in Vietnam is very similar to that of cavalry
forts in Westerns, and its demonization of the Vietcong also strongly resembles
that of Native Americans in earlier films and other media. The film heroized the
Green Berets – i.e., the US Army Special Forces, whose guerrilla and counterin-
surgency tactics were endorsed by the Kennedy administration – by representing
them as "a fused image of sophisticated contemporary professional and rough
Indian fighters" that embodied the "paradox of the genteel killer" and "the death-
dealing innocent" on the new frontier in Asia (Hellmann, *American Myth* 46/47).
John Wayne's son Michael, who produced the film, would later note in an interview: "Maybe we shouldn't have destroyed all those Indians, but when you are
making a picture, the Indians are the bad guys" (qtd. in Adair, *Hollywood's Vietnam* 35).

Thus, from a New Historicist perspective, *The Green Berets* can be read as a
film that makes sense of the 'Vietnam War' by employing the Western's mode
of representing the 'Indian Wars.' Other Vietnam War films also transpose the
myth of the West, and in particular the myth of the frontier, to Vietnam: Michael
Cimino's *The Deer Hunter* (1978) references James Fenimore Cooper's historical frontier romance *The Deerslayer* (1841); *First Blood* (1982) places its pro-

tagonist Rambo (Sylvester Stallone), a former Green Beret and traumatized war veteran, on the outskirts of a small American town in a quasi wilderness, thus rendering him an inverted Natty Bumppo; its sequel *Rambo: First Blood Part II* (1985), a latter-day American captivity narrative, once again stages Rambo as a prototypical 'Indian fighter' who this time is on a mission to liberate American soldiers from Vietnamese POW camps; *Apocalypse Now* (1979) by contrast uses the hardboiled detective genre – which can be considered to have transposed the 'Wild West' into an urban context – to more radically depict "Vietnam as a nightmare extension of American society" (Hellmann, *American Myth* 201), and further undermines "the idealistic self-concept embodied in the American hero" (ibid. 203) through its references to Joseph Conrad's novella *Heart of Darkness* (1899). Let me add in passing that we can also examine how the war in Southeast Asia changed the American Western proper; as a case in point we may consider *Little Big Man* (1970), an early revisionist Western based on Thomas Berger's 1964 novel of the same title that "portrayed the settling of the frontier as a succession of My Lai's" (Hellmann, *American Myth* 95).

As John Clark Pratt points out in a similar context, we can observe that "the literature of the Vietnam War is filled with American characters who enter Vietnam as traditional frontier huntsmen, then become men trying merely to survive in a wilderness they do not understand" ("Lost Frontier" 238). In many ways, Vietnam brought the American foundational mythic formula to a crisis, because the myth failed to successfully work the war into a coherent narrative; as many have noted, the war could not be easily contained in the language of the frontier myth, and moreover brought to the surface the 'origins' of the myth – the collectively dis- or misremembered 'Indian Wars' – which thus became the object of reinterpretation. "The war did what almost nothing else could have: it forced a major breach in consciousness" (Charles Reich qtd. in Hellmann, *American Myth* 76). Hellmann also suggests – in language echoing that of earlier Americanists – that Vietnam became "a landscape in the American consciousness that would have to be journeyed through many times over, self-consciously experienced through narrative art as myth and symbol" (ibid. 95). We may thus consider the war in Southeast Asia as an event that unsettled the heroic myth of the West in that it brought to the fore the violence inscribed into it as well as the utter 'ugliness' of US military engagement in Asia and elsewhere (cf. William Lederer and Eugene Burdick's 1958 political novel *The Ugly American*). However, official efforts at (re-)mythologizing Vietnam continue to this day, as president Obama's 2012 proclamation in commemoration of the 50th anniversary of the war show:

[W]e reflect with solemn reverence upon the valor of a generation that served with honor. We pay tribute to the more than 3 million servicemen and women who left their families to serve bravely, a world away from everything they knew and everyone they loved. From Ia Drang to Khe Sanh, from Hue to Saigon and countless villages in between, they pushed through jungles and rice paddies, heat and monsoon, fighting heroically to protect the ideals we hold dear as Americans. (Presidential Proclamation)

The doubts about individual and collective American identities triggered by the war were articulated in many forms; representatives of the American counter-culture and the peace movement argued that Vietnam revealed the pathological nature of the American empire, or, less radically, that it signified a loss of values. Activists and writers who visited North Vietnam, among them Susan Sontag, regarded Vietnam as "the America that no longer exists" (Hellmann, *American Myth* 85); the innocence yet also the 'primitiveness' and 'backward-ness' Sontag perceives are evident in many instances of her travel report *Trip to Hanoi* (1968), in which she pastoralizes Vietnam and describes its inhabitants as "children – beautiful, patient, heroic, martyred, stubborn children" (15). Whereas the 'Indians' of Vietnam are demonized in productions such as *The Green Berets*, they are infantilized by Sontag and other countercultural voices, which constitutes a form of othering that is hardly less problematical. Thus, we can see that the Vietnamese are still described within the bounds of the myth of the West – as evil or noble 'savages.'

Lastly, there is yet another aspect to the connection between Vietnam and the American Indian Wars which centers on Native American agency rather than on the objectification of 'natives.' In the midst of the 'Cold War,' 'Indian country' migrated back from Vietnam to the American heartland when Native American activists occupied the town of Wounded Knee, South Dakota, from February 27 to May 8, 1973. The protest of the American Indian Movement (AIM) at Wounded Knee focused on what many considered as America's racist imperial-ism at home (cf. Rosier, *Serving* 264) and was joined by a number of Native American veterans who had just returned from Vietnam. The protest in South Dakota soon appeared as a (semi-staged) re-creation of Vietnam which indicated that for the US, the 'Cold War' had both an international as well as a domestic side to it (ibid. 269). Woody Kipp, a member of the Blackfeet Nation and a US Marine Corps veteran who fought in Vietnam, would in his memoirs titled *Viet Cong at Wounded Knee: The Trail of a Blackfeet Activist* (2004) refer to this connection as the "pervasive issues of race and dominance [...] that have shaped and formed this country since its earliest days" (141).

Illustration 7: The Anti-Mad Cowboy

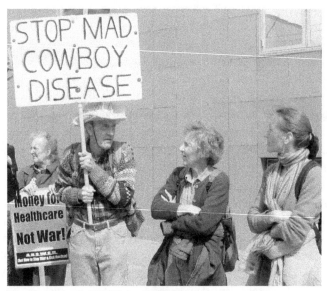

Photograph by Gail Williams (2005).

Clearly, and in spite of the most radical protest at the time of the war in South-east Asia, the frontier myth was not entirely debunked and much less destroyed, but perhaps it was expanded to the extent that post-Vietnam, it could include failure as well as triumph and victory. Beyond Vietnam, the US national security apparatus has continued to conflate 'Indians' with those it felt the need to frame as enemies, and to use the semantics of the frontier myth in acts of epistemic violence; the Old West revenge tale, for instance, has figured prominently in the political rhetoric of the 'War on Terror' ('dead or alive'), and it led protesters against the War in Iraq to chant "it's the Middle East, not the Wild West" (Kollin, "Introduction" x). A connection between the 'Indian Wars' and US foreign policy was established once again in May 2011 when 'Geronimo,' the name of an Apache leader, was used as a code word in the CIA-led operation that presumably resulted in the killing of Osama bin Laden.

8. CONCLUSION: THE TRANSNATIONAL WEST

> The west is everywhere.
> KRIS FRESONKE, *WEST OF EMERSON*

> There's a bit of the West in all of us.
> WRANGLER ADVERTISING SLOGAN

In his study *The Rhizomatic West*, Neil Campbell seeks to define "westness" (41) beyond a national paradigm and considers the West as a "travelling" and "mobile discourse" (ibid. 1) and, with James Clifford, as a "travelling concept" (*Routes* 4). Paul Giles has asked us to view "native [American] landscapes refracted or inverted in a foreign mirror" in order "to appreciate the assumptions framing these narratives and the ways they are intertwined with the construction and reproduction of national mythologies" (*Virtual Americas* 2). Similarly, the approach of critical regionalism – a term popularized by Kenneth Frampton (cf. "Towards") – allows us to focus on the West in its local and global dimensions simultaneously, and to look at the connections between both.

A transnational view would thus, first, privilege the cultural mobility and non-American appropriations of the American West: in Europe, the myth of the West has been affirmed in appropriations of the Western genre for instance by the German author Karl May and the Belgian cartoonist Maurice de Bevere (a.k.a. Morris), whose characters Winnetou and Lucky Luke have become iconic figures. Their re-articulation of the myth of the West is relevant in various cultural and temporal contexts; May's Winnetou stories are still staged yearly at the Karl May Festival in Bad Segeberg, and are parodied in *Der Schuh des Manitu* (2001), which to date is the greatest commercial success in German film history, while murals depicting scenes from the Lucky Luke comics series decorate houses in Brussels. Whereas Karl May's fictional West has been quite thoroughly studied (cf. Schmidt, *Sitara*; Sammons, *Ideology*), little cultural studies scholarship so far exists on Morris's work.

From a different vantage point we may also consider the Western not only as the prototypical US-American film genre but also as, in fact, a transnational genre, as classic Westerns have inspired eastern remakes, and vice versa. Japanese filmmaker Akira Kurosawa's *Yojimbo* (1961), which is indebted to Dashiell Hammett's novel *Red Harvest* (1929), in turn is the 'original' to Italian filmmaker Sergio Leone's *Per un pugno di dollari* (1964), which invested the genre with a new sense of irony and cynicism.

Kurosawa's films have served as models for American Western films time and again: His *Seven Samurai* (1954) served as the template for John Sturges's *The Magnificent Seven* (1960), and *Yojimbo* was adapted once again by Walter Hill as *Last Man Standing* (1996). At the same time, the so-called 'Eastern' has emerged as a global, commercially successful hybrid that fuses the formula of the Western with that of the martial arts film. In looking at these cultural productions, we may ask ourselves how we can conceive of such a mythic fusion critically in terms of orientalist as well as 'western' discourses, and how the myth of the West – either in its agrarian/pastoralist or in its expansionist version – can be transposed and translated into other (sub)cultural and (trans)national contexts; another question would be whether we should consider these translations and appropriations as affirmative or subversive in regard to canonical accounts of the myth of the West.

A transnational view, second, necessitates looking more closely at economic factors and the neoliberal logic that shapes the identity of regions and their international reception/consumption in a globalized world: Critical regionalist scholars have their eyes on processes of globalization that also 'produce' regions as marketable commodities, and the West – as (part of) a "corporate geography" (Cheryl Herr, *Critical Regionalism* 3) – has been such a commodity for a long time. Global enterprises attest to that, for instance the online shopping center New West Mall (newwestmall.com), or Disney, whose theme parks in Anaheim, Bay Lake, Tokyo, Paris, and Hong Kong include a so-called Frontierland made up of generic cowboys, pioneers, saloons, and other stereotypical 'Wild West' features. No explicit mention is made of Native Americans in the parks located in the US, where the so-called Indian Village that had previously been part of Frontierland has been removed. The biggest Frontierland is that in Disneyland Park (Paris), which also includes the so-called Pocahontas Indian Village. In Tokyo Disneyland, it is called Westernland, as 'frontier' does not adequately translate into Japanese; ironically, both theme parks in Asia focus on the history of mining in the West – a history that includes the large-scale exploitation of Asian immigrants who were being used as forced labor on the so-called mining frontier – which in the parks however is transfigured and symbolically and economically exploited once more.

A critique of local/global capitalism would have to go back to US expansionism in the West and to agrarianism, which have always been connected by commercial interests that upon closer inspection also demystify the myth of the garden and of manifest destiny, as Thorstein Veblen has noted:

The country town is a product and exponent of the American land system. In its beginning it is located and "developed" as an enterprise of speculation in land values; that is to say it is a businesslike endeavour to get something for nothing by engrossing as much as may be of the increment of land values due to the increase of population and the settlement and cultivation of the adjacent agricultural area. It never (hitherto) loses this character of real-estate speculation. This affords a common bond and a common ground of pecuniary interest, which commonly masquerades under the name of public patriotism, public spirit, civic pride, and the like. (*Imperial Germany* 334)

The ideology of manifest destiny is certainly an important part of the patriotic spirit Veblen describes. A number of cultural productions, among them the television series *Deadwood* (2004-2006), have recently addressed the capitalist logic of early settlement, which established still existing structures of economic exploitation in the West and at times outside the borders of the US. *Deadwood* has been applauded for its postwestern, critical representation of "life within a world ordered entirely around the marketplace" (Worden, "Neo-liberalism" 221), which points to the capitalist logic underlying Euro-American settlement in North America, and from which the standard heroism and nostalgia that continues to be an important dimension of the myth of the West is largely absent. With Daniel Worden, we can interpret the West as a national allegory that connects past, present, and future and that also reveals the violence at work in economic transformations within the larger "incorporation of America" (cf. Trachtenberg's book of the same title), an incorporation that does not stop at national borders.

A transnational critical regionalist framework, third, also pays new attention to comparative frameworks of analysis. The West and its myth(s) are analyzed from such angles, for instance, by The Comparative Wests Project at Stanford University, which researches "the common histories and shared contemporary issues among Indigenous populations and settler colonialists in Australia, New Zealand, Western South America, the Western United States, Canada, and the Pacific Islands" (comparativewests.stanford.edu). The American Midwest and Ireland have also been analyzed as two regions whose histories have been connected to and shaped each other over a long period of time (cf. Cheryl Herr, *Critical Regionalism*). Comparative border studies (cf. Sadowski-Smith, "Introduction") touch upon constructions of the American West and its borders with other regions, particularly those to the south. Russell Ward has probed Turner's thesis with regard to Australian history and the construction of an Australian frontier narrative in his study *The Australian Legend* (1958), which may well be seen as the search for an Australian Adam in analogy to R.W.B. Lewis's *The American Adam*, published only a few years earlier. From a historical perspective, Edward Watts urges us to study the West (in particular the Midwest) not only as an American region in an intranational context but also as a colony – or "hypercolony" – "within the context of the global European diaspora of the nineteenth century," as it shares certain features with other Dominions of the British Empire at the time ("Midwest" 166, 169, 174); Watts holds that it

turns more on the scholarly redefinition of what a colony is (and what its relationship to its metropolis is) than on whether the Midwest was ever a colony to the East the same way Massachusetts was a colony of the British Empire in 1776. A colony in the eighteenth century was one thing; in the nineteenth, another. And the Midwest can and should be studied alongside not just the other regions with whom it shares a nation, but also alongside the other colonies with whom it shared a century. (ibid. 187)

Critical regionalism thus calls for an internationalization of the study of regions in the US and for connecting the West as region, fantasy, and brand to concepts of (neo)colonialism and globalization.

9. STUDY QUESTIONS

1. Identify and discuss the different meanings of the American West. How can they be contrasted, and what do they have in common?
2. Why may mapping the West in geographical terms be difficult? What kind of maps can you think of that capture the (myth of the) American West?
3. Give a brief definition of what Frederick Jackson Turner refers to as "the significance of the frontier in American history."
4. Interpret Frances Flora Bond Palmer's *Across the Continent: "Westward the Course of Empire Makes Its Way"* (1868). How does it represent the West and westward expansion?

Illustration 8: Westward Expansion

Frances Flora Bond Palmer, *Across the Continent: "Westward the Course of Empire Takes Its Way"* (1868). (Philadelphia Museum of Art: Gift of Kathy and Ted Fernberger, 2009).

5. Read Stephen Crane's short stories "The Blue Hotel" and "The Bride Comes to Yellow Sky" and discuss how Crane's representations of the West undermine prevailing stereotypes of his (and our) time.
6. Watch and discuss commercials that use the myth of the West. A good place to start would be the "So God Made a Farmer" Ram Trucks commercial from Super Bowl 2013 with Paul Harvey, which is available on the internet.

7. Choose a Western movie and discuss its representation of the West and the frontier.

8. Discuss the implications of the myth of the West with regard to different ethnic groups in the US (Native Americans, Asian Americans, Mexican Americans, African Americans).

9. Give reasons for the success of Buffalo Bill's Wild West in Europe. Can you draw analogies to other, perhaps more recent phenomena?

10. The opening sequence of the television series *Star Trek* begins with a voice-over declaring "space" to be "the final frontier." Discuss this opening in the context of the frontier myth.

10. BIBLIOGRAPHY

Works Cited

Adair, Gilbert. *Hollywood's Vietnam*. New York: Proteus, 1981.

Adorno, Theodor, and Max Horkheimer. "The Culture Industry: Enlightenment as Mass Deception." *The Cultural Studies Reader*. Ed. Simon During. 3rd ed. London: Routledge, 2007. 405-15.

Algeo, Matthew. *Harry Truman's Excellent Adventure: The True Story of a Great American Road Trip*. Chicago: Chicago Review, 2009.

Apocalypse Now. Dir. Francis Ford Coppola. United Artists, 1979.

Appleby, Joyce. *Capitalism and a New Social Order: The Republican Vision of the 1790s*. New York: New York UP, 1984.

Armitage, Susan. "Through Women's Eyes: A New View of the West." *The Women's West*. Ed. Susan Armitage and Elizabeth Jameson. Norman: U of Oklahoma P, 1987. 9-18.

Bates, Milton J. *The Wars We Took to Vietnam: Cultural Conflict and Storytelling*. Berkeley: U of California P, 1996.

Berger, Thomas. *Little Big Man*. New York: Dial, 1964.

Berson, Misha. "Fighting the Religion of the Present: Western Motifs in the First Wave of Asian American Plays." *Reading the West: New Essays on the Literature of the American West*. Ed. Michael Kowalewski. Cambridge: Cambridge UP, 1996. 251-72.

Billington, Ray Allen. "Introduction." Billington, *Frontier Thesis* 1-8.

–, ed. *The Frontier Thesis: Valid Interpretation of American History?* New York: Holt, Rinehart, 1966.

Bourne, Randolph Silliman. "A Mirror of the Middle West." *The Radical Will: Selected Writings*. Berkeley: U of California P, 1992. 265-70.

Brokeback Mountain. Dir. Ang Lee. Focus Features, 2005.

Brown, Bill. "Introduction." Brown, *Reading* 1-40.

–, ed. *Reading the West: An Anthology of Dime Westerns*. Boston: Bedford/St. Martin's, 1997.

Brown, Dee. *Bury My Heart at Wounded Knee: An Indian History of the American West*. 1970. New York: Vintage, 1991.

–. *The Gentle Tamers: Women of the Old Wild West*. Lincoln: U of Nebraska P, 1958.

Calloway, Colin G. *Our Hearts Fell to the Ground: Plains Indians Views of How the West Was Lost*. Boston: Bedford/St. Martin's, 1996.

Campbell, Neil. *The Rhizomatic West: Representing the American West in a Transnational, Global, Media Age.* Lincoln: U of Nebraska P, 2008.

Cather, Willa. *My Ántonia.* 1918. Boston: Houghton, 1995.

–. *O Pioneers!* Boston: Houghton, 1913.

Cawelti, John G. *The Six-Gun Mystique.* Bowling Green: Bowling Green State U Popular P, 1975.

Cheung, King-Kok. *Articulate Silences: Hisaye Yamamoto, Maxine Hong Kingston, Joy Kogawa.* Ithaca: Cornell UP, 1993.

Clifford, James. *Routes: Travel and Translation in the Late Twentieth Century.* Cambridge: Harvard UP, 1997.

The Comparative Wests Project. comparativewests.stanford.edu. 22 Feb. 2014.

Cong. Rec. V. 144, Pt. 15, 22 Sept. 1998 to 26 Sept. 1998. *Google Books.* 30 Sept. 2013.

Conrad, Joseph. *Heart of Darkness.* Ed. Robert Kimbrough. New York: Norton, 1972.

Conzen, Kathleen Neils. "A Saga of Families." *The Oxford History of the American West.* Ed. Clyde A. Milner II, Carol A. O'Connor, and Martha A. Sandweiss. New York: Oxford UP, 1994. 315-58.

Cook, Nancy. "The Romance of Ranching; Or Selling Place-Based Fantasies in and of the West." Kollin, *Postwestern Cultures* 223-44.

Cooper, James Fenimore. *The Deerslayer, Or, The First War-Path.* Philadelphia: Lea and Blanchard, 1841.

–. *The Last of the Mohicans: A Narrative of 1757.* London: Miller, 1826.

Coyne, Michael. *The Crowded Prairie: American National Identity in the Hollywood Western.* London: I.B. Tauris, 1997.

Crane, Stephen. "The Blue Hotel." Crane, *Works* 142-70.

–. "The Bride Comes to Yellow Sky." Crane, *Works* 109-20.

–. *The Works of Stephen Crane.* Vol. 5. Charlotteville: UP of Virginia, 1970.

Crèvecoeur, J. Hector St. John de. *Letters from an American Farmer.* London: Dent, 1912.

Curtis, Christopher Michael. *Jefferson's Freeholders and the Politics of Ownership in the Old Dominion.* New York: Cambridge UP, 2012.

Dances with Wolves. Dir. Kevin Costner. Orion, 1990.

Dead Man. Dir. Jim Jarmusch. Miramax, 1995.

Deadwood. HBO, 2004-2006.

The Deer Hunter. Dir. Michael Cimino. Universal, 1978.

Der Schuh des Manitu. Dir. Michael Herbig. Constantin, 2001.

Django Unchained. Dir. Quentin Tarantino. Weinstein/Columbia, 2012.

Dorman, Robert L. *Hell of a Vision: Regionalism and the Modern American West*. Tucson: U of Arizona P, 2012.

Drayton, Michael. "To the Virginian Voyage." 1606. *Poetry Foundation*. http://www.poetryfoundation.org/poem/173426. 30 Sept. 2013.

Eastlake, William. *The Bamboo Bed*. New York: Simon, 1969.

Ellet, Elizabeth. *Pioneer Women of the West*. Philadelphia: Coates, 1901.

Ellis, Edward S. "Seth Jones; or, The Captives of the Frontier." 1860. Brown, *Reading* 169-268.

Eyal, Yonatan. *The Young America Movement and the Transformation of the Democratic Party, 1828-1861*. Cambridge: Cambridge UP, 2007.

Farnham, Eliza. *Life in Prairie Land*. New York: Harper, 1846.

Fees, Paul. "Wild West Shows: Buffalo Bill's Wild West." *Buffalo Bill Center of the West*. http://centerofthewest.org/learn/western-essays/wild-west-shows/. 1 Oct. 2013.

Fiedler, Leslie A. *The Return of the Vanishing American*. New York: Stein and Day, 1968.

First Blood. Dir. Ted Kotcheff. Orion, 1982.

Filson, John. "The Discovery, Settlement and Present State of Kentucke (1784): An Online Electronic Text Edition." *Electronic Texts in American Studies*. Ed. Paul Royster. http://digitalcommons.unl.edu/etas/3. 30 Sept. 2013.

Fox, William. *The Void, the Grid, and the Sign*. Salt Lake City: U of Utah P, 2000.

Frampton, Kenneth. "Towards a Critical Regionalism: Six Points for an Architecture of Resistance." *The Anti-Aesthetic: Essays on Postmodern Culture*. Ed. Hal Foster. Port Townsend: Bay, 1983. 16-30.

Frémont, John C. *Report of the Exploring Expedition to the Rocky Mountains and to Oregon and North California*. 1852. *Project Gutenberg*. http://www.gutenberg.org/dirs/etext05/8expr10h.htm. 30 Sept. 2013.

Fresonke, Kris. *West of Emerson: The Design of Manifest Destiny*. Berkeley: U of California P, 2003.

Gebhard, Caroline. "Comic Displacement: Caroline M. Kirkland's Satire on Frontier Democracy in *A New Home, Who'll Follow?*" *Women, America and Movement: Narratives of Relocation*. Ed. Susan L. Roberson. Columbia: U of Missouri P, 1998. 157-75.

Georgi-Findlay, Brigitte. *The Frontiers of Women's Writing: Women's Narratives and the Rhetoric of Westward Expansion*. Tucson: U of Arizona P, 1996.

Giles, Paul. *Virtual Americas: Transnational Fictions and the Transatlantic Imaginary*. Durham: Duke UP, 2002.

Gilman, Charlotte Perkins. *Herland.* 1915. *Project Gutenberg.* http://www.guten berg.org/ebooks/32. 30 Sept. 2013.

Glaspell, Susan. *Trifles.* 1916. *University of Virginia Library.* http://lib. virginia.edu/. 30 Sept. 2013.

Goldman, Anne E. *Continental Divides: Revisioning American Literature.* New York: Palgrave, 2010.

The Great Train Robbery. Dir. Edwin S. Porter. Edison Manufacturing, 1903.

The Green Berets. Dir. Ray Kellogg and John Wayne. Warner Bros.-Seven Arts, 1968.

Hammett, Dashiell. *Red Harvest.* New York: Knopf, 1929.

Hellmann, John. *American Myth and the Legacy of Vietnam.* New York: Columbia UP, 1986.

Herr, Cheryl. *Critical Regionalism and Cultural Studies: From Ireland to the American Midwest.* Gainesville: UP of Florida, 1996.

Herr, Michael. *Dispatches.* New York: Knopf, 1968.

Hietala, Thomas R. *Manifest Design: Anxious Aggrandizement in Late Jacksonian America.* Ithaca: Cornell UP, 1985.

Hine, Robert V., and John Mack Faragher. *The American West: A New Interpretive History.* New Haven, Yale UP, 2000.

Hofstadter, Richard. *The Age of Reform: From Bryan to F.D.R.* New York: Vintage, 1955.

–. "The Thesis Disputed." Billington, *Frontier Thesis* 100-106.

Hough, Emerson. *The Passing of the Frontier: A Chronicle of the Old West.* New Haven: Yale UP, 1921.

Houston, Velina Hasu. *Tea.* New York: Dramatist Play Service, 2007.

Jackson, John Brinckerhoff. *A Sense of Place, a Sense of Time.* New Haven: Yale UP, 1994.

Jameson, Elizabeth, and Susan Armitage, eds. *Writing the Range: Race, Class, and Culture in the Women's West.* Norman: U of Oklahoma P, 1997.

Jefferson, Thomas. "Notes on the State of Virginia." *The Selected Writings of Thomas Jefferson: Authoritative Texts, Contexts, Criticism.* Ed. Wayne Franklin. New York: Norton, 2010. 24-177.

Jeffords, Susan. *Hard Bodies: Hollywood Masculinity in the Reagan Era.* New Brunswick: Rutgers UP, 1994.

Jeffrey, Julie Roy. *Frontier Women: "Civilizing" the West? 1840-1880.* New York: Hill, 1979.

Kaplan, Amy. *The Anarchy of Empire in the Making of U.S. Culture.* Cambridge: Harvard UP, 2003.

Kennedy, John F. "Presidential Nomination Acceptance Speech." Democratic National Convention, Los Angeles, 15 July 1960. *John F. Kennedy Presidential Library and Museum.* http://www.jfklibrary.org/. 30 Sept. 2013.

Kipp, Woody. *Viet Cong at Wounded Knee: The Trail of a Blackfeet Activist.* Lincoln: U of Nebraska P, 2004.

Kirkland, Caroline M. *A New Home, Who'll Follow? Or, Glimpses of Western Life.* 1839. Ed. Sandra A. Zagarell. New Brunswick: Rutgers UP, 1990.

Kollin, Susan. "Introduction: Postwestern Studies, Dead or Alive." Kollin, *Postwestern Cultures* ix-xix.

–, ed. *Postwestern Cultures: Literature, Theory, Space.* Lincoln: U of Nebraska P, 2007.

Kolodny, Annette. *The Lay of the Land: Metaphor as Experience and History in American Life and Letters.* Chapel Hill: U of North Carolina P, 1975.

Lange, Dorothea. *An American Exodus: A Record of Human Erosion.* 1939. New York: Arno, 1975.

Last Man Standing. Dir. Walter Hill. New Line Cinema, 1996.

Lawlor, Mary. *Recalling the Wild: Naturalism and the Closing of the American West.* New Brunswick: Rutgers UP, 2000.

Lederer, William J., and Eugene Burdick. *The Ugly American.* New York: Norton, 1958.

Lepore, Jill. *The Story of America: Essays on Origins.* Princeton: Princeton UP, 2012.

Lewis, R.W.B. *The American Adam: Innocence, Tragedy, and Tradition in the Nineteenth Century.* Chicago: U of Chicago P, 1955.

Limerick, Patricia Nelson. "The Adventures of the Frontier in the Twentieth Century." *The Frontier in American Culture.* Ed. James R. Grossman. Berkeley: U of California P, 1994. 67-102.

–. *The Legacy of Conquest: The Unbroken Past of the American West.* New York: Norton, 1987.

–. *Something in the Soil: Legacies and Reckonings in the New West.* New York: Norton, 2000.

Little Big Man. Dir. Arthur Penn. National General, 1970.

Lopez, Barry. "The American Geographies." *About This Life: Journeys on the Threshold of Memory.* New York: Vintage, 1998.

Lowe, Lisa. *Immigrant Acts: On Asian American Cultural Politics.* Durham: Duke UP, 1996.

The Magnificent Seven. Dir. John Sturges. United Artists, 1960.

Mahoney, Timothy R., and Wendy J. Katz, eds. *Regionalism and the Humanities.* Lincoln: U of Nebraska P, 2008.

Marx, Leo. *The Machine in the Garden: Technology and the Pastoral Ideal in America*. New York: Oxford UP, 1964.

Matthews, John T. "What Was High About Modernism? The American Novel and Modernity." *The Companion to the Modern American Novel, 1900-1950*. Ed. John T. Matthews. Chichester: Wiley, 2009. 282-305.

McMurtry, Larry. *The Colonel and Little Missie: Buffalo Bill, Annie Oakley, and the Beginnings of Superstardom in America*. New York: Simon, 2005.

Meek's Cutoff. Dir. Kelly Reichardt. Oscilloscope, 2010.

Merish, Lori. "'The Hand of Refined Taste' in the Frontier Landscape: Caroline Kirkland's *A New Home, Who'll Follow?* and the Feminization of American Consumerism." *American Quarterly* 45.4 (1993): 485-523.

Miller, Perry. *Nature's Nation*. Cambridge: Belknap, 1967.

Miller, Susan Cummins, ed. *A Sweet, Separate Intimacy: Women Writers of the American Frontier, 1800-1922*. 2000. Salt Lake City: U of Utah P, 2007.

Mogen, David, Scott P. Sanders, and Joanne B. Karpinski. *Frontier Gothic: Terror and Wonder at the Frontier in American Literature*. Rutherford: Farleigh Dickinson UP, 1993.

Moore, Robin. *The Green Berets*. New York: Crown, 1965.

Muller, Dan. *My Life with Buffalo Bill*. Chicago: Reilly and Lee, 1948.

Myres, Sandra L. *Westering Women and the Frontier Experience, 1800-1915*. Albuquerque: U of New Mexico P, 1982.

Ngai, Mae M. *Impossible Subjects: Illegal Aliens and the Making of Modern America*. Princeton: Princeton UP, 2004.

Obama, Barack. Presidential Proclamation. Commemoration of the 50th Anniversary of the Vietnam War. *The White House*. http://www.whitehouse.gov/the-press-office/2012/05/25/presidential-proclamation-commemoration-50th-anniversary-vietnam-war. 10 March 2014.

Onuf, Peter S. *Jefferson's Empire: The Language of American Nationhood*. Charlottesville: UP of Virginia, 2001.

O'Sullivan, John L. "Annexation." *United States Magazine and Democratic Review* 17.1 (1845): 5-10.

Parkman, Francis. *The Oregon Trail: Sketches of Prairie and Rocky-Mountain Life*. 1849. Boston: Little and Brown, 1895.

Paul, Heike. *Mapping Migration: Women's Writing and the American Immigrant Experience from the 1950s to the 1990s*. Heidelberg: Winter, 1999.

Pearce, Roy Harvey. *Savagism and Civilization: A Study of the Indian and the American Mind*. 1953. Berkeley: U of California P, 1988.

Per un pugno di dollari. Dir. Sergio Leone. United Artists, 1964.

Pierson, George W. "Turner's Views Challenged." Billington, *Frontier Thesis* 31-40.

Pratt, John Clark. "The Lost Frontier: American Myth in the Literature of the Vietnam War." *The Frontier Experience and the American Dream: Essays on American Literature*. Ed. David Mogen, Mark Busby, and Paul Bryant. College Station: Texas A&M UP, 1989. 236-47.

Proulx, Annie. "Dangerous Ground: Landscape in American Fiction." Mahoney and Katz, *Regionalism* 6-25.

Rambo: First Blood Part II. Dir. George P. Cosmatos. Tri-Star, 1985.

Reynolds, Guy. "Willa Cather's Case: Region and Reputation." Mahoney and Katz, *Regionalism* 79-94.

Riley, Glenda. *The Female Frontier: A Comparative View of Women on the Prairie and the Plains*. Lawrence: UP of Kansas, 1988.

–. *Women and Indians on the Frontier, 1825-1915*. Albuquerque: U of New Mexico P, 1984.

Rogin, Michael. *Ronald Reagan, the Movie, and Other Episodes in Political Demonology*. Berkeley: U of California P, 1987.

Roosevelt, Theodore. *The Winning of the West: An Account of the Exploration and Settlement of Our Country from the Alleghanies to the Pacific*. 1889. *The Works of Theodore Roosevelt*. Vols. 8-9. New York: Scribner's, 1924.

Rosier, Paul C. *Serving Their Country: American Indian Politics and Patriotism in the Twentieth Century*. Cambridge: Harvard UP, 2012.

Sadowski-Smith, Claudia. "Introduction: Comparative Border Studies." *Comparative American Studies* 9.4 (2011): 273-87.

Sammons, Jeffrey. *Ideology, Mimesis, Fantasy: Charles Sealsfield, Friedrich Gerstäcker, Karl May, and Other German Novelists of America*. Chapel Hill: U of North Carolina P, 1998.

Schlissel, Lilian. *Women's Diaries of the Westward Journey*. New York: Schocken, 1982.

Schlissel, Lilian, Vicki Ruíz, and Janice J. Monk, eds. *Western Women: Their Land, Their Lives*. Albuquerque: U of New Mexico P, 1988.

Schmidt, Arno. *Sitara und der Weg dorthin: Eine Studie über Wesen, Werk und Wirkung Karl Mays*. Karlsruhe: Stahlberg, 1963.

Seven Samurai. Dir. Akira Kurosawa. Columbia, 1954.

Shannon, Fred A. "Not Even an Indirect Safety Valve Attracting Eastern Farmers." Billington, *Frontier Thesis* 41-50.

Slotkin, Richard. *The Fatal Environment: The Myth of the Frontier in the Age of Industrialization, 1800-1890*. Norman: U of Oklahoma P, 1998.

–. *Gunfighter Nation: The Myth of the Frontier in Twentieth-Century America*. Norman: U of Oklahoma P, 1992.

–. *Regeneration through Violence: The Mythology of the American Frontier, 1600-1860*. Norman: Oklahoma UP, 1973.

–. "Unit Pride: Ethnic Platoons and the Myths of American Nationality." *American Literary History* 13.3 (2001): 469-98.

Smith, Henry Nash. *Virgin Land: The American West as Symbol and Myth*. Cambridge: Harvard UP, 1950.

Smith-Rosenberg, Carroll. *This Violent Empire: The Birth of an American National Identity*. Chapel Hill: U of North Carolina P, 2010.

Sone, Monica. *Nisei Daughter*. Boston: Little, 1953.

Sontag, Susan. *Trip to Hanoi*. New York: Farrar, 1968.

Stagecoach. Dir. John Ford. United Artists, 1939.

Stephanson, Anders. *Manifest Destiny: American Exceptionalism and the Empire of Right*. New York: Hill, 1995.

Stewart, Catherine. *New Homes in the West*. Nashville: Cameron and Fall, 1843.

Streamas, John. "Frontier Mythology, Children's Literature, and Japanese American Incarceration." Kollin, *Postwestern Cultures* 172-85.

Sweetwater. Dir. Logan Miller. ARC Entertainment, 2013.

Thoreau, Henry David. "Walking." *Walden and Other Writings*. New York: Norton, 1966. 260-87.

Tompkins, Jane. *West of Everything: The Inner Life of Westerns*. New York: Oxford UP, 1992.

Trachtenberg, Alan. *The Incorporation of America: Culture and Society in the Gilded Age*. New York: Hill, 1982.

True Grit. Dir. Joel and Ethan Coen. Paramount, 2010.

Turner, Frederick Jackson. "The Significance of the Frontier in American History." 1893. *American Studies at the University of Virginia*. http://xroads. virginia.edu/~hyper/turner/chapter1.html. 3 Oct. 2013.

Uchida, Yoshiko. *Desert Exile: The Uprooting of a Japanese American Family*. Seattle: U of Washington P, 1982.

Unforgiven. Dir. Clint Eastwood. Warner Bros., 1992.

Veblen, Thorstein. *Imperial Germany and the Industrial Revolution*. New York: Viking, 1946.

Von Frank, Albert J. *The Sacred Game: Provincialism and Frontier Consciousness in American Literature, 1630-1860*. Cambridge: Cambridge UP, 1985.

Ward, Russell. *The Australian Legend*. Melbourne: Oxford UP, 1958.

Watts, Edward. "The Midwest as a Colony: Transnational Regionalism." Mahoney and Katz, *Regionalism* 166-89.

Whitman, Walt. "Pioneers! O Pioneers!" *Leaves of Grass.* Ed. Sculley Bradley and Harold W. Blodgett. New York: Norton, 1973. 229-32.

The Wild Bunch. Dir. Sam Peckinpah. Warner Bros.-Seven Arts, 1969.

Wilder, Laura Ingalls. *Little House on the Prairie.* 1935. New York: Harper, 1981.

Williams, Raymond. *The Country and the City.* New York: Oxford UP, 1973.

–. "Stuctures of Feeling." *Marxism and Literature.* Oxford: Oxford UP, 1977. 128-35.

Wister, Owen. *The Virginian: A Horseman of the Plains.* 1902. Introd. by Robert B. Parker. Afterword by Max Evans. New York: Penguin/Signet, 2010.

Worden, Daniel. "Neo-liberalism and the Western: HBO's *Deadwood* as National Allegory." *Canadian Review of American Studies* 39.2 (2009): 221-46.

Wrobel, David M. *Promised Lands: Promotion, Memory, and the Creation of the American West.* Lawrence: UP of Kansas, 2002.

Yamada, Mitsuye. "Block 4 Barrack 4 'Apt' C." *Camp Notes and Other Poems.* Latham: Kitchen Table, 1976. 19.

–. *Desert Run: Poems and Stories.* Latham: Kitchen Table, 1988.

Yamamoto, Hisaye. "Seventeen Syllables." *Seventeen Syllables and Other Stories.* Latham: Kitchen Table, 1988. 8-19.

Yamauchi, Wakako. *Songs My Mother Taught Me: Stories, Plays, and Memoirs.* New York: Feminist, 1994.

Yojimbo. Dir. Akira Kurosawa. Toho, 1961.

Zagarell, Sandra A. Introduction. *A New Home, Who'll Follow? Or, Glimpses of Western Life.* By Caroline Kirkland. New Brunswick: Rutgers UP, 1990. xi-xliii.

Further Reading

Armor, John, and Peter Wright. *Manzanar.* New York: Times, 1988.

Babcock, C. Merton. *The American Frontier: A Social and Literary Record.* New York: Holt, Rinehart and Winston, 1965.

Billington, Ray Allen. *Land of Savagery, Land of Promise: The European Image of the American Frontier in the Nineteenth Century.* New York: Norton, 1981.

–. *Westward Expansion: A History of the American Frontier.* New York: Macmillan, 1967.

Campbell, Neil. "Critical Regionalism, Third Space, and John Brinckerhoff Jackson's Western Cultural Landscapes." *Postwestern Cultures: Literature, Theory, Space.* Ed. Susan Kollin. Lincoln: U of Nebraska P, 2007. 59-81.

–. *The Cultures of the American New West*. Chicago: Fitzroy Dearborn, 2000.

Clark, Thomas D. *Frontier America: The Story of the Westward Movement*. New York: Scribner's, 1959.

Cody, Louisa Frederici. *Memories of Buffalo Bill by His Wife*. New York: Appleton, 1919.

Coues, Elliott. *History of the Expedition under the Command of Lewis and Clark to the Sources of the Missouri River*. 1893. Rpt. 3 vols. New York: Dover, 1964.

Durham, Philip, and Everett L. Jones, eds. *The Frontier in American Literature*. Indianapolis: Bobbs-Merrill, 1969.

Ellis, David M. *The Frontier in American Development: Essays in Honor of Paul Wallace Gates*. Ithaca: Cornell UP, 1969.

Fabian, Ann. "The West." *A Companion to American Cultural History*. Ed. Karen Halttunen. Malden: Blackwell, 2008. 125-38.

Fender, Stephen. *Plotting the Golden West: American Literature and the Rhetoric of the California Trail*. Cambridge: Cambridge UP, 1981.

Fussell, Edwin. *Frontier: American Literature and the American West*. Princeton: Princeton UP, 1965.

Gersdorf, Catrin. *The Poetics and Politics of the Desert*. Amsterdam: Rodopi, 2009.

Graulich, Melody. "'Cameras and Photographs Were Not Permitted in the Camps:' Photographic Documentation and Distortion in Japanese American Internment Narratives." *True West*. Ed. William Handley and Nathaniel Lewis. Lincoln: U of Nebraska P, 2004. 222-56.

Hawgood, John A. *America's Western Frontiers: The Exploration and Settlement of the Trans-Mississippi West*. New York: Knopf, 1967.

Hazard, Lucy Lockwood. *The Frontier in American Literature*. New York: Unger, 1927.

Hofstadter, Richard, and Seymour Martin Lipset. *Turner and the Sociology of the Frontier*. New York: Basic, 1968.

Hollon, W. Eugene. *Frontier Violence: Another Look*. London: Oxford UP, 1974.

Jackson, John Brinckerhoff. *Discovering the Vernacular Landscape*. New Haven: Yale UP, 1984.

–. *Landscape in Sight: Looking at America*. Ed. Helen Lefkowitz Horowitz. New Haven: Yale UP, 1997.

Kaufman, Polly Welts. *Women Teachers on the Frontier*. New Haven: Yale UP, 1984.

LeMenager, Stephanie. *Manifest and Other Destinies: Territorial Fictions of the Nineteenth-Century United States*. Lincoln: U of Nebraska P, 2004.

Lewis, Marvin, ed. *The Mining Frontier: Contemporary Accounts from the American West in the Nineteenth Century*. Norman: U of Oklahoma P, 1967.

A Literary History of the American West. Fort Worth: Texas Christian UP and the Western Literature Association, 1987.

Moore, Arthur K. *The Frontier Mind*. Lexington: U of Kentucky P, 1957.

Paxson, Frederic L. *History of the American Frontier, 1763-1893*. Boston: Houghton, 1924.

Reich, Charles A. *The Greening of America: How the Youth Revolution Is Trying to Make America Livable*. New York: Random, 1970.

Riegel, Robert E. *America Moves West*. New York: Holt, 1930.

Russell, Don. *The Lives and Legends of Buffalo Bill*. Norman: U of Oklahoma P, 1960.

Shepard, Sam. *True West*. London: Faber, 1981.

Stratton, Joanna L. *Pioneer Women: Voices from the Kansas Frontier*. New York: Simon, 1981.

Sullivan, Tom R. *Cowboys and Caudillos: Frontier Ideology of the Americas*. Bowling Green: Bowling Green State U Popular P, 1990.

Turner, Frederick Jackson. *America's Great Frontiers and Sections: Frederick Jackson Turner's Unpublished Essays*. Introd. Wilbur R. Jacobs. Lincoln: U of Nebraska P, 1965.

–. *The Frontier in American History*. Foreword by Ray Allen Billington. New York: Holt, Rinehart and Winston, 1967.

Chapter VII

Expressive Individualism and the Myth of the Self-Made Man

---

1. WHY THE SELF-MADE MAN?

> The legendary hero of America is the self-made man.
> IRVIN G. WYLLIE, *THE SELF-MADE MAN IN AMERICA*

> It is strange to see with what feverish ardour the Americans pursue their own
> welfare, and to watch the vague dread that constantly torments them lest they
> should not have chosen the shortest path which may lead to it.
> ALEXIS DE TOCQUEVILLE, *DEMOCRACY IN AMERICA*

Besides notions of religious predestination, political liberty, and social harmony,
the imagined economic promises of the 'new world' constitute another important
dimension of American exceptionalism and US foundational mythology. The
popular phrase 'rags to riches' describes social mobility in analogy to geographical mobility in the discourse of westward expansion, the difference being that the
latter refers to horizontal and the former to vertical mobility. Historically, the
notion that upward mobility in US society is unlimited regardless of inherited
social and financial status has been used to contrast the US to European societies
with rigidly stratified social hierarchies, and to support the claim that the American economic system leads to a higher standard of living in general as well as to
a higher degree of individual agency and economic opportunity; Myth and Symbol scholar David Potter, for example, described Americans within this framework of economic exceptionalism as a "people of plenty" and defined "economic
abundance" as a decisive "force in US history" (*People* 75). In the 19th century,
European visitors to the US, among them Alexis de Tocqueville (cf. *Democracy*), Joanna Trollope (cf. *Domestic Manners*), Harriet Martineau (cf. *Society*),
and James Bryce (cf. *American Commonwealth*) have remarked on the hectic
commercial activities of Americans and considered their peculiar pursuit of

material gain as an aspect of the American national character. In the 20th century, Theodor W. Adorno, who was more critical than many visitors before him, identified a culturally specific "barbarian success religion" in American society ("Tugendspiegel" 354). In its hegemonic version, the myth of the self-made man refers, first of all, to expressive individualism and individual success and de-scribes a cultural type that is often seen as an "American invention" and a "unique national product" (Cawelti, *Apostles* 1). Second, based on the assump-tion of competitive equality, the self-made man has often been connected to utopian visions of a classless society, or at least to a society that allows con-siderable social mobility. Upon closer examination, the mirage of classlessness is often connected to the belief that most Americans belong to the middle class, into which most Americans will group themselves even in the face of contra-dictory empirical evidence: very few "will willingly say that they are in any other class" (Robertson, *American Myth* 259; cf. Mead, *And Keep* 54). The illu-sive conceptualization of the middle class as "homogenous and proximate" (Robertson, *American Myth* 260) entails not only notions of classlessness but also of democracy, freedom, and equality. This phenomenon has been dissected by Barbara Ehrenreich and others as a kind of 'false consciousness' which impedes social change (cf. Ehrenreich, *Fear*) and may also explain the relative absence of class as a concept and object of analysis throughout much of US social and intellectual history. Thirdly, the culturally specific figure and formula of the self-made man thrives according to all empirical evidence on the illusion that the exception is the rule (cf. Koch-Linde, *Amerikanische Tagträume* 9) and thus follows and time and again re-inscribes a social Darwinist logic based on the quasi-natural selection of those fit to compete and succeed in a modern "post-stratificatory society" (cf. Helmstetter, "Viel Erfolg" 709). According to this logic, there is little collective responsibility for the well-being of individual citizens. The illusion of equality – or rather of the equality of opportunity – is at the core of hegemonic discourses that describe social and political hierarchies in American society as temporary rather than as structural (cf. Fluck and Werner, "Einführung" 9). The national type of the self-made man and the creed of American mobility imply "parity in competition" (Potter, *People* 92), and, in fact, "an endless race open to all" (Thernstrom, *Poverty* 63) despite the fact that not all start out even or compete on an equal footing, and have been used to bolster the assumption that there are no permanent classes in US society. In "the doctrine of the open race" (ibid.), the providential success of the self-made man was identified with the success of the national project, and expressive individual-ism was thus regarded not only as the basis for individual but also for collective success.

In many ways, the notion that individuals can determine their own future and change their lives for the better is a modern idea and presupposes modern notions of culture, society, and the individual along the lines of Immanuel Kant's enlightenment dictum that man will be 'what he makes of himself' (*Anthropologie* 29), which later, in Sartre's reformulation, becomes "[m]an is nothing else but what he makes of himself" (*Existentialism* 10). This notion is the result of large-scale and complex processes of secularization that are quite at odds with Christian ethics, as it often flaunts competition, self-help, and ambition as its driving forces: "The competitive society out of which the success myth and the self-made man have grown may accept the Christian virtues in principle but can hardly observe them in practice" (Hofstadter, "Abraham Lincoln" 94). This connection – or rather disjunction – of ethics, ambition, and success plays out in culturally specific ways. In the present context, the idea of personal success is closely linked to processes of nation-building. The "pursuit of happiness" (as famously formulated in the Declaration of Independence) and the "promise of American life" (cf. Croly's book of the same title) in their early exceptionalist logic transfer notions of happiness from the afterlife to one's earthly existence, i.e. to the present moment or at least the near future. Coupled with the Calvinist work ethic, the pursuit of happiness constructs the modern individual's path to happiness as the pursuit of property and allows for self-realization in new ways. This notion has already been at the center of 18th-century 'new world' promotional literature, which touted America as an earthly paradise. The self-made man as a foundational mythical figure personifies this promotional discourse, and has been used to allegorize the 'new world' social order since the late 18th and throughout the 19th century. Of course, this perspective is highly biased: the eighteenth-century enlightenment subject was conceptualized as white and male, and thus the myth of the self-made man historically applies to white men only; however, in this chapter we will also look at the ways in which this perspective has been revised or amended by other individuals and groups who have appropriated this myth.

The coinage of the term "self-made man" is commonly credited to Henry Clay, who wrote in 1832: "In Kentucky, almost every manufactory known to me is in the hands of enterprising self-made men, who have whatever wealth they possess by patient and diligent labor" ("Defence" 39). The term can thus be considered as yet another neologism of the early republic that speaks to specifically US-American cultural and economic patterns and is deeply intertwined with various aspects of American exceptionalism. There are contradictory forces at work in this notion, as it includes both aspects of self-denial (education, hard work, and discipline) and self-realization based on an ethic of self-interest that aims at the sheer accumulation of property, recognition, prestige, and personal gain without any concern for others. This contradiction is explored repeatedly in scholarly as well as literary texts and in popular culture as the basic conundrum of a myth that defines self-interest as the basis of the common good rather than as an immersion "in the *icy water* of *egotistical calculation*" (Marx and Engels, *Communist Manifesto*).

In this chapter, I will discuss, first, the history of the myth of the self-made man in the late 18th century and the foundational phase of the nation by reference to Benjamin Franklin's writings and self-fashioning, and second, the popularization of success stories (such as those by Horatio Alger) in the 19th century; I will, third, analyze numerous rise-and-fall narratives and narratives of failure that mark the transition from romantic to realist and modernist representations and that fictionalize and criticize hegemonic ideological manoeuvers in the context of industrialization, immigration, urbanization, and consumer culture; I will analyze, fourth, immigrant fiction, which is often similarly ambivalent, fifth, African American constructions of the self-made man, and sixth, the feminization of this prototypically male formula with respect to the self-made woman; I will, seventh, conclude with some remarks on the myth of the self-made man in the age of globalization.

2. BENJAMIN FRANKLIN, AMERICAN PARVENU

> The root of the matter is a peculiar sense of the self, at once buoyant and practical, visionary and manipulative. To make a self – such is the audacious undertaking that brings one into a world of masks and roles and shape-shifters, that requires one to manipulate beliefs and impressions, that elevates technical facility and gives one the heady sense of playing a game. The central document of such self making is Franklin's *Autobiography*.
> GARY LINDBERG, *THE CONFIDENCE MAN IN AMERICAN LITERATURE*

> Get what you can, and what you get, hold; 'Tis the stone that will turn all your lead into gold.
> BENJAMIN FRANKLIN

Benjamin Franklin (1706-1790) not only figures prominently in the myth of the Founding Fathers (cf. chapter 4) but has also typified the self-made man in American culture. As an autodidact who became one of the most respected Americans of his time (and beyond), he has often been considered the *homo americanus* par excellence, and has been called "a model representative of the American Dream" (Huang and Mulford, "Benjamin Franklin" 147) and "a liberal capitalist hero" (Newman, "Benjamin Franklin" 173). His writings have been extraordinarily popular, especially his *Poor Richard's Almanack*, of which 10.000 copies were printed each year from 1732 to 1758 and which by 1850 had been printed more than eighty times (cf. Huang and Mulford, "Benjamin Franklin" 150), and his *Autobiography*, which was published posthumously in English in 1793; both texts immediately turned into bestsellers, household names, and canonical material, and can be considered advice literature providing guidance on how to rise from "Obscurity" to "some Degree of Reputation in the World" (Franklin, *Autobiography* 1). Ever since the publication of Franklin's memoirs, "autobiography has been the authoritative mode within which to imagine the self-made man" (Decker, *Made in* xxvii). Structured in four parts, they were composed by the author at different times in his life but never finished. Part one covers the first 21 years of his life in Boston and Philadelphia and narrates his childhood in poverty, his apprenticeship as a printer, his first journey to London, his marriage to Deborah Read, and his first professional success as a printer in Philadelphia. Part two is short and consists mostly of a self-improvement scheme that Franklin purportedly practiced on a daily basis; this "famous system of moral book keeping" (Cawelti, *Apostles* 20) has been quoted and emulated many times and reveals the didacticism of the text. In part three, Franklin says much about his achievements, among them the publication of his almanac, his study of foreign languages, and his initiatives in public affairs; this part ends with another journey to London on behalf of the Pennsylvania Provincial Assembly. Part four is again brief and recounts his affairs in London; overall, Franklin's text thus is a relatively disparate genre-mix. As a success story which recounts the life of a printer's apprentice who becomes an internationally recognized statesman due to his "industry" and "frugality" (*Autobiography* 67), it displays the author's modest origins as a dimension of his virtue rather than seeking to hide them, and thus also recodes 'old-world' resentments against social upstarts and 'parvenus' into evidence and manifestations of greater liberty, equality, and social justice in America (cf. Weber, *Protestant Ethic* 57).

Even if some of the advice doled out by Franklin is tongue-in-cheek, he certainly represents an optimistic version of the American Dream of upward social mobility. His *Autobiography* has been received much in the vein of a success manual; the American frontiersman Davy Crockett apparently consulted it during the Battle of the Alamo (cf. Parini, *Promised Land* 79), and banker Thomas Mellon also speaks of having read the autobiography at a young and impressionable age and declares this experience "the turning point of my life" (qtd. in Wyllie, *Self-Made Man* 15). In the 20th century, it has been referenced by F. Scott Fitzgerald in his novel *The Great Gatsby* (1925) as well as by Dale Carnegie in his 1936 bestseller *How to Win Friends and Influence People*. In addition, "Franklin was a self-made man in far more than a literal sense: how he constructed and presented himself, and the ways in which such performances succeeded and failed, reveal a great deal about life and society in eighteenth-century British North America" (Newman, "Benjamin Franklin" 162). Franklin's self-fashioning celebrates individualism and free will against a deterministic social order, but it also affirms that everyone is responsible for their own fate and success in life: self-improvement and self-perfectability loom large in his texts, which were and still are part of US school curricula.

Franklin's audiences past and present read his ideas about the synergetic fusion of a paling Protestant religiosity (Franklin was a deist) and a Calvinist work ethic as enabling and fuelling a capitalist economy that promises individual and collective gain and well-being – the defense of capitalism is, time and again, the tacit subtext of the narratives of self-made men. It is this blend of religious ideas and economic aspects that the German sociologist Max Weber discusses prominently in his description of what he calls the Protestant Ethic in his book of the same title. According to Weber, Franklin embodies the new type of the *homo americanus* that has been molded in and advances the "spirit of capitalism" (cf. ibid.). This spirit – which Weber identifies in the North American colonies as early as 1632 (cf. ibid. 46) – is brought forth by Puritanism as well as by the economic development of the colonies, which together turned people into economic subjects ("Wirtschaftssubjekte") on the basis of an increasingly secularized logic of work-discipline, which, however, still took material wealth as a sign of God's blessing. Over time, though, success was less and less defined in religious terms, and instead became a kind of 'sublime' of the social world, a way of distinguishing one's self (cf. Helmstetter, "Viel Erfolg" 706). Self-improvement, in Franklin's and in Weber's argument, involves competition as well as processes of selection, but whereas Franklin sees "the necessity of a self-selecting and self-disciplining elite" (Cawelti, *Apostles* 14) and trusts the cultural and economic elite to work for the greater public good, Weber's retrospective reconstruction of the capitalist 'type' is much more skeptical.

Even as Franklin's writings are often seen as embodying the era and *zeitgeist* of the early republic, it becomes clear upon closer inspection that they also gloss over serious developments which ensued during Franklin's lifetime:

During his [Franklin's] lifetime wealth inequality rose in American towns and cities, and the economic security of craftsmen and unskilled labourers diminished. By the late eighteenth century the traditional route to competency and independence that many working men had dreamed of, and which Franklin and some others had travelled, had become increasingly difficult. (Newman, "Benjamin Franklin" 167)

Thus, Franklin's success can in and of itself be considered an exception to the rule; whereas he personified the self-made man in no uncertain terms, his reception is often strongly decontextualized and smoothes out many contradictions that mark his historical persona, his time, and his idealism. Defining individual gain in terms of the greater common good clearly ignores the tension between two very different kinds of interest.

3. Horatio Alger and the Popularization of the Success Narrative

> Only fools laugh at Horatio Alger, and his poor boys who make good. The wiser man who thinks twice about that sterling author will realize that Alger is to America what Homer was to the Greeks.
> Nathanael West/Boris Ingster, "A Cool Million"

> I felt that my foot was upon the ladder and that I was bound to climb.
> Andrew Carnegie

By the mid-19th century, the "ideology of mobility" was firmly entrenched in American society; it was the theme of "[e]ditorials, news stories, political speeches, commencement addresses, sermons, [and] popular fiction" (Thernstrom, *Poverty* 57-58). Representations of the self-made man in popular fiction are particularly prominent in this period in the oeuvre of Horatio Alger (1832-1899), who was not only a prolific writer but also worked as an editor, teacher, and pastor. The *American Heritage Dictionary* defines Horatio Alger as the author of popular fiction about "impoverished boys who through hard work and virtue achieve great wealth and respect" (43); often living with a single mother who depends on him for support, Alger's typical protagonist usually has a chance encounter with a gentleman, who becomes his mentor as the young protagonist shows his moral integrity, works hard, and thus appears to be deserving of help. At the end of the story, he ends up comfortably ensconced in middle-class America and "is established in a secure white-collar position, either as a clerk with the promise of a junior partnership or as a junior member of a successful mercantile establishment" (Cawelti, *Apostles* 109). Alger's novels pursue a thinly veiled didactic aim while they also cater to sensationalism, sentimentalism, and voyeurism. In the 19th century, the virtual "cult of the self-made man" (Wyllie, *Self-Made Man* 13) was certainly propelled and reinforced by "Algerism," as the popularity of the Horatio Alger stories came to be described, and even if his texts are hardly read anymore, Alger is still a household name today. Addressing a young, male audience, Alger's 135 books, among them the well-known Ragged Dick series which comprises six novels (1868-1870), have sold more than 300.000.000 copies.

They "have structured national discourse as a narrative of personal initiative, enterprise, financial responsibility, thrift, equal opportunity, hard-work ethic, education and self-education, and other similar values of Puritan-Calvinist and liberal extraction" (Moraru, *Rewriting* 57) in seeming opposition to – yet ultimately in conjunction with – the so-called "bad boy-books" by Mark Twain and others that focused on a nostalgic "figurative escape into the pastoral, imaginative life of a premodern, anticapitalist world, while also embodying the enterprising and unsentimental agency of the capitalist himself" (Salazar, *Bodies* 75). In the 19th century, Alger's books functioned as national allegories, since their adolescent protagonists' rites of passage could be paralleled with the young republic's struggle for independence (cf. Nackenoff, *Fictional Republic* 34, 38). Alger's success as a writer diminished towards the end of his life, when his books became the object of criticism by an 'anti-Alger movement' which rallied to have his books removed from public libraries because they were deemed too trivial, "harmful," and "bad," and to cause a "softening [of] the brain" (ibid. 256; cf. Hendler, *Public Sentiments* 87-91). Alger's stories became truly iconic in the first half of the 20th century, when the sales of his books, which were then used to identify the 'American way of life' in contrast to the 'un-American' notions of socialism and communism, rose sharply; 'Cold War' ideology thus enlisted Alger as "a patriotic defender of the social and political status quo and erstwhile advocate of laissez-faire capitalism" (Scharnhorst and Bales, *Lost Life* 152). It is during these decades that Algerism had its heyday. As Algerism came to signify "Americanism," in many crucial ways "[t]he word of Alger excluded the word of Marx" (Hartz, *Liberal Tradition* 248).

Illustration 1: Rags to Riches

Cover of *Sink or Swim* by H. Alger (Boston:
Loring, 1870).

Referring to the Horatio Alger stories as rags-to-riches narratives, however, may
be an oversimplification, as John Cawelti has pointed out: First, because their
protagonists never achieve success on their own but crucially rely on helper figures, a circumstance which somewhat mitigates the self-help impetus of Alger's
writings – Alger's typical protagonist has "an astounding propensity for chance
encounters with benevolent and useful friends, and his success is largely due to
their patronage and assistance" (Cawelti, *Apostles* 109); this reliance on "magical outside assistance" (Trachtenberg, *Incorporation* 81) has led scholars to
describe Alger's famous hero Ragged Dick as a "male Cinderella-character in a
postbellum America" (Moraru, *Rewriting* 56; cf. Nackenoff, *Fictional Republic*
275). Second, the protagonists of Alger's tales never become spectacularly rich
or successful – they rise from poverty to a comfortable middle-class status but
never beyond that, and thus do not follow the get-rich-quick formula; in fact, we

may consider the rather nostalgic hankering after a "return to the age of innocence" (Salmi, "Success" 601) that can be discerned in Alger's texts as
indicative of his critical attitude toward "the greed of the Gilded Age" (Cawelti,
Apostles 120), the large-scale "incorporation of America" (cf. Trachtenberg's
book of the same title), and the new mythology of "corporate individualism"
(Robertson, *American Myth* 176). Yet, there are a number of issues that Horatio
Alger stories evade, and these evasions carry ideological weight: Alger's virtuous and deserving heroes never experience bad luck and are never threatened by
downward mobility – they never become homeless tramps or drifters, or inhabit
any other seriously stigmatized and disadvantaged social space (cf. Nackenoff,
Fictional Republic 76); as they also typically strive for white-collar employment,
the factory and the "factory system" as a locus of labor is effaced altogether
(ibid. 88), and their success in the corporate world seems to be based solely on
personal virtue and ambition: "Serve your employer well, learn business as
rapidly as possible, don't fall into bad habits, and you'll get on" (Alger qtd. in
ibid. 91); yet, this corporate world is at times also cast in a negative light: "The
popular image of the business world held unresolved tensions; on the one hand,
it seemed the field of just rewards, on the other, a realm of questionable motives
and unbridled appetites" (Trachtenberg, *Incorporation* 80-81); thus Alger's
stories point to a fundamental conflict in the American experience which is
vicariously solved in these narratives even if they hardly ever address it directly.
Alger's stories moreover pay no attention to how class distinctions can be maintained more subtly through manners and habitus (cf. Veblen, *Theory*) and how
the lack of a particular habitus can prevent upward mobility; instead, they offer
"a potentially seductive message" produced by an "amalgamation of moral and
cultural elitism with egalitarianism" (Nackenoff, *Fictional Republic* 179) that
optimistically suggests the complete permeability of social boundaries and thus
mostly negate class differences proper. Satirical reworkings of the Horatio Alger
story, whose theme of social mobility is heavily imbued with social Darwinist
thinking, can be found, for instance, in Nathanael West's *A Cool Million: The
Dismantling of Lemuel Pitkin* (1934) and Robert Coover's *The Public Burning*
(1977), whose protagonist, a fictionalized version of Richard Nixon, is reminiscent of Alger's Ragged Dick. Alger's long-term influence can also be detected in
many other texts, genres, and stock characters in popular fiction, but he did not
invent the success story formula and self-help-ethic that he helped popularize; a
few success stories of the Alger kind had been published prior to the Civil War,
among them Paddy O'Flarrity's *A Spur to Youth; or, Davy Crockett Beaten*
(1834), Charles F. Barnard's *The Life of Collin Reynolds, the Orphan Boy and
Young Merchant* (1835), and J.H. Ingraham's *Jemmy Daily, or, The Little News*

Vender (1843), and it is in the 1850s that newsboys and bootblacks become common figures in popular literature (cf. Cawelti, *Apostles* 107). Yet, it is Alger among all self-help propagandists who lastingly shaped the cultural imaginary of Americans by adding to Franklin's advice register a new success formula with sentimental, affective appeal which celebrated "the pleasures of property" (Hendler, *Public Sentiments* 101) even more thoroughly.

Both Franklin's and Alger's formulas echo in many later representations of success in American culture, and have time and again been used as models for narrating success in the biographical and autobiographical vein. The self-made man as cultural script has been employed in order to describe individuals as different as Andrew Jackson (often referred to as the first self-made man in the White House), Abraham Lincoln, and Andrew Carnegie, who also used the formula in their own self-fashioning. Thus, for instance, Abraham Lincoln, who has often been viewed as the quintessential self-made man, "himself nurtured this tradition of humble origins to accentuate his own rise from obscurity to distinction" and fashioned himself as a 'common man' for political purposes, and many of his biographers have followed this lead (Winkle, "Abraham Lincoln"). Richard Hofstadter in this vein sees Lincoln as a "pre-eminent example of that self-help which Americans have always so admired" ("Abraham Lincoln" 92), and quotes from Lincoln's Address to the 166th Ohio Regiment: "I happen, temporarily, to occupy this White House. I am living witness that any one of your children may look to come here as my father's child had" (ibid.). Lincoln's rhetoric to some extent shares in the "glorification of poverty in the success cult's ideology" (Wyllie, *Self-Made Man* 24), yet "the most publicized actors during the late nineteenth century were not politicians but a dynamic breed of entrepreneurs, such as Astor, Gould, Vanderbilt, Carnegie, and Rockefeller" (Decker, *Made in* xxvii).

One of those entrepreneurs, steel magnate Andrew Carnegie, published an article in 1889 titled "Wealth" (commonly referred to as "The Gospel of Wealth"), in which he programmatically (and somewhat hypocritically) reconnects wealth to social responsibility in a Franklinesque manner. In addition, Carnegie feels justified in advising the readers of his autobiography (published in 1920) about self-reliance and morality by repeatedly interspersing his account of how he spectacularly rose from poverty to become one of the world's richest entrepreneurs with truisms such as "It is a great mistake not to seize the opportunity" (*Autobiography* 38) or "No kind action is ever lost" (ibid. 78), while failing to elaborate on certain less illustrious events in his life like his dubious role in the suppression of the 1892 Homestead Strike, which occurred at a steel works belonging to the Carnegie Steel Company. In order to evade and counteract the question of how extremely wealthy people like him, despite "having everything they wanted, [...] manage[d] to keep on wanting" (Michaels, "Corporate Fiction" 193), Carnegie turned to charity and welfare. His text is prefaced by his editor as follows:

Nothing stranger ever came out of the Arabian Nights than the story of this poor Scotch boy who came to America and step by step, through many trials and triumphs, became the great steel master, built up a colossal industry, amassed an enormous fortune, and then deliberately and systematically gave away the whole of it for the enlightenment and betterment of mankind. (Van Dyke, Editor's Note 5)

'Giving away' one's wealth, of course, retrospectively affirms once more that one had earned and owned it legitimately. Charity thus seeks to close the gap between self-interest and the common good by 'returning' to the general public what had previously been extracted from it through often exploitative practices. In similar fashion to Carnegie, the Rockefeller family is linked to both ruthless business practices *and* philanthropy (e.g. through the Rockefeller Foundation). Oil magnate John D. Rockefeller Sr.'s corrupt business practices (such as the large-scale blackmailing of competitors) have been minutely chronicled in the voluminous *History of the Standard Oil Company* (1905), whose author, journalist and historian Ida Tarbell, regretted that despite the exposure of his unlawful monopolization of the oil industry public opinion did not turn against him. Although the court proceedings against him did lead to Progressivist anti-trust legislation, as by that time "tensions between the business community and the rest of American society seemed to preoccupy the minds of many" (Kammen, *People* 266), Americans seem to admire Rockefeller as an impressive specimen of the self-made man even today.

Illustration 2: Self-Made Monopolist

C.J. Taylor, *King of the World* (n.d).

The myth of the self-made man – with a story based on trust in the incentives of the capitalist market, adherence to the Protestant work ethic, and luck – may be *the* prototypical modern American fairy tale. Decker points out how "stories of entrepreneurial success confer 'moral luck' – a secular version of divine grace – on their upwardly mobile protagonists" (*Made in* xxviii). Success stories thus can easily be considered American fairy tales with a providential twist, and as such they echo in and are invoked by many cultural productions from 19th-century popular fiction to 20th- and 21st-century Hollywood films. Their protagonist, the self-made man, personifies the American dream as wishful thinking and wish-fulfillment at the same time: "[T]he assumption that men were created equal, with an equal ability to make an effort and win an earthly reward, although denied every day by experience, is maintained every day by our folklore and dreams" (Mead, *And Keep* 68). As part dream, part fantasy, and part prophecy, the foundational myth of the self-made man seems to be powerful enough to defy the overwhelming evidence of its own baselessness.

4. CRISES OF SELF-MADE MANHOOD
IN AMERICAN LITERATURE SINCE THE 19TH CENTURY

> The moral flabbiness born of the exclusive worship of the bitch-goddess
> SUCCESS. That – with the squalid cash interpretation put on the word
> "success" – is our national disease.
> WILLIAM JAMES

> I didn't want you to think I was just some nobody.
> JAY GATSBY IN *THE GREAT GATSBY*

Success narratives and the 'new world' social order they project of course have
not gone unchallenged. In this section, I will exemplarily discuss literary texts –
short stories, novels, essays, and poetry – which from the beginning have
provided critical perspectives on the success myth. My first example will be
Nathaniel Hawthorne's short story "My Kinsman, Major Molineux" (1832);
written and published more than 40 years after Franklin's death, it offers a quite
skeptical view on the transitional process at the end of which the self-made man
emerged as a new cultural type in North America. An initiation story set in the
pre-revolutionary period, the text revolves around Robin, a young man who goes
to Boston, where his uncle, a high-ranking official in the colonial government –
titular character Major Molineux – is supposed to act on his behalf and help him
to settle in. Throughout the story, Robin is in search of his uncle and invokes
him as a paternal authority figure and benefactor, but when he finally meets him
at the story's traumatic climax, the Major has been tarred and feathered and is
paraded through the town by an angry revolutionary mob. Seeing that his uncle
has lost his position of authority, Robin does not even consider attempting to
establish himself in the city without the Major's support and wishes to return to
his home, yet a fatherly friend advises him to stay and try to "rise in the world,
without the help of your kinsman, Major Molineux" (19). The short story plays
off the notions of European social hierarchy and 'new world' equality against
each other and "takes part in the cultural process that constructs self-made manhood" (Walter, "Doing" 21) as it narrates the shift from "the social habits of
deferential hierarchy" (ibid. 23) to self-made manhood and democracy by having
Robin display the former throughout much of the story until in the end, he is
rudely confronted with the advent of the latter. Hawthorne's ambivalence regarding revolutionary upheaval has often been noted and is evident in the unflattering
depiction of the mob (cf. Bercovitch, *Office*); "My Kinsman, Major Molineux"
can thus also be read as a critique of the self-made man (cf. Leverenz, *Manhood*

235), as the story points to the violence that accompanies his emergence. While Franklin's projection of upward mobility seems rather enthusiastic and embraces the full spectrum of economic success, social respectability, and participation in public life for the greater common good, other writers of the early republic, such as Nathaniel Hawthorne, James Kirke Paulding, James Fenimore Cooper, and Washington Irving, were more ambivalent toward the abolition of established social hierarchies and less eager to celebrate the new national ideal of 'equality.'

Self-made manhood is accentuated in yet another way by Transcendentalist writers Ralph Waldo Emerson and Henry David Thoreau, who connect it to an inner-directed way of life rather than to notions of material success and social permeability. Both writers thus critically comment on Franklin's success credo by providing a decidedly anti-materialistic and spiritual perspective on self-culture and "self-reliance" (cf. Emerson's famous essay of the same title). In his late poem "Success," Emerson contrasts success based on "the exact laws of reciprocity" and the "sentiment of love and heroism" with success that rests on "a system of distrust, of concealment, of superior keenness, not of giving, but of taking advantage" (232); for Emerson, the focus on outward success in hegemonic conceptualizations of the self-made man produce and conceal self-estrangement and alienation. Henry David Thoreau picks up on this theme in *Walden* (1854) when he states that "[t]he mass of men lead lives of quiet desperation" (8). In *Walden*, which recounts how Thoreau lived for two years in solitude in a hut at Walden Pond near Concord, Massachusetts, the author seems to mock Franklin when he elaborates in the first lengthy chapter titled "Economy" on how he has to live frugally due to his limited financial means, and even offers the statistics he used to calculate his living expenses. Thoreau's concept of self-making can be considered anti-Franklinesque in that it rejects the rags-to-riches scheme by following a reverse trajectory that seemingly moves from 'riches' to 'rags' (cf. Parini, *Promised Land* 115-17). The 19th-century Transcendentalist tradition, of which Emerson and Thoreau are two of the most famous representatives, will in the following continue to critically flank more positive (and popular) representations of the self-made man in the American history of ideas and culture.

Another prominent and highly complex (if not enigmatic) 19th-century text that provides a critique of the widely celebrated culture of self-help, optimism, success, and the self-made man certainly is Herman Melville's "Bartleby, the Scrivener: A Story from Wall Street" (1853), which revolves around a young man who is hired by a successful elderly Wall Street lawyer (the story's narrator) as a copyist. This young man – the story's title character – refuses to function in a rationalized capitalist economy; when asked to perform certain tasks by his employer, he answers "I would prefer not to" (10). Bartleby's repetition of this speech act appears, as critics have pointed out, to bear some self-referential quality (cf. Deleuze, *Bartleby* 19); his regressive development, which is an unmaking rather than self-making, contrasts with the career path of his employer, who qualifies as a self-made man and whose worldview thus prevents him from making sense of Bartleby and his actions. Upon first meeting him, he comments: "I should have been quite delighted with his application, had he been cheerfully industrious. But he wrote on silently, palely, mechanically" (10). The themes of isolation and alienation have repeatedly been pointed out by critics such as Leo Marx, who has read the story as a critique of capitalism (cf. "Melville's Parable" 605), and Louise Barnett, who has called Bartleby an "alienated worker" in the "numbing world of capitalist profit and alienated labor" ("Bartleby" 385); and yet, Bartleby's self-assertion is neither compliance nor refusal in that it preserves a balance between affirmation and negation, as Giorgio Agamben has pointed out (cf. *Bartleby* 38). Michael Rogin calls attention to Bartleby's "passive resistance" (*Subversive Genealogies* 195), which is explicitly acknowledged in the story by his employer: "Nothing so aggravates an earnest person as a passive resistance" (13); Rogin thus considers the story in terms of its political message:

Bartleby protests, with "passive resistance," against his condition. In refusing to copy, he is copying Thoreau. "I simply wish to refuse allegiance," announced Thoreau, "to withdraw." Bartleby's "I prefer not to" is an echo of "Civil Disobedience." (*Subversive Genealogies* 195)

The connection between Melville's character Bartleby and Thoreau's writings has also been established by other critics: "Bartleby represents the only real, if ultimately ineffective, threat to society; his experience gives some support to Henry Thoreau's view that one lone intransigent man can shake the foundations of our institutions" (Marx, "Melville's Parable" 621). Whereas Dan McCall considers an exclusively economic interpretation of Melville's "Bartleby" as perhaps too narrow in view of the existential *angst* that this story confronts us with (cf. *Silence*), such an interpretation is certainly correct in pointing out that the story has the hegemonic discourse of the self-made man appear as profoundly lacking in the "humanity" that its narrator in the end proclaims upon the death of his former employee.

In the last decades of the 19th century – a period that in reference to Mark Twain and Charles Dudley Warner's novel of the same title has been called the Gilded Age – and in the early 20th century, class and class difference were explored by realist/naturalist writers such as William Dean Howells, Henry James,

Edith Wharton, and Theodore Dreiser, in whose works the US does not at all appear as an egalitarian but instead as a highly stratified society with finely-tuned mechanisms of inclusion and exclusion. These mechanisms are often examined by these authors with the aid of characters representing the businessman as the prototype of the self-made man in the emerging corporate America; one example of such a businessman is Silas Lapham, the title character of William Dean Howells's *The Rise of Silas Lapham* (1885), a so-called *nouveau riche* who, having made a fortune in the mineral paint business, seeks to increase his social status by building a mansion in a fashionable Boston neighborhood and by having one of his daughters marry Tom Corey, the son of a genteel family that has less economic but far more social and cultural capital than the Laphams; for the Coreys however, the fact that Lapham is a self-made millionaire does not compensate for his lack of etiquette and his proud and boastful manner. When Lapham finally makes a decision that is ethically right but costs him much of his fortune, the Laphams move back to their family home in the countryside and accept their financial decline that returns them to middle-class status, which in the logic of the novel is a return to moral integrity (cf. Fluck, *Inszenierte Wirklichkeit* 226). By construing capitalism and the "superabundance" connected to the self-made man as "a violation of the old ways and of the family itself" (Michaels, *Gold Standard* 39) and Lapham's bankruptcy as leading to his redemption (cf. ibid. 40), the novel reflects on the psychological costs of self-made manhood and suggests a chiastic relation between material success and moral self-realization, as upward mobility in economic terms comes at the cost of alienation and moral decline, whereas financial ruin leads to true self-discovery. Thus, the ending may be considered positive, if not happy (cf. Boesenberg, *Money* 137). Howell's novel can be described as an "inverted success story" (Fluck, *Inszenierte Wirklichkeit* 281) that reflects on changes in American culture; according to Donald Pease, the novel

provided a representative account of the conflict, following the transition from a predominantly agrarian to an industrialized nation, between the restraint of self-made men and the unrestrained self-interest of laissez-faire individualists. [...] In this transition, the self-made man was replaced by the competitive personality, who depended less on his faith in character and more on the power of his drives to get whatever he wanted. ("Introduction" 15-16)

The figure of the self-made man is used in Howells's novel to critique a historical turning point after which economic success was increasingly achieved through speculation rather than work; that Silas Lapham remains bound to a traditional work ethic eventually makes him lose his self-made status under the conditions of a changing economic system.

Stephen Crane's late short story "A Self-Made Man" (1899) is lighter in tone and offers an ironic perspective on the subject of upward mobility; in this "little parody" (Solomon, *Stephen Crane* 60), Tom, a young man without means, becomes successful after helping an illiterate old man he happens to meet on the street regain his property by posing as his lawyer; even if Tom realizes that "he had not succeeded sooner because he did not know a man who knew another man" (129) – adding connections, or social capital, to chance and deceit as reasons for his success – the narrator ironically remarks near the end of the story that Tom's "fame has spread through the land as a man who carved his way to fortune with no help but his undaunted pluck, his tireless energy, and his sterling integrity" (ibid.). That Crane satirizes the Horatio Alger formula as well as the genre of self-help and advice literature becomes even more obvious from the subtitle of the story – "An Example of Success That Any One Can Follow" – and from its ending, where its protagonist, who developed from "Tom" into "Thomas G. Somebody" (ibid.), "gives the best possible advice as to how to become wealthy" to "struggling young men" in newspaper articles (ibid.).

The (preliminary) endpoint of the self-made man's development from a rural to an industrial and finally to a market-oriented and corporate figure seems to have been reached with *The Great Gatsby* (1925), whose titular character in Lionel Trilling's view is an allegorical figure that "comes inevitably to stand for America itself" (*Liberal Imagination* 251). Much of the scholarship on Fitzgerald's novel has focused on the American dream, or rather "the withering of the American dream" (Tyson, *Critical Theory* 69). However, it is noteworthy to point out that 'American dream' as a catchword became popular only with the publication of James Truslow Adams's *The Epic of America* (1931); thus, Fitzgerald's novel, by using interconnected characters of different backgrounds – Gatsby, a self-made man who has acquired his status and wealth by using dubious means, narrator Nick Carraway, an ambitious young man, the upper-class Buchanans, and the working-class Wilsons – deconstructs an implicit exceptionalist understanding of success in US society years before it was explicated in Adams's book.

Self-made manhood in the context of corporate and consumer culture has also been paradigmatically embodied by the figure of the salesman. Whereas salesmen "were heralded as the self-made men of the new century" (Kimmel, *Manhood* 71), they were also used as allegorical figures in texts that critiqued success ideology; a prominent example of the latter is Arthur Miller's play *Death of a Salesman* (1949), which revolves around protagonist Willy Loman's futile attempts at self-making in a culture characterized by affluence, mass-production, and an economic rationale that ultimately considers human beings just as expendable as the (mass) goods they produce and sell. Loman's materialistic worldview renders him a paradigmatic specimen of what David Riesman, Nathan Glazer, and Reuel Denney refer to as "outer-directed" individuals in their sociological study of character in corporate America, *The Lonely Crowd* (1950). Beside Miller's play, there have been numerous literary texts (as well as other cultural productions) that have more or less critically dealt with corporate culture in the 20th and 21st centuries, among them for example Sinclair Lewis's *Babbit* (1922), Sloan Wilson's *The Man in the Gray Flannel Suit* (1955), Joseph Heller's *Something Happened* (1974), and, more recently, the television series *Mad Men* (2007-).

The works I discussed in this section exemplarily show that the self-made man has not only been a figure of consensus but also one of controversy and criticism. By expressing anxieties about the overthrow of established social hierarchies, offering spiritual conceptualizations of self-making, critiquing capitalism and corporatism, or warning of the fleeting nature of material wealth, all of these texts point to the precariousness of dominant white, masculinist, and individualist notions of self-made manhood in the US.

5. "LAND OF OPPORTUNITY"? IMMIGRANT STORIES OF SELF-MAKING

> The American dream, as the nineteenth and twentieth centuries under the impact of mass immigration came to understand it, was neither the dream of the American Revolution – the foundation of freedom – nor the dream of the French Revolution – the liberation of man; it was, unhappily, the dream of a "promised land" where milk and honey flow. And the fact that the development of modern technology was so soon able to realize this dream beyond anyone's wildest expectation quite naturally had the effect of confirming for the dreamers that they really had come to live in the best of all possible worlds.
>
> HANNAH ARENDT, *ON REVOLUTION*

The notions of upward social mobility and the pursuit of the American dream have often been connected to the immigrant experience. Despite the fact that stories in the Horatio Alger vein at times displayed a nativist streak, immigrant authors too used the narrative formula popularized by Alger to frame the topics of immigration and Americanization in the context of individual success and self-making. Beginning a new life in the US in these texts is represented as a process of (predominantly cultural) change and transformation, and is rendered in the same civil religious diction that also shapes many discussions of the melting pot (cf. chapter 5). However, even if immigrants often comment on the fact that the standard of living in the US is higher than in their countries of origin, they have no illusions as to the hierarchies that structure US society, even if these hierarchies may be relatively permeable.

For the sake of a systematic approach, I would like to identify four different patterns that underlie representations of the immigrant experience in American literature and popular culture from the mid-19th century to the present and that articulate different degrees of affirmation and critique of the myth of the self-made man.

The first consists of success narratives that mostly conclude with a happy ending and feature successful and well-adjusted (i.e. assimilated) protagonists that take pride in their own achievements in a society which is usually described as rewarding hard work, discipline, and stamina. Success may come in different forms and need not be limited to financial success – often, it is connected to gaining an education, overcoming particular obstacles in life, or to achieving public recognition (sometimes even fame). Among this first type of self-made narratives, I group Scottish American Andrew Carnegie's autobiography; early immigrant tales such as Jewish American Mary Antin's autobiography *The Promised Land* (1912) and Arab American Abraham Mitrie Rihbany's memoir *A Far Journey* (1914); and more contemporary texts such as Richard Rodriguez's assimilationist autobiography *Hunger of Memory* (1982) and Bharati Mukherjee's novel *Jasmine* (1989), which features a female immigrant protagonist. Self-made success can also be achieved through physical self-discipline, as Italian American Rocky Balboa's boxing pursuits in *Rocky* (1976) show. The career of Austrian American Arnold Schwarzenegger, who quite recently published his celebrity memoir *Total Recall: My Unbelievably True Life Story* (2012), points to yet other arenas of self-making; his remark that "[i]f there is one thing in this world that I despise, it's losers!" (Schwarzenegger qtd. in Halberstam, *Queer Art* 5) is symptomatic of a cult(ure) of self-made manhood that glorifies the success of individuals and denigrates those who are unsuccessful. Historically, immigrants used a number of metaphors to frame their experience of the 'new world;' Chinese Americans for example referred to Western North America as the 'Gold Mountain,' whereas arrivals from the East referred to Ellis Island as the "golden door" (cf. Emma Lazarus's 1883 poem "The New Colossus," which is engraved on a plaque inside the Statue of Liberty), even if there was little to idealize about the experience of internment, inspection, and admission immigrants had to endure there. Today, the Immigration Museum on Ellis Island hosts the Bob Hope Memorial Library in honor of the English-born entertainer who after arriving at Ellis Island in 1908 went on to become one of America's most famous and successful self-made celebrities – and one of the most patriotic ones too (cf. Zoglin, "Bob Hope"). To summarize, immigrant voices and stories of the type outlined above articulate the hegemonic version of the myth of the self-made man and affirm exceptionalist notions of the US as a society in which anyone can achieve success through individual talent, hard work, and discipline.

The second type of immigrant tales in contrast is less unequivocally committed to the American success mythology, and consists of narratives of upward mobility that end on not quite so happy a note or consider the downside of success – in fact, outward success may even be paired with a sense of failure, loss, and alienation. This discrepancy becomes evident, for instance, in Abraham Cahan's *The Rise of David Levinsky* (1917), in which the titular character and first-person narrator has to realize that money and success do not provide happiness (525-26); echoing the work of Cahan's mentor Howells, the novel constructs a chiastic relation between feelings of loss and economic gain, and offers an ironic commentary on the mythology of success and self-making. Similarly, Paule Marshall's novels about the Caribbean-American immigrant experience reveal the discrepancy between material aspirations and non-material longings, for instance in *Brown Girl, Brownstones* (1957), where we encounter a profound generation gap between the first-generation immigrant Silla, who pursues material success at any cost, and her daughter Selina, who dreams of less tangible things like falling in love and becoming a dancer. Self-making is addressed in a somewhat ironic as well as magical realist fashion in Sandra Cisneros's *The House on Mango Street* (1984), where the house referenced in the title, while superficially representing material gain and upward mobility, at closer inspection turns out to be a metaphor for belonging and shelter against male abuse. All of these texts thus represent immigrant perspectives from which notions of self-making and upward mobility appear problematic.

In contrast to those who can be (with all due modifications) considered as self-made personae, there is a third variant: stories that address the 'other' side of winning and self-making, a perspective that even more strongly articulates counter-hegemonic aspects. Scholars have pointed out that many of those immigrant narratives critical of the success myth were written in languages other than English even as they were printed in the US. Werner Sollors (cf. *Multilingual America*), Orm Øverland (cf. *Immigrant Minds*), and others have pointed to the connection between multilingualism and non-conformity in American literature, and Karen Majewski's reading of Polish-language immigrant writings by Alfons Chrostowski (e.g. "The Polish Slave"), Bronislaw Wrotnowski, and Helena Stas (e.g. "In the Human Market: A Polish-American Sketch") also points to this connection (cf. Majewski, "Crossings"). Often written in a naturalist mode, these narratives, of which some were recorded and fictionalized by Progressivist reformers, naturalist writers, and so-called muckraking journalists, are part of a discourse of failure that is situated at a distance from notions of American civil religion, patriotism, and exceptionalism. The slums of New York City, where much of the immigrant population lived at the turn of the 19th to the 20th century, have been famously captured by Danish American journalist and photographer Jacob Riis in his book *How the Other Half Lives* (1890). Similarly, Stephan Thernstrom chronicles the lives of those who are at the bottom of society in his *The Other Bostonians* (1973). Many American critics of the self-made myth in and around what Daniel Bell has described as "the 'golden age' of American socialism" (*Marxian Socialism* 55) – the years from 1902 to 1912 – had other ideas than laissez-faire capitalism for realizing a truly egalitarian society; "Chicago Will Be Ours!" is the socialist prophecy at the end of Upton Sinclair's naturalist novel *The Jungle* (1906), which provides another bleak vision of the immigrant experience in American society by describing the merciless exploitation and destruction of a Lithuanian family who works in the Chicago meat packing industry. The family, once full of enthusiasm for America, realizes that immigrant life is "no fairy tale" (143), as their attempts at improving their lot – and even at survival – are defeated: "They were beaten; they had lost the game, they were swept aside" (144). Narratives of immigrant failure thus are obviously at odds with the hegemonic version of the self-made man and expose the underside of the myth. They also reveal the myth's often unacknowledged social Darwinist underpinnings, as the myth's hegemonic version shrugs off the fact that it is not success and self-making but sheer survival that is at stake for many immigrants in a society that is characterized by gross class inequities.

Illustration 3: Muckraking Photography

Photograph from *How the Other Half Lives* by Jacob Riis (1890).

Lastly, a fourth kind of formula explores alternative modes of self-making and success that often transgress the bounds of legality, and thus also do not follow the dominant version of the success myth. These narratives acknowledge the difficulties of immigrant life in the US that arise from nativist resentments and other forms of discrimination against immigrants that often make assimilation impossible or undesirable, and thus locate success not within the American mainstream but in family- or ethnically-based criminal organizations and in plots revolving around a central gangster figure (cf. Dickstein, *Dancing* 313). A prominent example of this kind of tale is the *Godfather* saga (cf. Mario Puzo's novel and Francis Ford Coppola's film of the same title, as well as the sequels they spawned), which exemplifies an immigrant success formula based on maneuvering at the limits of (and beyond) legality and in socio-economic niches. In fact, as John Cawelti already argued in the 1970s, we find "a new mythology of crime" that reveals a fascination with power and corruption ("New Mythology" 335); this fascination, however, may be explained not only by the allure of glamorized depictions of organized crime but also by the fact that organized crime in many ways reflects rather than contrasts with what often hardly deserves to be called 'honest' business in the US: Daniel Bell argues that "organized crime resembles the kind of ruthless business enterprise which successful Americans have always carried on" (qtd. in ibid. 347); thus, "[t]he drama of the criminal gang has become a kind of allegory of the corporation and the corporate society" which conveys "the dark message that America is a society of criminals" (ibid. 353, 355). Seen in this light, immigrant gangs and robber barons may be more closely connected than is immediately evident. More recently, the Godfather formula was taken up in the television series *The Sopranos* (1999-2007) as well as by a host of other series who focus on the self-making of characters conventionally thought of as 'criminals.' Beside Italian American mafia dynasties, Irish Americans also figure prominently in this alternative success myth, for example in Martin Scorsese's *Gangs of New York* (2002), which dramatizes nativist and Irish gang life against the backdrop of the New York Draft Riots of 1863 and other contemporaneous historical events.

The four different 'success' patterns that we can detect in representations of the immigrant experience thus cover a broad spectrum of responses to the myth of the self-made man: affirmative ones that tend to mimic older rags-to-riches narratives; mildly affirmative ones that often substitute material gain with non-material notions of success; highly critical ones that mostly focus on failure (caused by adverse circumstances and discrimination) rather than success; and mildly critical ones that sidestep the legal framework of the success myth but champion material success nonetheless. In all of these versions, the self-made man (or woman) appears as a more or less contested prototype of American entrepreneurship, whereas social stratification and systemic inequality are more systematically addressed only selectively by writers and critics who are invested in a socialist agenda that often does not stop at national borders and thus more fundamentally critiques the myth of the self-made man along with notions of American exceptionalism.

6. THE MYTH OF SELF-MADE MEN (AND WOMEN) AND THE AFRICAN AMERICAN IMAGINATION

> To be a poor man is hard, but to be a poor race in a land of dollars is the very bottom of hardships.
> W.E.B. DuBois, *THE SOULS OF BLACK FOLK*

Conventional versions of the figure of the self-made man as white (and male) have excluded many groups and minorities, among them African Americans.

Yet, as the self-made man has been such a prominent figure of empowerment, emancipation, self-reliance, and autonomy in the American cultural imagination, it is perhaps not surprising that African American writers and intellectuals took up the image as well as its cultural scripts of success and appropriated them for their own ends. In this section, I will thus trace the critical as well as affirmative responses to the powerful cultural prototype of the self-made man that can be found in African American cultural criticism, literature, and popular culture from Frederick Douglass to Oprah Winfrey and Barack Obama.

Scholars of slavery have argued for viewing the early African American literary form of the slave narrative as a modification of the success myth: When using a broad definition of the self-made man, we may consider the author/narrator of the slave narrative as a subject that has refigured himself (or herself) as a free person. This kind of interpretation prioritizes notions of freedom and emancipation over ideas of upward mobility and economic abundance, and turns the African American freedman or runaway slave into a paradigmatic exemplum of the self-made man who triumphs over adversity due to his own strength and perseverance and infuses a strong moral sense into the discourse of the self-made man. Frederick Douglass (1817/18-1895) for instance documents in his autobiography his own process of emancipation in a way that strongly resonates with the myth of the self-made man. Douglass, who certainly had read Franklin (he quotes Franklin's aphorisms every once in a while in his own writings), and admired him, among other things, for being the President of the first Abolition Society in America, has often been called "a sort of Negro edition of Ben Franklin" (Alain Locke qtd. in Zafar, "Franklinian Douglass" 99). In his writings, Douglass himself reacted ambivalently to being called a self-made man:

I have sometimes been credited with having been the architect of my own fortune, and have pretty generally received the title of a "self-made man;" and while I cannot altogether disclaim this title, when I look back over the facts of my life, and consider the helpful influences exerted upon me, by friends more fortunately born and educated than myself, I am compelled to give them at least an equal measure of credit, with myself, for the success which has attended my labours in life. (*Life* 900)

Rather than identifying with notions of the self-made man, Douglass reacts to this appellation with modesty, and seeks to give credit for his success to a collective agency of helpers and supporters of the abolitionist cause. Focusing on the assistance and support needed to become a self-made man, Douglass thus modifies the myth of the self-made man to suggest that there is a collective of helpers surrounding self-made men that should not be ignored for the purpose of elevating the individual in an undue manner.

Apart from referring to the self-made myth in his autobiographical writings, Douglass also wrote a talk titled "The Trials and Triumphs of Self-Made Men," which he delivered in slightly different versions on more than 50 occasions in the US, Canada, and Great Britain between 1859 and 1893, and which has been referred to as his "most familiar lecture" (McFeely, *Frederick Douglass* 298). Even if "Douglass' standard speech on 'Self-Made Men' accentuated the morality of success rather than its economics" (Martin, "Images" 275), it has a slightly chauvinistic ring to it that stands in contrast to many other descriptions he offers about antebellum and postbellum American society. In fact, it is astounding that he writes the following lines in the pre-Civil War version of the talk:

I seldom find anything either in the ideas or institutions of that country, whereof to glory. [...] But pushing aside this black and clotted covering which mantles all our land, as with the shadow of death, I recognize one feature at least of special and peculiar excellence, and that is the relation of America to self-made men. America is, most unquestionably and pre-eminently, the home and special patron of self-made men. In no country in the world are the conditions more favourable to the production and sustenation of such men than in America. ("Trials" 297)

In the version of this lecture that is included in John Blassingame's edition of Frederick Douglass's collected writings, we find the self-made man positioned at the heart of a work ethic that Douglass formulates in often proverbial and metaphorical language which frequently refers to labor, exertion, necessity, self-reliance, good work habits, industry, and uplift (ibid. 294, 298). That Douglass shares in the exceptionalist discourse of the self-made man to such an extent is perhaps somewhat surprising, and it seems awkward, if not outright cynical, that he would sweep aside his criticism of slavery that can be found elsewhere in his writings in the process; as to how it was possible for an ex-slave and abolitionist intellectual to embrace the hegemonic version of the success myth remains open to speculation.

After Douglass's awkward affirmation of the self-made man despite the institution of slavery and rampant racism in US society, other African American intellectuals also referred to and appropriated the white success mythology. The title of Booker T. Washington's (1856-1915) *Up from Slavery: An Autobiography* (1901) for example clearly borrows from the notion of upward mobility, which in the book is connected to educational achievement and economic success. Like Franklin, Washington conceives of the public good and of republican virtue as compatible with economic self-interest and material gain, and many contemporaneous reviewers of his book – e.g. in the *Nation* (April 4, 1901), the *New York Times* (June 15, 1901), and *Atlantic Monthly* (June 1901) – pointed out exactly this parallel (cf. Kafka, *Great White* 9). Phillipa Kafka similarly holds that "Booker T. Washington was the mediator for African Americans of the European American success mythology as personified by Benjamin Franklin" (ibid. 3). She considers *Up from Slavery* as the narrative of a self-made man seeking to expand white success mythologies, as the text begins with the statement that "[m]y life had its beginning in the midst of the most miserable, desolate, and discouraging surroundings" (*Up from* 15) and ends with Washington's account of being awarded an honorary degree from Harvard University in 1896 (he is also invited to dine at the White House by US president Theodore Roosevelt in 1901). In statements such as "I believe that any man's life will be filled with constant, unexpected encouragements of this kind if he makes up his mind to do his level best each day of his life" (*Up from* 133), Washington's wording echoes Franklin's aphorisms. In contrast to more critical assessments of Washington's accommodationist views, Houston Baker sees him as providing a "*how-to* manual, setting forth strategies of address (ways of talking black and back) designed for Afro-American empowerment" (*Modernism* 32) based on a realistic assessment of the options of African Americans in the Southern US at the time.

Even if Douglass and Washington, two of the most prominent figures who contributed to the discourse of black self-making, exemplify the tendency in the African American history of ideas to conceive of self-made success figures as male (just as in its hegemonic white counterpart), we find female embodiments as well, for example in Ann Petry's naturalistic novel *The Street* (1946), whose protagonist, Lutie Johnson, a self-supporting, single mother, tries to emulate the ideal of self-making. At one point, having just found new employment, she imagines herself in Benjamin Franklin's footsteps – almost:

She walked slowly, avoiding the moment when she must enter the apartment and start fixing dinner. She shifted the packages into a more comfortable position and feeling the hard roundness of the rolls through the paper bag, she thought immediately of Ben Franklin and his loaf of bread. And grinned thinking, You and Ben Franklin. You ought to take one out and start eating it as you walk along 116th Street. Only you ought to remember while you eat that you're in Harlem and he was in Philadelphia a pretty long number of years ago. Yet she couldn't get rid of the feeling of self-confidence and she went on thinking that if Ben Franklin could live on a little bit of money and could prosper, then so could she. [...]

You better get your dinner started, Ben Franklin, she said to herself and walked past the children who were jumping rope. (64)

As a Black woman, the novel suggests, the odds are against her, however hard she may try to make a living for herself and her son, and she begins to completely lose her sense of agency as she realizes that despite all her efforts at self-improvement she will forever be kept down by the structural forces of racism and classism:

All those years, going to grammar school, going to high school, getting married, having a baby, going to work for the Chandlers, leaving Jim because he got himself another woman – all those years she'd been heading straight as an arrow for that street or some other street just like it. (426)

Petry, who was associated with the Communist Party, as Alan Wald points out (cf. *American Night* 88), addresses "the postwar crisis of the vision of the 1930s in relation to Black America" (ibid. 155). Failure, rather than success, is explored in her oeuvre, and this is also true for many other texts by African American women writers such as Gloria Naylor, Toni Cade Bambara, and Gayle Jones. Somewhat in contrast to Petry's account of a failed self-made woman stands Alice Walker's epistolary novel *The Color Purple* (1982), which narrates the story of two sisters, Celie and Nettie; even if their lives are characterized by acts of the most brutal patriarchal violence, abuse, and oppression, the novel ends fairly happy, with Celie becoming a self-made woman who supports herself as a tailor and owns her own house. The novel has been criticized for both its explicit depiction of violence and sexual abuse (according to the American Library Association, it is one of the most frequently challenged books) and for its somewhat implausible, (pseudo-)emancipatory happy ending.

Hollywood films constitute another arena in which we find many representations of black social mobility and immobility. It is noteworthy that even quite recent productions often depict African American characters as being content with holding subordinate social positions, even if they are the protagonists of the films in question. In *Driving Miss Daisy* (1989) for example, the African American Hoke (Morgan Freeman) is happy to be employed as a chauffeur by the elderly Miss Daisy (Jessica Tandy), and even though the film acknowledges racism and anti-Semitism, it also affirms a racially stratified social order. The controversially discussed adaptation of Kathryn Stockett's 2009 bestseller *The Help* (2011), which again portrays African American characters in a position of servitude, arguably similarly downplays past and present racial discrimination and black subordination by way of a sentimental politics of representation. Another puzzling example that calls for a thorough critique of black representation is *The Pursuit of Happyness* (2006) starring Will Smith as Chris Gardner, a homeless African American salesman and single parent who against all odds lands an unpaid internship at a brokerage firm, is then taken on as a paid employee, and finally goes on to become a millionaire. Instead of using its premise – unemployment, social insecurity, and poverty in an increasingly finance-driven economy – to formulate a critique of the financial sector in particular and of US society at large, the film thus turns out to be yet another celebration of individualism and self-reliance. Gardner tells his son: "Don't ever let somebody tell you, you can't do something. [...] You got a dream, you gotta protect it. [...] If you want something, go get it. Period." This American Dream narrative may well be described as postracial, if only for the very fact that it does not acknowledge the blackness of its protagonist: as Gardner is never interpellated as black and racism is never explicitly addressed in the film (cf. Gerund and Koetzing, "This Part" 203), *The Pursuit of Happyness* seems to deny race as a factor that co-determines social (im)mobility by once more celebrating the exception as the rule.

Self-making as a cultural script has been used to fashion African Americans as heroes and heroines not only in the realm of business and enterprise but also in many other areas such as the entertainment industry, sports, and – less often – politics. Media personality Oprah Winfrey for instance, who grew up in rural poverty, went on to become one of the richest self-made women in the US, and can easily be considered to be the most prominent icon of black female success. In her talks, she affirms notions of expressive individualism and the myth of self-making by once more reiterating the claims that hard work, moral integrity, and discipline lead to material success and that experiences of crisis and failure – rather than being indicative of larger social, political, and economic problems – constitute chances for self-improvement. In this sense, her philanthropy and the laudatory discourse within and by which her philanthropic and charitable activities are framed and promoted (not least by herself) function as complementing and enhancing her own success myth: philanthropy and charity become part of an entrepreneurial scheme that – not unlike Rockefeller's and Carnegie's approach – attempts to forestall and defuse any critique of structural injustice and inequality. Again, because Oprah Winfrey has her own autobiographical narrative of success and conversion to offer and to share, she can speak with the authority of experience about the business of self-making, adding positive thinking and pop psychology in "a trademark combination of pathos and uplift"

(Watts, *Self-Help Messiah* 495) as enabling forces to the myth while figuring as a living exemplum herself.

Barack Obama – whose rise to the highest political office in the US has often been rendered according to the standard narrative formula of the success myth – has also himself appropriated the myth of the self-made man in many instances, for example in the following passage from the speech he gave in Berlin on July 24, 2008:

I know that I don't look like the Americans who've previously spoken in this great city. The journey that led me here is improbable. My mother was born in the heartland of America, but my father grew up herding goats in Kenya. His father – my grandfather – was a cook, a domestic servant to the British. ("World")

Whereas Obama here appropriates the cultural script of the white success mythology to frame his own family's story (from domestic servant to US president in the course of two generations) and more generally contributes to the mythic discourse of the land of opportunity in his book *The Audacity of Hope: Thoughts on Reclaiming the American Dream* (2006), he has also somewhat inconsistently and provocatively issued criticism of the myth of the self-made man, for instance in a speech he held in the course of his re-election campaign on July 13, 2012 in Roanoke, Virginia:

[L]ook, if you've been successful, you didn't get there on your own. You didn't get there on your own. I'm always struck by people who think, well, it must be because I was just so smart. There are a lot of smart people out there. It must be because I worked harder than everybody else. Let me tell you something — there are a whole bunch of hard-working people out there. If you were successful, somebody along the line gave you some help. There was a great teacher somewhere in your life. Somebody helped to create this unbelievable American system that we have that allowed you to thrive. Somebody invested in roads and bridges. If you've got a business — you didn't build that. Somebody else made that happen. The Internet didn't get invented on its own. Government research created the Internet so that all the companies could make money off the Internet. You [wealthy people] moved your goods on roads the rest of us paid for. You hired workers the rest of us paid to educate. You were safe in your factory because of police forces and fire forces the rest of us paid for. ("Remarks")

Even if phrases such as "this unbelievable American system" reinforce long-standing assumptions about America's exceptionality, they at the same time also emphasize the public sector and communal efforts as prerequisites for individual success, and thus counter the hegemonic version of the myth of the self-made man. Obama's speech has been denounced as a call for "massive redistribution" (Goodman, "Obama") and as "contradict[ing] the belief in American exceptionalism, that is: Laissez faire economics, equality of opportunity, individualism, and popular but limited self-government" (Stepman, "Obama's Philosophy"); these responses reveal that remarks that challenge the ideology of individual success, whose function it is after all to provide a justification for the social order, will be immediately perceived as a threat to the economic status quo by conservatives like the above-quoted critics, who thus attempt to bolster the myth of self-making by evading and intentionally blurring the question as to whether wealth is actually distributed fairly in a capitalist system.

In sum, we can thus identify different aims for which the myth of the self-made man has been used in African American intellectual history, culture, and individual (self)-representations, for example, to construct a positive image of black masculinity and to claim recognition for African American individual and collective achievement, but also to point to the limits of the model of expressive individualism in US society.

7. AMERICAN CINDERELLAS? THE CASE OF THE SELF-MADE WOMAN

Workin' 9 to 5
What a way to make a livin'
Barely gettin' by
It's all takin'
And no givin'
They just use your mind
And they never give you credit
It's enough to drive you
Crazy if you let it.
[...]
It's a rich man's game
No matter what they call it
And you spend your life
Puttin' money in his wallet.
DOLLY PARTON, "9 TO 5"

They can beg and they can plead, but they can't see the light,
cuz the boy with the cold, hard cash is always Mr. Right!
Cuz we are living in a material world, and I am a material girl.
MADONNA, "MATERIAL GIRL"

The myth of the self-made man can also be related to women, as has already become clear by the (more or less successful) self-made women we have already encountered in this chapter. Still, there seem to be crucial points in which the female success myth departs from the hegemonic male one, to which it appears to be connected asymmetrically and in complementary fashion. For one thing, self-made women are not part of the foundational narrative of self-making, and even more recent female exemplars often follow a skewed logic that tends to define female success not in terms of work as productivity, but more often in terms of the kind of work that goes into maintaining and improving one's physical attractiveness. Thus, we may well speak of the prototype of the self-made woman as being shaped somewhat paradoxically by a process of 'othering.' Ann Douglas has diagnosed a "feminization of American Culture" as having accompanied the shift to an increasingly consumption-oriented economy in the 19th century that lastingly gendered the relations of production and consumption: The "sentimentalization" of culture "was an inevitable part of the self-evasion of a society both committed to laissez-faire industrial expansion and disturbed by its consequences. [...] [S]entimentalism provided the inevitable rationalization of the economic order" (*Feminization* 12). In that sense, women were both

> the stewards and prisoners of sentimental culture; theoretically reduced to affect and relegated to domestic space, women oversaw the cultural role of their own social and ontological captivity, which provided the moral rationale for an increasingly economically competitive society. (Gould, "Revisiting" ii)

Being interpellated not as producers/workers but as "consuming angels" (cf. Lori Anne Loeb's book of the same title) by the discourse of economic wealth and social mobility which propped up the newly emergent consumer economy, women entered it as customers and as male status symbols – i.e. as passive subjects or rather objectified non-subjects – or not at all. Women's upward mobility thus depended on their relations to men: The boy in the Alger story who becomes the protégé of an older benefactor is replaced by a young, attractive girl/woman who is similarly elevated through male assistance according to a patriarchal logic in which women's function is precisely not to become independently successful but to further highlight male success by yielding to men's efforts at changing women according to their ideals. American cultural productions also often use an Americanized version of the Cinderella tale to circumscribe female success, for example Theodore Dreiser's *Sister Carrie* (1901), in which the titular character, a country girl who goes on to become a successful actress, however ultimately leaves both male mentor figures with whom she has relations in the course of the novel; Anita Loos's *Gentlemen Prefer Blondes* (1925), which ends with protagonist Lorelei Lee, another provincial girl, marrying into high society; or Garry Marshall's Hollywood romance *Pretty Woman* (1990), which tells the love story between Vivian Ward, a prostitute, and a rich businessman. Whether Carrie Meeber, Lorelei Lee, and Vivian Ward would more aptly be called self-made women, businesswomen, or "sexual entrepreneurs" (Harvey and Gill, "Spicing" 52) is a question that cannot easily be answered. As female success often seems circumscribed by and limited to marriage as an arena in which the exchange/ circulation of social capital, economic capital, and libidinal energies is only thinly veiled by the ideology of romantic love, it is no wonder that we also encounter more critical treatments of marriage in American literature and culture, for example in Edith Wharton's *House of Mirth* (1905), which ends with the tragic death of protagonist Lily Bart, a young woman who refuses marriage and fails to live up to the (double) moral standards of New York high society. With regard to Wharton's novel, Lauren Berlant notes that "the linkage between conventional gendering and failure feels both melodramatic and mundane," and wonders, "what are the consequences if you try to 'quote' the normal practices identified with your gender and you fail [...]?" (*Desire/Love* 61). In the context of a newly emerging women's movement in the late 19th and early 20th centuries, women themselves critiqued white middle-class women for partaking in relationships based on what Olive Schreiner for instance has called "sex parasitism" (*Woman* 78); after all, these women could be considered to be complicit in maintaining their own socio-economic dependency, which Charlotte Perkins Gilman described as follows:

We are the only animal species in which the female depends on the male for food, the only animal species in which the sex-relation is also an economic relation. With us an entire sex lives in a relation of economic dependence upon the other sex, and the economic relation is combined with the sex-relation. The economic status of the human female is relative to the sex-relation. (*Women* 5)

From a gender-specific perspective, the Cinderella story as the (inverted) correlate of the male success myth thus defines the capital and opportunities of women differently from the capital and opportunities of men. Whereas we do find straightforward narratives of upward mobility, more often we encounter narratives of self-making that are concerned with women's outward appearance and with the work that needs to be invested in order to conform to socially defined beauty standards. Beauty contests constitute a notorious example of socially accepted cultural practices and forms of female self-making aiming at recognition, fame, and economic gain, of which the Miss America pageant is especially prominent. Invented as a marketing strategy by Atlantic City hotel owners to extend the holiday season beyond the Labor Day weekend, it took place for the first time in 1921 and, in spite of several interruptions, is still an extremely profitable venture. Ironically, 1921 was also the year women were allowed to vote in national elections for the first time, as Susan Faludi notes (cf. *Backlash* 50), which shows that emancipatory efforts conflicted and overlapped with discourses and practices that objectified and commodified women and their bodies. More broadly, Lois Banner suggests that

[t]he history of beauty contests tells us much about American attitudes toward physical appearance and women's expected roles. Rituals following set procedures, beauty contests have long existed to legitimize the Cinderella mythology for women, to make it seem that beauty is all a woman needs for success and, as a corollary, that beauty ought to be a major pursuit of all women. (*American Beauty* 249)

Banner goes on to say that "the Miss America pageant is a striking example both of the breakdown of Victorian prudery in the early twentieth century and the strength of Victorianism in a specific setting" (ibid.). In order to ameliorate the overtly sexist, objectifying implications of the beauty contest, which to this day is considered the most important part of the competition, the winner of the pageant is now awarded a college scholarship.

Overall, female self-making runs counter to the conventional American work ethic. Rita Freedman comments on the Disney television film *Cinderella* (1997): "Hard at work in her clogs, Cinderella was ignored. Transformed by her satins and slippers, she conquered the world" (*Beauty Bound* 68). Thus, we may even speak of a somewhat perverted work ethic that encourages women to spend all their material resources and time on the exhaustive and narcissistic task of self-managing and self-disciplining their bodies (cf. Gill and Scharff, "Introduction" 7). The fact that more and more women undergo surgical treatment before entering the Miss America contest (cf. Wolf, *Beauty Myth* 266-67) has given rise to renewed criticism of the competition.

Illustration 4: Margaret Gorman, the First Miss America

(1922) © Bettmann/CORBIS

In a more recent postfeminist discourse, female self-making more radically (and quite literally) refers to self-transformations achieved through cosmetic surgery.

Thus, Elizabeth Atwood Gailey discusses as "self-made" the women who undergo cosmetic surgery on reality television series such as *The Swan*, *Extreme Makeover*, and *Dr. 90210* for "the promise of status elevation and enhanced economic opportunity" ("Self-Made Women" 109). Here, as Gailey points out, "[w]omen are either portrayed as material objects – little more than a collection of (often almost cartoonishly) formulaic body parts – or, equally limiting and pathological – as self-exploitative, entrepreneurial agents who are more than willing to use their bodies to 'get ahead'" (ibid. 110) or to have signs of aging or pregnancy and childbirth removed in a spirit of "responsible self-management and care" (ibid.). This sort of female self-making constitutes "a liberation requiring utter submission to social authority" and complete conformity to normative gender ideals:

Performing perhaps the ultimate act of the "self-made" subject, women who undergo cosmetic surgery on these shows not only personify the exercise of political power through women's bodies, they reveal themselves as paragons of the neo-liberal doctrines of self-help and self-sufficiency. They are, in every way, then, "self-made women," products of the hegemonic alliance of patriarchy and global capitalism. (ibid. 118)

Speaking to individualist, neo-liberal notions of empowerment, emancipation, and agency, this kind of self-making in the spirit of a "postfeminist sensibility" (Gill, "Postfeminist" 147) at the same time can also be considered as a practice which enforces conformity rather than individuality and deprives women not only of their agency, but possibly even of their lives, as made-over women, by being surgically remade again and again, ultimately may literally come undone.

Another cultural script about female self-making addresses women conventionally as wives and assigns them a supporting role in their husbands' self-making and rising in the world. In *How to Help Your Husband Get Ahead in His Social and Business Life* (1953), a book adhering to the prototypical "conformist sensibility of the 1950s" (Watts, *Self-Help Messiah* 485), Dorothy Carnegie, who tellingly refers to herself rather as Mrs. Dale Carnegie, counsels wives on how to increase their husbands' success by making them comfortable at home, boosting their egos, and – most importantly – by not pursuing careers of their own, while she herself de facto took over her ailing husband's business around the time of her book's publication. Beside patriarchal conceptualizations of female/wifely success as coextensive with the success of their husbands, there are also other – quite ambivalent – images of the self-made woman for example in cinema, in which career women are often represented negatively as deficient single females.

In the 1950s, a watershed moment for gender conservatism, movie stars like Doris Day in many films played businesswomen who give up their careers for the sake of a man, and in the 1980s, successful female professionals are also often confined to narrow stereotypes, for example in *Fatal Attraction* (1987), in which Alex (Glenn Close), the successful editor of a publishing company, starts terrorizing Dan (Michael Douglas) and his family after he refuses to continue their affair; Susan Faludi compellingly reads Alex's deterioration as signifying the pathologization of the businesswoman in American culture (cf. *Backlash* 112-13, 122-23): Self-making and professional emancipation in the film's logic lead to the character's psycho-social disintegration because her career cannot compensate for her lack of a husband and family. The romantic comedy *Working Girl* (1988), in which we follow Tess McGill's (Melanie Griffith's) rise from secretary to successful businesswoman, represents female professional ambition and success rather positively; however, the character of Katharine Parker (Sigourney Weaver), Tess's boss, does reinforce the stereotype of the scheming and callous career woman, and as she is also Tess's major antagonist furthermore disavows any notion of female solidarity (cf. Faludi, *Backlash* 128-29). Whereas "Hollywood representation is characterised by an insistent equation between working women, women's work, and some form of sexual(ised) performance" (Tasker, *Working Girls* 3), in *Working Girl*, this performance is ultimately relegated to the sidelines, as the protagonist in the end earns her deserved recognition, which is symbolized by her moving into an office of her own in the final scene. It should be noted though that this largely positive representation of female professional success must be considered as more of an exception than the rule in Hollywood films as well as American popular culture in general.

Investigating self-made women in relation to self-made men obviously operates within a binary opposition; J. Halberstam has noted that "success in a heteronormative, capitalist society equates too easily to specific forms of reproductive maturity combined with wealth accumulation" (*Queer Art* 2). Beyond the reproductive paradigm, Lauren Berlant is asking us in her book of the same title to consider the "cruel optimism" that underlies the American dream of success and prosperity, which is as alluring as it is out of reach for most people: "The fantasies that are fraying include, particularly, upward mobility, job security, political and social equality, and lively, durable intimacy" (3). In fact, focusing on the avenues of self-making heralded by hegemonic versions of the success myth may just accustom one to a sense of permanent anxiety, or what Berlant calls "crisis ordinary" (ibid. 9). Rather than to adjust and succumb to this sense of crisis, J. Halberstam suggests reading failure "as a refusal of mastery, a critique of the intuitive connections within capitalism between success and profit, and as a counterhegemonic discourse of losing" (*Queer Art* 12). A feminist and/or queer studies perspective on self-making can contribute to such a critical reading by asking us not merely to include women into the dominant logic of self-making, but to question the premises of growth, reproduction, success, and gain that connect the success myth to capitalism and to normative conceptualizations of social structures and institutions such as the family.

8. CONCLUSION

> But what I want to see above all is that this country remains a country where someone can always get rich. That's the thing that we have and that must be preserved.
> RONALD REAGAN

> Of course we need the rich. We always have: to ogle and envy and imitate. They are our spectacle and our joy because in the head of every American lies the thought *That could be me*. The rich constitute our mythos, after all, our fairy tale, our hymn to success.
> SIRI HUSTVEDT, *THE BLAZING WORLD*

> Why is it that the wealthiest nation in the world finds it so hard to keep its promise and faith with its weakest citizens?
> BRUCE SPRINGSTEEN

Throughout this chapter it has become evident that the myth of the self-made man strongly affirms an ideology of expressive individualism as well as individual achievement and success that conceptualizes the "pursuit of happiness" (cf. the Declaration of Independence) as the pursuit of property. By claiming that self-making also contributes to the greater common good, hegemonic versions of this powerful myth – or fairy tale – of social mobility still very successfully obscure its role in legitimizing and perpetuating immense structural social inequalities.

In the age of global capitalism and the new social media, corporate success on a grand scale has once more become concretized and personalized in 'self-made' individuals such as Bill Gates, Steve Jobs, or Mark Zuckerberg (again, self-made *men*), who are turned into celebrities and high priests of the American civil religion of success, albeit with a new global dimension. In *The Road Ahead* (1995), Bill Gates fashions himself as such a high priest of the new age by using the semantics of a "peaceful revolution" to describe the effects of the computer and the internet on US society (and the world at large) and by affirming his company's supposedly democratic commitment to making it affordable for people to have "a computer on every desk and in every home" (4) – which, of course, is only in the corporate interest and need not necessarily be a blessing for humanity. Based on the success formula of the self-made man, Gates' develops a notion of "friction-free capitalism" (ibid. 180):

Capitalism, demonstrably the greatest of the constructed economic systems, has in the past decade clearly proved its advantages over the alternative systems. As the internet evolves into a broadband, global, interactive network, those advantages will be magnified. [...] I think Adam Smith would be pleased. (207)

It is telling that Gates invokes Adam Smith, whose *The Wealth of Nations* is a key text of laissez-faire capitalism, rather than Thomas Jefferson and The Declaration of Independence, which constitutes a key text of a very different kind even if both were published only a few months apart, in March and July of 1776, respectively. Gates's reference to Smith attests to his own global neoliberal capitalist vision (exceeding the nation state and the national market) in which there are supposedly only winners, as everybody profits from the new 'democratizing' technologies and the workings of Smith's proverbial invisible hand. Gates thus romanticizes the conditions of consumption and the role of consumers and entrepreneurs while obscuring the conditions of production and the economic vulnerability of those involved in it. In *Steve Jobs: Life Changing Lessons! Steve Jobs on How to Achieve Massive Success, Develop Powerful Leadership Skills and Unleash Your Wildest Creativity* (2014), William Wyatt similarly taps into the tradition of idolizing self-made men in a quite narrow ideological framework and regardless of Apple's numerous manufacturing and tax scandals and its dubious labor policies abroad (condoning for example deplorable working conditions at its suppliers in China). In spite of somewhat critical representations of his personality and entrepreneurial strategies for example in *The Social Network* (2010), Mark Zuckerberg's achievement also has been much applauded in biographies and advice literature such as George Beahm's *Billionaire Boy: Mark Zuckerberg in His Own Words* (2013) and Lev Grossman's *The Connector: How Facebook's Mark Zuckerberg Rewired Our World and Changed the Way We Live* (2010).

These more recent embodiments of the self-made man indicate that the myth has weathered the storms of capitalism's periodic crises and may have in fact even been instrumental in providing the ideological glue which maintains the quasi civil religious belief that upward mobility can be achieved by all. In turn, in the logic of this myth, financial and economic crises are not considered as part and parcel of a dynamic that is built into the increasingly globalized capitalist US economic system, but as somehow random and contingent or caused by outside economic influences. Nancy Fraser has called this false attribution of responsibility for structural inequalities "misframing" ("Post-Polanyische Reflektionen" 103); according to her argument, the intrinsic problems of a market economy are often credited to adverse outside factors allegedly skewed against the self-made man as object and agent of American exceptionalism. In view of a transnational perspective, scholars have also pointed out that many other societies are much more permissive and less socially deterministic than the US, which however has not lastingly affected specifically American notions of the self-made man and competitive equality. Even more fundamentally, sociologist Pitirim A. Sorokin has asserted that an "unstratified society with real equality of its members is a myth which has never been realized in the history of mankind. [...] The forms and proportions of stratification may vary, but its essence is permanent" (qtd. in Potter, *People* 99). Like so many aspects of American exceptionalism, the myth of the self-made man is as unrealistic as it is powerful. As we have seen in this as well as the preceding chapters, the foundational mythology of the US – Margaret Mead describes it as "our compensatory mythology" (*And Keep* 50) – creates a usable past and a hopeful future by bypassing the manifold discrepancies between mythic text and lived reality. Closing this gap is the ideological function of myth and the ongoing cultural work it performs.

9. STUDY QUESTIONS

1. Define the cultural type of the self-made man, and explain its ideological function.
2. Give a definition of Algerism, and discuss and contextualize the statement "Horatio Alger must die" from Michael Moore's *Dude, Where's My Country?* (2003).
3. Discuss how F. Scott Fitzgerald's *The Great Gatsby* and its 1974 and 2013 film adaptations represent class in American society.
4. How does the meaning of the phrase "pursuit of happiness" change when we focus on the notion of "pursuit" instead of "happiness"?
5. In the context of the Great Depression many texts about the experience of migrants offer a profound counter-narrative to that of expressive individualism and success. Studs Terkel writes: "Failure was as unforgivable then as it is now. Perhaps that's why so many of the young were never told about the depression; were, as one indignant girl put it, 'denied our history'" (*American Dreams* xxiv). Discuss the 1930s and the Great Depression in light of the myth of the self-made man.
6. Analyze the particular ways in which Bobbie Carlyle's sculpture *Self-Made Man* visualizes the myth. You may also refer to the artist's website: http://selfmademan.bobbiecarlylesculpture.com/.

Illustration 5: Self-Creation

Bobbie Carlyle, *Self-Made Man* (1988).

7. What distinguishes self-made women (in the dominant cultural logic) from self-made men? Give examples and discuss *Little Miss Sunshine* (2006) as a film about and a comment on beauty pageants.

8. How do self-help books connect to the ideology of self-making and to the myth of the self-made man? Discuss the self-help genre with regard to social, cultural, and economic aspects, and analyze *How to Win Friends and Influence People* (1936) by Dale Carnegie, who has been considered as having created a new and attractive blend of "success ideology, charismatic personality and self-fulfillment, positive thought, human relations, and therapeutic well-being" (Watts, *Self-Help Messiah* 7).

9. How are success and failure represented in advertising? Compare, for instance, Nike's "Failure" commercial with Michael Jordan and Citibank-City "Moments of Success" commercial (both to be found on the web).

10. Discuss how the rules, options, and gratifications of the board game Monopoly connect to American ideas of self-making, classlessness, and success.

10. BIBLIOGRAPHY

Works Cited

Adams, James Truslow. *The Epic of America*. 1931. New York: Blue Ribbon, 1941.

Adorno, Theodor W. "Tugendspiegel." *Minima Moralia: Reflexionen aus dem beschädigten Leben*. Frankfurt/Main: Suhrkamp, 1951. 349-54.

Agamben, Giorgio. *Bartleby oder die Kontingenz*. Berlin: Merve, 1998.

Alger, Horatio. *Ragged Dick; or, Street Life in New York*. New York: Loring, 1868.

"Alger, Horatio." *The American Heritage Dictionary*. 5th ed. 2011.

Antin, Mary. *The Promised Land*. Boston: Houghton, 1912.

Arendt, Hannah. *On Revolution*. London: Faber, 1963.

Baker, Houston. *Modernism and the Harlem Renaissance*. Chicago: Chicago UP, 1987.

Banner, Lois W. *American Beauty*. New York: Knopf, 1983.

Barnard, Charles F. *The Life of Collin Reynolds, the Orphan Boy and Young Merchant*. Boston: Simpkins, 1835.

Barnett, Louise K. "Bartleby as Alienated Worker." *Studies in Short Fiction* 11 (1974): 379-95.

Beahm, George. *Billionaire Boy: Mark Zuckerberg in His Own Words*. Richmond: Hardie Grant, 2013.

Bell, Daniel. *Marxian Socialism in the United States*. Princeton: Princeton UP, 1967.

Bercovitch, Sacvan. *The Office of the Scarlet Letter*. Baltimore: Johns Hopkins UP, 1991.

Berlant, Lauren. *Cruel Optimism*. Durham: Duke UP, 2012.

–. *Desire/Love*. Brooklyn: Punctum, 2012.

Boesenberg, Eva. *Money and Gender in the American Novel, 1850-2000*. Heidelberg: Winter, 2010.

Bryce, James. *The American Commonwealth*. 2 vols. Completely rev. ed. New York: Macmillan, 1923.

Cahan, Abraham. *The Rise of David Levinsky*. 1917. Introd. Jules Chametzky. New York: Penguin, 1993.

Carnegie, Andrew. *The Autobiography of Andrew Carnegie and the Gospel of Wealth*. Introd. Gordon Hutner. New York: Signet, 2006.

Carnegie, Dale. *How to Win Friends and Influence People*. 1936. New York: Simon, 1981.

Carnegie, Dorothy. *How to Help Your Husband Get Ahead in His Social and Business Life.* Salem: Pyramid, 1957.

Cawelti, John. *Apostles of the Self-Made Man: Changing Concepts of Success in America.* Chicago: U of Chicago P, 1965.

–. "The New Mythology of Crime." *boundary 2* 3.2 (1975): 324-57.

Cinderella. Dir. Robert Iscove. ABC, 2 Nov. 1997.

Cisneros, Sandra. *The House on Mango Street.* 1984. New York: Vintage, 1991.

Clay, Henry. "Defence of the American System." 1832. *The Life and Speeches of Henry Clay of Kentucky.* Vol. 2. New York: James B. Swaine, 1843. 9-67.

Coover, Robert. *The Public Burning.* New York: Viking, 1977.

Crane, Stephen. "A Self-Made Man." *The Works of Stephen Crane.* Vol. 8. Charlotteville: UP of Virginia, 1973. 124-29.

Croly, Herbert. *The Promise of American Life.* New York: Macmillan, 1909.

Decker, Jeffrey Louis. *Made in America: Self-Styled Success from Horatio Alger to Oprah Winfrey.* Minneapolis: U of Minnesota P, 1997.

Declaration of Independence. *Library of Congress.* http://www.loc.gov/rr/program/bib/ourdocs/DeclarInd.html. 30 Aug. 2013.

Deleuze, Gilles. *Bartleby oder die Formel.* Berlin: Merve, 1994.

Dickstein, Morris. *Dancing in the Dark: A Cultural History of the Great Depression.* New York: Norton, 2009.

Douglas, Ann. *The Feminization of American Culture.* New York: Knopf, 1977.

Douglass, Frederick. "The Trials and Triumphs of Self-Made Men." *The Frederick Douglass Papers.* Vol. 3: 1855-63. Ed. John Blassingame. New Haven: Yale UP, 1985. 289-300.

–. *The Life and Times of Frederick Douglass.* 1881. *Autobiographies.* New York: Penguin, 1996. 453-1048.

Dreiser, Theodore. *Sister Carrie.* 1901. Ed. Donald Pizer. New York: Norton, 1991.

Driving Miss Daisy. Dir. Bruce Beresford. Warner Bros., 1989.

DuBois, W.E.B. *The Souls of Black Folk.* 1903. Greenwich: Fawcett, 1969.

Ehrenreich, Barbara. *Fear of Falling.* New York: Harper, 1989.

Emerson, Ralph Waldo. "Self-Reliance." *Complete Works.* Vol. 2. Boston: Houghton, 1903. 43-90.

–. "Success." *Complete Works.* Vol. 7. Boston: Houghton, 1904. 281-312.

Faludi, Susan. *Backlash: The Undeclared War against American Women.* New York: Anchor, 1992.

Fatal Attraction. Dir. Adrian Lync. Paramount, 1987.

Fitzgerald, F. Scott. *The Great Gatsby.* 1925. New York: Scribner, 1992.

Fluck, Winfried. *Inszenierte Wirklichkeit: Der amerikanische Realismus 1865-1900*. München: Fink, 1992.

Fluck, Winfried, and Welf Werner. "Einführung." *Wieviel Ungleichheit verträgt die Demokratie? Armut und Reichtum in den USA*. Ed. Winfried Fluck and Welf Werner. Frankfurt/Main: Campus, 2003. 7-22.

Franklin, Benjamin. *Benjamin Franklin's Autobiography*. Ed. J.A. Leo Lemay and P.M. Zall. New York: Norton, 1986.

–. *Poor Richard's Almanack*. Waterloo: U.S.C., 1914. *Internet Archive.* http://archive.org/stream/poorrichardsalma00franrich/. 18 April 2013.

Fraser, Nancy. "Post-Polanyianische Reflektionen über die Krise des Kapitalismus." *American Dream? Eine Weltmacht in der Krise*. Ed. Andreas Etges and Winfried Fluck. Frankfurt/Main: Campus, 2011. 89-110.

Freedman, Rita. *Beauty Bound*. Lexington: Heath, 1986.

Gailey, Elizabeth Atwood. "Self-Made Women: Cosmetic Surgery Shows and the Construction of Female Psychopathology." *Makeover Television: Realities Remodelled*. Ed. Dana Heller. London: Tauris, 2007. 107-18.

Gangs of New York. Dir. Martin Scorsese. Miramax, 2002.

Gates, Bill. *The Road Ahead*. New York: Viking, 1995.

Gerund, Katharina, and Stephen Koetzing. "'This Part of My Life, This Part Here, It's Called Running:' Social and Geographical (Im)Mobility in *The Pursuit of Happyness* (2006)." *Kritische Perspektiven: 'Turns,' Trends und Theorien*. Ed. Michael Gubo. Berlin: LIT, 2011. 194-217.

Gill, Rosalind. "Postfeminist Media Culture: Elements of a Sensibility." *European Journal of Cultural Studies* 10 (2007): 147-66.

Gill, Rosalind, and Christina Scharff. "Introduction." Gill and Scharff, *New Femininities* 1-17.

–, eds. *New Femininities: Postfeminism, Neoliberalism, and Subjectivity*. Houndmills: Palgrave Macmillan, 2011.

Gilman, Charlotte Perkins. *Women and Economics: A Study of the Economic Relation between Men and Women as a Factor in Social Evolution*. Boston: Small, 1900.

The Godfather. Dir. Francis Ford Coppola. Paramount, 1972.

Goodman, John C. "Obama: There Are No Self-Made Men?" 21 July 2012. *Townhall.* http://www.townhall.com/columnists/johncgoodman/2012/07/21/obama_there_are_no_selfmade_men/page/full. 2 Feb. 2014.

Gould, Philip. "Revisiting the 'Feminization' of American Culture: Introduction." *differences* 11.3 (1999): i-xii.

The Great Gatsby. Dir. Jack Clayton. Paramount, 1974.

The Great Gatsby. Dir. Baz Luhrmann. Warner Bros./Roadshow Entertainment, 2013.

Grossman, Lev. *The Connector: How Facebook's Mark Zuckerberg Rewired Our World and Changed the Way We Live*. Introd. Richard Stengel. New York: Time, 2010.

Halberstam, Jack. *The Queer Art of Failure*. Durham: Duke UP, 2011.

Hartz, Louis. *The Liberal Tradition in America: An Interpretation of American Political Thought Since the Revolution*. New York: Harcourt, Brace and World, 1955.

Harvey, Laura, and Rosalind Gill. "Spicing It Up: Sexual Entrepreneurs and *The Sex Inspector*." Gill and Scharff, *New Femininities* 52-67.

Hawthorne, Nathaniel. "My Kinsman, Major Molineux." 1832. *Nathaniel Hawthorne's Tales*. Ed. James McIntosh. New York: Norton, 2013. 3-19.

Heller, Joseph. *Something Happened*. New York: Knopf, 1974.

Helmstetter, Rudolf. "Viel Erfolg." *Merkur* 8 (2013): 706-19.

The Help. Dir. Tate Taylor. Disney, 2011.

Hendler, Glenn. *Public Sentiments: Structures of Feeling in Nineteenth-Century American Literature*. Chapel Hill: North Carolina UP, 2001.

Hofstadter, Richard. "Abraham Lincoln and the Self-Made Myth." *The American Political Tradition and the Men Who Made It*. New York: Knopf, 1951. 92-134.

Howells, William Dean. *The Rise of Silas Lapham*. 1895. Ed. Don L. Cook. New York: Norton, 1982.

Huang, Nian-Sheng, and Carla Mulford. "Benjamin Franklin and the American Dream." *The Cambridge Companion to Benjamin Franklin*. Ed. Carla Mulford. New York: Cambridge UP, 2008. 145-58.

Hustvedt, Siri. *The Blazing World*. New York: Simon, 2014.

Ingraham, J.H. *Jemmy Daily, or, The Little News Vender*. Boston: Brainard, 1843.

Kafka, Phillipa. *The Great White Way: African American Women Writers and American Success Mythologies*. New York: Garland, 1993.

Kammen, Michael. *People of Paradox: An Inquiry into the Origins of American Civilization*. New York: Knopf, 1975.

Kant, Immanuel. *Anthropologie in pragmatischer Hinsicht*. 1798. Ed. and introd. Wolfgang Becker. Stuttgart: Reclam, 1983.

Kimmel, Michael. *Manhood in America: A Cultural History*. New York: Free, 1996.

Koch-Linde, Brigitta. *Amerikanische Tagträume: Success und Self-Help Literatur der USA*. Frankfurt/Main: Campus, 1984.

Lazarus, Emma. "The New Colossus." 1883. *The Norton Anthology of Poetry.* 4th edition. Ed. Margaret Ferguson, Mary Jo Salter, and Jon Stallworthy. New York: Norton, 1996. 1172.

Leverenz, David. *Manhood and the American Renaissance.* Ithaca: Cornell UP, 1989.

Lewis, Sinclair. *Babbit.* New York: Harcourt, 1922.

Lindberg, Gary. *The Confidence Man in American Literature.* New York: Oxford UP, 1982.

Little Miss Sunshine. Dir. Jonathan Dayton and Valerie Faris. Fox Searchlight, 2006.

Loeb, Lori Anne. *Consuming Angels: Advertising and Victorian Women.* Oxford: Oxford UP, 1994.

Loos, Anita. *Gentlemen Prefer Blondes: The Intimate Diary of a Professional Lady.* 1925. Introd. by Candica Bushnell. Illustr. by Ralph Barton. New York: Liveright, 1998.

Mad Men. AMC, 2007-.

Majewski, Karen. "Crossings and Double-Crossings: Polish-Language Immigrant Narratives of the Great Migration." Sollors, *Multilingual America* 246-54.

Marshall, Paule. *Brown Girl, Brownstones.* New York: Random, 1959.

Martin, Waldo E. "Images of Frederick Douglass in the Afro-American Mind: The Recent Black Freedom Struggle." Sundquist, *Frederick Douglass* 271-85.

Martineau, Harriet. *Society in America.* 1837. Cambridge: Cambridge UP, 2009.

Marx, Karl, and Friedrich Engels. *The Communist Manifesto.* 1848. *Marxists Internet Archive.* http://www.marxists.org/archive/marx/works/download/pdf/Manifesto.pdf. 2 Feb. 2014.

Marx, Leo. "Melville's Parable of the Walls." *Sewanee Review* 61.4 (1953): 602-27.

McCall, Dan. *The Silence of Bartleby.* Ithaca: Cornell UP, 1989.

McFeely, William. *Frederick Douglass.* New York: Norton, 1991.

Mead, Margaret. *And Keep Your Powder Dry: An Anthropologist Looks at America.* New York: Morrow, 1942.

Melville, Herman. "Bartleby, the Scrivener." 1853. *Melville's Short Novels.* Ed. Dan McCall. New York: Norton, 2002. 3-34.

Michaels, Walter Benn. "Corporate Fiction: Norris, Royce, and Arthur Machen." *Reconstructing American Literary History.* Ed. Sacvan Bercovitch. Cambridge: Harvard UP, 1986. 189-219.

–. *The Gold Standard and the Logic of Naturalism: American Literature at the Turn of the Century.* Berkeley: U of California P, 1987.

Miller, Arthur. *Death of a Salesman.* New York: Viking, 1949.

Moore, Michael. *Dude, Where's My Country?* London: Penguin, 2003.

Moraru, Christian. *Rewriting: Postmodern Narrative and Cultural Critique in the Age of Cloning.* New York: State U of New York P, 2001.

Mukherjee, Bharati. *Jasmine.* New York: Grove, 1989.

Nackenoff, Carol. *The Fictional Republic: Horatio Alger and American Political Discourse.* New York: Oxford UP, 1994.

Newman, S.P. "Benjamin Franklin and the Leather-Apron Men: The Politics of Class in Eighteenth-Century Philadelphia." *Journal of American Studies* 43.2 (2009): 161-75.

Obama, Barack. *The Audacity of Hope: Thoughts on Reclaiming the American Dream.* New York: Crown/Three Rivers, 2006.

–. "Remarks by the President at a Campaign Event in Roanoke, Virginia." Roanoke Fire Station #1, Roanoke, Virginia. 13 July 2012. *The White House.* http://www.whitehouse.gov/the-press-office/2012/07/13/remarks-president-campaign-event-roanoke-virginia. 18 April 2013.

–. "A World That Stands As One." Berlin, Germany. 24 July 2008. *Nahostblog.* http://www.transatlantikblog.de/2008/07/25/barack-obama-rede-berlin-siegessaeule-luftbruecke-2008/. 2 Feb. 2014.

O'Flarrity, Paddy. *A Spur to Youth; or, Davy Crockett Beaten.* Washington, D.C.: n.p., 1834.

Øverland, Orm. *Immigrant Minds, American Identities: Making the United States Home, 1870-1930.* Urbana: U of Illinois P, 2000.

Parini, Jay. *Promised Land: Thirteen Books That Changed America.* New York: Anchor, 2008.

Pease, Donald E. "Introduction." *New Essays on* The Rise of Silas Lapham. Ed. Donald E. Pease. New York: Cambridge UP, 1991. 1-28.

Petry, Ann. *The Street.* Boston: Houghton, 1946.

Potter, David M. *People of Plenty: Economic Abundance and the American Character.* Chicago: U of Chicago P, 1954.

Pretty Woman. Dir. Garry Marshall. Buena Vista, 1990.

The Pursuit of Happyness. Dir. Gabriele Muccino. Columbia, 2006.

Puzo, Mario. *The Godfather.* New York: Putnam, 1969.

Riesman, David, with Nathan Glazer and Reuel Denney. *The Lonely Crowd.* New Haven: Yale UP, 1950.

Rihbany, Abraham Mitrie. *A Far Journey.* Boston: Houghton, 1914.

Riis, Jacob. *How the Other Half Lives: Studies among the Tenements of New York*. 1890. New York: Hill, 1968.

Robertson, James Oliver. *American Myth, American Reality*. New York: Hill, 1980.

Rocky. Dir. John G. Avildsen. United Artists, 1976.

Rodriguez, Richard. *Hunger of Memory: The Education of Richard Rodriguez*. Boston: Godine, 1982.

Rogin, Michael. *Subversive Genealogies: The Politics and Art of Herman Melville*. Berkeley: U of California P, 1985.

Salazar, James B. *Bodies of Reform: The Rhetoric of Character in Gilded Age America*. New York: New York UP, 2010.

Salmi, Hannu. "Success and the Self-Made Man." *The Columbia Companion to American History on Film: How the Movies Have Portrayed the American Past*. Ed. Peter C. Rollins. New York: Columbia UP, 2003. 596-602.

Sartre, Jean Paul. *Existentialism and Human Emotions*. New York: Philosophical Library, 1957. *David Banach's Course Center*. http://dbanach.com/exist.htm. 2 Feb. 2014.

Scharnhorst, Gary, and Jack Bales. *The Lost Life of Horatio Alger, Jr.* Bloomington: Indiana UP, 1985.

Schreiner, Olive. *Woman and Labour*. London: T. Fisher Unwin, 1911.

Schwarzenegger, Arnold. *Total Recall: My Unbelievably True Life Story*. New York: Simon, 2012.

Sinclair, Upton. *The Jungle*. 1906. Ed. Clare Virginia Eby. New York: Norton, 2003.

Smith, Adam. *An Inquiry into the Nature and Causes of the Wealth of Nations*. 1776. Ed. and introd. Kathryn Sutherland. Oxford: Oxford UP, 1993.

The Social Network. Dir. David Fincher. Columbia, 2010.

Sollors, Werner, ed. *Multilingual America: Transnationalism, Ethnicity, and the Languages of America*. New York: New York UP, 1998.

Solomon, Eric. *Stephen Crane: From Parody to Realism*. Cambridge: Harvard UP, 1966.

The Sopranos. HBO, 1999-2007.

Stepman, Jarrett. "Obama's Philosophy Out of Step with American History's 'Self-Made Men.'" 24 July 2012. *Human Events – Conservative News, Views & Books*. http://www.humanevents.com/2012/07/24/obamas-philosophy-out-of-step-with-american-historys-self-made-men. 18 April 2013.

Stockett, Kathryn. *The Help*. New York: Berkley, 2009.

Sundquist, Eric J., ed. *Frederick Douglass: New Literary and Historical Essays*. Cambridge: Cambridge UP, 1991.

Tarbell, Ida. *The History of the Standard Oil Company.* New York: McClure, 1905.

Tasker, Yvonne. *Working Girls: Gender and Sexuality in Popular Cinema.* London: Taylor and Francis, 2002.

Terkel, Studs. *American Dreams: Lost and Found.* New York: New, 1980.

Thernstrom, Stephan. *The Other Bostonians: Poverty and Progress in the American Metropolis, 1880-1970.* Cambridge: Harvard UP, 1973.

–. *Poverty and Progress: Social Mobility in a Nineteenth-Century City.* Cambridge: Harvard UP, 1964.

Thoreau, Henry David. *Walden, Civil Disobedience, and Other Writings.* Ed. William Rossi. New York: Norton, 2008.

Tocqueville, Alexis de. *Democracy in America.* 2 vols. Ed. Daniel Boorstein. New York: Vintage, 1990.

Trachtenberg, Alan. *The Incorporation of America: Culture and Society in the Gilded Age.* New York: Hill, 1982.

Trilling, Lionel. *The Liberal Imagination.* Garden City: Doubleday, 1950.

Trollope, Joanna. *Domestic Manners of the Americans.* 1832. London: Century, 1984.

Twain, Mark, and Charles Dudley Warner. *The Gilded Age: A Tale of Today.* Chicago: American, 1873.

Tyson, Lois. *Critical Theory Today: A User-Friendly Guide.* New York: Routledge, 2006.

Van Dyke, John C. Editor's Note to *The Autobiography of Andrew Carnegie and the Gospel of Wealth.* Carnegie, *Autobiography* 5-6.

Veblen, Thorstein. *The Theory of the Leisure Class.* New York: Macmillan, 1899.

Wald, Alan. *American Night: The Literary Left in the Era of the Cold War.* Chapel Hill: U of North Carolina P, 2012.

Walker, Alice. *The Color Purple.* New York: Harcourt Brace Jovanovich, 1982.

Wall Street. Dir. Oliver Stone. 20th Century Fox, 1987.

Walter, Herbert T. "Doing Cultural Work: 'My Kinsman Major Molineux' and the Construction of the Self-Made Man." *Studies in the Novel* 23.1 (1991): 20-27.

Washington, Booker T. *Up from Slavery.* 1901. Ed. William L. Andrews. New York: Norton, 1995.

Watts, Steven. *Self-Help Messiah: Dale Carnegie and Success in Modern America.* New York: Othcr, 2013.

Weber, Max. *The Protestant Ethic and the Spirit of Capitalism.* Ed. Richard Swedberg. New York: Norton, 2009.

West, Nathanael. *A Cool Million: The Dismantling of Lemuel Pitkin*. 1934. *The Complete Works of Nathanael West*. Introd. Alan Ross. New York: Farrar, 1957. 143-255.

Wharton, Edith. *The House of Mirth*. 1905. Ed. Elizabeth Ammons. New York: Norton, 1990.

Wilson, Sloan. *The Man in the Gray Flannel Suit*. New York: Simon, 1955.

Winkle, Kenneth J. "Abraham Lincoln: Self-Made Man." *Journal of the Abraham Lincoln Association* 21.2 (2000): 1-16. http://hdl.handle.net/2027/spo.2629860.0021.203. 2 Feb. 2014.

Wolf, Naomi. *The Beauty Myth*. New York: Morrow, 1991.

The Wolf of Wall Street. Dir. Martin Scorsese. Paramount Pictures/Universal Pictures/Roadshow Entertainment, 2013.

Working Girl. Dir. Mike Nichols. 20th Century Fox, 1988.

Wyatt, William. *Steve Jobs: Life Changing Lessons! Steve Jobs on How to Achieve Massive Success, Develop Powerful Leadership Skills and Unleash Your Wildest Creativity*. E-book/Kindle edition. 2014.

Wyllie, Irvin G. *The Self-Made Man in America: The Myth of Rags to Riches*. 1954. New York: Free, 1966.

Zafar, Rafia. "Franklinian Douglass: The Afro-American as Representative Man." Sundquist, *Frederick Douglass* 99-117.

Zoglin, Richard. "Bob Hope: America's Most Famous Immigrant." *Time* 13 Oct. 2010. http://content.time.com/time/arts/article/0,8599,2025095,00.html. 2 Feb. 2014.

Further Reading

Banta, Martha. *Failure and Success in America: A Literary Debate*. Princeton: Princeton UP, 1978.

Baraka, Amiri. "The Death of Horatio Alger." *The Fiction of LeRoi Jones/Amiri Baraka*. Chicago: Lawrence Hill, 2000. 159-64.

Benziman, Galia. "Success, Law, and the Law of Success: Reevaluating *Death of a Salesman*'s Treatment of the American Dream." *South Atlantic Review* 70.2 (2005): 20-40.

Carter, Everett. *The American Idea: The Literary Response to American Optimism*. Chapel Hill: North Carolina UP, 1977.

Catano, James V. *Ragged Dicks: Masculinity, Steel, and the Rhetoric of the Self-Made Man*. Carbondale: Southern Illinois UP, 2001.

Dolby, Sandra K. *Self-Help Books: Why Americans Keep Reading Them*. Urbana: U of Illinois P, 2005.

Fahey, William A. *F. Scott Fitzgerald and the American Dream.* New York: Thomas Crowell, 1973.

Fluck, Winfried. "Was ist eigentlich so schlecht daran, reich zu sein? Zur Darstellung des Reichtums in der amerikanischen Kultur." *Wieviel Ungleichheit verträgt die Demokratie? Armut und Reichtum in den USA.* Ed. Winfried Fluck and Welf Werner. Frankfurt/Main: Campus, 2003. 267-303.

Haltunen, Karen. *Confidence Men and Painted Women.* New Haven: Yale UP, 1982.

Harlan, Louis R. *Booker T. Washington: The Making of a Black Leader.* New York: Oxford UP, 1972.

Hochschild, Jennifer L. *Facing Up the American Dream: Race, Class, and the Soul of the Nation.* Princeton: Princeton UP, 1995.

Kaplan, Amy. *The Social Construction of American Realism.* Chicago: U of Chicago P, 1988.

Kenworthy, Lane. *Social Democratic America.* Oxford: Oxford UP, 2014.

Lawson, Andrew. *Downwardly Mobile: The Changing Fortunes of American Realism.* New York: Oxford UP, 2012.

Lynd, Robert S., and Helen Merrell. *Middletown: A Study in Modern American Culture.* San Diego: Harcourt Brace, 1929.

–. *Middletown in Transition.* New York: Harcourt Brace, 1937.

Melville, Herman. *The Confidence Man: His Masquerade.* Ed. Hershel Parker. New York: Norton, 1971.

Michaels, Walter Benn. "Romance and Real Estate." *The American Renaissance Reconsidered.* Ed. Walter Benn Michaels and Donald Pease. Baltimore: Johns Hopkins UP, 1985. 156-82.

Mieder, Wolfgang. "'Paddle Your Own Canoe:' Frederick Douglass's Proverbial Message in His 'Self-Made Men' Speech." *Midwestern Folklore* 27 (2001): 21-40.

Pizer, Donald, ed. *The Cambridge Companion to American Realism and Naturalism: Howells to London.* Cambridge: Cambridge UP, 1995.

Rubin, Gretchen. *The Happiness Project.* New York: Harper, 2009.

Smith, Hedrick. *Who Stole the American Dream?* New York: Random, 2012.

Voorhees, Matthew. "Imitating Franklin: Booker T. Washington's Gospel of Wealth." Western Political Science Association 2010 Annual Meeting Paper. *SSRN.* http://ssrn.com/abstract=1581025. 2 Feb. 2014.

Wall, Wendy. *Inventing the "American Way."* New York: Oxford UP, 2008.

Watson, Elwood, and Darcy Martin. "The Miss America Pageant: Pluralism, Femininity, and Cinderella All in One." *Journal of Popular Culture* 34.1 (2000): 105-26.

Wysong, Earl, Robert Perrucci, and David Wright. *The New Class Society: Goodbye American Dream?* 4th ed. Lanham: Rowman and Littlefield, 2014.

By Way of Conclusion

Twenty-Five More Study Questions

1. Beside those American foundational myths that I have discussed in this book, many other US myths about individuals, groups, documents, buildings, and historical events could be identified. Give examples for each of those five categories, and describe their national, subnational, and/or transnational dimensions.

2. American sociologist Robert Bellah writes in *The Broken Covenant* (1975): "[W]hen we look closely at the beginning time of the American republic we find not a simple unitary myth of origin but a complex and richly textured mythical structure with many inner tensions" (4). Discuss this statement especially with regard to the "inner tensions" that Bellah refers to.

3. Identify the civil religious dimension of the myths discussed in this book, and relate it to the notions of a 'national spirituality.'

4. American foundational mythology provides a meaningful past as well as future for the US nation. Compare the ways in which the myths discussed in this book conceptualize national pasts and/or futures.

5. Historian and geographer David Lowenthal reminds us in his book of the same title that "the past is a foreign country" to which we have only limited access. Discuss how the myths addressed in this book attempt to presentify this "foreign country," and in how far these attempts succeed (or fail).

6. Contextualize and interpret the quotations by Gertrude Stein, Henry David Thoreau, and Studs Terkel with which this book opens, and relate them to the book's overall analysis of foundational mythology.

7. In *Marxism and Literature*, Raymond Williams describes "dominant," "residual," and "emergent" forms of culture. Use these concepts to analyze the making, remaking and unmaking of US foundational mythology in general as well as one specific myth of your choosing in particular.

8. Discuss the following paragraph from Amy Kaplan's *The Anarchy of Empire in the Making of US Culture* in the context of foundational mythological constructions of the US as both democracy and empire.

> A key paradox informs the ideology of American exceptionalism: it defines America's radical difference from other nations as something that goes beyond the separateness and uniqueness of its own particular heritage and culture. Rather, its exceptional nature lies in its exemplary status as the apotheosis of the nation-form itself and as a model for the rest of the world. American exceptionalism is in part an argument for boundless expansion, where national particularism and international universalism converge. [...] If the fantasy of American imperialism aspires to a borderless world where it finds its own reflection everywhere, then the fruition of this dream shatters the coherence of national identity, as the boundaries that distinguish it from the outside world promise to collapse. (16)

9. In an editorial published in the February 17, 1941 issue of *Life*, *Time* magazine co-founder Henry Luce called the 20th century the "American Century." Contextualize this claim and discuss its implications. Also discuss 1898 and 2001 as possibly marking the beginning and the end of the 'American Century' in light of foundational American myths.

10. Relate the following definition of the American dream from James Truslow Adams's *The Epic of America* (1931) to notions of American exceptionalism and to the foundational myths discussed in this book.

> The American Dream is that dream of a land in which life should be better and richer and fuller for every man, with opportunity for each according to ability or achievement. It is a difficult dream for the European upper classes to interpret adequately, also too many of us ourselves have grown weary and mistrustful of it. It is not a dream of motor cars and high wages merely, but a dream of social order in which each man and each woman shall be able to attain to the fullest stature of which they are innately capable, and be recognized by others for what they are, regardless of the fortuitous circumstances of birth or position. (317)

11. Many writers and critics have employed the metaphor of the American nightmare to counter the ideology of the American dream. Discuss for instance Henry Miller's essay collection *The Air-Conditioned Nightmare* (1945), the first chapter of *The Autobiography of Malcolm X* (1965, which is titled "Nightmare"), Norman Mailer's *An American Dream* (1965), or Adam Simon's film *American Nightmare* (2000). What kinds of grievances are articulated in these texts, and what exactly is it that they deem nightmarish about the US?

12. One of the most iconic manifestations of American exceptionalism is the Statue of Liberty in New York Harbor. For all its national symbolic capital, it is, in fact, a transnational symbol. Research its history, and analyze the following description in light of the statue's iconicity:

> She sits like a great witch at the gate of the country, showing her alluring white face and hiding her crooked hands and feet under folds of her wide garments – constantly enticing thousands from far within, and tempting those who come from across the seas to go no farther. And all these become the victims of her caprice. Some she at once crushes beneath her cruel feet; others she condemns to a fate like that of galley slaves; a few she favors and fondles, riding them high on the bubbles of fortune; then with a sudden breath she blows the bubbles out and laughs mockingly as she watches them fall. (Johnson, *Autobiography* 65)

13. In this book, I have repeatedly discussed the foundational quality of artistic representations in and around the US Capitol. Among the rotunda paintings I have not discussed are William Powell's *Discovery of the Mississippi by De Soto* and John Trumbull's paintings of the *Surrender of General Burgoyne* as well as the *Surrender of Lord Cornwallis*. How do these three paintings fit (or do not fit) into the framework of a foundational mythology? Along similar lines, discuss the Frieze of American History (which is also to be found in the United States Capitol rotunda). What kind of mythic and "usable" past do the frieze's 19 scenes convey? Which scenes do you find conventional and expectable, which surprising?

14. At the age of 87, Robert Frost read his poem "The Gift Outright" (1942) at the inauguration of John F. Kennedy on January 20, 1961. For the occasion, it was requested that Frost change the "would" in the last line of his poem to "will" in order for it to end on a more optimistic note. Analyze the poem with regard to its references to US mythology, and research and discuss its performance at the presidential inauguration.

The land was ours before we were the land's.
She was our land more than a hundred years
Before we were her people. She was ours
In Massachusetts, in Virginia,
But we were England's, still colonials,
Possessing what we still were unpossessed by,
Possessed by what we now no more possessed.
Something we were withholding made us weak
Until we found out that it was ourselves
We were withholding from our land of living,

And forthwith found salvation in surrender.
Such as we were we gave ourselves outright
(The deed of gift was many deeds of war)
To the land vaguely realizing westward,
But still unstoried, artless, unenhanced,
Such as she was, such as she would become.

15. Memorial culture plays a major role in the foundational mythology of the US. Research and analyze one of the memorials on the National Mall in Washington, D.C. in light of the 'myths that made America.'

16. Early Americanist scholars have been described collectively as the American studies *movement* (Wise, "'Paradigm Dramas'" 294). What does this appellation imply? Characterize the differences between a movement and a discipline and relate them to the development of the field of American studies in the United States.

17. Browse the official website of the American Studies Association (ASA) and discuss the description of American studies as well as of the organization itself that are provided there (www.theasa.net). Also look at the list of past ASA presidents (www.theasa.net/about/page/past_presidents) and research the titles of their presidential addresses. How do they reflect the history and development of the field of American studies?

18. How can the notions of repetition and seriality be related to the processes through which the myths discussed in this book have been appropriated and re-appropriated time and again?

19. Discuss the connection between myth and narrative (or myth *as* narrative), and relate your discussion to the following excerpt from Leslie Marmon Silko's novel *Ceremony* (1977):

I will tell you something about stories,
[he said]
They aren't just entertainment.
Don't be fooled.
They are all we have, you see,
All we have to fight off illness and death.
You don't have anything if you don't have the stories. (2)

20. Outline how a counter-hegemonic, women-centered foundational US mythology would possibly look like.

21. Michael Novak famously referred to the American president as "priest," "prophet," and "king" (cf. *Choosing*). Discuss the role of the president in the American political system and in political culture as well as popular rep-

resentations of the presidency (e.g. in Hollywood films and television series) in light of Novak's assessment.

22. In *Frames of War*, Judith Butler analyzes the means and the results of the so-called "War on Terror" after 9/11 with regard to its media portrayal. How can this "War" (as it manifests itself in names such as Guantanamo and Abu Ghraib) be related to US-foundational mythology on the whole and/or to individual myths in particular?

23. From architectural styles in the early republic (as evidenced by buildings and monuments on the National Mall) to contemporary mass cultural poductions (*Gladiator* [2005], *Troy* [2004], *Rome* [2005-07]), US culture has appropriated classicist forms and themes and retold classicist (mythic) narratives. How do the references to ancient Greece and Rome time and again play out with regard to US foundational mythology?

24. In the context of the so-called transnational American Studies, various perspectives have been introduced. Research and discuss the following: Hemispheric American Studies, Planetary American Studies, and Cosmic American Studies.

25. How can we approach US foundational mythology from an intercultural and comparative perspective? Identify non-American national myths that are comparable to those of the US, and describe their (structural) similarities as well as (culturally specific) differences. How can we envision a foundational mythology or mythic repertoire with regard to other than national entities? Identify and discuss European myths.

WORKS CITED

Adams, James Truslow. *The Epic of America*. New York: Little, 1931.

The American Nightmare. Dir. Adam Simon. Minerva, 2000.

Bellah, Robert. *The Broken Covenant: American Civil Religion in Time of Trial*. Chicago: U of Chicago P, 1975.

Butler, Judith. *Frames of War: When Is Life Grievable?* London: Verso, 2009.

Frost, Robert. "The Gift Outright." *Complete Poems of Robert Frost*. New York: Holt, 1949. 467.

Gladiator. Dir Ridley Scott. DreamWorks/Universal, 2000.

Kaplan, Amy. *The Anarchy of Empire in the Making of US Culture*. Cambridge: Harvard UP, 2005.

Johnson, James Weldon. *The Autobiography of an Ex-Colored Man*. 1912. New York: Penguin, 1990.

Lowenthal, David. *The Past Is a Foreign Country*. Cambridge: Cambridge UP, 1985.

Luce, Henry. "The American Century." *Life Magazine* 17 Feb. 1941. 61-65.

Mailer, Norman. *An American Dream*. New York: Dial, 1965.

Miller, Henry. *The Air-Conditioned Nightmare*. New York: New Directions, 1945.

Novak, Michael. *Choosing Our King: Powerful Symbols in Presidential Politics*. New York: Macmillan, 1974.

Rome. BBC/HBO/Rai Fiction, 2005-07.

Silko, Leslie Marmon. *Ceremony*. New York: Penguin, 1977.

Troy. Dir Wolfgang Petersen. Warner Bros., 2004.

Williams, Raymond. *Marxism and Literature*. London: Routledge, 1977.

Wise, Gene. "'Paradigm Dramas' in American Studies: A Cultural and Institutional History of the Movement." *American Quarterly* 31.3 (1979): 293-337.

X, Malcolm, with Alex Haley. *The Autobiography of Malcolm X*. New York: Grove, 1965.

Index

Index note: page references in *italics* indicate a bibliographical entry

H

Z